English Lessons Through Literature

Discerning

Kathy Jo DeVore

Copyright © 2017 by Kathy Jo DeVore. The eBook version may be printed for the use of one household and may not be resold. The print version may not be reproduced.

Clipart images Copyright © GraphicsFactory.com

ad majorem Dei gloriam

et liberis meis

Table of Contents

Introduction 11

Level D: Discerning Literature List 17

1. Introduction to the Thesaurus 19
2. Parts of Speech: Nouns 23
3. Literary Analysis 27
4. Parts of Speech: Verbs 31
5. How to Write a Condensed Narrative 35
6. Condensed Narrative: How We Got the Name "Spider Tales" .. 39
7. Parts of Speech: Pronouns 41
8. The Sentence 45
9. Descriptive Writing 51
10. The Four Types of Sentences, Part 1 57
11. Parts of Speech: Adjectives; Articles 61
12. Condensed Narrative: Anansi and Nothing 65
13. The Four Types of Sentences, Part 2 67
14. Linking Verbs; Predicate Nominatives 71
15. Literary Analysis 77
16. Adjectives That Tell Which One and Whose 81
17. Predicate Adjectives 85
18. Condensed Narrative: Why We See Ants Carrying Bundles 89
19. Helping Verbs 91
20. Plurals With -f and -fe 95
21. Descriptive Writing 101
22. Direct Objects 105
23. Plurals With -o 109
24. Amplified Narrative: The Fox and the Grapes 113
25. Nouns as Adjectives 115

26. Diagramming Interrogative Sentences 119

27. Literary Analysis 125

28. Compound Subjects and Predicates 129

29. Quotations 135

30. Amplified Narrative: The Bundle of Sticks 139

31. Diagramming Imperative Sentences 141

32. Parts of Speech: Adverbs 145

33. Descriptive Writing 151

34. Adverbs That Tell How and When 155

35. Adverbs That Tell Where and How Often 161

36. Amplified Narrative: The Leap at Rhodes 165

37. Adverbs That Tell to What Extent 169

38. Writing an Outline 173

39. Literary Analysis 177

40. The Paragraph 181

41. Point of View 185

42. Point of View Narration: The Humble Bee's Nest 189

43. Phrases and Clauses 191

44. Parts of Speech: Conjunctions 195

45. Descriptive Writing 201

46. Parts of Speech: Interjections; Nouns of Direct Address 205

47. Appositives 211

48. Point of View Narration: A Frog's Life 215

49. Commas in a Series 217

50. Writing an Outline 221

51. Literary Analysis 227

52. Homonyms 231

53. Parts of Speech: Prepositions 237

54. Point of View Narration: The Greedy Stranger 241

55. Object of the Preposition 243

56. Diagramming Prepositions 247

57.	Descriptive Writing	253
58.	Prepositions and Adverbs	257
59.	Slant Narratives	261
60.	Slant Narrative: The Ants and the Grasshopper	265
61.	Noun and Pronouns Cases	267
62.	Pronoun Cases: Correct Usage	273
63.	Literary Analysis	279
64.	Interrogative Adverbs	281
65.	The Principal Parts of the Verb	287
66.	Slant Narrative: The Town Mouse and the Country Mouse	291
67.	The Infinitive; Verb Properties: Person	293
68.	Verb Properties: Number	297
69.	Descriptive Writing	303
70.	Verb Properties: Tense	307
71.	Properties of Nouns and Pronouns	313
72.	Slant Narrative: The Hare and the Tortoise	317
73.	Collective Nouns	319
74.	Subject-Verb Agreement	325
75.	Literary Analysis	329
76.	Comparatives	333
77.	Superlatives	337
78.	Scientific Narration: Snow	341
79.	Irregular Verbs	343
80.	Tenses: Negatives and Questions	349
81.	Descriptive Writing	355
82.	To Be	359
83.	To Do and To Go	367
84.	Scientific Narration: Silk	373
85.	To See and To Come	375
86.	To Have	381
87.	Literary Analysis	387

88.	Other Irregular Verbs	391
89.	Subordinate Conjunctions	397
90.	Scientific Narration: Sound	401
91.	Compound Sentences	405
92.	Review: Phrases and Clauses	411
93.	Descriptive Writing	417
94.	Complex Sentences	421
95.	Indirect Objects	427
96.	Historical Narration: Hieroglyphics	433
97.	Review: Compound and Complex Sentences	435
98.	Commas After Introductory Elements	441
99.	Literary Analysis	445
100.	Relative Pronouns	449
101.	Rhythm in Poetry	453
102.	Historical Narration: The Nile Valley	457
103.	Rhyme in Poetry	459
104.	Sit and Set	465
105.	Descriptive Writing	471
106.	Lie and Lay	475
107.	Well and Good	481
108.	Historical Narration: Greek Life	485

Exercise Answers	487
Appendix A: Memory Work	521
Appendix B: Correct Use of Words	527
Appendix C: Diagramming Reference	531
Appendix D: Irregular Verbs	539
Appendix E: Tenses	543
Appendix F: Editing	545

Introduction

English Lessons Through Literature has three lessons per week for thirty-six weeks. This is a total of 108 lessons per year. A total of eight levels of *English Lessons Through Literature* have been planned which will take children through elementary and middle school grammar and composition. Lessons also include literature and poetry, handwriting through copywork, and spelling through prepared dictation, making it a complete language arts program.

Level C is intended for 3rd grade and up; Level D is intended for 4th grade and up; and Level E is intended for 5th grade and up. Each of these levels reviews all previously taught material, including the parts of speech, so there is no prerequisite to any of these levels.

In the optional workbook for Level C, students are given the lines for diagramming, making it a "fill in the diagram" exercise. Without the workbook, parents can provide the same by copying the diagram lines from the answer key in the back of the book. Oral exercises are included in Level C to practice new concepts without the additional stress of having to write the answers because it is best to transition children gently into doing new things. In writing, this means that first we talk, then we write. Students of this age can continue to give their narrations orally, then they can take the first sentence as dictation. See the section on dictation for instructions.

Literature Selections

The literature suggested in this book is in the public domain in the United States, and the full text of each story and book can be found online. Most are also available as audio books. A complete reading list appears at the beginning of each level.

Since most of the examples and part of the daily copywork come directly from the literature, reading the literature is an important component of this program. However, there is certainly room to skip books that the child does not like. It is up to the parents to determine whether or not a recommended resource is right for their family. My homeschooling motto has long been, "Use the curriculum; don't let the curriculum use you." I recommend the motto more highly than I recommend any of the literature selections in this book.

I do recommend reading the literature prior to the lesson. The examples and the copywork almost always come from the reading selection from that day.

Copywork and Commonplace Book

ELTL contains a great deal of copywork. Students should not do more copywork than they can complete perfectly and neatly. If you find this is too much copywork for your young students, there are several options:

1. Skip part of the copywork. Decide which portions of the copywork are most important to your goals, and have your child do only those.

2. If you'd rather have your child do all of the copywork, have him do the copywork portions five days a week instead of three.

3. Have your child do half the copywork in the morning and the other half in the afternoon.

In Levels E and up, the commonplace book completely replaces copywork. A commonplace book is a book for copying poetry and passages from literature, scripture, history, science, or the student's free reading. A simple composition book can be used for this purpose.

Each model story has a commonplace book exercise, a passage from the story to copy. Students can also begin to add to the commonplace book from other reading. My children choose their own passages to copy, passages which speak to them in some way. For my oldest son, it was often something philosophical or political. For my second son, it is usually something funny. For my third son, it is usually popular fiction—we are still careful to find well-written passages. And for my youngest son, it is often his children's Bible. Unlike copywork, the commonplace book is tailored to the student's personality and interests.

Narrations

Narrations occur throughout all levels of *English Lessons Through Literature*. Once the student is comfortable with narrating, you can include narration exercises from history and science reading as well.

The procedure for doing the narrations is quite simple: After hearing the story, students tell the story back to their instructors in their own words. For students who are new to narration, prompting them with questions at first may help. Ask questions such as, "What happened first?" and, "Then what happened?" Help them get the details of the story in the proper order.

For students in Level C, since the instructor is doing the writing for the student, the student has no need to worry about spelling or punctuation. At this stage, I correct nothing more than grammatical errors—the sort that I would correct during normal conversation—and, occasionally, a detail from the story. These are best done at the end of the narration to avoid interrupting the child's train of thought.

Lessons and Exercises

Ideally, *English Lessons Through Literature* narrations should be in addition to oral and written narrations in other areas, such as history and science.

The writing lessons follow a two-week (six-day) repeating pattern:

> **Day 1**: The model story for the next two weeks (six lessons) is in this lesson. The student reads and orally narrates the new model story.
>
> **Day 2**: In Level C, the student has a "Playing With Words" exercise. In Levels D and up, the student outlines the new model story.
>
> **Day 3**: In Levels D and up, the student has either a literary analysis or descriptive writing exercise.
>
> **Day 4**: The student has a sentence-rewriting copia exercise.
>
> **Day 5**: The student has a commonplace book entry from the model story.
>
> **Day 6**: The student uses the outline to complete the writing project.

Prepared Dictation

I recommend prepared dictation—and only prepared dictation. In prepared dictation, students type or write a passage after studying it for five to ten minutes. Without this preparation, the exercise is not a teaching exercise—it is a test. In *Home Education*, Charlotte Mason went further, describing dictation without preparation as "a fertile cause of bad spelling" (241).

Like copywork, dictation is a form of studying grammar, spelling, and the mechanics of writing. However, dictation requires students to take a more active role and actually study and think about the material as opposed to passively taking it in through copywork. Students who type can type their dictations instead. This simplifies the process for students who hate writing.

I know that dictation can sound like a huge, time-consuming exercise, especially with multiple students. It is not. We do prepared dictation twice a week, on the "off" days from grammar. Each of my boys studies his exercise for about 10 minutes. He chooses, sometimes with my help, two or three words to analyze. A passage should not have more than three or four unknown words to be studied. He adds these to his **Spelling Journal**, writing each word with a space between the syllables, which helps him to analyze each word syllable by syllable. The **Spelling Journal** organizes words according to phonogram or spelling rule, and it is a free download on my site.

Dictations may be written or typed. My boys type their dictations. The spelling and grammar checks are turned off in our word processing program, and we increase the font size to 20+ points so that I can read over their shoulders. I read the passages while each boy takes his turn at the keyboard. I stand behind them so that I can immediately catch and correct any mistakes.

English Lessons Through Literature includes two dictation exercises each week. Sources include the literature and poems in ELTL. If you prefer, choose dictation exercises from history, science, or free reading.

Watch as the student writes to catch mistakes immediately. Mistakes imprint on a student's mind just as correctly written material does, and this confusion is difficult to correct, as some of us have found while using poor spelling programs which ask students still learning the basics to proofread a passage. In *Home Education*, Charlotte Mason writes:

> Once the eye sees a misspelt word, that image remains; and if there is also the image of the word rightly spelt, we are perplexed as to which is which. Now we see why there could not be a more ingenious way of making bad spellers than 'dictation' as it is commonly taught. Every misspelt word is an image in the child's brain not to be obliterated by the right spelling. It becomes, therefore, the teacher's business to prevent false spelling, and, if an error has been made, to hide it away, as it were, so that the impression may not become fixed (242).

Memory Work and Reference Pages

Memory work is an important part of this program; I do not consider it an optional component. Students cannot properly analyze sentences when they do not remember the difference between a verb and an adverb, or a phrase and a clause, or if they cannot remember which verbs are linking verbs. When it comes to learning the basics of any subject, vocabulary is king.

At the back of the book, you will find pages that have all the definitions and lists from ELTL to make it easy to learn and review the information. Students can simply read through the material each week. Over time, they will memorize the material or at least become very familiar with it.

Students can also actively memorize the lists and definitions. New material can be read three times every lesson day until it is memorized. Newly learned material should be reviewed regularly at first, perhaps once a week. Material which has been learned for a longer time should be reviewed every month to six weeks, but if it stops being automatic, it should go back to the frequent review list.

As for poetry memorization, this book includes more than one hundred poems. My suggestion is to select a poem, preferably one the student enjoys, and begin to memorize it. When he has memorized it, move on to a new one.

Appendix B has sentences to read weekly for correct use of words. I highly recommend this. The purpose is akin to that of copywork in that it is intended to imprint certain grammatical concepts into the student's mind just through repetition. Saying these sentences aloud regularly will help the correct forms to "sound" right to our children and to ourselves. My advice is to read these sentences approximately once a week for the school year.

In the appendices, Levels D and up also include diagramming reference pages, a list of irregular verbs, verb tense reference pages, and the editing protocol that students use after each writing project.

Picture Study

Charlotte Mason recommended having the student look at the picture without interruption for several minutes, then putting the picture away, and having the student describe the picture. It is, in essence, a picture narration. Afterwards, bring the picture back out and see if he notices anything else. This is not art criticism, though. It is learning to attend to detail and to form a love and appreciation for art.

Each artist has six paintings studied with new paintings added every other week, so you have a full twelve weeks to enjoy each artist and to include additional activities if desired. For example, you could read a short biography of the artist and view some additional works. More paintings can often be found at www.wikiart.org, or just do an internet search for the artist's name.

All pictures of paintings in this book are, by necessity, black and white. For your convenience, color copies of the paintings are provided on my site at no cost. These can be viewed on screen or printed so that you can display the picture for the two weeks between new paintings. You can find a link to the free art files on my website; choose the "Freebies" link from the menu.

In the past, we have also used the pictures as backgrounds on my computer. However, my oldest son did tell me once that it was strange seeing a particular painting without the computer icons.

Optional Workbook

The suggested exercises and copywork are included in this book, so the workbook is truly optional. The benefits of purchasing the workbook are as follows:

1. The PDF version of the workbook is a file that may be printed out for all the children in your family. It may not be resold.

2. In Levels A through D, the copywork is already typed in a handwriting font so that you don't have to type or write it for the child to copy. There are five popular handwriting styles from which to choose.

Level D

Level D: Discerning Literature List

All the literature selections suggested herein are in the public domain in the United States of America and are probably available at your local library. The complete texts can also be found online from Project Gutenberg (www.gutenberg.org) and/or the Baldwin Project (www.mainlesson.com). Most are available as audio books, and free audio book versions may be found online from LibriVox (www.librivox.org).

This list shows in which lesson each book begins in parentheses after the book title.

The Book of Dragons by E. Nesbit (Lesson 1)

Black Beauty by Anna Sewell (Lesson 9)

Ozma of Oz by L. Frank Baum (Lesson 42)

"The Reluctant Dragon" by Kenneth Grahame (Lesson 63)
    "The Reluctant Dragon" is part of the book *Dream Days* by Kenneth Grahame on Gutenberg.org. It is also available commercially as an illustrated book.

Heidi by Johanna Spyri (Lesson 68)

Tanglewood Tales by Nathaniel Hawthorne (Lesson 91)

All the fables in Level D are African folk tales from *West African Folk-Tales* by William H. Barker and *South-African Folk-Tales* by James A. Honey.

The artists studied in Level D are Edgar Degas, South African artist (of Dutch descent) Pieter Wenning to complement the stories in this level, and Claude Monet. (Note: I would have preferred a born and bred African painter, but I am limited by what is in the public domain.)

1. Introduction to the Thesaurus

• The Book of Dragons, Chapter 1

Like the dictionary, the **thesaurus** is a book of words. But while the purpose of the dictionary is to define words, the purpose of the thesaurus is to help you find the best word for your writing.

The thesaurus includes both **synonyms** and **antonyms**. Synonyms are words which have the same or similar meanings, while antonyms have opposite meanings. In *The Book of Dragons*, young Lionel apologizes to the Prime Minister for **vexing** him.

> "Well, I'm sorry if I've **vexed** you," said Lionel. "Come, let's kiss and be friends."

Roget's Thesaurus at www.thesaurus.com lists both synonyms and antonyms for the word **vex**:

> Synonyms: afflict, agitate, annoy, displease, disquiet, disturb, embarrass, exasperate, gall, infuriate, irk, irritate, offend, peeve, perplex, rile, torment
>
> Antonyms: aid, appease, calm, comfort, delight, ease, help, make happy, please, quiet, soothe

Look at how we could change that sentence with this information:

> "Well, I'm sorry if I've **agitated** you," said Lionel.
>
> "Well, I'm sorry if I've **exasperated** you," said Lionel.
>
> "Well, I'm sorry if I **didn't help** you," said Lionel.
>
> "Well, I'm sorry if I **didn't appease** you," said Lionel.

Within the lists above, we have shades of meaning. The synonyms do not mean exactly the same thing, and the antonyms are not perfect opposites. Using the thesaurus, we can find the best word to express the exact meaning we want to convey.

The thesaurus can also help us to vary our word choice so that we are not using the same words over and over again.

Today, get acquainted with the thesaurus. Look up a few words and find different ways to say them.

New Feet Within My Garden Go

By Emily Dickinson

New feet within my garden go,
New fingers stir the sod;
A troubadour upon the elm
Betrays the solitude.
New children play upon the green,
New weary sleep below;
And still the pensive spring returns,
And still the punctual snow!

Writing: Oral Narration

A model story is one which you will be using as a model for your own writing. When you get a new model story, you will read it and give an oral narration of it. Over the following five lessons, you will have other exercises with the model story, finally producing a written narration from it.

This story is from a book called *West-African Folk Tales*. A folktale is a story that is part of the oral tradition of a people. That means it originally got passed around by people telling it orally, not by being printed in a book. Many cultures which do not have a written language still have rich storytelling traditions.

Read your new model story below, and then give your instructor an oral narration of it.

How We Got the Name "Spider Tales"

From *West-African Folk Tales* by William H. Barker

In the olden days, all the stories which men told were stories of Nyankupon, the chief of the gods. Spider, who was very conceited, wanted the stories to be told about him.

Accordingly, one day he went to Nyankupon and asked that, in future, all tales told by men might be Anansi stories instead of Nyankupon stories. Nyankupon agreed—on one condition. He told Spider (or Anansi) that he must bring him three things: the first was a jar full of live bees; the second was a boa constrictor; and the third was a tiger. Spider gave his promise.

He took an earthen vessel and set out for a place where he knew he could find numbers of bees. When he came in sight of the bees, he began saying to himself, "They will not be able to fill this jar"—"Yes, they will be able"— "No, they will not be able." At last the bees came up to him and said, "What are you talking about, Mr. Anansi?" He thereupon explained to them that Nyankupon and he had had a great dispute. Nyankupon had said the bees could not fly into the jar—Anansi had said they could. The bees immediately declared that of course they could fly into the jar—which they at once did. As soon as they were safely inside, Anansi sealed up the jar and sent it off to Nyankupon.

Next day he took a long stick and set out in search of a boa constrictor. When he arrived at the place where one lived, he began speaking to himself again. "He will just be as long as this stick"—"No, he will not be so long as this"—"Yes, he will be as long as this." These words he repeated several times, till the boa came out and asked him what was the matter. "Oh, we have been having a dispute in Nyankupon's town about you. Nyankupon's people say you are not as long as this stick. I say you are. Please let me measure you by it." The boa innocently laid himself out straight, and Spider lost no time in tying him on to the stick from end to end. He then sent him to Nyankupon.

The third day he took a needle and thread and sewed up his eye. He then set out for a den where he knew a tiger lived. As he approached the place he began to shout and sing so loudly that the tiger came out to see what was the matter. "Can you not see?" said Spider. "My eye is sewn up, and now I can see such wonderful things that I must sing about them."

"Sew up my eyes," said the tiger. "Then I too can see these surprising sights." Spider immediately did so. Having thus made the tiger helpless, he led him straight to Nyankupon's house.

Nyankupon was amazed at Spider's cleverness in fulfilling the three conditions. He immediately gave him permission for the future to call all the old tales Anansi tales.

Commonplace Book

With your instructor's approval, add the passage below to your commonplace book, or choose your own passage from a work of fiction. This can be from either school reading or free reading.

> When the people in the town saw the Dragon fly off after the Hippogriff and the King, they all came out of their houses to look, and when they saw the two disappear, they made up their minds to the worst and began to think what they would wear for Court mourning.

Dictation

> At last came a Saturday when the Dragon actually walked into the Royal nursery and carried off the King's own pet Rocking Horse. Then the King cried for six days, and on the seventh, he was so tired that he had to stop. He heard the Blue Bird singing among the roses and saw the Butterfly fluttering among the lilies, and he said, "Nurse, wipe my face, please. I am not going to cry any more."

2. Parts of Speech: Nouns

• The Book of Dragons, Chapter 2

> Definition: A noun is the name of a
> person, place, thing, or idea.

Nouns are naming words. Everything and everybody has a name, and all of those names are nouns. Some nouns name people, like **Princess Mary Ann**, a little **girl**, and **Tom**, the gardener's **boy**. Some words name places, like **castle**, **Zoological Gardens**, and **Rotundia**. Some words name things, like **pet** and **rhinoceros**, two words we thankfully do not normally see together. And some words name ideas, like **wickedness** and **love**.

Look at the following passage from *The Book of Dragons*. The underlined words are all nouns.

> What with the **elephant**, and the Princess's **affection**, and the **knowledge** that the very next **day** he would receive the **History of Rotundia**, beautifully bound, with the Royal **arms** on the **cover**, **Tom** could hardly sleep a **wink**. And, besides, the **dog** did bark so terribly. There was only one **dog** in **Rotundia**—the **kingdom** could not afford to keep more than one.

In this sentence, we have a person: Tom. We have places: kingdom and Rotundia. We have things: elephant, *History of Rotundia*, arms, cover, wink, and dog. And we have ideas: affection and knowledge. All of these words are nouns.

Nouns can be either **common** or **proper**. Common nouns like **girl** and **boy** could refer to any child at all, but **Princess Mary Ann** and **Tom** refer to very specific children. Many **kingdoms** exist, but no other like **Rotundia**. Many **elephants** are in the world, but only **Fido** is six inches tall and can fit into your pocket. Common nouns are general. Proper nouns are specific and point out an individual person, place, thing, or idea. Proper nouns always begin with a capital letter.

Some authors capitalize nouns that are not ordinarily capitalized. For instance, the animal names in Aesop are always capitalized. We have stories about the Tortoise and

23

the Hare, and even the Ants and the Grasshopper. He used the common names as if they were the proper names for his characters. If the author treats a noun as a proper noun by capitalizing it, I also treat it as a proper noun in the exercises.

You will be learning the definitions for all the parts of speech as well as lists of important material. It is important to know this information well.

The Fairy in Winter

By Walter De La Mare

There was a Fairy—flake of winter—
Who, when the snow came, whispering, Silence,
Sister crystal to crystal sighing,
Making of meadow argent palace,
Night a star-sown solitude,
Cried 'neath her frozen eaves, "I burn here!"

Wings diaphanous, beating bee-like,
Wand within fingers, locks enspangled,
Icicle foot, lip sharp as scarlet,
She lifted her eyes in her pitch-black hollow—
Green as stalks of weeds in water—
Breathed: stirred.

Rilled from her heart the ichor, coursing,
Flamed and awoke her slumbering magic.
Softlier than moth's her pinions trembled;
Out into blackness, light-like, she flittered,
Leaving her hollow cold, forsaken.

In air, o'er crystal, rang twangling night-wind.
Bare, rimed pine-woods murmured lament.

How Mushrooms First Grew

From *West African Folk-Tales* by William H. Barker

Part I

Long, long ago there dwelt in a town two brothers whose bad habits brought them much trouble. Day by day they got more deeply in debt. Their creditors gave them no peace, so at last they ran away into the woods and became highway robbers.

But they were not happy. Their minds were troubled by their evil deeds. At last they decided to go home, make a big farm, and pay off their debts gradually.

They accordingly set to work and soon had quite a fine farm prepared for corn. As the soil was good, they hoped the harvest would bring them in much money.

Unfortunately, that very day a bushfowl came along. Being hungry, it scratched up all the newly planted seeds and ate them.

The two poor brothers, on arriving at the field next day, were dismayed to find all their work quite wasted. They put down a trap for the thief. That evening the bushfowl was caught in it. The two brothers, when they came and found the bird, told it that now all their debts would be transferred to it because it had robbed them of the means of paying the debts themselves.

Writing: Copia, Playing With Words

Part of writing is developing what the ancient Greeks called copia, which means an abundance of words and phrases. The writing exercises are meant to help you develop copia, so in addition to writing narrations, you will also be playing with words and sentences so that you will learn a variety of ways to say things.

Take each of the following words from your model story and look them up in the thesaurus. Give two or three different ways to say each word.

> earthen, vessel, cleverness, conditions, stories

Exercise

Review memory work. This can be an oral exercise. Find the nouns in this passage. Which nouns are proper nouns, and which are common?

> "Come, little birthday present," he said tenderly. "The dragon will be so pleased. And I'm glad to see you're not crying. You know, my child, we cannot begin too young to learn to think of the happiness of others rather than our own. I should not like my dear little niece to be selfish or to wish to deny a trivial pleasure to a poor, sick dragon, far from his home and friends."

Commonplace Book

With your instructor's approval, add this part of today's poem to your commonplace book, or choose your own poem.

> There was a Fairy—flake of winter—
> Who, when the snow came, whispering, Silence,
> Sister crystal to crystal sighing,
> Making of meadow argent palace,
> Night a star-sown solitude,
> Cried 'neath her frozen eaves, "I burn here!"

Dictation

> Act in haste and repent at leisure.

Women on a Cafe Terrace in the Evening by Edgar Degas

Picture Study

1. Read the title and the name of the artist. Study the picture for several minutes, then put the picture away.

2. Describe the picture.

3. Look at the picture again. Do you notice any details that you missed before? What do you like or dislike about this painting? Does it remind you of anything?

3. Literary Analysis

- The Book of Dragons, Chapter 3

Writing: Literary Analysis

This is an oral exercise. With your instructor's approval, choose a story from *The Book of Dragons* or one of the other books you are currently reading, and answer the following questions.

If you could trade places with one of the characters, which one would it be, and why?

It is important to tell why you feel this way. Give examples from the story. For instance, do not say that you liked a character because he was nice. Instead, give an example from the story that shows that he was nice. For example, consider the two men in yesterday's fable who wanted to pay back their debts. Were they good men? If I wanted to write about that fable, I might say one of the following sentences.

> I think the two men were trying to be good. They stopped thieving and started farming to pay back their debts.

> I think the men were still bad. They said they wanted to pay back their debts, but when they bushfowl ate their crop, they claimed that the debts they had run up were now his.

Bluebells

By Walter De La Mare

Where the bluebells and the wind are,
Fairies in a ring I spied,
And I heard a little linnet
Singing near beside.

Where the primrose and the dew are,
Soon were sped the fairies all:

Only now the green turf freshens,
And the linnets call.

How Mushrooms First Grew

From *West African Folk-Tales* by William H. Barker

Part II

The poor bird—in great trouble at having such a burden thrust upon it—made a nest under a silk-cotton tree. There it began to lay eggs, meaning to hatch them and sell the young birds for money to pay off the debts.

A terrible hurricane came, however, and a branch of the tree came down. All the eggs were smashed. As a result, the bushfowl transferred the debts to the tree as it had broken the eggs.

The silk-cotton tree was in dismay at having such a big sum of money to pay off. It immediately set to work to make as much silk cotton as it possibly could so that it might sell it.

An elephant, not knowing all that had happened, came along. Seeing the silk cotton, he came to the tree and plucked down all its bearings. By this means the debts were transferred to the poor elephant.

The elephant was very sad when he found what he had done. He wandered away into the desert, thinking of a way to make money. He could think of none.

As he stood quietly under a tree, a poor hunter crept up. This man thought he was very lucky to find such a fine elephant standing so still. He at once shot him.

Just before the animal died, he told the hunter that now the debts would have to be paid by him. The hunter was much grieved when he heard this as he had no money at all.

He walked home wondering what he could do to make enough money to pay the debts. In the darkness he did not see the stump of a tree which the overseers had cut down in the road. He fell and broke his leg. By this means the debts were transferred to the tree-stump.

Not knowing this, a party of white ants came along next morning and began to eat into the tree. When they had broken it nearly to the ground, the tree told them that now the debts were theirs as they had killed it.

The ants, being very wise, held a council together to find out how best they could make money. They decided each to contribute as much as possible. With the proceeds, one of their young men would go to the nearest market and buy pure linen thread. This they would weave and sell and the profits would go to help pay the debts.

This was done. From time to time all the linen in stock was brought and spread out in the sunshine to keep it in good condition. When men see this linen lying out on the ant-hills, they call it "mushroom" and gather it for food.

Exercise

Review memory work. This can be an oral exercise. Find the nouns in this passage. Which nouns are proper nouns, and which are common?

"We must go and look," said Harry boldly. "You shall wear a dragonproof frock, made of stuff like the curtains. And I will smear myself all over with the best dragon poison, and—"

Effie clasped her hands, and skipped with joy, and cried: "Oh, Harry! I know where we can find St. George!"

Commonplace Book

With your instructor's approval, add the passage below to your commonplace book, or choose your own passage from a work of non-fiction. This can be from religious scriptures, a biography, or one of your history or science books.

> Then they joined hands and set out to walk to St. George's Church. As you know, there are many St. George's churches, but fortunately they took the turning that leads to the right one and went along in the bright sunlight, feeling very brave and adventurous.

4. Parts of Speech: Verbs

• The Book of Dragons, Chapter 4

> Definition: A verb is a word that shows
> action or a state of being.

Verbs are what we do. They show action. Can you **speak, hop, listen,** and **talk**? These are all action verbs. If you can do it, it is a verb. Look at the following sentences from *The Book of Dragons*. The action verbs are underlined. Notice that I use a double underline for verbs.

> The fairy spears of light <u>twinkled</u> and <u>gleamed</u>.

> George <u>kicked</u> his boots against the fencing.

Some actions are invisible. Can you **love, wonder,** and **believe**? Of course you can, but no one can see these actions. What two invisible action verbs are in the sentence below?

> Very few people know this, though you would think they could tell it by the ice in the jugs of a morning.

In the sentence above, the two invisible action verbs are **think** and **know**. Although you can do these things, the action cannot be seen by others. Can you think of other invisible action verbs?

Not all verbs show action. Some verbs merely show that something or someone exists. We call these verbs **state of being verbs**.

> The state of being verbs are am, are,
> is, was, were, be, being, been.

I am. You are. He is. These sentences show existence, not action, but they are still verbs. Often, they are used to answer questions.

31

Is it the North Pole? It is.

Were the children naughty to go there? They were.

For You, Mother
By Hilda Conkling

I have a dream for you, Mother,
Like a soft thick fringe to hide your eyes.
I have a surprise for you, Mother,
Shaped like a strange butterfly.
I have found a way of thinking
To make you happy;
I have made a song and a poem
All twisted into one.
If I sing, you listen;
If I think, you know.
I have a secret from everybody in the world full of people
But I cannot always remember how it goes;
It is a song
For you, Mother,
With a curl of cloud and a feather of blue
And a mist
Blowing along the sky.
If I sing it some day, under my voice,
Will it make you happy?

The Dance for Water or Rabbit's Triumph
From *South-African Folk-Tales* by James A. Honey

There was a frightful drought. The rivers after a while dried up, and even the springs gave no water. The animals wandered around seeking drink, but to no avail. Nowhere was water to be found.

A great gathering of animals was held: Lion, Tiger, Wolf, Jackal, Elephant, all of them came together. What was to be done? That was the question. One had this plan, and another had that; but no plan seemed of value.

Finally one of them suggested: "Come, let all of us go to the dry river bed and dance; in that way we can tread out the water."

Good! Everyone was satisfied and ready to begin instantly, excepting Rabbit, who said, "I will not go and dance. All of you are mad to attempt to get water from the ground by dancing."

The other animals danced, and danced, and ultimately danced the water to the surface. How glad they were. Everyone drank as much as he could, but Rabbit did not dance with them. So it was decided that Rabbit should have no water.

He laughed at them: "I will nevertheless drink some of your water."

That evening he proceeded leisurely to the river bed where the dance had been and drank as much as he wanted. The following morning the animals saw the footprints of

Rabbit in the ground, and Rabbit shouted to them: "Aha! I did have some of the water, and it was most refreshing and tasted fine."

Quickly all the animals were called together. What were they to do? How were they to get Rabbit in their hands? All had some means to propose; the one suggested this, and the other that.

Finally old Tortoise moved slowly forward, foot by foot: "I will catch Rabbit."

"You? How? What do you think of yourself?" shouted the others in unison.

"Rub my shell with pitch, and I will go to the edge of the water and lie down. I will then resemble a stone so that when Rabbit steps on me, his feet will stick fast."

"Yes! Yes! That's good."

And in a one, two, three, Tortoise's shell was covered with pitch, and foot by foot, he moved away to the river. At the edge, close to the water, he lay down and drew his head into his shell.

Rabbit, during the evening, came to get a drink. "Ha!" he chuckled sarcastically. "They are, after all, quite decent. Here they have placed a stone so now I need not unnecessarily wet my feet."

Rabbit trod with his left foot on the stone, and there it stuck. Tortoise then put his head out. "Ha! Old Tortoise! And it's you, is it, that's holding me. But here I still have another foot. I'll give you a good clout." Rabbit gave Tortoise what he said he would with his right fore foot, hard and straight; and there his foot remained.

"I have yet a hind foot, and with it I'll kick you." Rabbit drove his hind foot down. This also rested on Tortoise where it struck.

"But still another foot remains, and now I'll tread you." He stamped his foot down, but it stuck like the others.

He used his head to hammer Tortoise and his tail as a whip, but both met the same fate as his feet so there he was, tight and fast down to the pitch.

Tortoise now slowly turned himself round and, foot by foot, started for the other animals with Rabbit on his back.

"Ha! Ha! Ha! Rabbit! How does it look now? Insolence does not pay after all," shouted the animals.

Now advice was sought. What should they do with Rabbit? He certainly must die. But how? One said, "Behead him"; another, "Some severe penalty."

"Rabbit, how are we to kill you?"

"It does not affect me," Rabbit said. "Only a shameful death please do not pronounce."

"And what is that?" they all shouted.

"To take me by my tail and dash my head against a stone; that, I pray and beseech you, don't do."

"No, but just so you'll die. That is decided."

It was decided Rabbit should die by taking him by his tail and dashing his head to pieces against some stone. But who is to do it?

Lion, because he is the most powerful one. Good! Lion should do it. He stood up and walked to the front, and poor Rabbit was brought to him. Rabbit pleaded and beseeched that he couldn't die such a miserable death.

Lion took Rabbit firmly by the tail and swung him around. The white skin slipped off from Rabbit, and there Lion stood with the white bit of skin and hair in his paw. Rabbit was free.

Writing: Copia

Take the following sentence and play with it. Remember that the point is not necessarily to make the sentence better. The point is to play with the sentence and make it different. Make a new sentence for each number, using at least one change from that category. For number 1, change the grammar in one of the ways listed. For number 2, use synonyms or antonyms. New categories and different types of changes will be added as you learn more.

Spider, who was very conceited, wanted the stories to be told about him.

1. Change the grammar.
   • Change the nouns from common to proper and vice versa. You can make up names for this exercise if you want.
   • Change the nouns from singular to plural and vice versa.

2. Use synonyms and antonyms.
   • Substitute synonyms.
   • Say the opposite thing using antonyms.

Exercise

Review memory work. This can be an oral exercise. Find the verbs in this passage.

"Tumble for your life!" cried George, and he fell down at once because it is the only way to stop. Jane fell on top of him—and then they crawled on hands and knees to the snow at the edge of the slide—and there was a sportsman, dressed in a peaked cap and a frozen moustache, like the one you see in the pictures about Ice-Peter, and he had a gun in his hand.

Commonplace Book

With your instructor's approval, add the passage below to your commonplace book, or choose your own passage from a work of fiction. This can be from either school reading or free reading.

"Well, well," said he. "Here's a whole Arctic expedition thrown away! I shall have to go home and fit out another. And that means a lot of writing to the papers and things. You seem to be a singularly thoughtless little girl."

Dictation

All around the Pole, making a bright ring about it, were hundreds of little fires, and the flames of them did not flicker and twist, but went up blue and green and rosy and straight, like the stalks of dream lilies.
Jane said so, but George said they were as straight as ramrods.

5. How to Write a Condensed Narrative

- The Book of Dragons, Chapter 5

Today you will learn how to write a condensed narrative. A condensed narrative is also called a **summary**. When you write a summary, you leave out all the details and only include the most important information.

Read the following story.

Tit for Tat

From *West African Folk-Tales* by William H. Barker

There had been a great famine in the land for many months. Meat had become so scarce that only the rich chiefs had money enough to buy it. The poor people were starving. Anansi and his family were in a miserable state.

One day, Anansi's eldest son—Kweku Tsin—to his great joy, discovered a place in the forest where there were still many animals. Knowing his father's wicked ways, Kweku told him nothing of the matter. Anansi, however, speedily discovered that Kweku was returning loaded, day after day, to the village. There he was able to sell the meat at a good price to the hungry villagers. Anansi immediately wanted to know the secret—but his son wisely refused to tell him. The old man determined to find out by a trick.

Slipping into his son's room one night, when he was fast asleep, he cut a tiny hole in the corner of the bag which Kweku always carried into the forest. Anansi then put a quantity of ashes into the bag and replaced it where he had found it.

Next morning, as Kweku set out for the forest, he threw the bag, as usual, over his shoulder. Unknown to him, at each step, the ashes were sprinkled on the ground. Consequently, when Anansi set out an hour later, he was easily able to follow his son by means of the trail of ashes. He, too, arrived at the animals' home in the forest and found Kweku there before him. He immediately drove his son away, saying that, by the law of the land, the place belonged to him. Kweku saw how he had been tricked and determined to have the meat back.

He accordingly went home, made a tiny image, and hung little bells round its neck. He then tied a long thread to its head and returned toward the hunting-place.

When about halfway there, he hung the image to a branch of a tree in the path and hid himself in the bushes near by—holding the other end of the thread in his hand.

The greedy father, in the meantime, had killed as many animals as he could find, being determined to become rich as speedily as possible. He then skinned them and prepared the flesh to carry it to the neighboring villages to sell. Taking the first load, he set off for his own village. Halfway there, he came to the place where the image hung in the way. Thinking this was one of the gods, he stopped. As he approached, the image began to shake its head vigorously at him. He felt that this meant that the gods were angry. To please them, he said to the image, "May I give you a little of this meat?" Again the image shook its head. "May I give you half of this meat?" he then inquired. The head shook once more. "Do you want the whole of this meat?" he shouted fiercely. This time the head nodded, as if the image were well pleased. "I will not give you all my meat," Anansi cried. At this the image shook in every limb as if in a terrible temper. Anansi was so frightened that he threw the whole load on the ground and ran away. As he ran, he called back, "Tomorrow I shall go to Ekubon—you will not be able to take my meat from me there, you thief."

But Kweku had heard where his father intended to go next day and set the image in his path as before. Again Anansi was obliged to leave his whole load—and again he called out the name of the place where he would go the following day.

The same thing occurred, day after day, till all the animals in the wood were killed. By this time, Kweku Tsin had become very rich—but his father Anansi was still very poor. He was obliged to go to Kweku's house every day for food.

When the famine was over, Kweku gave a great feast and invited the entire village. While all were gathered together, Kweku told the story of his father's cunning and how it had been overcome. This caused great merriment among the villagers. Anansi was so ashamed that he readily promised Kweku to refrain from his evil tricks for the future. This promise, however, he did not keep long.

A story has a beginning, a middle, and an end. Can you identify the beginning, middle, and end of today's story?

    Beginning: A great famine was in the land, and meat was scarce.

    Middle: Kweku found a place where there were still many animals. His father, Anansi, tried to trick Kweku into telling him where the animals were, but Kweku instead tricked Anansi.

    End: Kweku gave a great feast when the famine was over and told the story of how he had overcome his father's cunning.

Notice that in our condensed version, I've left out all the details about Anansi's trickery and how Kweku overcame it. These details make the story more interesting, but they are unnecessary in a summary because the summary only tells the main parts.

When we put the parts together as a paragraph, we have a **condensed narrative** or a **summary paragraph**. The original story was almost two pages, but the summary is only a few sentences long.

> A great famine was in the land, and meat was scarce. Kweku found a place where there were still many animals. His father, Anansi, tried to trick Kweku into telling him where the animals were, but Kweku instead tricked Anansi and kept his secret. Kweku gave a great feast when the famine was over and told the story of how he had overcome his father's cunning.

The Lonesome Wave

By Hilda Conkling

There is an island
In the middle of my heart,
And all day comes lapping on the shore
A long silver wave.
It is the lonesome wave;
I cannot see the other side of it.
It will never go away
Until it meets the glad gold wave
Of happiness!

Wandering over the monstrous rocks,
Looking into the caves,
I see my island dark, all cold,
Until the gold wave sweeps in
From a sea deep blue,
And flings itself on the beach.
Oh, it is joy, then!
No more whispers like sorrow,
No more silvery lonesome lapping of the long wave . . .

Exercise

Review memory work. This can be an oral exercise. Find the verbs in this passage.

> The stuff in the cauldron boiled up in foaming flashes of yellow and blue and red and white and silver and sent out a sweet scent, and presently the witch poured it out into a pot and set it to cool in the doorway among the snakes.

Writing: Commonplace Book

Add the passage below from your model story to your commonplace book.

> Nyankupon agreed—on one condition. He told Spider (or Anansi) that he must bring him three things: the first was a jar full of live bees; the second was a boa constrictor; and the third was a tiger. Spider gave his promise.

Dictation

Use the first stanza of today's poem for dictation.

6. Condensed Narrative: How We Got the Name "Spider Tales"

• The Book of Dragons, Chapter 6

Write "How We Got the Name 'Spider Tales'" as a condensed narrative, or summary. Remember, just include the main content of the story and leave out unnecessary details. What is the beginning, the middle, and the end of "How We Got the Name 'Spider Tales'"?

Down-Adown-Derry

By Walter De Le Mare

Down-adown-derry,
Sweet Annie Maroon,
Gathering daisies
In the meadows of Doone,
Hears a shrill piping,
Elflike and free,
Where the waters go brawling
In rills to the sea;
Singing down-adown-derry.

Down-adown-derry,
Sweet Annie Maroon,
Through the green grasses
Peeps softly; and soon
Spies under green willows
A fairy whose song
Like the smallest of bubbles
Floats bobbing along;
Singing down-adown-derry.

Down-adown-derry,
Her cheeks were like wine,
Her eyes in her wee face

Like water-sparks shine,
Her niminy fingers
Her sleek tresses preen,
The which in the combing
She peeps out between;
Singing down-adown-derry.

Down-adown-derry,
Shrill, shrill was her tune:—
"Come to my water-house,
Annie Maroon:
Come in your dimity,
Ribbon on head,
To wear siller seaweed
And coral instead";
Singing down-adown-derry.

"Down-adown-derry,
Lean fish of the sea,
Bring lanthorns for feasting
The gay Faërie;
'Tis sand for the dancing,
A music all sweet
In the water-green gloaming
For thistledown feet";
Singing down-adown-derry.

Down-adown-derry,
Sweet Annie Maroon
Looked large on the fairy
Curled wan as the moon
And all the grey ripples
To the Mill racing by,
With harps and with timbrels
Did ringing reply;
Singing down-adown-derry.

"Down-adown-derry,"
Sang the Fairy of Doone,
Piercing the heart
Of Sweet Annie Maroon;
And lo! When like roses
The clouds of the sun
Faded at dusk, gone
Was Annie Maroon;
Singing down-adown-derry.

Down-adown-derry,
The daisies are few;
Frost twinkles powdery
In haunts of the dew;
And only the robin
Perched on a thorn,
Can comfort the heart
Of a father forlorn;
Singing down-adown-derry.

Down-adown-derry,
There's snow in the air;
Ice where the lily
Bloomed waxen and fair;
He may call o'er the water,
Cry—cry through the Mill,
But Annie Maroon, alas!
Answer ne'er will;
Singing down-adown-derry.

Editing

- Did you meet the goal of this writing exercise?

7. Parts of Speech: Pronouns

- The Book of Dragons, Chapter 7

> Definitions: A pronoun is a word used in the place of a noun. An antecedent is the noun that a pronoun replaces in a sentence.

We use pronouns so that we do not have to keep using the same noun over and over again. The noun replaced by a pronoun is called the **antecedent**. Consider the following sentence from *The Book of Dragons* which has had its pronouns removed:

> Sabrinetta's name was Sabrinetta, and Sabrinetta's grandmother was Sabra, who married St. George after St. George had killed the dragon, and by real rights all the country belonged to Sabrinetta.

With its pronouns, the sentence is much easier to read:

> **Her** name was Sabrinetta, and **her** grandmother was Sabra, who married St. George after **he** had killed the dragon, and by real rights all the country belonged to **her**.

In the sentence above, the antecedent for the pronoun **her** in each case is **Sabrinetta**. The antecedent of the pronoun **he** is **St. George**. Notice, though, that the sentence has a mix of nouns and pronouns. If you use too many pronouns, the antecedent may not be clear, and you may end up wondering if Sabra married St. George or the dragon.

Different pronouns are necessary for speaking about different people. We use first person pronouns when we talk about ourselves. I can talk only about myself and use the singular form, or I can talk about myself and others with the plural form.

> The first person pronouns are I, me, my, mine, we, us, our, ours.

We use second person pronouns to refer to the person we are talking to. Singular and plural pronouns are the same in the second person.

> The second person pronouns are you, your, yours.

We use third person pronouns to refer to people and things which we are talking about.

The third person pronouns are he, him, his, she, her, hers, it, its, they, them, their, theirs.

If—

By Rudyard Kipling

If you can keep your head when all about you
Are losing theirs and blaming it on you;
If you can trust yourself when all men doubt you,
But make allowance for their doubting too;
If you can wait and not be tired by waiting,
Or being lied about, don't deal in lies,
Or being hated, don't give way to hating,
And yet don't look too good, nor talk too wise;

If you can dream—and not make dreams your master;
If you can think—and not make thoughts your aim,
If you can meet with Triumph and Disaster
And treat those two impostors just the same;
If you can bear to hear the truth you've spoken
Twisted by knaves to make a trap for fools,
Or watch the things you gave your life to, broken,
And stoop and build 'em up with worn-out tools;

If you can make one heap of all your winnings
And risk it on one turn of pitch-and-toss,
And lose, and start again at your beginnings
And never breathe a word about your loss;
If you can force your heart and nerve and sinew
To serve your turn long after they are gone,
And so hold on when there is nothing in you
Except the Will which says to them: 'Hold on!'

If you can talk with crowds and keep your virtue,
Or walk with Kings—nor lose the common touch,
If neither foes nor loving friends can hurt you,
If all men count with you, but none too much;
If you can fill the unforgiving minute
With sixty seconds' worth of distance run,
Yours is the Earth and everything that's in it,
And—which is more—you'll be a Man, my son!

Writing: Oral Narration

Read your new model story below, and then give your instructor an oral narration of it.

Anansi and Nothing

From West African Folk-Tales *by William H. Barker*

Near Anansi's miserable little hut, there was a fine palace where lived a very rich man called Nothing. Nothing and Anansi proposed, one day, to go to the neighboring town to get some wives. Accordingly, they set off together.

Nothing, being a rich man, wore a very fine velvet cloth, while Anansi had a ragged cotton one. While they were on their way, Anansi persuaded Nothing to change clothes for a little while, promising to give back the fine velvet before they reached the town. He delayed doing this, however—first on one pretext, then on another—till they arrived at their destination.

Anansi, being dressed in such a fine garment, found no difficulty in getting as many wives as he wished. Poor Nothing, with his ragged and miserable cloth, was treated with great contempt. At first he could not get even one wife. At last, however, a woman took pity on him and gave him her daughter. The poor girl was laughed at very heartily by Anansi's wives for choosing such a beggar as Nothing appeared to be. She wisely took no notice of their scorn.

The party set off for home. When they reached the crossroads leading to their respective houses, the women were astonished. The road leading to Anansi's house was only half cleared. The one which led to Nothing's palace was, of course, wide and well made. Not only so, but his servants had strewn it with beautiful skins and carpets in preparation for his return. Servants were there, awaiting him, with fine clothes for himself and his wife. No one was waiting for Anansi.

Nothing's wife was queen over the whole district and had everything her heart could desire. Anansi's wives could not even get proper food; they had to live on unripe bananas with peppers. The wife of Nothing heard of her friends' miserable state and invited them to a great feast in her palace. They came and were so pleased with all they saw that they agreed to stay there. Accordingly, they refused to come back to Anansi's hut.

He was very angry and tried in many ways to kill Nothing, but without success. Finally, however, he persuaded some rat friends to dig a deep tunnel in front of Nothing's door. When the hole was finished, Anansi lined it with knives and broken bottles. He then smeared the steps of the palace with okro to make them very slippery, and he withdrew to a little distance.

When he thought Nothing's household was safely in bed and asleep, he called to Nothing to come out to the courtyard and see something. Nothing's wife, however, dissuaded him from going. Anansi tried again and again, and each time she bade her husband not to listen. At last Nothing determined to go and see this thing. As he placed his foot on the first step, of course he slipped, and down he fell into the hole. The noise alarmed the household. Lights were fetched, and Nothing was found in the ditch, so much wounded by the knives that he soon died. His wife was terribly grieved at his untimely death. She boiled many yams, mashed them, and took a great dishful of them round the district. To every child she met, she gave some so that the child might help her to cry for her husband. This is why, if you find a child crying and ask the cause, you will often be told he is "crying for Nothing."

Exercise

Review memory work. This can be an oral exercise. Find the pronouns in this passage. What is the antecedent of each pronoun?

It only came out for a minute, but she saw it quite plainly, and she said to herself: "Dear me, what a curious, shiny, bright-looking creature! If it were bigger, and if I didn't know that there have been no fabulous monsters for quite a long time now, I should almost think it was a dragon."

Commonplace Book

With your instructor's approval, add the passage below to your commonplace book, or choose your own passage from a work of fiction. This can be from either school reading or free reading.

"I wish it had not been in such a hurry to get back into the wood," said Sabrinetta. "Of course, it's quite safe for me, in my dragon-proof tower; but if it is a dragon, it's quite big enough to eat people, and today's the first of May, and the children go out to get flowers in the wood."

Dictation

The little white Princess always woke in her little white bed when the starlings began to chatter in the pearl gray morning. As soon as the woods were awake, she used to run up the twisting turret-stairs with her little bare feet, and stand on the top of the tower in her white bed-gown, and kiss her hands to the sun and to the woods and to the sleeping town, and say, "Good morning, pretty world!"

8. The Sentence

• The Book of Dragons, Chapter 8

> Definition: A sentence is a group of words
> that expresses a complete thought.

To be a sentence, a group of words must express a complete thought. To express a complete thought, a sentence must have two parts. The first part of the sentence is called the **subject**, and it tells who or what the sentence is about. The second part is called the **predicate**, and it tells what the subject is (state of being verb) or is doing (action verb).

Complete Subject	Complete Predicate
And now the cockatrice	stirred it with his tail

Above, you can see the **complete subject** and the **complete predicate** of a sentence from *The Book of Dragons*. The complete subject includes all the words which tell who or what the sentence is about. The complete predicate includes all the words that tell what the subject is or is doing.

The sentence also has a **simple subject** and a **simple predicate**. The simple subject is the main word—a noun or pronoun—which tells who or what the sentence is about. The simple predicate is the main word—a verb— which tells what the subject is or is doing.

Who is this sentence about? The **cockatrice**. What is he doing? He **stirred**. The simple subject of the sentence is **cockatrice**, and the simple predicate is **stirred**.

We can draw a word picture, called a diagram, to show the parts of a sentence. We start with a long line divided in half. On the left hand side, we write the simple subject. On the right hand side, we write the simple predicate.

| cockatrice | stirred |

Name the simple subject and simple predicate from each of the following sentences.

So the cockatrice began.

And Edmund ate his eggs and his turnover.

He told the boys at school about the cockatrice.

When you do your exercises, you will double underline the simple predicate and underline the simple subject. Label each part of speech: nouns N, proper nouns PN, pronouns PRO, and verbs V. If a part of speech is more than one word, make arms stretched out to include the whole thing, like this:

———PN———

Then you will diagram the simple subject and the simple predicate of each sentence.

       n   v
So the cockatrice began.

     pn   v
And Edmund ate his eggs and his turnover.

pro v
He told the boys at school about the cockatrice.

| cockatrice | began |

| Edmund | ate |

| He | told |

The Bee Is Not Afraid of Me

By Emily Dickinson

The bee is not afraid of me,
I know the butterfly;
The pretty people in the woods
Receive me cordially.

The brooks laugh louder when I come,
The breezes madder play.
Wherefore, mine eyes, thy silver mists?
Wherefore, O summer's day?

The World's Reward

From *South-African Folk-Tales* by James A. Honey

Part I

Once there was a man that had an old dog, so old that the man desired to put him aside. The dog had served him very faithfully when he was still young, but ingratitude is the world's reward, and the man now wanted to dispose of him. The old dumb creature, however, ferreted out the plan of his master, and so at once he resolved to go away of his own accord.

After he had walked quite a way he met an old bull in the veldt.

"Don't you want to go with me?" asked the dog.

"Where?" was the reply.

"To the land of the aged," said the dog, "where troubles don't disturb you and thanklessness does not deface the deeds of man."

"Good," said the bull, "I am your companion."

The two now walked on and found a ram.

The dog laid the plan before him, and all moved off together until they afterwards came successively upon a donkey, a cat, a rooster, and a goose. These joined their company, and the seven set out on their journey.

Late one night, they came to a house, and through the open door, they saw a table spread with all kinds of nice food, of which some robbers were having their fill. It would help nothing to ask for admittance, and seeing that they were hungry, they must think of something else.

Therefore the donkey climbed up on the bull, the ram on the donkey, the dog on the ram, the cat on the dog, the goose on the cat, and the rooster on the goose, and with one accord they all let out terrible noises. The bull began to bellow, the donkey to bray, the dog to bark, the ram to bleat, the cat to mew, the goose to giggle gaggle, and the rooster to crow, all without cessation.

The people in the house were frightened perfectly limp. They glanced out through the front door, and there they stared on the strange sight. Some of them took to the ropes over the back lower door; some disappeared through the window; and in a few counts, the house was empty.

Then the seven old animals climbed down from one another, stepped into the house, and satisfied themselves with the delicious food.

Writing: Copia, Playing With Words

Take each of the following words from your model story and look them up in the thesaurus. Give two or three different ways to say each word.

> garment, scorn, wounded, miserable, rich

Exercise

Review memory work. This can be an oral exercise. Find the pronouns in this passage. What is the antecedent of each pronoun?

> Now, one day Edmund made a new lantern out of something chemical that he sneaked from the school laboratory. And with it, he went exploring again to see if he could find the things that made the other sorts of noises.

Copy each sentence below. Double underline the predicate, and underline the subject. Label the part of speech of each Noun, N; Proper Noun, PN; Pronoun, PRO; Verb, V. Diagram the simple subject and simple predicate from each sentence.

> The next moment Edmund turned a corner.

> He told him about mines and treasures and geological formations.

> He pointed out of the window.

Commonplace Book

With your instructor's approval, add this part of today's poem to your commonplace book, or choose your own poem.

> The bee is not afraid of me,
> I know the butterfly;
> The pretty people in the woods
> Receive me cordially.
>
> The brooks laugh louder when I come,
> The breezes madder play.
> Wherefore, mine eyes, thy silver mists?
> Wherefore, O summer's day?

Dictation

The smaller the mind, the greater the conceit.

A Woman Seated Beside a Vase of Flowers by Edgar Degas

Picture Study

1. Read the title and the name of the artist. Study the picture for several minutes, then put the picture away.

2. Describe the picture.

3. Look at the picture again. Do you notice any details that you missed before? What do you like or dislike about this painting? Does it remind you of anything?

9. Descriptive Writing

- Black Beauty, Chapter 1

Today we are going to look at a **descriptive passage**. A descriptive passage is one which describes a person, place, thing, idea, or event. The author creates a picture with words.

The descriptive passage we will be looking at is the beginning of *Black Beauty*. In this passage, Black Beauty describes the first home he can remember:

> The first place that I can well remember was a large pleasant meadow with a pond of clear water in it. Some shady trees leaned over it, and rushes and water-lilies grew at the deep end. Over the hedge on one side, we looked into a plowed field, and on the other we looked over a gate at our master's house, which stood by the roadside; at the top of the meadow was a grove of fir trees, and at the bottom was a running brook overhung by a steep bank.

The description does not tell us which side the master's house is on and which side the field is on. It does not tell us exactly where the pond is located or which end is the deep end. However, it still gives us enough details so that we can have a general idea of the layout of the meadow that Black Beauty remembers.

Since a descriptive passage paints a word picture, you should be able to draw a picture from a good description. Try to draw a picture of your own from the first paragraph of *Black Beauty* before looking at the example on the next page. The point is not to create a perfect picture, so do not worry if you think that you do not draw well. The point is to draw a representation of what is described in the passage. Later on, this picture will help you to write your own description about Black Beauty's memory.

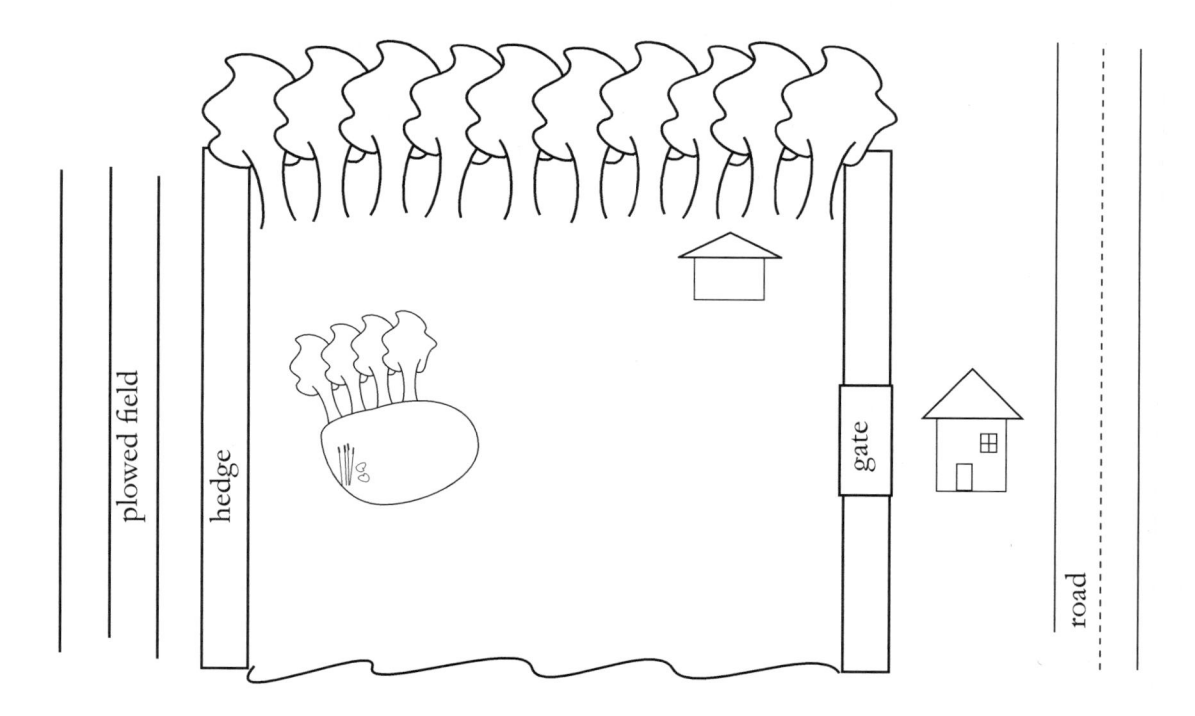

If you need to keep up with details sometimes, and you do not want to draw a picture, you can also make a few notes with words instead.

- A large meadow
- Pond in meadow with shady trees along one side and rushes and water lilies at the deep end
- Plowed field on one side
- Master's house on the other side by the road
- Grove of fir trees at the top of the meadow
- Running brook with a steep bank at the bottom of the meadow

Writing: Descriptive Writing

Read the passage below and write a narration from it. Notice the words that Anna Sewell uses to create a word picture. Use your picture to remember the details of the meadow. This passage describes not only the meadow, but also some of Black Beauty's early memories.

Black Beauty

The first place that I can well remember was a large pleasant meadow with a pond of clear water in it. Some shady trees leaned over it, and rushes and water-lilies grew at the deep end. Over the hedge on one side, we looked into a plowed field, and on the other we looked over a gate at our master's house, which stood by the roadside; at the top of the meadow was a grove of fir trees, and at the bottom was a running brook overhung by a steep bank.

While I was young, I lived upon my mother's milk, as I could not eat grass. In the daytime, I ran by her side, and at night, I lay down close by her. When it was hot, we used to stand by the pond in the shade of the trees, and when it was cold, we had a nice warm shed near the grove.

As soon as I was old enough to eat grass, my mother used to go out to work in the daytime and come back in the evening.

There were six young colts in the meadow besides me; they were older than I was; some were nearly as large as grown-up horses. I used to run with them and had great fun; we used to gallop all together round and round the field as hard as we could go. Sometimes we had rather rough play, for they would frequently bite and kick as well as gallop.

The Band

By C. J. Dennis

Hey, there! Listen awhile! Listen awhile, and come.
Down in the street there are marching feet, and I hear the beat of a drum.
Bim! Boom!! Out of the room! Pick up your hat and fly!
Isn't it grand? The band! The band! The band is marching by!

Oh, the clarinet is the finest yet, and the uniforms are gay.
    Tah, rah! We don't go home—
    Oom, pah! We won't go home—
Oh, we shan't go home, and we can't go home when the band begins to play.

Oh, see them swinging along, swinging along the street!
Left, right! buttons so bright, jackets and caps so neat.
Ho, the Fire Brigade, or a dress parade of the Soldier-men is grand;
But everyone, for regular fun, wants a Big-Brass-Band.

The slide-trombone is a joy alone, and the drummer! He's a treat!
    So, Rackety-rumph! We don't go home—
    Boom, Bumph! We won't go home—
Oh, we shan't go home, and we can't go home while the band is in the street.
    Tooral-ooral, Oom-pah!
    The band is in the street!

The World's Reward

From *South-African Folk-Tales* by James A. Honey

Part II

But when they had finished, there still remained a great deal of food, too much to take with them on their remaining journey, and so together they contrived a plan to hold their position until the next day after breakfast.
    The dog said, "See here, I am accustomed to watch at the front door of my master's house," and thereupon flopped himself down to sleep.
    The bull said, "I go behind the door," and there he took his position.
    The ram said, "I will go up on to the loft."
    The donkey said, "I will be at the middle door."
    The cat said, "I will be in the fireplace."
    The goose said, "I will be in the back door."
    And the rooster said, "I am going to sleep on the bed."
    The captain of the robbers, after a while, sent one of his men back to see if these creatures had yet left the house. The man came very cautiously into the neighborhood,

listened and listened, but he heard nothing; he peeped through the window and saw in the grate just two coals still glimmering and started to walk through the front door.

There the old dog seized him by the leg. He jumped into the house, but the bull was ready; he swept him up with his horns and tossed him on to the loft. Here the ram received him and pushed him off the loft again. Reaching ground, he made for the middle door, but the donkey set up a terrible braying and, at the same time, gave him a kick that landed him in the fireplace, where the cat flew at him and scratched him nearly to pieces. He then jumped out through the back door, and here the goose got him by the trousers. When he was some distance away, the rooster crowed. He then ran so that you could hear the stones rattle in the dark.

Purple and crimson and out of breath, he came back to his companions.

"Frightful, frightful!" was all that they could get from him at first, but after a while, he told them.

"When I looked through the window, I saw in the fireplace two bright coals shining, and when I wanted to go through the front door to go and look, I stepped into an iron trap. I jumped into the house, and there someone seized me with a fork and pitched me up on to the loft. There again, someone was ready and threw me down on all fours. I wanted to fly through the middle door, but there someone blew on a trumpet and smote me with a sledge hammer so that I did not know where I landed; but coming to very quickly, I found I was in the fireplace, and there another flew at me and scratched the eyes almost out of my head. I then fled out of the back door, and lastly I was attacked on the leg by the sixth with a pair of fire tongs, and when I was still running away, someone shouted out of the house, 'Stop him, stop h—i—m!'"

Exercise

Review memory work. This can be an oral exercise. Find the pronouns in this passage. What is the antecedent of each pronoun?

> There were six young colts in the meadow besides me; they were older than I was; some were nearly as large as grown-up horses. I used to run with them and had great fun; we used to gallop all together round and round the field as hard as we could go. Sometimes we had rather rough play, for they would frequently bite and kick as well as gallop.

Copy each sentence below. Double underline the predicate, and underline the subject. Label the part of speech of each word. Noun, N; Proper Noun, PN; Pronoun, PRO; Verb, V. Diagram the simple subject and simple predicate from each sentence.

> He gave us good food, good lodging, and kind words.

> My mother always took him to the town.

> We trotted up nearer to see what went on.

Commonplace Book

With your instructor's approval, add the passage below to your commonplace book, or choose your own passage from a work of non-fiction. This can be from religious scriptures, a biography, or one of your history or science books.

"I hope you will grow up gentle and good and never learn bad ways; do your work with a good will, lift your feet up well when you trot, and never bite or kick even in play."

I have never forgotten my mother's advice; I knew she was a wise old horse, and our master thought a great deal of her. Her name was Duchess, but he often called her Pet.

Editing

- Did you meet the goal of this writing exercise?

- Look at your word choice. Is there a good mixture of nouns and pronouns? Is the antecedent of each pronoun clear?

10. The Four Types of Sentences, Part 1

- Black Beauty, Chapters 2-3

We have four types of sentences, and today we will talk about two of them.

1. A declarative sentence makes a statement. It ends with a period.

To declare means to state or announce something. The purpose of a **declarative sentence** is to give information.

> She never would go to that part of the field afterward.

2. An interrogative sentence asks a question. It ends with a question mark.

To interrogate means to ask questions. You may have read or seen a story in which criminal suspects were **interrogated** by law enforcement. The purpose of an **interrogative sentence** is to ask for information.

> "What hare?" I said.

We can change sentences from one type to another. Look at the example sentences above from *Black Beauty*. Can you make the first one a question and the second one a statement? You might need to change a word or two to make it work. Here is a way that we could change each of those sentences:

> Would she ever would go to that part of the field afterward?

> "That hare," I said.

When the sentence type changes, the meaning of the sentence also changes. The sentence type helps to give meaning to the sentence.

The Ruin

By Walter De La Mare

When the last colors of the day
Have from their burning ebbed away,
About that ruin, cold and lone,
The cricket shrills from stone to stone;
And scattering o'er its darkened green,
Bands of the fairies may be seen,
Chattering like grasshoppers, their feet
Dancing a thistledown dance round it:
While the great gold of the mild moon
Tinges their tiny acorn shoon.

Thunder and Anansi

From *West African Folk-Tales* by William H. Barker

Part I

    There had been a long and severe famine in the land where Anansi lived. He had been quite unable to obtain food for his poor wife and family. One day, gazing desperately out to sea, he saw, rising from the midst of the water, a tiny island with a tall palm tree upon it. He determined to reach this tree—if any means proved possible—and climb it in the hope of finding a few nuts to reward him. How to get there was the difficulty.

    This, however, solved itself when he reached the beach, for there lay the means to his hand, in the shape of an old broken boat. It certainly did not look very strong, but Anansi decided to try it.

    His first six attempts were unsuccessful—a great wave dashed him back on the beach each time he tried to put off. He was persevering, however, and at the seventh trial was successful in getting away. He steered the battered old boat as best he could, and at length reached the palm tree of his desire. Having tied the boat to the trunk of the tree—which grew almost straight out of the water—he climbed toward the nuts. Plucking all he could reach, he dropped them, one by one, down to the boat. To his dismay, everyone missed the boat and fell, instead, into the water until only the last one remained. This he aimed even more carefully than the others, but it also fell into the water and disappeared from his hungry eyes. He had not tasted even one, and now all were gone.

    He could not bear the thought of going home empty-handed, so in his despair, he threw himself into the water, too. To his complete astonishment, instead of being drowned, he found himself standing on the sea-bottom in front of a pretty little cottage. From the latter came an old man who asked Anansi what he wanted so badly that he had come to Thunder's cottage to seek it. Anansi told his tale of woe, and Thunder showed himself most sympathetic.

    He went into the cottage and fetched a fine cooking-pot which he presented to Anansi, telling him that he need never be hungry again. The pot would always supply enough food for himself and his family. Anansi was most grateful and left Thunder with many thanks.

Being anxious to test the pot at once, Anansi only waited till he was again seated in the old boat to say, "Pot, pot, what you used to do for your master, do now for me." Immediately good food of all sorts appeared. Anansi ate a hearty meal, which he very much enjoyed.

On reaching land again, his first thought was to run home and give all his family a good meal from his wonderful pot. A selfish, greedy fear prevented him. "What if I should use up all the magic of the pot on them and have nothing more left for myself! Better keep the pot a secret—then I can enjoy a meal when I want one." So, his mind full of this thought, he hid the pot.

Writing: Copia

Take the following sentence and play with it. Remember that the point is not necessarily to make the sentence better. The point is to play with the sentence and make it different. Make one new sentence from each of the following categories.

> The wife of Nothing heard of her friends' miserable state and invited them to a great feast in her palace.

1. Change the grammar.
   - Change the nouns from common to proper and vice versa.
   - Change the nouns from singular to plural and vice versa.
   - Change the sentence type.

2. Condense the sentence.

3. Use synonyms and antonyms.
   - Substitute synonyms.
   - Say the opposite thing using antonyms.

Exercise

Review memory work. Find the pronouns in this passage. What is the antecedent of each pronoun?

> When I was four years old, Squire Gordon came to look at me. He examined my eyes, my mouth, and my legs; he felt them all down; and then I had to walk and trot and gallop before him. He seemed to like me and said, "When he has been well broken in, he will do very well."

Copy each sentence below. Double underline the predicate, and underline the subject. Label the part of speech of each word. Noun, N; Proper Noun, PN; Pronoun, PRO; Verb, V. Diagram the simple subject and simple predicate from each sentence.

> My master sent me for a fortnight to a neighboring farmer's.

> I galloped to the further side of the meadow.

> My master often drove me in double harness with my mother.

Commonplace Book

With your instructor's approval, add the passage below to your commonplace book, or choose your own passage from a work of fiction. This can be from either school reading or free reading.

> When I was four years old, Squire Gordon came to look at me. He examined my eyes, my mouth, and my legs; he felt them all down; and then I had to walk and trot and gallop before him. He seemed to like me and said, "When he has been well broken in, he will do very well."

Dictation

Before I was two years old, a circumstance happened which I have never forgotten. It was early in the spring; there had been a little frost in the night, and a light mist still hung over the woods and meadows. I and the other colts were feeding at the lower part of the field when we heard, quite in the distance, what sounded like the cry of dogs.

11. Parts of Speech: Adjectives; Articles

• Black Beauty, Chapter 4

> Definition: An adjective is a word that modifies a noun or a pronoun. Adjectives tell what kind, how many, which one, and whose.

Adjectives point out and describe nouns and pronouns. Do you ever have an apple for a snack? Do you like your apple **big** or **small**? Do you prefer **red** or **green**? Do you like your apple **juicy** or **dried**? All of the bold words are adjectives which tell us more about the apple.

Look at the following sentence from *Black Beauty*. The large, bold words are adjectives.

> The **first** stall was a **large square** one, shut in behind with a **wooden** gate; the others were **common** stalls, **good** stalls, but not nearly so **large**.

Adjectives tell what kind, how many, which one, and whose. Today, we are talking about adjectives that tell **what kind** and **how many**.

Adjectives that tell **what kind** are descriptive in nature. What kind of ball? The **red, striped, bouncy** ball or the **hard, heavy, bowling** ball? What kind of pet? The **large, furry** dog or the **bald, scaly** lizard? Adjectives tell **what kind**.

What kind of stall did Beauty have? One which was **large** and **square**. The others were **common** stalls, **good** but not as **large**. Using adjectives, the author tells us more about Beauty's new home.

Adjectives also tell **how many**. Numbers are adjectives that tell how many, but we have other words which describe an amount of something as well, such as **plenty, some, several, few,** and **much**. **None** is also an adjective that tells **how many**.

> But I need only describe the stable into which I was taken; this was very roomy, with **four** good stalls.

> He gave me **some** very nice oats; he patted me, spoke kindly, and then went away.

Articles are the most common adjectives that you will see.

The articles are a, an, the. Articles are adjectives.

The is the **definite** article, while **a** and **an** are called **indefinite** articles. **The** is specific in nature, while **a** and **an** are non-specific in nature. In other words, "a book" may refer to any book at all, but "the book" implies a specific book. **A** is used before words which begin with a consonant, and **an** is used before words which begin with a vowel.

An adjective is diagrammed by placing it on a slanted line below the noun or pronoun which it modifies.

The kindly groom patted me.

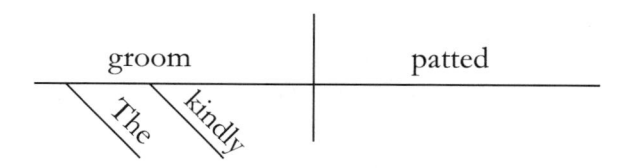

```
   groom    |    patted
  \   \     |
 The  kindly
```

The Nightingale and the Glow-worm
By William Cowper

A nightingale, that all day long
Had cheered the village with his song,
Nor yet at eve his note suspended,
Nor yet when eventide was ended,
Began to feel, as well he might,
The keen demands of appetite;
When, looking eagerly around,
He spied far off, upon the ground,
A something shining in the dark,
And knew the glow-worm by his spark;
So, stooping down from hawthorn top,
He thought to put him in his crop.
The worm, aware of his intent,
Harangued him thus, right eloquent:
  "Did you admire my lamp," quoth he,
  "As much as I your minstrelsy,
You would abhor to do me wrong,
As much as I to spoil your song;
For 'twas the self-same power divine,
Taught you to sing and me to shine;
That you with music, I with light,
Might beautify and cheer the night."
The songster heard his short oration,
And warbling out his approbation,
Released him, as my story tells,
And found a supper somewhere else.

Thunder and Anansi

From *West African Folk-Tales* by William H. Barker

Part II

He reached home, pretending to be utterly worn out with fatigue and hunger. There was not a grain of food to be had anywhere. His wife and poor children were weak with want of it, but selfish Anansi took no notice of that. He congratulated himself at the thought of his magic pot, now safely hidden in his room. There he retired from time to time when he felt hungry and enjoyed a good meal. His family got thinner and thinner, but he grew plumper and plumper. They began to suspect some secret and determined to find it out. His eldest son, Kweku Tsin, had the power of changing himself into any shape he chose; so he took the form of a tiny fly and accompanied his father everywhere. At last, Anansi, feeling hungry, entered his room and closed the door. Next he took the pot and had a fine meal. After replacing the pot in its hiding-place, he went out on the pretence of looking for food.

As soon as he was safely out of sight, Kweku Tsin fetched out the pot and called all his hungry family to come at once. They had as good a meal as their father had had. When they had finished, Mrs. Anansi—to punish her husband—said she would take the pot down to the village and give everybody a meal. This she did—but alas! In working to prepare so much food at one time, the pot grew too hot and melted away. What was to be done now? Anansi would be so angry! His wife forbade everyone to mention the pot.

Anansi returned, ready for his supper and, as usual, went into his room, carefully shutting the door. He went to the hiding-place—it was empty. He looked around in consternation. No pot was to be seen anywhere. Someone must have discovered it. His family must be the culprits; he would find a means to punish them.

Saying nothing to anyone about the matter, he waited till morning. As soon as it was light, he started off towards the shore, where the old boat lay. Getting into the boat, it started of its own accord and glided swiftly over the water—straight for the palm tree. When he arrived there, Anansi attached the boat as before and climbed the tree. This time, unlike the last, the nuts almost fell into his hands. When he aimed them at the boat, they fell easily into it—not one dropping into the water as before. He deliberately took them and threw them overboard, immediately jumping after them. As before, he found himself in front of Thunder's cottage, with Thunder waiting to hear his tale. This he told, and the old man showed the same sympathy as he had previously done.

This time, he presented Anansi with a fine stick and bade him goodbye. Anansi could scarcely wait till he got into the boat, so anxious was he to try the magic properties of his new gift. "Stick, stick," he said. "What you used to do for your master, do for me also." The stick began to beat him so severely that, in a few minutes, he was obliged to jump into the water and swim ashore, leaving boat and stick to drift away where they pleased. Then he returned sorrowfully homeward, bemoaning his many bruises and wishing he had acted more wisely from the beginning.

Exercise

Review memory work. Copy each sentence below. Double underline the predicate, and underline the subject. Label the part of speech of each word. Noun, N; Proper Noun, PN; Pronoun, PRO; Verb, V; Adjective, ADJ; Article, ART. Diagram each sentence.

Handsome Merrylegs turned.

The colt spoke.

Ill-tempered Ginger snapped.

Writing: Commonplace Book

Add the passage below from your model story to your commonplace book.

> While they were on their way, Anansi persuaded Nothing to change clothes for a little while, promising to give back the fine velvet before they reached the town. He delayed doing this, however, first on one pretext, then on another—till they arrived at their destination.

Dictation

Use part of today's poem for dictation.

12. Condensed Narrative: Anansi and Nothing

- Black Beauty, Chapters 5-6

Write "Anansi and Nothing" as a condensed narrative, or summary. Remember, just include the main content of the story and leave out unnecessary details. What is the beginning, the middle, and the end of the story?

Sleepyhead

By Walter De La Mare

As I lay awake in the white moonlight
I heard a faint singing in the wood,
"Out of bed,
Sleepyhead,
Put your white foot, now;
Here are we
Beneath the tree
Singing round the root now."

I looked out of window, in the white moonlight,
The leaves were like snow in the wood—
"Come away,
Child, and play
Light with the gnomies;
In a mound,
Green and round,
That's where their home is.

"Honey sweet,
Curds to eat,
Cream and frumenty,
Shells and beads,
Poppy seeds,
You shall have plenty."

But, as soon as I stooped in the dim moonlight
To put on my stocking and my shoe,
The sweet shrill singing echoed faintly away,
And the grey of the morning peeped through,
And instead of the gnomies there came a red robin
To sing of the buttercups and dew.

Editing

- Did you meet the goal of this writing exercise?
- Look at your word choice. Is there a good mixture of nouns and pronouns? Is the antecedent of each pronoun clear?

13. The Four Types of Sentences, Part 2

- Black Beauty, Chapter 7

You have learned about the first two types of sentences. Can you remember what they are?

1. A declarative sentence makes a statement. It ends with a period. The purpose of a declarative sentence is to give information.

2. An interrogative sentence asks a question. It ends with a question mark. The purpose of an interrogative sentence is to ask for information.

Today, we will be talking about the last two types of sentences.

3. An exclamatory sentence shows sudden or strong feeling. It ends with an exclamation mark.

To exclaim means to cry out suddenly. The purpose of an **exclamatory sentence** is to show that sudden or strong feelings are involved.

"How good that mash was!"

4. An imperative sentence gives a command or makes a request. It ends with a period.

An *imperator* was a Roman general. Do you know what generals do? They give commands! The purpose of an **imperative sentence** is to get someone to do something.

"Come along, lassie, come along."

Sometimes, a sentence seems to be both an exclamatory and an imperative sentence, like this one:

"Stand still, stand still!"

It gives a command, but it also shows sudden or strong feeling. Since it ends with an exclamation mark, we count it as an exclamatory sentence. Exclamatory sentences end with exclamation marks, and imperative sentences end with periods.

Look at the following sentences from *Black Beauty*. Name each sentence type, then change it to another type.

> Ginger stamped her foot as if the very thought of him made her angry.

> "Stand back," said the master.

> "Didn't you know that Farmer Grey's old Duchess was the mother of them both?"

Here is one way to change each of the sentences. Your answers may have been different depending on which type of sentence you changed each one into.

> Ginger stamped her foot as if the very thought of him made her angry!

> "Should you stand back?" asked the master.

> "You did not know that Farmer Grey's old Duchess was the mother of them both."

Angels in the Early Morning
By Emily Dickinson

Angels in the early morning
May be seen the dews among,
Stooping, plucking, smiling, flying:
Do the buds to them belong?
Angels when the sun is hottest
May be seen the sands among,
Stooping, plucking, sighing, flying;
Parched the flowers they bear along.

Writing: Oral Narration

Read your new model story below, and then give your instructor an oral narration of it.

Why We See Ants Carrying Bundles as Big as Themselves
From *West African Folk-Tales* by William H. Barker

Part I

Kweku Anansi and Kweku Tsin—his son—were both very clever farmers. Generally they succeeded in getting fine harvests from each of their farms. One year, however, they were very unfortunate. They had sown their seeds as usual, but no rain had fallen for more than a month after, and it looked as if the seeds would be unable to sprout.

Kweku Tsin was walking sadly through his fields one day looking at the bare, dry ground and wondering what he and his family would do for food if they were unable to get any harvest. To his surprise, he saw a tiny dwarf seated by the roadside. The little hunchback asked the reason for his sadness, and Kweku Tsin told him. The dwarf promised to help him by bringing rain on the farm. He bade Kweku fetch two small sticks and tap him lightly on the hump, while he sang:

"O water, go up! O water, go up, And let rain fall, and let rain fall!"

To Kweku's great joy, rain immediately began to fall and continued till the ground was thoroughly well soaked. In the days following, the seeds germinated, and the crops began to promise well.

Anansi soon heard how well Kweku's crops were growing—while his own were still bare and hard. He went straightway to his son and demanded to know the reason. Kweku Tsin, being an honest fellow, at once told him what had happened.

Anansi quickly made up his mind to get his farm watered in the same way and accordingly set out toward it. As he went, he cut two big, strong sticks, thinking, "My son made the dwarf work with little sticks. I will make him do twice as much with my big ones." He carefully hid the big sticks, however, when he saw the dwarf coming toward him. As before, the hunchback asked what the trouble was, and Anansi told him. "Take two small sticks and beat me lightly on the hump," said the dwarf. "I will get rain for you."

But Anansi took his big sticks and beat so hard that the dwarf fell down dead. The greedy fellow was now thoroughly frightened, for he knew that the dwarf was jester to the King of the country and a very great favorite of his. He wondered how he could fix the blame on someone else. He picked up the dwarf's dead body and carried it to a kola-tree. There he laid it on one of the top branches and sat down under the tree to watch.

By and by Kweku Tsin came along to see if his father had succeeded in getting rain for his crops. "Did you not see the dwarf, father?" he asked as he saw the old man sitting alone.

"Oh, yes!" replied Anansi. "But he has climbed this tree to pick kola. I am now waiting for him."

"I will go up and fetch him," said the young man who immediately began to climb. As soon as his head touched the body, the latter, of course, fell to the ground.

"Oh! What have you done, you wicked fellow?" cried his father. "You have killed the King's jester!"

"That is all right," quietly replied the son, who saw that this was one of Anansi's tricks. "The King is very angry with him and has promised a bag of money to anyone who would kill him. I will now go and get the reward."

"No! No! No!" shouted Anansi. "The reward is mine. I killed him with two big sticks. I will take him to the King."

"Very well," was the son's reply. "As you killed him, you may take him."

Off set Anansi, quite pleased with the prospect of getting a reward. He reached the King's court only to find the King very angry at the death of his favorite. The body of the jester was shut up in a great box, and Anansi was condemned, as a punishment, to carry it on his head for ever. The King enchanted the box so that it could never be set down on the ground. The only way in which Anansi could ever get rid of it was by getting some other man to put it on his head. This, of course, no one was willing to do.

At last, one day when Anansi was almost worn out with his heavy burden, he met the Ant. "Will you hold this box for me while I go to market and buy some things I need badly?" said Anansi to Mr. Ant.

"I know your tricks, Anansi," replied Ant. "You want to be rid of it."

"Oh, no, indeed, Mr. Ant," protested Anansi. "Indeed I will come back for it, I promise."

Mr. Ant, who was an honest fellow and always kept his own promises, believed him. He took the box on his head, and Anansi hurried off. Needless to say, the sly fellow had not the least intention of keeping his word. Mr. Ant waited in vain for his return and was obliged to wander all the rest of his life with the box in his head. That is the reason we so often see ants carrying great bundles as they hurry along.

Exercise

Review memory work. Copy each sentence below. Double underline the predicate, and underline the subject. Label the part of speech of each word. Noun, N; Proper Noun, PN; Pronoun, PRO; Verb, V; Adjective, ADJ; Article, ART. Diagram each sentence.

Strong, tall, bold Samson boasted.

The kindly old master helped.

Steady, thoughtful Job trained.

Commonplace Book

With your instructor's approval, add the passage below to your commonplace book, or choose your own passage from a work of fiction. This can be from either school reading or free reading.

> "He looked closely at it, shook his head, and told the man to fetch a good bran mash and put some meal into it. How good that mash was, and so soft and healing to my mouth. He stood by all the time I was eating, stroking me and talking to the man."

Dictation

> "He was a very fine old gentleman with quite white hair, but his voice was what I should know him by among a thousand. It was not high, nor yet low, but full, and clear, and kind, and when he gave orders, it was so steady and decided that everyone knew, both horses and men, that he expected to be obeyed."

14. Linking Verbs; Predicate Nominatives

- Black Beauty, Chapters 8-9

> The linking verbs are am, are, is, was, were,
> be, being, been, become, seem.

The linking verb list is almost identical to the list of state of being verbs. While the state of being verbs just state that something exists, the linking verbs link the subject of the sentence together with interesting information about the subject.

When a noun or pronoun follows a linking verb, we call it a **predicate nominative**. It renames the subject of the sentence.

Black Beauty is a horse.

As for Merrylegs, he and I soon became great friends.

The predicate nominative answers the question **who** or **what** after a linking verb. Notice that the noun which follows the linking verb may have modifiers. Black Beauty is what? A **horse**. He and I became what? Great **friends**.

We mark linking verbs LV. We diagram a predicate nominative by placing a slanted line after the linking verb and placing the predicate nominative after it—like the slanted line, the predicate nominative points back to the subject.

```
    ——pn——   lv art  n
Black Beauty is  a  horse.
```

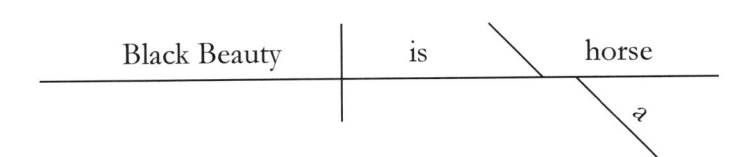

Black Beauty	is \ horse
	a

Jack Frost

By Hannah Flagg Gould

The Frost looked forth, one still, clear night,
And whispered, "Now I shall be out of sight;
So through the valley and over the height,
  In silence I'll take my way:
I will not go on with that blustering train,
The wind and the snow, the hail and the rain,
Who make so much bustle and noise in vain,
  But I'll be as busy as they."

Then he flew to the mountain and powdered its crest;
He lit on the trees, and their boughs he dressed
In diamond beads—and over the breast
  Of the quivering lake he spread
A coat of mail, that it need not fear
The downward point of many a spear
That hung on its margin far and near,
  Where a rock could rear its head.

He went to the windows of those who slept,
And over each pane, like a fairy, crept;
Wherever he breathed, wherever he slept,
  By the light of the moon were seen
Most beautiful things—there were flowers and trees;
There were bevies of birds and swarms of bees;
There were cities with temples and towers, and these
  All pictured in silver sheen!

But he did one thing that was hardly fair;
He peeped in the cupboard, and finding there
That all had forgotten for him to prepare—
  "Now just to set them a-thinking,
I'll bite this basket of fruit," said he,
  "This costly pitcher I'll burst in three,
And the glass of water they've left for me
  Shall 'tchich!' to tell them I'm drinking."

How Beasts and Serpents First Came Into the World

From *West African Folk-Tales* by William H. Barker

Part I

The famine had lasted nearly three years. Kweku Tsin, being very hungry, looked daily in the forest in the hope of finding food. One day he was fortunate enough to discover three palm-kernels lying on the ground. He picked up two stones with which to crack them. The first nut, however, slipped when he hit it and fell into a hole behind him. The same thing happened to the second and to the third. Very much annoyed at his loss, Kweku determined to go down the hole to see if he could find his lost nuts.

To his surprise, however, he discovered that this hole was really the entrance to a town of which he had never before even heard. When he reached it he found absolute silence everywhere. He called out, "Is there nobody in this town?" and presently heard a voice in answer. He went in its direction and found an old woman sitting in one of the houses. She demanded the reason of his appearance, which he readily gave.

The old woman was very kind and sympathetic, and promised to help him. "You must do exactly as I tell you," said she. "Go into the garden and listen attentively. You will hear the yams speak. Pass by any yam that says, 'Dig me out, dig me out!' But take the one that says, 'Do not dig me out!' Then bring it to me."

When he brought it, she directed him to remove the peel from the yam and throw the latter away. He was then to boil the rind, and while boiling, it would become yam. It did actually do so, and they sat down to eat some of it. Before beginning their meal, the old woman requested Kweku not to look at her while she ate. Being very polite and obedient, he did exactly as he was told.

In the evening, the old woman sent him into the garden to choose one of the drums which stood there. She warned him: "If you come to a drum which says, 'Ding-ding,' on being touched—take it. But be very careful not to take one which sounds, 'Dong-dong.'" He obeyed her direction in every detail. When he showed her the drum, she looked pleased and told him, to his great delight, that he had only to beat it if at any time he were hungry. That would bring him food in plenty. He thanked the old woman heartily and went home.

As soon as he reached his own hut, he gathered his household together and then beat the drum. Immediately, food of every description appeared before them, and they all ate as much as they wished.

The following day, Kweku Tsin gathered all the people of the village together in the Assembly Place and then beat the drum once more. In this way, every family got sufficient food for their wants, and all thanked Kweku very much for thus providing for them.

Writing: Copia, Playing With Words

Take each of the following words from your model story and look them up in the thesaurus. Give two or three different ways to say each word.

> condemn, punishment, reward, favorite, quiet

Exercise

Review memory work. Copy each sentence below. Double underline the predicate, and underline the subject. Label the part of speech of each word. Noun, N; Proper Noun, PN; Pronoun, PRO; Verb, V; Linking Verb, LV; Adjective, ADJ; Article, ART. Diagram each sentence.

> "I am the best riding-master."

> "We were colts."

> "He was a good master."

Commonplace Book

With your instructor's approval, add this part of today's poem to your commonplace book, or choose your own poem.

> The Frost looked forth, one still, clear night,
> And whispered, "Now I shall be out of sight;
> So through the valley and over the height,
>   In silence I'll take my way:
> I will not go on with that blustering train,
> The wind and the snow, the hail and the rain,
> Who make so much bustle and noise in vain,
>   But I'll be as busy as they."

Dictation

Doubt is the beginning, not the end, of wisdom.

Ballet Class: The Dance Hall by Edgar Degas

Picture Study

1. Read the title and the name of the artist. Study the picture for several minutes, then put the picture away.

2. Describe the picture.

3. Look at the picture again. Do you notice any details that you missed before? What do you like or dislike about this painting? Does it remind you of anything?

15. Literary Analysis

• Black Beauty, Chapter 10

Writing: Literary Analysis

This is an oral exercise. With your instructor's approval, choose *Black Beauty* or one of the other books you are currently reading, and answer the following questions.

What is the book about? Give a brief summary, just a few sentences. Do you have sympathy for any of the characters? Why or why not?

How Beasts and Serpents First Came Into the World

From *West African Folk-Tales* by William H. Barker

Part II

Kweku's father, however, was not at all pleased to see his son thus able to feed the whole village. Anansi thought he, too, ought to have a drum. Then the people would be grateful to him instead of to Kweku Tsin. Accordingly, he asked the young man where the wonderful drum had come from. His son was most unwilling to tell him, but Anansi gave him no peace until he had heard the whole story. He then wasted no time, but set off at once toward the entrance hole. He had taken the precaution to carry with him an old nut which he pretended to crack. Then throwing it into the hole, he jumped in after it and hurried along to the silent village. Arrived at the first house, he shouted, "Is there no one in this town?" The old woman answered as before, and Anansi entered her house.

He did not trouble to be polite to her, but addressed her most rudely, saying, "Hurry up, old woman, and get me something to eat." The woman quietly directed him to go into the garden and choose the yam which should say, "Do not dig me out." Anansi laughed in her face and said, "You surely take me for a fool. If the yam does not want me to dig it out, I will certainly not do so. I will take the one which wants to be gathered." This he did.

When he brought it to the old woman she told him, as she told his son, to throw away the inside and boil the rind. Again he refused to obey. "Who ever heard of such a silly thing as throwing away the yam? I will do nothing of the sort. I will throw away the peel and boil the inside." He did so, and the yam turned into stones. He was then obliged to do as she first suggested and boil the rind. The rind, while boiling, turned into yam. Anansi turned angrily to the old woman and said, "You are a witch." She took no notice of his remark, but went on setting the table. She placed his dinner on a small table, lower than her own, saying. "You must not look at me while I eat." He rudely replied, "Indeed, I will look at you if I choose. And I will have my dinner at your table, not at that small one." Again she said nothing—but she left her dinner untouched. Anansi ate his own then took hers and ate it also.

When he had finished, she said, "Now go into the garden and choose a drum. Do not take one which sounds, 'Dong-dong'; only take one which says, 'Ding-ding.'" Anansi retorted, "Do you think I will take your advice, you witch? No, I will choose the drum which says, 'Dong-dong.' You are just trying to play a trick on me."

He did as he wished. Having secured the drum, he marched off without so much as a "thank you" to the old woman.

No sooner had he reached home than he longed to show off his new power to the villagers. He called all to the Assembly Place, telling them to bring dishes and trays as he was going to provide them with food. The people in great delight hurried to the spot. Anansi, proudly taking his position in the midst of them, began to beat his drum. To his horror and dismay, instead of the multitude of food-stuffs which Kweku had summoned, Anansi saw, rushing toward him, beasts and serpents of all kinds. Such creatures had never been seen on the earth before.

The people fled in every direction—all except Anansi, who was too terrified to move. He speedily received fitting punishment for his disobedience. Fortunately, Kweku, with his mother and sisters, had been at the outer edge of the crowd and so easily escaped into shelter. The animals presently scattered in every direction, and ever since, they have roamed wild in the great forests.

Exercise

Review memory work. Copy each sentence below. Double underline the predicate, and underline the subject. Label the part of speech of each word. Noun, N; Proper Noun, PN; Pronoun, PRO; Verb, V; Linking Verb, LV; Adjective, ADJ; Article, ART. Diagram each sentence.

"They were a valuable kind."

"Men are blockheads."

"Blinkers are dangerous things."

Commonplace Book

With your instructor's approval, add the passage below to your commonplace book, or choose your own passage from a work of non-fiction. This can be from religious scriptures, a biography, or one of your history or science books.

> Oh! If people knew what a comfort to horses a light hand is, and how it keeps a good mouth and a good temper, they surely would not chuck, and drag, and pull at the rein as they often do. Our mouths are so tender that where they

have not been spoiled or hardened with bad or ignorant treatment, they feel the slightest movement of the driver's hand, and we know in an instant what is required of us.

16. Adjectives That Tell Which One and Whose

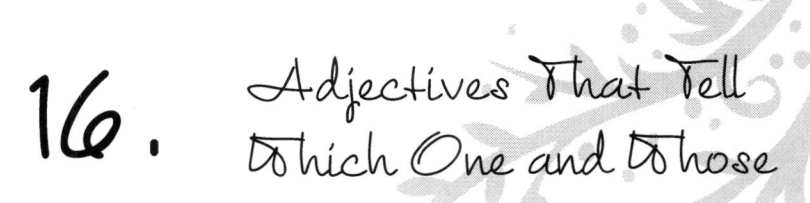

• Black Beauty, Chapters 11-12

> Definition: An adjective is a word that modifies
> a noun or a pronoun. Adjectives tell what kind,
> how many, which one, and whose.

You have learned about adjectives that tell **what kind** and **how many**. Adjectives that tell **what kind** are descriptive in nature, like **red** or **bouncy**. Adjectives that tell **how many** can either be specific numbers, or they can give a general idea, like **plenty** or **several**.

Adjectives also tell **which one** and **whose**. Adjectives that tell **which one** modify nouns and pronouns by pointing towards them. **This, that, these,** and **those** are adjectives that tell **which one**. Ordinal numbers—first, second, third—are also adjectives that tell **which one**. Which boy? **That** boy. Which girl? The **third** girl. Other adjectives that tell **which one** are words like **first** and **last**.

Oh, what a good supper he gave me **that** night.

But the moment my feet touched the **first** part of the bridge, I felt sure there was something wrong.

Adjectives that tell **whose** modify nouns and pronouns by telling to whom they belong; they show ownership of things or relationship to people—you do not own your mother, but she still belongs to you. Possessive nouns and pronouns are adjectives that tell **whose**. To make a noun possessive, we add an apostrophe and an *s* (*'s*).

"It only shows the **creature's** memory and intelligence."

We met a Captain Langley, a friend of our **master's**.

Pronouns take a different form to show possession. These are the possessive pronouns:

First person: my, mine, our, ours
Second person: your, yours
Third person: his, her, hers, its, their, theirs

"You have often driven that pony up to **my** place," said master.

"I should like **your** opinion."

"I like to see my horses hold **their** heads up."

Since possessive nouns and pronouns tell **whose**, they are adjectives. Label them adjectives when you do your exercises.

          adj
John went with his master.

       adj
The master's business engaged him a long time.

The Owl

By Alfred Tennyson

When cats run home and light is come,
  And dew is cold upon the ground,
And the far-off stream is dumb,
  And the whirring sail goes round,
  And the whirring sail goes round;
Alone and warming his five wits,
The white owl in the belfry sits.

When merry milkmaids click the latch,
  And rarely smells the new-mown hay,
And the cock hath sung beneath the thatch
  Twice or thrice his roundelay,
  Twice or thrice his roundelay;
Alone and warming his five wits,
The white owl in the belfry sits.

"Morning Sunrise"

From *West African Folk-Tales* by William H. Barker

    A man in one of the villages had a very beautiful daughter. She was so lovely that people called her Morning Sunrise. Every young man who saw her wanted to marry her. Three, in particular, were very anxious to have her for their wife. Her father found it difficult to decide among them. He determined to find out by a trick which of the three was most worthy of her.

He bade her lie down on her bed as if she were dead. He then sent the report of her death to each of the three lovers, asking them to come and help him with her funeral.

The messenger came first to Wise Man. When he heard the message, he exclaimed, "What can this man mean? The girl is not my wife. I certainly will not pay any money for her funeral."

The messenger came next to the second man. His name was Wit. The latter at once said, "Oh dear, no! I shall not pay any money for her funeral expenses. Her father did not even let me know she was ill." So he refused to go.

Thinker was the third young man. When he received the message, he at once got ready to go. "Certainly I must go and mourn for Morning Sunrise," said he. "Had she lived, surely she would have been my wife." So he took money with him and set out for her home.

When he reached it, her father called out, "Morning Sunrise, Morning Sunrise. Come here. This is your true husband."

That very day the betrothal took place, and soon after the wedding followed. Thinker and his beautiful wife lived very happily together.

Writing: Copia

Take the following sentence and play with it. Remember that the point is not necessarily to make the sentence better. The point is to play with the sentence and make it different. Make a new sentence for each number, using at least one change from that category.

> He reached the King's court only to find the King very angry at the death of his favorite.

1. Change the grammar.
   - Change the nouns from common to proper and vice versa.
   - Change the nouns from singular to plural and vice versa.
   - Change the sentence type.
   - Change the adjectives from articles to descriptive to possessive, etc.

2. Condense the sentence.
   - Remove details.
   - Remove modifiers.

3. Use synonyms and antonyms.
   - Substitute synonyms.
   - Say the opposite thing using antonyms.

Exercise

Review memory work. Copy each sentence below. Double underline the predicate, and underline the subject. Label the part of speech of each word. Noun, N; Proper Noun, PN; Pronoun, PRO; Verb, V; Linking Verb, LV; Adjective, ADJ; Article, ART. Diagram each sentence.

"They are a handsome pair."

"You are a military man."

My master rode.

Commonplace Book

With your instructor's approval, add the passage below to your commonplace book, or choose your own passage from a work of fiction. This can be from either school reading or free reading.

> "Well, sir, we can't drive over that tree, nor yet get round it; there will be nothing for it but to go back to the four crossways, and that will be a good six miles before we get round to the wooden bridge again; it will make us late, but the horse is fresh."

Dictation

The squire and Farmer Grey had worked together, as they said, for more than twenty years to get check-reins on the cart-horses done away with, and in our parts you seldom saw them; and sometimes, if mistress met a heavily laden horse with his head strained up, she would stop the carriage, and get out, and reason with the driver in her sweet, serious voice, and try to show him how foolish and cruel it was.

17. Predicate Adjectives

• Black Beauty, Chapter 13

The linking verbs are am, are, is, was, were,
be, being, been, become, seem.

When a noun or pronoun follows a linking verb, we call it a **predicate nominative**. It renames the subject of the sentence.

When an adjective follows a linking verb, we call it a **predicate adjective**. It modifies or describes the subject of the sentence.

> They were kind.

> The river banks were high.

Predicate nominatives and predicate adjectives are both **subject complements**. A subject complement completes the subject. Notice the spelling of the word **complement**, and consider a similar word, **compliment**. These two words are so alike in spelling that people often confuse them. Let's look at them closely and learn a way to remember which is which.

> compliment
> complement

> A complement completes something.
> A compliment is what I give to praise you.

Remember to mark linking verbs LV. This will help you recognize subject complements because they always follow linking verbs.

We diagram a predicate adjective the same way we diagram a predicate nominative, by placing a slanted line after the linking verb and placing the predicate adjective after it—like the slanted line, the predicate adjective points back to the subject.

>   lv
> The river banks were high.

```
           banks    |   were  \   high
         /    \     |          \
        The   river
```

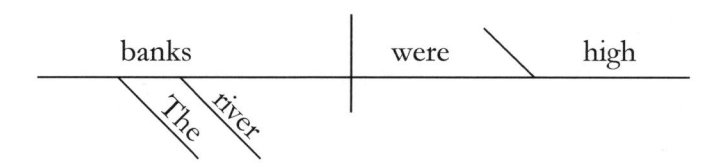

Robert of Lincoln

By William Cullen Bryant

Merrily swinging on brier and weed,
  Near to the nest of his little dame,
Over the mountain-side or mead,
  Robert of Lincoln is telling his name.
  Bob-o'-link, bob-o'-link,
    Spink, spank, spink,
Snug and safe is this nest of ours,
Hidden among the summer flowers.
    Chee, chee, chee.

Robert of Lincoln is gayly dressed,
  Wearing a bright, black wedding-coat;
White are his shoulders, and white his crest,
  Hear him call in his merry note,
  Bob-o'-link, bob-o'-link,
    Spink, spank, spink,
Look what a nice, new coat is mine;
Sure there was never a bird so fine.
    Chee, chee, chee.

Robert of Lincoln's Quaker wife,
  Pretty and quiet, with plain brown wings,
Passing at home a patient life,
  Broods in the grass while her husband sings,
  Bob-o'-link, bob-o'-link,
    Spink, spank, spink,
Brood, kind creature, you need not fear
Thieves and robbers while I am here.
    Chee, chee, chee.

Modest and shy as a nun is she;
  One weak chirp is her only note;
Braggart, and prince of braggarts is he,
  Pouring boasts from his little throat,
  Bob-o'-link, bob-o'-link,
    Spink, spank, spink,
Never was I afraid of man,
Catch me, cowardly knaves, if you can.
    Chee, chee, chee.

Six white eggs on a bed of hay,
  Flecked with purple, a pretty sight:
There as the mother sits all day,
  Robert is singing with all his might,
  Bob-o'-link, bob-o'-link,
  Spink, spank, spink,
Nice good wife that never goes out,
Keeping house while I frolic about.
  Chee, chee, chee.

Soon as the little ones chip the shell,
  Six wide mouths are open for food;
Robert of Lincoln bestirs him well,
  Gathering seeds for the hungry brood:
  Bob-o'-link, bob-o'-link,
  Spink, spank, spink,
This new life is likely to be
Hard for a gay young fellow like me.
  Chee, chee, chee.

Robert of Lincoln at length is made
  Sober with work, and silent with care,
Off is his holiday garment laid,
  Half forgotten that merry air,
  Bob-o'-link, bob-o'-link,
  Spink, spank, spink,
Nobody knows but my mate and I,
Where our nest and our nestlings lie.
  Chee, chee, chee.

Summer wanes; the children are grown;
  Fun and frolic no more he knows;
Robert of Lincoln's a hum-drum drone;
  Off he flies, and we sing as he goes,
  Bob-o'-link, bob-o'-link,
  Spink, spank, spink,
When you can pipe that merry old strain,
Robert of Lincoln, come back again.
  Chee, chee, chee.

Why the Sea-Turtle When Caught Beats Its Breast With Its Forelegs

From *West African Folk-Tales* by William H. Barker

    Many centuries ago, the people of this earth were much troubled by floods. The sea used to overflow its usual boundaries and sweep across the low, sandy stretches of land which bordered it. Time and again this happened, with many lives being lost at each flood. Mankind was very troubled to find an escape from this oft-repeated disaster. He could think of no way of avoiding it.

Fortunately for him, the wise turtle came to his help. "Take my advice," said she, "and plant rows of palms along the sea-coast. They will bind the sand together and keep it from being washed so easily away." He did so, with great success. The roots of the palms kept the sand firmly in its place. When the time came again for the sea to overflow, it washed just to the line of trees and came no farther. Thus many lives were saved annually by the kind forethought of the turtle.

In return—one would think—mankind would protect and cherish this poor animal. But no! Each time a turtle comes to the seashore to lay her eggs among the sand, she is caught and killed for the sake of her flesh. It is the thought of the ingratitude of mankind to her which makes her beat her breast with her forelegs when she is caught. She seems to be saying, "Ah! This is all the return I get for my kindness to you."

Exercise

Review memory work. Copy each sentence below. Double underline the predicate, and underline the subject. Label the part of speech of each word. Noun, N; Proper Noun, PN; Pronoun, PRO; Verb, V; Linking Verb, LV; Adjective, ADJ; Article, ART. Diagram each sentence.

"The horse is fresh."

"The bridge is broken."

"That young fellow is a liar."

Writing: Commonplace Book

Add the passage below from your model story to your commonplace book.

> Mr. Ant, who was an honest fellow and always kept his own promises, believed him. He took the box on his head, and Anansi hurried off. Needless to say, the sly fellow had not the least intention of keeping his word. Mr. Ant waited in vain for his return and was obliged to wander all the rest of his life with the box in his head.

Dictation

Use part of today's poem for dictation.

18. Condensed Narrative: Why We See Ants Carrying Bundles

- Black Beauty, Chapters 14-15

Write "Why We See Ants Carrying Bundles" as a condensed narrative, or summary. Remember, just include the main content of the story and leave out unnecessary details. What is the beginning, the middle, and the end of the story?

Berries

By Walter De La Mare

There was an old woman
Went blackberry picking
Along the hedges
From Weep to Wicking.
Half a pottle—
No more she had got,
When out steps a Fairy
From her green grot;
And says, "Well, Jill,
Would 'ee pick 'ee mo?"
And Jill, she curtseys,
And looks just so.
"Be off," says the Fairy,
"As quick as you can,
Over the meadows
To the little green lane,
That dips to the hayfields
Of Farmer Grimes:
I've berried those hedges
A score of times;
Bushel on bushel
I'll promise 'ee, Jill,
This side of supper
If 'ee pick with a will."

She glints very bright,
And speaks her fair;
Then lo, and behold!
She has faded in air.

Be sure old Goodie
She trots betimes
Over the meadows
To Farmer Grimes.
And never was queen
With jewelry rich
As those same hedges
From twig to ditch;
Like Dutchmen's coffers,
Fruit, thorn, and flower—
They shone like William
And Mary's bower.
And be sure Old Goodie
Went back to Weep,
So tired with her basket
She scarce could creep.

When she comes in the dusk
To her cottage door,
There's Towser wagging
As never before,
To see his Missus

So glad to be
Come from her fruit-picking
Back to he.
As soon as next morning
Dawn was grey,
The pot on the hob
Was simmering away;
And all in a stew
And a hugger-mugger
Towser and Jill
A-boiling of sugar,
And the dark clear fruit
That from Faërie came,
For syrup and jelly
And blackberry jam.

Twelve jolly gallipots
Jill put by;
And one little teeny one,
One inch high;
And that she's hidden
A good thumb deep,
Half way over
From Wicking to Weep.

Editing

- Did you meet the goal of this writing exercise?
- Look at your word choice. Is there a good mixture of nouns and pronouns? Is the antecedent of each pronoun clear?

19. Helping Verbs

• Black Beauty, Chapter 16

The helping verbs are
am, are, is,   was, were,   be, being, been,
do, does, did,   have, has, had,   may, might, must,
can, could,   shall, should,   will, would.

Helping verbs come before the main verb in the sentence. They "help" by providing more specific information. Consider this sentence from *Black Beauty*:

> I heard Ginger coughing.

In the above sentence, we have a simple verb with no helpers. Look at how the meaning of the sentence changes when we add helping verbs.

> I had heard Ginger coughing.

> I have heard Ginger coughing.

> I should have heard Ginger coughing.

> I must have heard Ginger coughing.

Each of these sentences means something slightly different than what the verb can say without helping verbs.

Sometimes, helping verbs are separated from the main verb by other words, and you have to play Verb Roundup. The word **not** especially loves to sit in this position.

> The first horse would not go with him.

> He could not yet speak.

When you label sentences for your exercises, make arms to spread over the main verb and all of its helpers. If the parts of the verb are separated, double underline the main verb as well as any helping verbs, and label the helping verbs HV.

⎯⎯v⎯⎯
I have heard Ginger coughing.

     hv   v
He could not yet speak.

Like action verbs, linking verbs can have helping verbs. They are still linking verbs, linking the subject to its subject complement.

"You have been my best friend."

Helping verbs are part of the verb. They are diagrammed with the main verb, even when they are separated in the sentence.

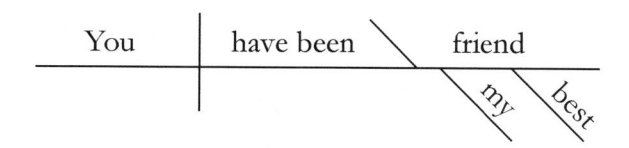

```
You | have been \ friend
                 \ my \ best
```

The Butterfly and the Bee
By William Lisle Bowles

Methought I heard a butterfly
  Say to a laboring bee:
    "Thou hast no colors of the sky
  On painted wings like me."

  "Poor child of vanity! Those dyes,
  And colors bright and rare,"
With mild reproof, the bee replies,
  "Are all beneath my care.

  "Content I toil from morn to eve,
  And scorning idleness,
To tribes of gaudy sloth I leave
  The vanity of dress."

Writing: Oral Narration

Read your new model story below, and then give your instructor an oral narration of it.

The Fox and the Grapes

From *The Aesop for Children* illustrated by Milo Winter

A Fox one day spied a beautiful bunch of ripe grapes hanging from a vine trained along the branches of a tree. The grapes seemed ready to burst with juice, and the Fox's mouth watered as he gazed longingly at them.

The bunch hung from a high branch, and the Fox had to jump for it. The first time he jumped, he missed it by a long way. So he walked off a short distance and took a running leap at it, only to fall short once more. Again and again he tried, but in vain.

Now he sat down and looked at the grapes in disgust.

"What a fool I am," he said. "Here I am wearing myself out to get a bunch of sour grapes that are not worth gaping for."

And off he walked very, very scornfully.

There are many who pretend to despise and belittle that which is beyond their reach.

Exercise

Review memory work. Copy each sentence below. Double underline the predicate, and underline the subject. Label the part of speech of each word. Noun, N; Proper Noun, PN; Pronoun, PRO; Verb, V; Linking Verb, LV; Adjective, ADJ; Article, ART. Diagram each sentence.

"He is a brave lad."

A fine horse had died.

Our mistress had been alarmed.

Commonplace Book

With your instructor's approval, add the passage below to your commonplace book, or choose your own passage from a work of fiction. This can be from either school reading or free reading.

> "And now," said master, "when you have got your breath, James, we'll get out of this place as quickly as we can." And we were moving toward the entry, when from the market-place there came a sound of galloping feet and loud rumbling wheels.

Dictation

We got out as fast as we could into the broad quiet market-place; the stars were shining, and except the noise behind us, all was still. Master led the way to a large hotel on the other side, and as soon as the hostler came, he said, "James, I must now hasten to your mistress. I trust the horses entirely to you; order whatever you think is needed." And with that, he was gone. The master did not run, but I never saw mortal man walk so fast as he did that night.

20. Plurals with -f and -fe

- Black Beauty, Chapters 17-18

Today's lesson is on forming plurals with words that end in *f* or *fe*. First, though, let's review forming other plurals.

In most cases, forming the plural of a noun is simple and straightforward: just add an *s*:

    boy→boys   girl→girls

If the word hisses at the end (ends with *ch*, *sh*, *s*, *x*, or *z*), add *es*:

    branch→branches   fox→foxes

Sometimes, *ch* says /k/. When it does, it doesn't hiss, so just add *s*:

    epoch→epochs   monarach→monarchs

Words that end in *y* form plurals in two different ways. If a vowel comes before the *y*, then we just add an *s*. That's because *ay*, *ey*, and *oy* are **phonograms**—the two letters work together to form a sound.

    play→plays   monkey→monkeys   toy→toys

But when a consonant comes before the *y*, we change the *y* to *i* and add *-es*. *Y* is acting as a vowel in these words, saying either /ē/ or /ī/.

    spy→spies   baby→babies

Of course, a few irregular words either change completely or do not change at all when forming plurals. **Mouse** becomes **mice**, but **deer** remains **deer**. In most of cases, however, a straightforward rule tells you what to do when a word ends in a certain sound or combination of letters.

Words which end in *f* or *fe* also have rules to determine how they form plurals. When the word ends in two vowels plus *f*, in most cases, just add an *s*:

    Two vowels + *f*   chief→chiefs   spoof→spoofs

95

When the word ends in **ff**, just add **s**.

      cliff→cliffs   tiff→tiffs

However, when a word ends in a consonant plus **f**, or a single vowel plus **fe**, change the **f** or **fe** to **ves**.

      Consonant + **f**   wolf→wolves

      Single vowel + **fe**   knife→knives

Occasionally, you will find exceptions to these rules. For instance, the word leaf has two vowels plus an **f**, but it forms a plural by changing the **f** to **ves**, like the words above:

      Two vowels + **f** exception   leaf→leaves

If you listen closely, you can hear when **f** should change to **v**. The sound changes, not just the spelling.

When in doubt about forming a plural, always check the dictionary.

Old Grimes

By Albert Gorton Greene

Old Grimes is dead; that good old man,
  We ne'er shall see him more;
He used to wear a long, black coat,
  All buttoned down before.

His heart was open as the day,
  His feelings all were true;
His hair was some inclined to gray,
  He wore it in a queue.

He lived at peace with all mankind,
  In friendship he was true;
His coat had pocket-holes behind,
  His pantaloons were blue.

He modest merit sought to find,
  And pay it its desert;
He had no malice in his mind,
  No ruffles on his shirt.

His neighbors he did not abuse,
  Was sociable and gay;
He wore large buckles on his shoes,
  And changed them every day.

His knowledge, hid from public gaze,
  He did not bring to view,

Nor make a noise town-meeting days,
  As many people do.

His worldly goods he never threw
  In trust to fortune's chances,
But lived (as all his brothers do)
  In easy circumstances.

Thus undisturbed by anxious cares
  His peaceful moments ran;
And everybody said he was
  A fine old gentleman.

Adzanumee and Her Mother

From *West African Folk-Tales* by William H. Barker

There once lived a woman who had one great desire. She longed to have a daughter—but alas! She was childless. She could never feel happy because of this unfulfilled wish. Even in the midst of a feast, the thought would be in her mind—"Ah! If only I had a daughter to share this with me!"

One day, she was gathering yams in the field, and it chanced that she pulled out one which was very straight and well shaped. "Ah!" she thought to herself. "If only this fine yam were a daughter, how happy I should be!"

To her astonishment, the yam answered, "If I were to become your daughter, would you promise never to reproach me with having been a yam?" She eagerly gave her promise, and at once the yam changed into a beautiful, well-made girl. The woman was overjoyed and was very kind to the girl. She named her Adzanumee. The latter was exceedingly useful to her mother. She would make the bread, gather the yams, and sell them at the market-place.

One day, when she had been detained longer than usual, her mother became impatient at her absence and angrily said, "Where can Adzanumee be? She does not deserve that beautiful name. She is only a yam."

A bird singing near by heard the mother's words and immediately flew off to the tree under which Adzanumee sat. There he began to sing:

>"Adzanumee! Adzanumee!
>Your mother is unkind—she says you are only a yam,
>You do not deserve your name!
>Adzanumee! Adzanumee!"

The girl heard him and returned home weeping. When the woman saw her she said, "My daughter, my daughter! What is the matter?" Adzanumee replied:

>"O my mother! My mother!
>You have reproached me with being a yam.
>You said I did not deserve my name.
>O my mother! My mother!"

With these words, she made her way toward the yam-field. Her mother, filled with fear, followed her, wailing:

"Nay, Adzanumee! Adzanumee!
Do not believe it—do not believe it.
You are my daughter, my dear daughter
Adzanumee!"

But she was too late. Her daughter, still singing her sad little song, quickly changed back into a yam. When the woman arrived at the field there lay the yam on the ground, and nothing she could do or say would give her back the daughter she had desired so earnestly and treated so inconsiderately.

Writing: Copia, Playing With Words

Take each of the following words from your model story and look them up in the thesaurus. Give two or three different ways to say each word.

> leap, disgust, fox, ripe, burst

Exercise

Review memory work. Make the following words plural.

> kerchief, reef, bluff, scarf

Review memory work. Copy each sentence below. Double underline the predicate, and underline the subject. Label the part of speech of each word. Noun, N; Proper Noun, PN; Pronoun, PRO; Verb, V; Linking Verb, LV; Adjective, ADJ; Article, ART. Diagram each sentence.

> "I will be ready."

> "Black Beauty will go."

> We had left.

Commonplace Book

With your instructor's approval, add this part of today's poem to your commonplace book, or choose your own poem.

> His heart was open as the day,
>   His feelings all were true;
> His hair was some inclined to gray,
>   He wore it in a queue.

> He lived at peace with all mankind,
>   In friendship he was true;
> His coat had pocket-holes behind,
>   His pantaloons were blue.

Dictation

Not my circus, not my monkeys.

Ballet School by Edgar Degas

Picture Study

1. Read the title and the name of the artist. Study the picture for several minutes, then put the picture away.

2. Describe the picture.

3. Look at the picture again. Do you notice any details that you missed before? What do you like or dislike about this painting? Does it remind you of anything?

21. Descriptive Writing

• Black Beauty, Chapter 19

Writing: Descriptive Writing

The purpose of descriptive writing is to describe a person, place, thing, or event so well that an image forms in the mind of the reader.

In today's chapter of *Black Beauty*, Ginger explains the reasons for her bad temper. Read that passage below, paying close attention to the details that make a vivid picture in your mind, and then write a narration of it. How does she describe her old master? Look at the descriptive words she uses to describe his voice when he speaks to her and again when he speaks to Samson. Does the tone of his voice change? How does the author let us know?

Add details if you wish. Remember, the point of this exercise is to write as descriptively as possible, not just to narrate the passage exactly.

Black Beauty

"At last, just as the sun went down, I saw the old master come out with a sieve in his hand. He was a very fine old gentleman with quite white hair, but his voice was what I should know him by among a thousand. It was not high, nor yet low, but full, and clear, and kind, and when he gave orders, it was so steady and decided that everyone knew, both horses and men, that he expected to be obeyed. He came quietly along, now and then shaking the oats about that he had in the sieve, and speaking cheerfully and gently to me: 'Come along, lassie, come along, lassie; come along, come along.' I stood still and let him come up; he held the oats to me, and I began to eat without fear; his voice took all my fear away. He stood by, patting and stroking me while I was eating, and seeing the clots of blood on my side, he seemed very vexed. 'Poor lassie! It was a bad business, a bad business;' then he quietly took the rein and led me to the stable; just at the door stood Samson. I laid my ears back and snapped at him. 'Stand back,' said the master, 'and keep out of her way; you've done a bad day's work for this filly.' He growled out something about a vicious brute. 'Hark ye,' said the father. 'A bad-tempered man will never make a good-tempered horse. You've not learned your trade yet, Samson.' Then he led me into my box, took off the saddle and bridle with his own hands, and tied me up; then he called for a pail of warm water and a sponge and took off his coat, and while the stable-man held the pail, he sponged my sides a good while, so tenderly that I was sure he knew how sore and bruised they were. 'Whoa! My pretty one,' he said. 'Stand still, stand still.' His very voice did me good, and the bathing was very comfortable. The skin was so broken at the corners of my mouth that I could not eat the hay; the stalks hurt me. He looked closely at it, shook his head, and told the man to fetch a good bran mash and put some meal into it. How good that mash was! And so soft and healing to my mouth. He stood by all the time I was eating, stroking me and talking to the man. 'If a high-mettled creature like this,' said he, 'can't be broken by fair means, she will never be good for anything.'

"After that, he often came to see me, and when my mouth was healed, the other breaker, Job, they called him, went on training me; he was steady and thoughtful, and I soon learned what he wanted."

The Mocking Fairy

By Walter De La Mare

"Won't you look out of your window, Mrs. Gill?"
Quoth the Fairy, nidding, nodding in the garden;
"Can't you look out of your window, Mrs. Gill?"
Quoth the Fairy, laughing softly in the garden;
But the air was still, the cherry boughs were still,
And the ivy-tod 'neath the empty sill,
And never from her window looked out Mrs. Gill
On the Fairy shrilly mocking in the garden.

"What have they done with you, you poor Mrs. Gill?"
Quoth the Fairy, brightly glancing in the garden;
"Where have they hidden you, you poor old Mrs. Gill?"
Quoth the Fairy dancing lightly in the garden;
But night's faint veil now wrapped the hill,
Stark 'neath the stars stood the dead-still Mill,
And out of her cold cottage never answered Mrs. Gill
The Fairy mimbling mambling in the garden.

Honorable Minu

From *West African Folk-Tales* by William H. Barker

It happened one day that a poor Akim-man had to travel from his own little village to Accra—one of the big towns on the coast. This man could only speak the language of his own village—which was not understood by the men of the town. As he approached Accra, he met a great herd of cows. He was surprised at the number of them and wondered to whom they could belong. Seeing a man with them, he asked him, "To whom do these cows belong?" The man did not know the language of the Akim-man, so he replied, "Minu," which means, "I do not understand." The traveler, however, thought that Minu was the name of the owner of the cows and exclaimed, "Mr. Minu must be very rich."

He then entered the town. Very soon he saw a fine large building and wondered to whom it might belong. The man he asked could not understand his question, so he also answered, "Minu."

"Dear me! What a rich fellow Mr. Minu must be!" cried the Akim-man.

Coming to a still finer building with beautiful gardens round it, he again asked the owner's name. Again came the answer, "Minu."

"How wealthy Mr. Minu is!" said our wondering traveler.

Next he came to the beach. There he saw a magnificent steamer being loaded in the harbor. He was surprised at the great cargo which was being put on board and inquired of a bystander, "To whom does this fine vessel belong?"

"Minu," replied the man.

"To the Honorable Minu also! He is the richest man I ever heard of!" cried the Akim-man.

Having finished his business, the Akim-man set out for home. As he passed down one of the streets of the town, he met men carrying a coffin and followed by a long procession, all dressed in black. He asked the name of the dead person, and received the usual reply, "Minu."

"Poor Mr. Minu!" cried the Akim-man. "So he has had to leave all his wealth and beautiful houses and die just as a poor person would do! Well, well—in future I will be content with my tiny house and little money." And the Akim-man went home quite pleased to his own hut.

Exercise

Review memory work. Make the following words plural.

> life, cliff, roof, dwarf

Review memory work. Copy each sentence below. Double underline the predicate, and underline the subject. Label the part of speech of each word. Noun, N; Proper Noun, PN; Pronoun, PRO; Verb, V; Linking Verb, LV; Adjective, ADJ; Article, ART. Diagram each sentence.

> "The boy is broken-hearted."

> "It was only ignorance."

> He was feeling better.

Commonplace Book

With your instructor's approval, add the passage below to your commonplace book, or choose your own passage from a work of non-fiction. This can be from religious scriptures, a biography, or one of your history or science books.

> Ginger and Merrylegs had been moved into the other stable so that I might be quiet, for the fever made me very quick of hearing; any little noise seemed quite loud, and I could tell everyone's footstep going to and from the house. I knew all that was going on. One night John had to give me a draught; Thomas Green came in to help him.

22. Direct Objects

• Black Beauty, Chapters 20-21

Definition: A direct object is the noun or pronoun
that receives the action of the verb.

When a noun or pronoun follows a linking verb, it is a predicate nominative. A predicate nominative renames the subject, telling us **who** or **what** the subject is.

Nouns and pronouns can also follow action verbs. They receive the action of the verb, answering the question **whom** or **what**. Look at these sentences from *Black Beauty*:

Master gave the address.

They hugged poor Merrylegs.

The master gave what? The **address**. **Address** is the direct object because it receives the action of the verb; it is what the master gave. The girls hugged whom? Poor **Merrylegs**. **Merrylegs** is the direct object because he receives the action of the verb; he is whom the girls hugged.

Follow this procedure for analyzing sentences:

- What is the predicate? The main verb is often easier to find than its subject, so find it first. Double underline it.

- Is the verb an action verb or a linking verb? Label it.

- What is the subject? Underline it once.

- For action verbs, is there a direct object?

- For linking verbs, is there a subject complement—a predicate nominative or a predicate adjective?

The direct object is diagrammed in a similar way to the predicate nominative. Instead of following a linking verb and a slanted line, it follows an action verb and a straight line. As always, place the modifiers on slanted lines under the words they modify.

Master gave the address.

```
    Master    |    gave    |   address
              |         \the
```

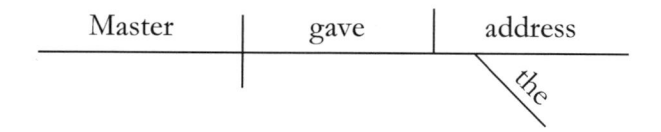

They <u>hugged</u> poor Merrylegs.

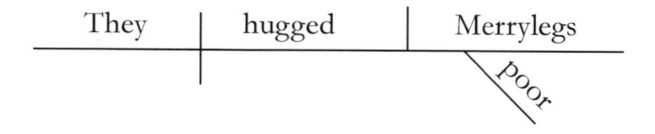

```
    They    |    hugged    |   Merrylegs
            |         \poor
```

Song of Life
By Charles Mackay

A traveler on a dusty road
  Strewed acorns on the lea;
And one took root and sprouted up,
  And grew into a tree.
Love sought its shade at evening-time,
  To breathe its early vows;
And Age was pleased, in heights of noon,
  To bask beneath its boughs.
The dormouse loved its dangling twigs,
  The birds sweet music bore—
It stood a glory in its place,
  A blessing evermore.

A little spring had lost its way
  Amid the grass and fern;
A passing stranger scooped a well
  Where weary men might turn.
He walled it in, and hung with care
  A ladle on the brink;
He thought not of the deed he did,
  But judged that Toil might drink.
He passed again; and lo! The well,
  By summer never dried,
Had cooled ten thousand parched tongues,
  And saved a life beside.

A nameless man, amid the crowd
  That thronged the daily mart,
Let fall a word of hope and love,
  Unstudied from the heart,
A whisper on the tumult thrown,
  A transitory breath,

It raised a brother from the dust,
  It saved a soul from death.
O germ! O fount! O word of love!
  O thought at random cast!
Ye were but little at the first,
  But mighty at the last.

Why the Moon and the Stars Receive Their Light From the Sun

From *West African Folk-Tales* by William H. Barker

Part I

  Once upon a time, there was great scarcity of food in the land. Father Anansi and his son, Kweku Tsin, being very hungry, set out one morning to hunt in the forest. In a short time, Kweku Tsin was fortunate enough to kill a fine deer, which he carried to his father at their resting place. Anansi was very glad to see such a supply of food, and he requested his son to remain there on guard while he went for a large basket in which to carry it home. An hour or so passed without his return, and Kweku Tsin became anxious. Fearing lest his father had lost his way, he called out loudly, "Father, father!" to guide him to the spot. To his joy, he heard a voice reply, "Yes, my son," and immediately, he shouted again, thinking it was Anansi. Instead of the latter, however, a terrible dragon appeared. This monster breathed fire from his great nostrils and was altogether a dreadful sight to behold. Kweku Tsin was terrified at his approach and speedily hid himself in a cave near by.

  The dragon arrived at the resting place and was much annoyed to find only the deer's body. He vented his anger in blows upon the latter and went away. Soon after, Father Anansi made his appearance. He was greatly interested in his son's tale and wished to see the dragon for himself. He soon had his desire, for the monster, smelling human flesh, hastily returned to the spot and seized them both. They were carried off by him to his castle, where they found many other unfortunate creatures also awaiting their fate. All were left in charge of the dragon's servant—a fine, white rooster which always crowed to summon his master if anything unusual happened in the latter's absence. The dragon then went off in search of more prey.

Writing: Copia

  Take the following sentence and play with it. Remember that the point is not necessarily to make the sentence better. The point is to play with the sentence and make it different. Make a new sentence for each number, using at least one change from that category.

> The grapes seemed ready to burst with juice, and the Fox's mouth watered as he gazed longingly at them.

1. Change the grammar.
   - Change the nouns from common to proper and vice versa.
   - Change the nouns from singular to plural and vice versa.
   - Change the sentence type.
   - Change the adjectives from articles to descriptive to possessive, etc.

2. Condense the sentence.
   - Remove details.
   - Remove modifiers.

3. Use synonyms and antonyms.
   - Substitute synonyms.
   - Say the opposite thing using antonyms.

Exercise

Review memory work. Copy each sentence below. Double underline the predicate, and underline the subject. Label the part of speech of each word. Noun, N; Proper Noun, PN; Pronoun, PRO; Verb, V; Linking Verb, LV; Adjective, ADJ; Article, ART. Diagram each sentence.

> The master gave some directions.

> "You understand horses."

> The last sad day had come.

Commonplace Book

With your instructor's approval, add the passage below to your commonplace book, or choose your own passage from a work of fiction. This can be from either school reading or free reading.

> It was wonderful what a change had come over Joe. John laughed and said he had grown an inch taller in that week, and I believe he had. He was just as kind and gentle as before, but there was more purpose and determination in all that he did, as if he had jumped at once from a boy into a man.

Dictation

> Joe Green went on very well; he learned quickly and was so attentive and careful that John began to trust him in many things; but as I have said, he was small of his age, and it was seldom that he was allowed to exercise either Ginger or me; but it so happened one morning that John was out with Justice in the luggage cart, and the master wanted a note to be taken immediately to a gentleman's house, about three miles distant.

23. Plurals with -o

- Black Beauty, Chapter 22

When a word ends in *o*, we form the plural by adding either *s* or *es*. As with words ending in *f*, the way we form plurals for words ending in *o* often depends on what letter comes before the *o*. We use *s* when the word ends in a vowel plus *o*.

    Vowel + *o*   radio→radios

When a consonant comes before the *o*, add *es*.

    Consonant + *o*   potato→potatoes

However, some words break these rules. **Piano** is actually short for **pianoforte**. When an abbreviated word ends in *o*, the plural is formed by adding just an *s*.

    Abbreviated word   piano→pianos

And for some words, both endings are correct!

    zeros→zeroes   halos→haloes   banjos→banjoes

When in doubt, always check the dictionary for information on forming plurals.

Fairy Song

By John Keats

Shed no tear! O shed no tear!
The flower will bloom another year.
Weep no more! O, weep no more!
Young buds sleep in the root's white core.
Dry your eyes! Oh! Dry your eyes!
For I was taught in Paradise
To ease my breast of melodies—
Shed no tear.

Overhead! Look overhead!
  'Mong the blossoms white and red—
Look up, look up. I flutter now
On this flush pomegranate bough.
See me! 'tis this silvery bell
Ever cures the good man's ill.
Shed no tear! O, shed no tear!
The flowers will bloom another year.
Adieu, adieu—I fly, adieu,
I vanish in the heaven's blue—
Adieu, adieu!

Why the Moon and the Stars Receive Their Light From the Sun

From *West African Folk-Tales* by William H. Barker

Part II

    Kweku Tsin now summoned all his fellow-prisoners together to arrange a way of escape. All feared to run away because of the wonderful powers of the monster. His eyesight was so keen that he could detect a fly moving miles away. Not only that, but he could move over the ground so swiftly that none could outdistance him. Kweku Tsin, however, being exceedingly clever, soon thought of a plan.

    Knowing that the white rooster would not crow as long as he has grains of rice to pick up, Kweku scattered on the ground the contents of forty bags of grain which were stored in the great hall. While the rooster was thus busily engaged, Kweku Tsin ordered the spinners to spin fine hemp ropes to make a strong rope ladder. One end of this he intended to throw up to heaven, trusting that the gods would catch it and hold it fast while he and his fellow-prisoners mounted.

    While the ladder was being made, the men killed and ate all the cattle they needed—reserving all the bones for Kweku Tsin at his express desire. When all was ready, the young man gathered the bones into a great sack. He also procured the dragon's fiddle and placed it by his side.

    Everything was now ready. Kweku Tsin threw one end of the ladder up to the sky. It was caught and held. The dragon's victims began to mount, one after the other, while Kweku remained at the bottom.

    By this time, however, the monster's powerful eyesight showed him that something unusual was happening at his abode. He hastened his return. On seeing his approach, Kweku Tsin also mounted the ladder—with the bag of bones on his back and the fiddle under his arm. The dragon began to climb after him. Each time the monster came too near, the young man threw him a bone. The monster, being very hungry, was obliged to descend to the ground to eat.

    Kweku Tsin repeated this performance till all the bones were gone, by which time the people were safely up in the heavens. Then he mounted himself, as rapidly as possible, stopping every now and then to play a tune on the wonderful fiddle. Each time he did this, the dragon had to return to earth, to dance as he could not resist the magic music. When Kweku was quite close to the top, the dragon had very nearly reached him again. The brave youth bent down and cut the ladder away below his own feet. The dragon was dashed to the ground, but Kweku was pulled up into safety by the gods.

The latter were so pleased with his wisdom and bravery in giving freedom to his fellowmen that they made him the sun, the source of all light and heat to the world. His father, Anansi, became the moon, and his friends became the stars. Thereafter, it was Kweku Tsin's privilege to supply all these with light, each being dull and powerless without him.

Exercise

Review memory work. Make the following words plural. Use the dictionary if necessary!

wife, staff, stereo, tomato, photo

Copy each sentence below. Double underline the predicate, and underline the subject. Label the part of speech of each word. Noun, N; Proper Noun, PN; Pronoun, PRO; Verb, V; Linking Verb, LV; Adjective, ADJ; Article, ART. Diagram each sentence.

He took the reins.

He mounted the box.

His voice was sad.

Writing: Commonplace Book

Add the passage below from your model story to your commonplace book.

The bunch hung from a high branch, and the Fox had to jump for it. The first time he jumped, he missed it by a long way. So he walked off a short distance and took a running leap at it, only to fall short once more. Again and again he tried, but in vain.

Dictation

Use the first stanza of today's poem for dictation.

24. Amplified Narrative: The Fox and the Grapes

• Black Beauty, Chapters 23-24

So far, your narrations have been **condensed**, which means that you shortened the stories. Your next three narrations will be the opposite. You will **amplify** the stories, which means that you will expand the stories and make them longer.

Today, write "The Fox and the Grapes" as an amplified narrative. For this narration, amplify the narrative by adding descriptive detail. Be careful to actually add descriptive detail. Do not just throw in a couple of adjectives! Add the kind of details that will paint a picture in the reader's mind.

You can choose which types of details to add. What was the fox like, both in appearance and character? What time of day was it? What was the landscape like? What did the grapes look like? How did the fox try to get the grapes? What was his appearance and attitude as he walked away?

The Enchanted Hill

By Walter De La Mare

From height of noon, remote and still,
The sun shines on the empty hill.
No mist, no wind, above, below;
No living thing strays to and fro.
No bird replies to bird on high,
Cleaving the skies with echoing cry.
Like dreaming water, green and wan,
Glassing the snow of mantling swan,
Like a clear jewel encharactered
With secret symbol of line and word,
Asheen, unruffled, slumbrous, still,
The sunlight streams on the empty hill.
But soon as Night's dark shadows ride
Across its shrouded Eastern side,
When at her kindling, clear and full,
Star beyond star stands visible;

Then course pale phantoms, fleet-foot deer
Lap of its waters icy-clear;
Mounts the large moon, and pours her beams
On bright-fish-flashing, singing streams;
Voices re-echo; coursing by,
Horsemen, like clouds, wheel silently.
Glide then from out their pitch-black lair
Beneath the dark's ensilvered arch,
Witches becowled into the air;
And iron pine and emerald larch,
Tents of delight for ravished bird,
Are by loud music thrilled and stirred.
Winging the light, with silver feet,
Beneath their bowers of fragrance met,
In dells of rose and meadowsweet,
In mazed dance the fairies flit;
While drives his share the Ploughman high
Athwart the daisy-powdered sky:
Till far away, in thickening dew,
Piercing the Eastern shadows through
Rilling in crystal clear and still,
Light 'gins to tremble on the hill.
And like a mist on faint winds borne,
Silent, forlorn, wells up the morn.
Then the broad sun with burning beams
Steeps slope and peak and gilded streams.
Then no foot stirs; the brake shakes not;
Soundless and wet in its green grot
As if asleep, the leaf hangs limp;
The white dews drip untrembling down,
From bough to bough, orblike, unblown;
And in strange quiet, shimmering and still,
Morning enshrines the empty hill.

Editing

- Did you meet the goal of this writing exercise?
- Look at your word choice. Is there a good mixture of nouns and pronouns? Is the antecedent of each pronoun clear?

25. Nouns as Adjectives

• Black Beauty, Chapter 25

You have already learned that the possessive form of nouns and pronouns act as adjectives. Other nouns can also act as adjectives.

When nouns act as adjectives, they usually answer the question **what kind** for another noun.

What kind of chair? A **wicker** chair.

What kind of ball? A **soccer** ball.

What kind of cake? A **birthday** cake.

Look at the following sentence from *Black Beauty*:

His poor wife and little children had to turn out of the pretty cottage by the **park** gate and go where they could.

Here, the word **park** is an adjective that tells which gate. The property has multiple gates, and each gate may be identified based on something that it is near, like the park.

Just as some nouns can be proper, some adjectives can be as well. A possessive proper noun, such as **Farmer Grey's**, is a proper adjective, and so are other adjectives made from proper nouns, such as **American**.

The part of speech of a word is determined by the job it is performing, so even though these words are normally nouns, they are adjectives when they modify other nouns. Label such a word ADJ and diagram it on a slanted line under the noun it modifies, like other adjectives.

Beauty remembered Farmer Grey's pleasant meadow.

```
  Beauty | remembered | meadow
                        \Farmer Grey's  \pleasant
```

115

The Mountain

By Emily Dickinson

The mountain sat upon the plain
In his eternal chair,
His observation omnifold,
His inquest everywhere.
The seasons prayed around his knees,
Like children round a sire:
Grandfather of the days is he,
Of dawn the ancestor.

Writing: Oral Narration

Read your new model story below, and then give your instructor an oral narration of it.

The Bundle of Sticks

From *The Aesop for Children* illustrated by Milo Winter

A certain Father had a family of Sons who were forever quarreling among themselves. No words he could say did the least good, so he cast about in his mind for some very striking example that should make them see that discord would lead them to misfortune.

One day, when the quarreling had been much more violent than usual and each of the Sons was moping in a surly manner, he asked one of them to bring him a bundle of sticks. Then handing the bundle to each of his Sons in turn, he told them to try to break it. But although each one tried his best, none was able to do so.

The Father then untied the bundle and gave the sticks to his Sons to break one by one. This they did very easily.

"My Sons," said the Father, "do you not see how certain it is that if you agree with each other and help each other, it will be impossible for your enemies to injure you? But if you are divided among yourselves, you will be no stronger than a single stick in that bundle."

In unity is strength.

Exercise

Review memory work. Make the following words plural. Use the dictionary if necessary!

video, mango, studio, echo, hero

Copy each sentence below. Double underline the predicate, and underline the subject. Label the part of speech of each word. Noun, N; Proper Noun, PN; Pronoun, PRO; Verb, V; Linking Verb, LV; Adjective, ADJ; Article, ART. Diagram each sentence.

The roads were stony.

He was a handsome man.

He had pleasant manners.

Commonplace Book

With your instructor's approval, add the passage below to your commonplace book, or choose your own passage from a work of fiction. This can be from either school reading or free reading.

> At the station, the colonel put some money into Smith's hand and bid him goodbye, saying, "Take care of your young mistress, Reuben, and don't let Black Auster be hacked about by any random young prig that wants to ride him; keep him for the lady."

Dictation

> We left the carriage at the maker's, and Smith rode me to the White Lion, and ordered the hostler to feed me well, and have me ready for him at four o'clock. A nail in one of my front shoes had started as I came along, but the hostler did not notice it till just about four o'clock. Smith did not come into the yard till five, and then he said he should not leave till six, as he had met with some old friends. The man then told him of the nail and asked if he should have the shoe looked to.

26. Diagramming Interrogative Sentences

- Black Beauty, Chapters 26-27

Interrogative sentences, or questions, are a type of **inverted** sentence. **Inverted** just means that the normal word order is reversed. Normally, the subject of the sentence comes before the verb, but in a question, a helping verb often comes before the subject.

Look at the following interrogative sentences from *Black Beauty*, and notice the inversion of the subject and verb:

"Can you ride?"

Which way had she turned?

To diagram a question, first put the sentence into normal word order. The subject and predicate then become obvious.

You can ride.

```
    you      |  Can ride
─────────────┼─────────────
             |
```

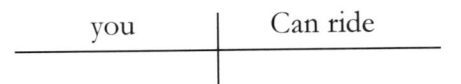

She had turned which way.

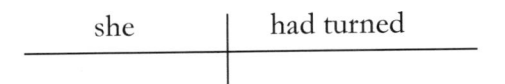

```
    she      |  had turned
─────────────┼─────────────
             |
```

Interrogative sentences can have subject complements—predicate nominatives and predicate adjectives—or direct objects, just as other sentences can. These parts of the sentence are also easier to see when the words of the sentence are in their normal order.

Remember that a subject complement renames (predicate nominative) or modifies (predicate adjective) the subject of the sentence. The linking verb acts like an equal sign in math. Like the slanted line that it follows on the diagram, the subject complement points back to the subject.

"Are you tired?"

You are tired.

You = tired

```
   you   |  Are  \  tired
_____|_____
         |
```

The direct object, on the other hand, is what the verb acts upon. It receives the action of the verb, whether it is a ball being kicked or a letter being given.

Would they ask this question?

They would ask this question.

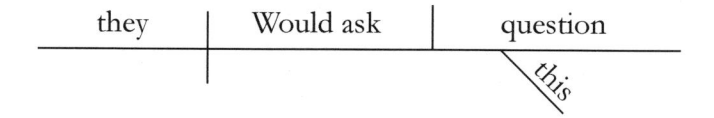

```
  they   | Would ask | question
_____|_____|_____
         |           \ this
```

A Boy's Song

By James Hogg

Where the pools are bright and deep,
Where the gray trout lies asleep,
Up the river and o'er the lea,
That's the way for Billy and me.

Where the blackbird sings the latest,
Where the hawthorn blooms the sweetest,
Where the nestlings chirp and flee,
That's the way for Billy and me.

Where the mowers mow the cleanest,
Where the hay lies thick and greenest,
There to trace the homeward bee,
That's the way for Billy and me.

Where the hazel bank is steepest,
Where the shadow falls the deepest,
Where the clustering nuts fall free.
That's the way for Billy and me.

Why the boys should drive away,
Little sweet maidens from the play,
Or love to banter and fight so well,
That's the thing I never could tell.

But this I know, I love to play,
Through the meadow, among the hay;
Up the water and o'er the lea,
That's the way for Billy and me.

How the Tortoise Got Its Shell

From *West African Folk-Tales* by William H. Barker

A few hundred years ago, the chief Mauri (God) determined to have a splendid yam festival. He therefore sent his messengers to invite all his chiefs and people to the gathering, which was to take place on Fida (Friday).

On the morning of that day, he sent some of his servants to the neighboring towns and villages to buy goats, sheep, and cows for the great feast. Mr. Klo, the tortoise, who was a tall and handsome fellow, was sent to buy palm wine. He was directed to the palm-fields of Koklovi, the chicken.

At that time Klo was a very powerful traveler; he speedily reached his destination although it was many miles distant from Mauri's palace.

When he arrived, Koklovi was taking his breakfast. When they had exchanged polite salutations, Koklovi asked the reason of Klo's visit. He replied, "I was sent by His Majesty Mauri, the ruler of the world, to buy him palm wine."

"Whether he's ruler of the world or not," answered Koklovi, "no one can buy my wine with money. If you want it, you must fight for it. If you win, you can have it all and the palm trees too."

This answer delighted Klo as he was a very strong fighter. Koklovi was the same, so the fighting continued for several hours before Klo was able to overcome Koklovi. He was at last successful, however, and securely bound Koklovi before he left him.

Then, taking his great pot, he filled it with wine. Finding that there was more wine than the pot would hold, Klo foolishly drank all the rest. He then piled the palm trees on his back and set out for the palace with the pot of wine. The amount which he had drunk, however, made him feel so sleepy and tired that he could not walk fast with his load. Added to this, a terrible rain began to fall, which made the ground very slippery and still more difficult to travel over.

By the time Klo succeeded in reaching his master's palace, the gates were shut and locked. Mauri, finding it so late, had concluded that everyone was inside.

There were many people packed into the great hall, and all were singing and dancing. The noise of the concert was so great that no one heard Klo's knocking at the gate, and there he had to stay with his great load of wine and palm trees.

The rain continued for nearly two months and was so terrible that the people all remained in the palace till it had finished. By that time, Klo had died under the weight of his load which he had been unable to get off his back. There he lay, before the gate, with the pile of palm trees on top of him.

When the rain ceased and the gates were opened, the people were amazed to see this great mound in front of the gate where before there had been nothing. They fetched spades and began to shovel it away.

When they came to the bottom of the pile, there lay Klo. His earthenware pot and the dust had caked together and formed quite a hard cover on his back. He was taken into the palace, and by the use of many wonderful medicines, he was restored to life. But since that date, he has never been able to stand upright. He has been a creeping creature with a great shell on his back.

Writing: Copia, Playing With Words

Take each of the following words from your model story and look them up in the thesaurus. Give two or three different ways to say each word.

> quarrel, discord, misfortune, surly, unity

Exercise

Review memory work. Copy each sentence below. Double underline the predicate, and underline the subject. Label the part of speech of each word. Noun, N; Proper Noun, PN; Pronoun, PRO; Verb, V; Linking Verb, LV; Adjective, ADJ; Article, ART. Diagram each sentence.

> Did Beauty enjoy the sweet grass?

> Had they become fast friends?

> Was Beauty lonely?

Commonplace Book

With your instructor's approval, add this part of today's poem to your commonplace book, or choose your own poem.

> Where the pools are bright and deep,
> Where the gray trout lies asleep,
> Up the river and o'er the lea,
> That's the way for Billy and me.
>
> Where the blackbird sings the latest,
> Where the hawthorn blooms the sweetest,
> Where the nestlings chirp and flee,
> That's the way for Billy and me.

Dictation

A man's reach should exceed his grasp.

Racehorses at Longchamp by Edgar Degas

Picture Study

1. Read the title and the name of the artist. Study the picture for several minutes, then put the picture away.

2. Describe the picture.

3. Look at the picture again. Do you notice any details that you missed before? What do you like or dislike about this painting? Does it remind you of anything?

27. Literary Analysis

• Black Beauty, Chapter 28

Writing: Literary Analysis

This is an oral exercise. With your instructor's approval, choose *Black Beauty* or one of the other books you are currently reading, and answer the following questions.

What is the book about? Give a brief summary, just a few sentences. Who is your favorite character? Why?

The Rainbow

By Thomas Campbell

Triumphal arch, that fills the sky
  When storms prepare to part,
I ask not proud Philosophy
  To teach me what thou art.

Still seem, as to my childhood's sight,
  A midway station given,
For happy spirits to alight,
  Betwixt the earth and heaven.

The Hunter and the Tortoise

From *West African Folk-Tales* by William H. Barker

A village hunter had one day gone farther afield than usual. Coming to a part of the forest with which he was unacquainted, he was astonished to hear a voice singing. He listened; this was the song:

> "It is man who forces himself on things,
>   Not things which force themselves on him."

The singing was accompanied by sweet music which entirely charmed the hunter's heart.

When the little song was finished, the hunter peeped through the branches to see who the singer could be. Imagine his amazement when he found it was none other than a tortoise with a tiny harp slung in front of her. Never had he seen such a marvellous thing.

Time after time, he returned to the same place in order to listen to this wonderful creature. At last he persuaded her to let him carry her back to his hut so that he might enjoy her singing daily in comfort. This she permitted only on the understanding that she sang to him alone.

The hunter did not rest long content with this arrangement, however. Soon he began to wish that he could show off this wonderful tortoise to all the world, and thereby thought he would gain great honor. He told the secret, first to one, then to another, until finally it reached the ears of the chief himself. The hunter was commanded to come and tell his tale before the Assembly. When, however, he described the tortoise who sang and played on the harp, the people shouted in scorn. They refused to believe him.

At last he said, "If I do not speak truth, I give you leave to kill me. Tomorrow I will bring the tortoise to this place, and you may all hear her. If she cannot do as I say, I am willing to die."

"Good," replied the people. "And if the tortoise can do as you say, we give you leave to punish us in any way you choose."

The matter being then settled, the hunter returned home, well pleased with the prospect. As soon as the morrow dawned, he carried tortoise and harp down to the Assembly Place, where a table had been placed ready for her. Everyone gathered round to listen. But no song came. The people were very patient and quite willing to give both tortoise and hunter a chance. Hours went by, and to the hunter's dismay and shame, the tortoise remained mute. He tried every means in his power to coax her to sing, but in vain. The people at first whispered, then spoke outright, in scorn of the boaster and his claims.

Night came on and brought with it the hunter's doom. As the last ray of the setting sun faded, he was beheaded. The instant this had happened, the tortoise spoke. The people looked at one another in troubled wonder: "Our brother spoke truth, then, and we have killed him."

The tortoise, however, went on to explain. "He brought his punishment on himself. I led a happy life in the forest, singing my little song. He was not content to come and listen to me. He had to tell my secret, which did not at all concern him, to all the world. Had he not tried to make a show of me, this would never have happened."

"It is man who forces himself on things,
Not things which force themselves on him."

Exercise

Review memory work. Copy each sentence below. Double underline the predicate, and underline the subject. Label the part of speech of each word. Noun, N; Proper Noun, PN; Pronoun, PRO; Verb, V; Linking Verb, LV; Adjective, ADJ; Article, ART. Diagram each sentence.

These drivers are careless.

He lifted his hat.

Did he have a stone?

Commonplace Book

With your instructor's approval, add the passage below to your commonplace book, or choose your own passage from a work of non-fiction. This can be from religious scriptures, a biography, or one of your history or science books.

> Besides, a slovenly way of driving gets a horse into bad and often lazy habits, and when he changes hands, he has to be whipped out of them with more or less pain and trouble. Squire Gordon always kept us to our best paces and our best manners. He said that spoiling a horse and letting him get into bad habits was just as cruel as spoiling a child, and both had to suffer for it afterward.

28. Compound Subjects and Predicates

- Black Beauty, Chapters 29-30

Sometimes, a sentence can have more than one subject or predicate. This is called a **compound subject** or a **compound predicate**. In grammar, **compound** just means that we have more than one of something. Look at this sentence from *Black Beauty*:

Mr. Gordon or John would have seen.

In this sentence, the simple predicate is **would have seen**. Who would have seen? Mr. Gordon or John. This is a compound subject joined by the word **or**. To diagram sentences with compound structures, we have to add extra lines to the diagram.

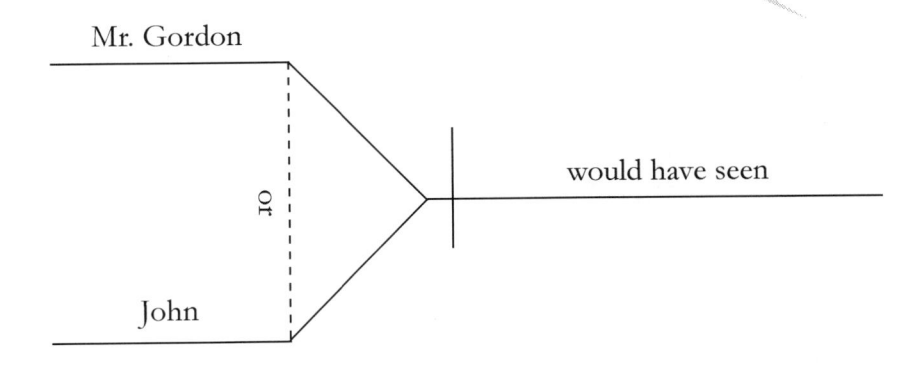

```
Mr. Gordon
           \
            \
        or   >——|—— would have seen
            /
           /
John
```

And and **or** are conjunctions, which we will talk about in another lesson. Label them CJ in your exercises.

```
——pn—— cj  pn  ———v———
Mr. Gordon or John would have seen.
```

Now look at this sentence:

```
adj   n    v   cj    v      n    cj   n
His wife bred and fattened poultry and rabbits.
```

In this sentence, the simple subject is **wife**. What did his wife do? She **bred** and **fattened** poultry and rabbits. This is a compound predicate joined by the word **and**.

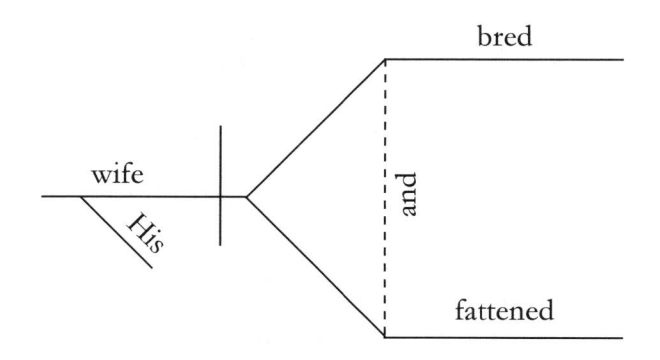

All compound structures are diagrammed in a similar way, by adding the additional lines for the extra words. The sentence above with the compound predicate also has a direct object. The way we diagram a compound predicate with a direct object—or a subject complement—depends on a couple of factors. First, does the compound predicate share the direct object? In this case, the two verbs do share the direct object. She bred poultry, and she fattened poultry. The diagram shows it like this:

His <u>wife</u> <u>bred</u> and <u>fattened</u> poultry.

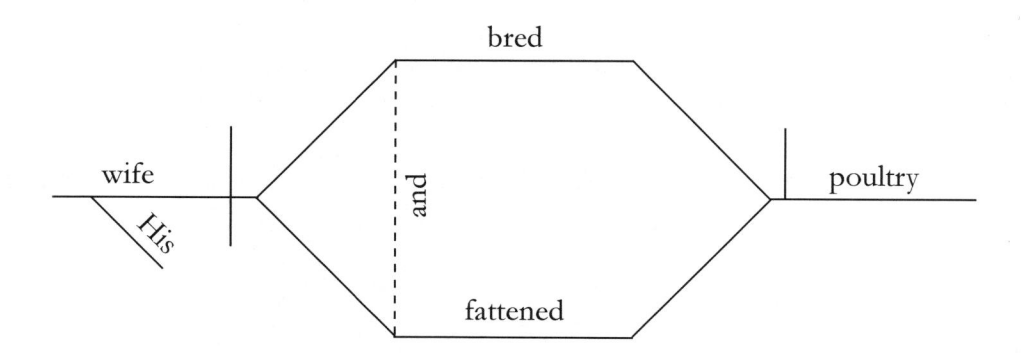

But wait a minute. She did not just breed and fatten poultry, did she? A sentence can have multiple compound structures. In this sentence, she bred and fattened poultry **and** rabbits. This is a compound direct object joined by the word **and**.

His <u>wife</u> <u>bred</u> and <u>fattened</u> poultry and rabbits.

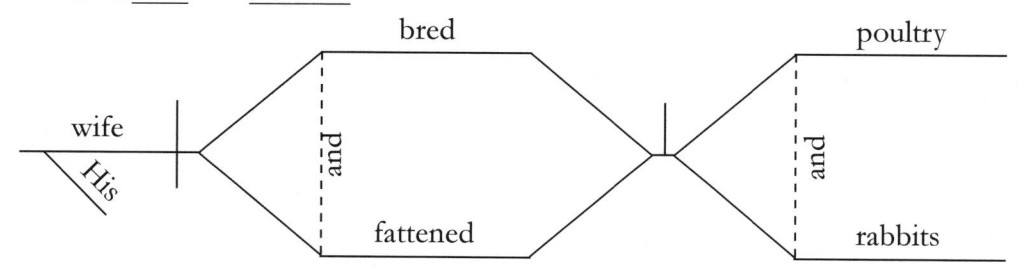

The direct object, or direct objects, will not always be shared by the verbs. Consider this sentence.

His <u>wife</u> <u>bred</u> poultry and <u>fattened</u> rabbits.

Now the direct objects are not shared. Each part of the compound predicate has its own direct object. We diagram it like this:

[Diagram: "His wife bred poultry and fattened rabbits"]

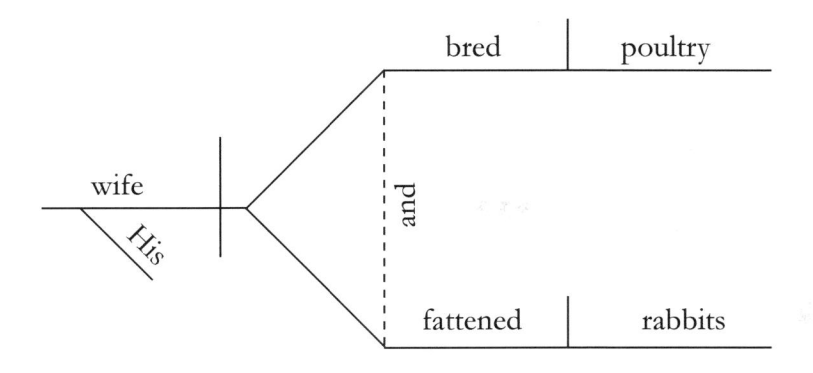

The differences in how to diagram all depend on whether or not the sentence has a direct object or subject complement, and if it has one, whether or not it is shared.

And here is one more, just for fun. This sentence has a compound subject, a compound predicate, and a compound direct object.

He and his wife bred and fattened poultry and rabbits.

[Diagram: "He and his wife bred and fattened poultry and rabbits"]

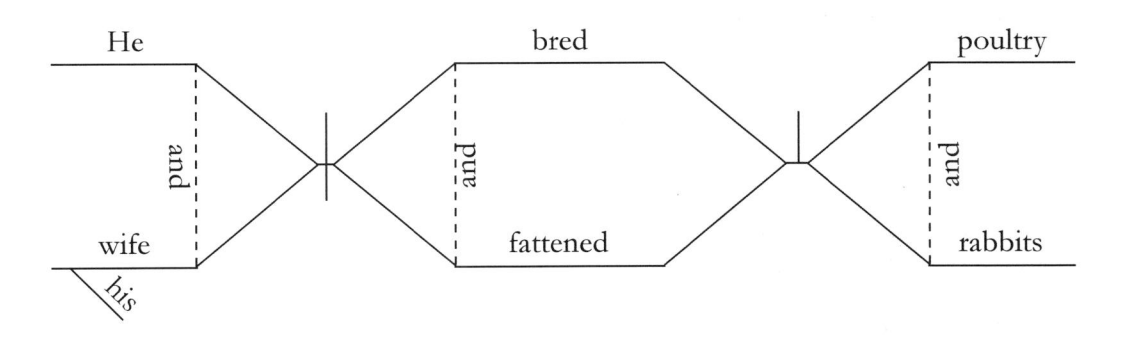

Old Ironsides

By Oliver Wendell Holmes

Ay, tear her tattered ensign down!
  Long has it waved on high,
And many an eye has danced to see
  That banner in the sky;
Beneath it rung the battle shout,
  And burst the cannon's roar;—
The meteor of the ocean air
  Shall sweep the clouds no more.

Her deck, once red with heroes' blood,
  Where knelt the vanquished foe,
When winds were hurrying o'er the flood
  And waves were white below.
No more shall feel the victor's tread,
  Or know the conquered knee;
The harpies of the shore shall pluck
  The eagle of the sea!

O, better that her shattered hulk
  Should sink beneath the wave;

Her thunders shook the mighty deep,
  And there should be her grave;
Nail to the mast her holy flag,
  Set every threadbare sail,
And give her to the god of storms,
  The lightning and the gale!

Kwofi and the Gods

From *West African Folk-Tales* by William H. Barker

Kwofi was the eldest son of a farmer who had two wives. Kwofi's mother had no other children. When the boy was three years old, his mother died. Kwofi was given to his stepmother to mind. After this, she had many children. Kwofi, of course, was the eldest of all.

When he was about ten years, old his father also died. Kwofi now had no relative but his stepmother, for whom he had to work.

As he grew older, she saw how much more clever and handsome he was than her own children, and she grew very jealous of him. He was such a good hunter that, day after day, he came home laden with meat or with fish.

Every day she treated him in the same way. She cooked the meat then portioned it out. She gave to each a large helping, but when it came to Kwofi's turn, she would say, "Oh, my son Kwofi, there is none left for you! You must go to the field and get some ripe paw-paw." Kwofi never complained. Never once did he taste any of the meat he had hunted. At every meal, the others were served, but there was never enough for him.

One evening, when the usual thing had happened, Kwofi was preparing to go to the field to fetch some paw-paw for his supper. All at once, one of the gods appeared in the village, carrying a great bag over his shoulder. He summoned all the villagers together with these words: "Oh, my villagers, I come with a bag of death for you!"

Thereupon he began to distribute the contents of his bag among them. When he came to Kwofi he said: "Oh, my son Kwofi, there was never sufficient meat for you; neither is there any death."

As he said these words everyone in the village died except Kwofi. He was left to reign there in peace, which he did very happily.

Writing: Copia

Take the following sentence and play with it. Remember that the point is not necessarily to make the sentence better. The point is to play with the sentence and make it different. Make a new sentence for each number, using at least one change from that category.

> The Father then untied the bundle and gave the sticks to his Sons to break one by one.

1. Change the grammar.
   - Change the nouns from common to proper and vice versa.
   - Change the nouns from singular to plural and vice versa.
   - Change the sentence type.
   - Change the adjectives from articles to descriptive to possessive, etc.
   - Change a quotation from direct to indirect and vice versa.

2. Condense the sentence.
   - Remove details.
   - Remove modifiers.

3. Amplify the sentence.
   - Add details.
   - Add modifiers.

4. Use synonyms and antonyms.
   - Substitute synonyms.
   - Say the opposite thing using antonyms.

Exercise

Review memory work. Copy each sentence below. Double underline the predicate, and underline the subject. Label the part of speech of each word. Noun, N; Proper Noun, PN; Pronoun, PRO; Verb, V; Linking Verb, LV; Adjective, ADJ; Article, ART; Adverb, ADV; Conjunctions, CJ; Interjections, INJ. Diagram each sentence.

"Has he been well?"

The farmer dismounted and held his rein.

Beauty and Peggy pulled the carriage.

Commonplace Book

With your instructor's approval, add the passage below to your commonplace book, or choose your own passage from a work of fiction. This can be from either school reading or free reading.

> "He is as warm and damp as a horse just come up from grass. I advise you to look into your stable a little more. I hate to be suspicious, and, thank heaven, I have no cause to be, for I can trust my men, present or absent; but there are mean scoundrels, wicked enough to rob a dumb beast of his food. You must look into it."

Dictation

My new master was an unmarried man. He lived at Bath and was much engaged in business. His doctor advised him to take horse exercise, and for this purpose, he bought me. He hired a stable a short distance from his lodgings and engaged a man named Filcher as groom. My master knew very little about horses, but he treated me well, and I should have had a good and easy place but for circumstances of which he was ignorant.

29. Quotations

- Black Beauty, Chapter 31

Today's lesson is about **quotations**. In a story, quotations tell us what the characters are saying to one another. Quotations can be either direct or indirect. Look at these two sentences from *Black Beauty*:

> One day his master came in and said, "Alfred, the stable smells rather strong."

> He said that spoiling a horse and letting him get into bad habits was just as cruel as spoiling a child.

Both sentences report what someone has said. The first sentence is a direct quotation because it reports the exact words that someone used. The second sentence is an indirect quotation because it reports what someone has said without using his exact words.

Direct quotations need quotation marks, but indirect quotations do not. Indirect quotations often use the word **that** to indicate an indirect quotation.

Sentences can be changed from direct to indirect and vice versa. Look again at the sentences above. How would you change them?

Here is one way that you could change each of them:

> One day his master came in and said **that** the stable smelled rather strong.

> He said**,** **"**Spoiling a horse and letting him get into bad habits is just as cruel as spoiling a child.**"**

Direct quotations are set apart from the rest of the sentence by quotation marks, and they also use some additional punctuation. Consider these sentences:

> One day his master came in and said, "Alfred, the stable smells rather strong."

> "Then send for the bricklayer and have it seen to," said his master.

135

"Well," said his master, "I should not like him to take cold."

Look again at the sentences above. In the first, the author states who is speaking at the beginning of the sentence. In the second, the author states who is speaking at the end of the sentence. And in the third, the author states who is speaking in the middle of the sentence!

Notice that the quoted sentences still begin with a capital letter. The first sentence still ends with a period, which comes before the ending quotation mark. But look at the second sentence. Where the period would be normally is a comma, and it is followed by a quotation mark. In the third sentence, two commas are required to separate the quotation from the reference to the speaker. The comma travels with the word in front of it. That means that if the word in front of the comma is in quotation marks, then the comma is also inside. If the word in front of the comma is outside the quotation marks, then the comma is also outside.

Do you know why you do copywork? You do copywork partially to practice your handwriting, but it also helps you to learn rules about capitalizing words and how to punctuate sentences. We call this the **mechanics of writing**. You learn proper mechanics when you copy correctly written sentences. Pay close attention to where the punctuation marks are when you do your copywork.

The Mermaids

By Walter De La Mare

Sand, sand; hills of sand;
And the wind where nothing is
Green and sweet of the land;
No grass, no trees,
No bird, no butterfly,
But hills, hills of sand,
And a burning sky.

Sea, sea, mounds of the sea,
Hollow, and dark, and blue,
Flashing incessantly
The whole sea through;
No flower, no jutting root,
Only the floor of the sea,
With foam afloat.

Blow, blow, winding shells;
And the watery fish,
Deaf to the hidden bells,
In the water splash;
No streaming gold, no eyes,
Watching along the waves,
But far-blown shells, faint bells,
From the darkling caves.

The Lion and the Wolf

From *West African Folk-Tales* by William H. Barker

A certain old lady had a very fine flock of sheep. She had fed and cared for them so well that they became famous for their fatness. In time a wicked wolf heard of them and determined to eat them.

Night after night he stole up to the old dame's cottage and killed a sheep. The poor woman tried her best to save her animals from harm, but failed.

At last there was only one sheep left of all the flock. Their owner was very sad. She feared that it, too, would be taken away from her, in spite of all she could do.

While she was grieving over the thought of this, a lion came to her village. Seeing her sad face, he asked the reason of it. She soon told him all about it. He thereupon offered to do his best to punish the wicked wolf. He himself went to the place where the sheep was generally kept while the latter was removed to another place.

In the meantime, the wolf was on his way to the cottage. As he came, he met a fox. The fox was somewhat afraid of him and prepared to run away. The wolf, however, told him where he was going and invited him to go too. The fox agreed, and the two set off together. They arrived at the cottage and went straight to the place where the sheep generally slept. The wolf at once rushed upon the animal while the fox waited a little behind. Just as the fox was deciding to enter and help the wolf, there came a bright flash of lightning. By the light of it, the fox could see that the wolf was attacking—not a sheep—but a lion. He hastily ran away, shouting as he went: "Look at his face! Look at his face!"

During the flash, the wolf did look at the pretend sheep. To his dismay, he found he had made a great mistake. At once he began to make humble apologies—but all in vain. Lion refused to listen to any of his explanations and speedily put him to death.

Exercise

Review memory work. Copy each sentence below. Double underline the predicate, and underline the subject. Label the part of speech of each word. Noun, N; Proper Noun, PN; Pronoun, PRO; Verb, V; Linking Verb, LV; Adjective, ADJ; Article, ART; Adverb, ADV; Conjunctions, CJ; Interjections, INJ. Diagram each sentence.

"I will attend the hoof and direct your man."

He was ignorant and conceited.

The bricklayer came and pulled many bricks.

Writing: Commonplace Book

Add the passage below from your model story to your commonplace book.

"My Sons," said the Father, "do you not see how certain it is that if you agree with each other and help each other, it will be impossible for your enemies to injure you? But if you are divided among yourselves, you will be no stronger than a single stick in that bundle."

Dictation

Use part of today's poem for dictation.

30. Amplified Narrative: The Bundle of Sticks

• Black Beauty, Chapters 32-33

Today, write "The Bundle of Sticks" as an amplified narrative. For this narration, amplify the narrative by adding **dialogue**, which is conversation between the characters. What do you think the father said to his sons? How would the sons have responded to their father, and what might they have said to one another? Use at least one direct quote and at least one indirect quote.

The Gnomies

By Walter De La Mare

As I lay awake in the white moonlight,
I heard a sweet singing in the wood—
'Out of bed,
Sleepyhead,
Put your white foot now,
Here are we,
'Neath the tree,
Singing round the root now!'
I looked out of window in the white moonlight,
The trees were like snow in the wood—
'Come away
Child and play,
Light wi' the gnomies;
In a mound,
Green and round,
That's where their home is!
'Honey sweet,
Curds to eat,
Cream and frumenty,
Shells and beads,
Poppy seeds,
You shall have plenty.'

But soon as I stooped in the dim moonlight
To put on my stocking and my shoe,
The sweet, sweet singing died sadly away,
And the light of the morning peep'd through:
Then instead of the gnomies there came a red robin
To sing of the buttercups and dew.

Editing

- Did you meet the goal of this writing exercise?
- Look at your word choice. Is there a good mixture of nouns and pronouns? Is the antecedent of each pronoun clear?

31. Diagramming Imperative Sentences

• Black Beauty, Chapter 34

An imperative sentence gives a command or makes a request. Look at the following sentences from *Black Beauty*.

"Send for the bricklayer and have it seen to," said his master.

"Say twenty-five, and you shall have him."

Can you find the subject in those sentences? When we give a command or make a request, the subject is always the person we are talking to. Do you remember what pronoun we use for the person we are talking to?

You! The word **you** is always the subject of an imperative sentence. Sometimes it is stated, but sometimes, it is understood to be the subject even though it is not actually in the sentence. When we diagram an imperative sentence, we put the understood **you** in parentheses to show that it was not actually in the sentence.

Say twenty-five.

```
(you)  |  Say  |  twenty-five
```

Sometimes, **you** is stated in the sentence. In that case, the parentheses on the diagram are not necessary.

You say twenty-five.

```
You  |  say  |  twenty-five
```

The Wind

By Emily Dickinson

Of all the sounds despatched abroad,
There's not a charge to me
Like that old measure in the boughs,
That phraseless melody
The wind does, working like a hand
Whose fingers brush the sky,
Then quiver down, with tufts of tune
Permitted gods and me.
When winds go round and round in bands,
And thrum upon the door,
And birds take places overhead,
To bear them orchestra,
I crave him grace, of summer boughs,
If such an outcast be,
He never heard that fleshless chant
Rise solemn in the tree,
As if some caravan of sound
On deserts, in the sky,
Had broken rank,
Then knit, and passed
In seamless company.

Writing: Oral Narration

Read your new model story below, and then give your instructor an oral narration of it.

The Leap at Rhodes

From *The Aesop for Children* illustrated by Milo Winter

A certain man who visited foreign lands could talk of little when he returned to his home except the wonderful adventures he had met with and the great deeds he had done abroad.

One of the feats he told about was a leap he had made in a city called Rhodes. That leap was so great, he said, that no other man could leap anywhere near the distance. A great many persons in Rhodes had seen him do it and would prove that what he told was true.

"No need of witnesses," said one of the hearers. "Suppose this city is Rhodes. Now show us how far you can jump."

Deeds count, not boasting words.

Exercise

Review memory work. Copy each sentence below. Double underline the predicate, and underline the subject. Label the part of speech of each word. Noun, N; Proper

Noun, PN; Pronoun, PRO; Verb, V; Linking Verb, LV; Adjective, ADJ; Article, ART; Adverb, ADV; Conjunctions, CJ; Interjections, INJ. Diagram each sentence.

He was a good-humored, sensible man.

My master and I understood each other. [Hint: **each other** is a two-word pronoun.]

"Open the gates."

Commonplace Book

With your instructor's approval, add the passage below to your commonplace book, or choose your own passage from a work of fiction. This can be from either school reading or free reading.

> "Fearful as it was, no one stopped; no one turned back. Every moment the ranks were thinned, but as our comrades fell, we closed in to keep them together; and instead of being shaken or staggered in our pace, our gallop became faster and faster as we neared the cannon."

Dictation

> "It was one autumn morning, and as usual, an hour before daybreak, our cavalry had turned out, ready caparisoned for the day's work, whether it might be fighting or waiting. The men stood by their horses waiting, ready for orders. As the light increased, there seemed to be some excitement among the officers; and before the day was well begun, we heard the firing of the enemy's guns."

32. Parts of Speech: Adverbs

- Black Beauty, Chapters 35-36

>Definition: An adverb is a word that modifies a verb, an adjective, or another adverb. Adverbs tell how, when, where, how often, and to what extent.

Nouns and pronouns have adjectives to tell more about them. Verbs and adjectives have adverbs. Adverbs modify verbs, adjectives, and other adverbs by telling **how, when, where, how often,** and **to what extent**. We will be looking at each type of adverb in upcoming lessons.

Look at the following sentences from *Black Beauty*:

>I **never** knew a better man.

In this sentence, the adverb **never** modifies the verb **knew**; it tells **when** he knew.

>He was **so** good-tempered.

In this sentence, the adverb **so** modifies the adjective **good-tempered**; it tells **to what extent** he was good-tempered.

>She spoke **very slowly**.

In this sentence, the adverb **very** modifies the adverb **slowly**; it tells **to what extent** she spoke slowly. The adverb **slowly** modifies the verb **spoke**; it tells **how** she spoke.

Many adverbs are formed by adding *ly* to adjectives, like **slowly** above. Can you think of some other *ly* words or any other adverbs? Be careful, though. Adjectives sometimes end in *ly*, too.

>The boy ran **quickly**, but he did **poorly** on a test.

>The sun shone **brightly**.

All of the adverbs in the sentences above are formed by adding *ly* to an adjective.

145

From the lesson on helping verbs, do you remember that sometimes other words come between a verb and its helpers? These words are adverbs. **Not** is a common adverb which likes to sit between the verb and its helpers, but other adverbs will sit in that position as well. **Not** is always an adverb, and it always modifies the verb.

He could **not** bear any careless loitering.

Like an adjective, an adverb is diagrammed by placing it on a slanted line underneath the word it modifies.

I **never** knew a better man.

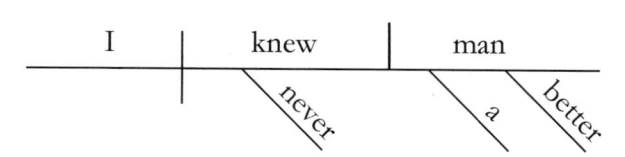

He was **so** good-tempered.

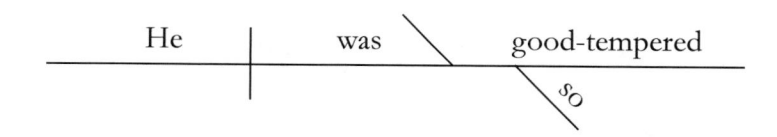

Adjectives and adverbs are often already on slanted lines, so when these words are modified to tell **to what extent**, we add a slanted line to the slanted line.

She spoke **very slowly**.

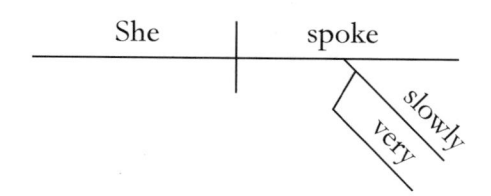

The Wind and the Moon

George MacDonald

Said the Wind to the Moon, "I will blow you out,
   You stare
   In the air
   Like a ghost in a chair,
Always looking what I am about—
I hate to be watched; I'll blow you out."

The Wind blew hard, and out went the Moon.
   So, deep
   On a heap
   Of clouds to sleep,

Down lay the Wind, and slumbered soon,
Muttering low, "I've done for that Moon."

He turned in his bed; she was there again!
   On high
   In the sky,
   With her one ghost eye,
The Moon shone white and alive and plain.
Said the Wind, "I will blow you out again."

The Wind blew hard, and the Moon grew dim.
   "With my sledge,
   And my wedge,
   I have knocked off her edge!
If only I blow right fierce and grim,
The creature will soon be dimmer than dim."

He blew and he blew, and she thinned to a thread.
   "One puff
   More's enough
   To blow her to snuff!
One good puff more where the last was bred,
And glimmer, glimmer, glum will go the thread."

He blew a great blast, and the thread was gone
   In the air
   Nowhere
   Was a moonbeam bare;
Far off and harmless the shy stars shone—
Sure and certain the Moon was gone!

The Wind he took to his revels once more;
   On down,
   In town,
   Like a merry-mad clown,
He leaped and hallooed with whistle and roar—
   "What's that?" The glimmering thread once more!

He flew in a rage—he danced and blew;
   But in vain
   Was the pain
   Of his bursting brain;
For still the broader the Moon-scrap grew,
The broader he swelled his big cheeks and blew.

Slowly she grew—till she filled the night,
   And shone
   On her throne
   In the sky alone,
A matchless, wonderful silvery light,
Radiant and lovely, the queen of the night.

Said the Wind: "What a marvel of power am I
   With my breath,
   Good faith!
   I blew her to death—
First blew her away right out of the sky—
Then blew her in; what strength have I!"

But the Moon she knew nothing about the affair;
   For high
   In the sky,
   With her one white eye,
Motionless, miles above the air,
She had never heard the great Wind blare.

Maku Mawu and Maku Fia

From *West African Folk-Tales* by William H. Barker

Part I

   Once upon a time there were two men who were such great friends that they were almost always together. If one was seen, the other was sure to be near. They had given one another special names which were to be used only by themselves. One name, Maku Mawu, meant, "I will die God's death," and the other, Maku Fia, meant, "I will die the King's death."

   By and by, however, the other villagers heard these names and gradually everyone got into the habit of calling the two friends by the nicknames in preference to the real ones. Finally, the King of the country heard of them and wished to see the men who had chosen such strange titles. He sent for them to Court, and they came together. He was much pleased with the one who had chosen the name of "Maku Fia," but he was annoyed at the other man's choice and sought a chance of punishing him.

   When he had talked to them a little while, he invited both to a great feast which he was to give in three days' time. As they went away, he gave a fine large yam to Maku Mawu and only a small round stone to his own favorite. The latter felt somewhat aggrieved at getting only a stone while his friend got such a fine yam. Very soon he said, "Oh, dear! I do not think it is any use carrying this stone home. How I wish it were a yam! Then I could cook it for dinner."

   Maku Mawu, being very generous, immediately replied, "Then change with me, for I am quite tired of carrying my great yam." They exchanged, and each went off to his own home. Maku Fia cut up his yam and cooked it. Maku Mawu broke his stone in half and found inside some beautiful ornaments which the King had hidden there. He thought that he would play a trick on the King, so he told nobody what had been in the stone.

   On the third day, they dressed to go to the King's feast. Maku Mawu put on all the beautiful ornaments out of the stone. Maku Fia dressed himself just as usual.

   When they reached the palace, the King was amazed to see the wrong man wearing his ornaments, and he determined to punish him more effectually next time. He asked Maku Fia what he had done with the stone, and the man told him he had exchanged it for his friend's yam.

At first the King could not think of any way to punish Maku Mawu as, of course, the latter had not done anything wrong. He soon had an idea, however. He pretended to be very pleased with the poor man and presented him with a beautiful ring from his own finger. He then made him promise to come back in seven days and show the ring to the King again, to let the king see that it was not lost. If by any chance he could not produce the ring, he would lose his head. This the King did, meaning to get hold of the ring in some way, and so get the young man killed.

Writing: Copia, Playing With Words

Take each of the following words from your model story and look them up in the thesaurus. Give two or three different ways to say each word.

> foreign, adventures, deeds, abroad, witness

Exercise

Review memory work. Copy each sentence below. Double underline the predicate, and underline the subject. Label the part of speech of each word. Noun, N; Proper Noun, PN; Pronoun, PRO; Verb, V; Linking Verb, LV; Adjective, ADJ; Article, ART; Adverb, ADV; Conjunctions, CJ; Interjections, INJ. Diagram each sentence.

> I never knew a better man.

> "They are not religious."

> "I do not believe."

Commonplace Book

With your instructor's approval, add this part of today's poem to your commonplace book, or choose your own poem.

> Said the Wind to the Moon, "I will blow you out,
> >   You stare
> >   In the air
> >   Like a ghost in a chair,
> Always looking what I am about—
> I hate to be watched; I'll blow you out."
>
> The Wind blew hard, and out went the Moon.
> >   So, deep
> >   On a heap
> >   Of clouds to sleep,
> Down lay the Wind, and slumbered soon,
> Muttering low, "I've done for that Moon."

Dictation

> A little knowledge is a dangerous thing.

The Dance Class by Edgar Degas

Picture Study

1. Read the title and the name of the artist. Study the picture for several minutes, then put the picture away.

2. Describe the picture.

3. Look at the picture again. Do you notice any details that you missed before? What do you like or dislike about this painting? Does it remind you of anything?

33. Descriptive Writing

• Black Beauty, Chapter 37

Writing: Descriptive Writing

Remember that the purpose of descriptive writing is to describe a person, place, thing, or event so well that an image forms in the mind of the reader.

Your last six picture studies have been on paintings by Edgar Degas. Today, choose one of his paintings, either one from this book or one from another source, and write a description of it. Imagine that you are describing the picture to someone who has never seen it before. Get creative if you wish. Write a description for a museum catalog or as part of a police report describing stolen merchandise. Or get really creative. Imagine that the painting is a window to another dimension, and you have just been pulled in. Describe the environment in which you find yourself. Or, write a story about the picture or about your experiences within it. Be as creative as you want. Just do not forget to describe the picture!

Peacock Feathers

By Hilda Conkling

On trees of fairyland
Grow peacock feathers of daylight colors
Like an Austrian fan.
But there is a strange thing!
I have heard that night gathers these feathers
For her cloak;
I have heard that the stars, the moon,
Are the eyes of peacock feathers
From fairy trees.
It is a thing that may be,
But I should not be sure of it, my dear,
If I were you!

Maku Mawu and Maku Fia

From West African Folk-Tales by William H. Barker

Part II

Maku Mawu saw what the King's design was, so he determined to hide the ring. He made a small hole in the wall of his room, put the ring in it, and carefully plastered over the place again. No one could see that the wall had been touched.

After two days, the King sent for the wife of Maku Mawu and asked her to find the ring. He promised her a large sum of money for it—not telling her, of course, what would happen to her husband if the ring were lost. The woman went home and searched diligently, but found nothing. The next day she tried again with no better success. Then she asked her husband what he had done with it. He innocently told her it was in the wall. The next day, when he was absent, she searched so carefully that at last she found it.

Delighted, she ran off to the King's palace and gave the ring to him. She got the promised money and returned home, never dreaming that she had really sold her husband's life.

On the sixth day, the King sent a message to Maku Mawu, telling him to prepare for the next day. The poor man thought of the ring and went to look to make sure it was still safe. To his despair, the hole was empty. He asked his wife and his neighbors. All denied having seen it. He made up his mind that he must die.

In the meantime, the King had laid the ring in one of the dishes in his palace and promptly forgot about it. When the seventh morning had arrived, he sent messengers far and wide to summon the people to come and see a man punished for disobeying the King's orders. Then he commanded his servants to set the palace in order and to take the dishes out of his room and wash them.

The careless servants—never looking to see if the dishes were empty or not—took them all to a pool nearby. Among them was the dish containing the ring. Of course, when the dish was being washed, out fell the ring into the water—without being noticed by the servants.

When the palace was all in readiness, the King went to fetch the ring. It was nowhere to be found, and he was obliged to go to the Assembly without it.

When everyone was ready, the poor man, Maku Mawu, was called to come forward and show the ring. He walked boldly up to the King and knelt down before him, saying, "The ring is lost, and I am prepared to die. Only grant me a few hours to put my house in order."

At first the king was unwilling to grant even that small favor, but finally he said, "Very well, you may have four hours. Then you must return here and be beheaded before the people."

The innocent man returned to his home and put everything in order. Then, feeling hungry, he thought, "I may as well have some food before I die. I will go and catch a fish in the pool."

He accordingly took his fishnet and bait and started off to the very pool where the King's dishes had been washed. Very soon he caught a fine large fish. When he had cut it open to clean it, you can imagine his delight at finding the lost ring inside it.

At once he ran off to the palace, crying: "I have found the ring! I have found the ring!"

When the people heard him, they all shouted in joy: "He named himself rightly 'Maku Mawu,' for see—the death God has chosen for him, that only will he die." So the King had no excuse to harm him, and he went free.

Exercise

Review memory work. Copy each sentence below. Double underline the predicate, and underline the subject. Label the part of speech of each word. Noun, N; Proper Noun, PN; Pronoun, PRO; Verb, V; Linking Verb, LV; Adjective, ADJ; Article, ART; Adverb, ADV; Conjunctions, CJ; Interjections, INJ. Diagram each sentence.

"Her mother is dangerously ill."

"She must go directly."

"It would be a rare treat."

Commonplace Book

With your instructor's approval, add the passage below to your commonplace book, or choose your own passage from a work of non-fiction. This can be from religious scriptures, a biography, or one of your history or science books.

> When my harness was taken off, I did not know what I should do first—whether to eat the grass, or roll over on my back, or lie down and rest, or have a gallop across the meadow out of sheer spirits at being free; and I did all by turns. Jerry seemed to be quite as happy as I was; he sat down by a bank under a shady tree and listened to the birds, then he sang himself and read out of the little brown book he is so fond of.

34. Adverbs That Tell How and When

- Black Beauty, Chapters 38-39

> Definition: An adverb is a word that modifies a verb, an adjective, or another adverb. Adverbs tell how, when, where, how often, and to what extent.

Just as we have different types of adjectives to give different types of information about nouns and pronouns, we also have different types of adverbs to give different types of information about verbs, adjectives, and other adverbs. Adverbs tell **how, when, where, how often,** and **to what extent**. If you memorize this list, and understand what each one means, adverbs will be easy to find in sentences.

First, adverbs tell **how**. Adverbs that tell **how** tell us how something is done. These adverbs are the most descriptive of the adverbs. Adverbs which are formed by adding *ly* to adjectives are usually adverbs that tell **how**. Look at the following sentence from *Black Beauty*:

Jerry thanked him **kindly**.

Jerry thanked who? **Him**; **him** is the direct object because it receives the action of the verb. He thanked him **how**? **Kindly**; **kindly** is the adverb that modifies **thanked**. It tells **how** he thanked him.

Adverbs that tell **how** do not have to end in *ly*. **Well** and **hard** are also adverbs which tell how.

He worked **hard**.

She did **well**.

Adverbs that tell **how** tell **how something was done**, so they modify the verb of the sentence.

Adverbs also tell **when**. Adverbs that tell **when** tell us when something is done. Words like **sometimes, never,** and **always** are adverbs that tell **when**.

Now we know.

Adverbs that tell **when** tell **when something was done**, so they modify the verb of the sentence.

Some adverbs which modify the verb can move around the sentence without changing the meaning of the sentence. Consider these changes to the sentence above. The word order is different, but the meaning is the same.

We **now** know.

We know **now**.

Some other adverbs that tell when are after, afterwards, already, before, ever, finally, later, now, soon, still, then, today, tomorrow, when, and yesterday.

This is not a complete list, but you should understand now how adverbs can tell **when**. Pick three of the words from the list above and make sentences with them. Tell what word your adverb that tells **when** modified.

The Ivy Green
By Charles Dickens

O, a dainty plant is the ivy green,
  That creepeth o'er ruins old!
Of right choice food are his meals, I ween,
  In his cell so lone and cold.
The walls must be crumbled, the stones decayed.
  To pleasure his dainty whim;
And the moldering dust that years have made
  Is a merry meal for him.
Creeping where no life is seen,
A rare old plant is the ivy green.

Fast he stealeth on, though he wears no wings,
  And a staunch old heart has he!
How closely he twineth, how tight he clings
  To his friend, the huge oak tree!
And slyly he traileth along the ground,
  And his leaves he gently waves,
And he joyously twines and hugs around
  The rich mould of dead men's graves.
Creeping where no life is seen,
A rare old plant is the ivy green.

Whole ages have fled, and their works decayed,
  And nations have scattered been;
But the stout old ivy shall never fade
  From its hale and hearty green.
The brave old plant in its lonely days
  Shall fatten upon the past;
For the stateliest building man can raise
  Is the ivy's food at last.

Creeping where no life is seen,
A rare old plant is the ivy green.

The Leopard and the Ram

From *West African Folk-Tales* by William H. Barker

A Ram once decided to make a clearing in the woods and build himself a house. A leopard who lived near also made up his mind to do the very same thing.

Unknown to each other, they both chose the same site. Ram came one day and worked at the clearing. Leopard arrived after Ram had gone and was much surprised to find some of his work already done. However, he continued what Ram had begun. Each was daily surprised at the progress made in his absence, but concluded that the fairies had been helping him. He gave them thanks and continued with his task.

Thus the matter went on—the two working alternately at the building and never seeing one another. At last the house was finished to the satisfaction of both.

The two prepared to take up their abode in the new home. To their great astonishment, they met. Each told his tale, and after some friendly discussion, they decided to live together.

Both Leopard and Ram had sons. These two young animals played together while their parents hunted. The leopard was very much surprised to find that every evening, his friend Ram brought home just as much meat or venison from the hunt as he himself did. He did not dare, however, to ask the other how he obtained it.

One day, before setting out to hunt, Leopard requested his son to find out, if possible, from young Ram, how his father managed to kill the animals. Accordingly, while they were at play, little Leopard inquired how Father Ram, having neither claws nor sharp teeth, succeeded in catching and killing the beasts. Ram refused to tell unless young Leopard would promise to show his father's way also. The latter agreed. Accordingly they took two large pieces of plantain stem and set out into the woods.

Young Leopard then took one piece and placed it in position. Then, going first to the right, then to the left—bowing and standing on his hind legs and peeping at the stem just as his father did—he took aim, sprang toward the stem, and tore it.

Young Ram then took the other piece and placed it in position. Wasting no time, he went backward a little way, took aim, then ran swiftly forward, pushing his head against the stem and tearing it to pieces. When they had finished, they swept the place clean and went home.

In the evening, the leopard obtained all the information about the hunt from his son. The latter warned him that he must always be careful when he saw the Ram go backward. He kept this in mind, and from that day watched the Ram very closely.

Some time afterward, it rained, making the floor of the house very slippery. The Leopard called the Ram, as usual, to dine with him. As he was coming, the Ram slipped backward on the wet floor. The Leopard, seeing this, thought the other was about to kill him. Calling to his son to follow, he sprang with all his might over the wall of the house and fled to the woods. The Ram called him back, but he did not listen. From that time, leopards have made their abode in the woods while rams have remained at home.

Writing: Copia

Take the following sentence and play with it. Remember that the point is not necessarily to make the sentence better. The point is to play with the sentence and make it different. Make a new sentence for each number, using at least one change from that category.

> One of the feats he told about was a leap he had made in a city called Rhodes.

1. Change the grammar.
   - Change the nouns from common to proper and vice versa.
   - Change the nouns from singular to plural and vice versa.
   - Change the sentence type.
   - Change the adjectives from articles to descriptive to possessive, etc.
   - Change a quotation from direct to indirect and vice versa.

2. Condense the sentence.
   - Remove details.
   - Remove modifiers.

3. Amplify the sentence.
   - Add details.
   - Add dialogue.
   - Add modifiers.

4. Use synonyms and antonyms.
   - Substitute synonyms.
   - Say the opposite thing using antonyms.

Exercise

Review memory work. Copy each sentence below. Double underline the predicate, and underline the subject. Label the part of speech of each word. Noun, N; Proper Noun, PN; Pronoun, PRO; Verb, V; Linking Verb, LV; Adjective, ADJ; Article, ART; Adverb, ADV; Conjunctions, CJ; Interjections, INJ. Diagram each sentence.

Winter came early.

The high-wheeled gig ran easily.

Dinah's family lived there.

Commonplace Book

With your instructor's approval, add the passage below to your commonplace book, or choose your own passage from a work of fiction. This can be from either school reading or free reading.

> "You that have your own horses and cabs, or drive for good masters, have a chance of getting on and a chance of doing right; I haven't. We can't charge

more than sixpence a mile after the first, within the four-mile radius. This very morning I had to go a clear six miles and only took three shillings."

Dictation

"If the police have any business with the matter, it ought to be with the masters who charge us so much or with the fares that are fixed so low. If a man has to pay eighteen shillings a day for the use of a cab and two horses, as many of us have to do in the season, and must make that up before we earn a penny for ourselves, I say 'tis more than hard work; nine shillings a day to get out of each horse before you begin to get your own living."

35. Adverbs That Tell Where and How Often

• Black Beauty, Chapter 40

Definition: An adverb is a word that modifies a verb, an adjective, or another adverb. Adverbs tell how, when, where, how often, and to what extent.

Today, we will be talking about adverbs that tell **where** and **how often**.

Adverbs tell us **where** something is done. Words like **here**, **there**, and **outside** are all adverbs that tell **where**. Look at the following sentences from *Black Beauty*:

"I'm **here** instead."

There were bags and boxes enough to have brought in a good many twopences if they had been put **outside**.

In the first sentence above, the adverb **here** tells **where** the speaker is. In the second sentence above, the adverb **outside** tells **where** the bags and boxes should have been put.

Adverbs that tell **where** tell **where something was done**, so they modify the verb of the sentence.

Some other adverbs that tell where are abroad, anywhere, downstairs, everywhere, here, in, inside, nowhere, out, somewhere, there, underground, and upstairs.

Pick three of the words from the list above and make sentences with them, and tell what word your adverb that tells **where** modified.

Adverbs also tell **how often** an event occurs. Words such as **daily**, **frequently**, and **occasionally** are adverbs that tell **how often**.

Ginger coughed **frequently**.

"I **often** feel like an old man."

Adverbs that tell **how often** tell **how often something was done**, so they modify the verb of the sentence.

Some other adverbs that tell how often are constantly, generally, infrequently, often, normally, once, periodically, rarely, regularly, seldom, sometimes, twice, usually, weekly, and yearly.

Pick three of the words from the list above and make sentences with them, and tell what word your adverb that tells **how often** modified.

Adverbs that tell **where** and **how often** are diagrammed like other adverbs, on slanted lines under the words they modify.

Now look again at this sentence.

"I'm here instead."

In this sentence, notice that our subject and verb have formed a contraction. To diagram the contraction, we un-contract it. I like to label contractions with the abbreviation for the first part of speech, an apostrophe, then the abbreviation for the second part of speech, like this:

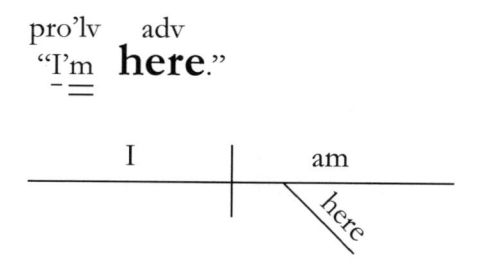

pro'lv   adv
"I'm **here**."

     I | am
                \here

Ginger coughed **frequently**.

     Ginger | coughed
                        \frequently

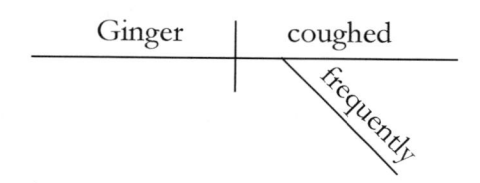

Tartary

By Walter De La Mare

If I were Lord of Tartary,
Myself and me alone,
My bed should be of ivory,
Of beaten gold my throne;
And in my court should peacocks flaunt,
And in my forests tigers haunt,
And in my pools great fishes slant
Their fins athwart the sun.

If I were Lord of Tartary,
Trumpeters every day
To all my meals should summon me,
And in my courtyards bray;
And in the evenings lamps should shine,

Yellow as honey, red as wine,
While harp, and flute, and mandoline,
Made music sweet and gay.

If I were Lord of Tartary,
I'd wear a robe of beads,
White, and gold, and green they'd be—
And small, and thick as seeds;
And ere should wane the morning-star,
I'd don my robe and scimitar,
And zebras seven should draw my car
Through Tartary's dark glades.

Lord of the fruits of Tartary,
Her rivers silver-pale!
Lord of the hills of Tartary,
Glen, thicket, wood, and dale!
Her flashing stars, her scented breeze,
Her trembling lakes, like foamless seas,
Her bird-delighting citron-trees
In every purple vale!

Why the Leopard Can Only Catch Prey on Its Left Side

From *West African Folk-Tales* by William H. Barker

At one time leopards did not know how to catch animals for food. Knowing that the cat was very skilful in this way, Leopard one day went to Cat and asked very politely if she would teach him the art. Cat readily consented.

The first thing Leopard had to learn was to hide himself among the bushes by the roadside so that he would not be seen by any animal passing by. Next, he must learn how to move noiselessly through the woods. He must never allow the animal he chased to know that he was following it. The third great principle was how to use his left paws and side in springing upon his prey.

Having taught him these three things, Cat requested him to go and practice them well. When he had learned them thoroughly, he could return to her, and she would give him more lessons in hunting.

Leopard obeyed. At first he was very successful and obtained all the food he wanted. One day, however, he was unable to catch anything at all.

Being very hungry, he bethought himself what he could have for dinner. Suddenly he remembered that the cat had quite a large family. He went straight to her home and found her absent.

Never thinking of her kindness to him—Leopard only remembered that he was hungry—he ate all her kittens. Puss, on discovering this dreadful fact, was so angry that she refused to have anything more to do with the great creature.

Consequently the leopard has never been able to learn how to catch animals that pass him on the right side.

Exercise

Review memory work. Copy each sentence below. Double underline the predicate, and underline the subject. Label the part of speech of each word. Noun, N; Proper Noun, PN; Pronoun, PRO; Verb, V; Linking Verb, LV; Adjective, ADJ; Article, ART; Adverb, ADV; Conjunctions, CJ; Interjections, INJ. Diagram each sentence.

"Yesterday he was raving."

Now he took his handkerchief out.

They often lost a fare.

Writing: Commonplace Book

Add the passage below from your model story to your commonplace book.

> One of the feats he told about was a leap he had made in a city called Rhodes. That leap was so great, he said, that no other man could leap anywhere near the distance. A great many persons in Rhodes had seen him do it and would prove that what he told was true.

Dictation

Use part of today's poem for dictation.

36. Amplified Narrative: The Leap at Rhodes

- Black Beauty, Chapters 41-42

Today, write "The Leap at Rhodes" as an amplified narrative. For this narration, amplify the narrative by adding both dialogue and descriptive detail. Remember, add details, not just adjectives!

In the story, a man describes a leap he made at Rhodes. Imagine the conversation that took place. You can describe the people and the setting where this conversation takes place. You can also have the man, in his dialogue, describe the scene at Rhodes. Be sure to use at least one direct quotation and one indirect quotation.

The Flying Squirrel

Mary E. Burt

Of all the woodland creatures,
  The quaintest little sprite
Is the dainty flying squirrel
  In vest of shining white,
In coat of silver gray,
  And vest of shining white.

His furry Quaker jacket
  Is trimmed with stripe of black;
A furry plume to match it
  Is curling o'er his back;
New curved with every motion,
  His plume curls o'er his back.

No little new-born baby
  Has pinker feet than he;
Each tiny toe is cushioned
  With velvet cushions three;
Three wee, pink, velvet cushions
  Almost too small to see.

Who said, "The foot of baby
  Might tempt an angel's kiss"?
I know a score of school-boys
  Who put their lips to this,—
This wee foot of the squirrel,
  And left a loving kiss.

The tiny thief has hidden
  My candy and my plum;
Ah, there he comes unbidden
  To gently nip my thumb,—
Down in his home (my pocket)
  He gently nips my thumb.

How strange the food he covets,
  The restless, restless wight;—
Fred's old stuffed armadillo
  He found a tempting bite,
Fred's old stuffed armadillo,
  With ears a perfect fright.

The Lady Ruth's great bureau,
  Each foot a dragon's paw!
The midget ate the nails from
  His famous antique claw.
Oh, what a cruel beastie
  To hurt a dragon's claw!

To autographic copies
  Upon my choicest shelf,—
To every dainty volume
  The rogue has helped himself.
My books! Oh dear! No matter!
  The rogue has helped himself.

And yet, my little squirrel,
  Your taste is not so bad;
You've swallowed Caird completely
  And psychologic Ladd.
Rosmini you've digested,
  And Kant in rags you've clad.

Gnaw on, my elfish rodent!
  Lay all the sages low!
My pretty lace and ribbons,
  They're yours for weal or woe!
My pocket-book's in tatters
  Because you like it so.

Editing

- Did you meet the goal of this writing exercise?
- Look at your word choice. Is there a good mixture of nouns and pronouns? Is the antecedent of each pronoun clear?

37. Adverbs That Tell to What Extent

• Black Beauty, Chapter 43

Definition: An adverb is a word that modifies a verb, an adjective, or another adverb. Adverbs tell how, when, where, how often, and to what extent.

The final kind of adverbs tell **to what extent**. While the other kinds of adverbs only modify verbs, adverbs that tell **to what extent** can modify verbs, adjectives, and other adverbs. When these adverbs modify verbs, they tell us to what degree something was done.

He had **just** eaten.

She had **barely** started.

When adverbs that tell **to what extent** modify adjectives and other adverbs, they strengthen or weaken the other modifiers.

Time passed **so** slowly.

They ran **very** fast.

Look at the following sentences from *Black Beauty*:

He had **scarcely** begun when a gentleman held up his umbrella.

It was a **very** rare thing for anyone to notice the horse that had been working for him.

What horse would **not** do his best for such a master?

Notice that the adverb **not** is on of our adverbs which tell **to what extent**. Some other adverbs that tell to what extent are almost, barely, entirely, extremely, not, quite, so, rather, terribly, too, and very.

Pick three of the words from the list above and make sentences with them, and tell what word your adverb that tells **to what extent** modified.

The Rolling-in of the Wave

By Hilda Conkling

It was night when the sky was dark blue
And the water came in with a wavy look
Like a spider's web.
The point of the slope came down to the water's edge;
It was green with a fairy ring of forget-me-not and fern.
The white foam licked the side of the slope
As it came up and bent backward;
It curled up like a beautiful cinder-tree
Bending in the wind.

Writing: Oral Narration

Read your new model story below, and then give your instructor an oral narration of it.

This is a story about a group of young people who find a humble bee's nest, what we call a bumble bee now. The story has two parts. The first part is the narrative portion. It tells about the events—who found the nest, what they did, what they said. The second part is the scientific discovery portion. It tells about the observations made about the life cycle of the bumble bee.

The Humble Bee's Nest

From *Wild Life in Woods and Fields* by Arabella B. Buckley

Last March, when the days began to be warm, we saw a big Humble Bee, or Bumble Bee as the little ones call it, buzzing along across the field.

"Look out, Peter," said Peggy. "That is a mother humble bee who has been asleep all the winter. She must be making a nest." So Peter followed her. She flew to a bank and went in among some tufts of grass. Peter put a large stick there, and we went to see her every day.

We used to find her dragging in little pieces of moss. But we did not look in for fear she should go away. After a fortnight, Paul said we might look, and hidden in the grass, we found a small round patch of moss lined with beeswax. It was like a tiny saucer turned upside down. We lifted it up and found under it a few round flat pockets, some as big as a halfpenny, some not larger than a farthing. (1) They were made of brown, sticky wax, and when we opened one we found inside seven tiny eggs, as small as poppy seeds, and some little brown balls. The balls, Paul said, were made of honey and of the yellow dust from flowers. In another pocket, we found grubs which had already been hatched from eggs. These were feeding on the brown balls near them.

The mother bee was very uneasy while we were looking at her nest. She sat down quite near. We could see how big and stout she was. She was so handsome. Her brown body was covered with soft yellow hairs, with stripes of black hairs between. Her wings were broad and shone so brightly in the sun. She did not sting us. Paul says that humble bees are very gentle. But she was afraid we would hurt the grubs, which were going to grow up into working bees. We put the cover back and waited two months. Then it was June. We were afraid the horses might tread on the nest when the hay was cut. So we went to look at it.

(2) Oh! How big it was now. There was a large round moss roof. It was lined with wax, and was so strong that we had to cut it with a knife. The only way for the bees to get into it was by a long tunnel just under the ground. (3) Under the roof were a number of dirty yellow silk cocoons. In these were the grubs, growing into humble bees. The cocoons were stuck together with wax. Some of them were open, for the young bees had come out. These had honey in them.

(4) There were a great many humble bees going in and out. These had all come from eggs laid by the mother bee in two months. They were very busy bringing in honey and bee-bread for the grubs to eat. But Paul says they do not store honey, like our hive-bees. For when the cold damp weather comes, they all die, except a few mothers. These creep into holes in the trees or into a warm haystack and sleep till the spring comes again.

About Christmas time we went to look at the nest. The roof was broken, and the cells all crushed. There was not one humble bee to be found.

Exercise

Review memory work. Copy each sentence below. Double underline the predicate, and underline the subject. Label the part of speech of each word. Noun, N; Proper Noun, PN; Pronoun, PRO; Verb, V; Linking Verb, LV; Adjective, ADJ; Article, ART; Adverb, ADV; Conjunctions, CJ; Interjections, INJ. Diagram each sentence.

Jerry and I had not eaten many mouthfuls.

Presently she approached Jerry.

Had she been Polly's mistress?

Commonplace Book

With your instructor's approval, add the passage below to your commonplace book, or choose your own passage from a work of fiction. This can be from either school reading or free reading.

"No, sir, no; I can't do that, thank you, I have only just money enough to get back with. Please tell me the way."

"Look you here, missis," said Jerry, "I've got a wife and dear children at home, and I know a father's feelings; now get you into that cab, and I'll take you there for nothing. I'd be ashamed of myself to let a woman and a sick child run a risk like that."

Dictation

And they soon were gone, for when they understood Jerry's dodge, they got out, calling him all sorts of bad names and blustering about his number and getting a summons. After this little stoppage, we were soon on our way to the hospital, going as much as possible through by-streets. Jerry rung the great bell and helped the young woman out.

"Thank you a thousand times," she said. "I could never have got here alone."

38. Writing an Outline

• Black Beauty, Chapters 44-45

An outline is a special way to write down details. You can write an outline of a story to list the main details, or you can write an outline of something you want to write to help you remember all the points you want to include.

In this lesson, we are going to outline a portion of "The Dragonfly and His Companions." Then, you will outline part of "The Humble Bee's Nest," your new model story from the last lesson. From now on, you will be outlining each new model story.

Like a summary, a one-level outline includes only the main content from a narrative. For this lesson, we are going to focus only on the changes that the dragonfly goes through. First, read the story below.

The Dragonfly and His Companions

From *By Pond and River* by Arabella B. Buckley

If you go often in April to a pond where dragonflies are, you may perhaps see one begin its life in the air. This is how it happens.

(1) Under the water a large insect crawls up the stem of a plant. He has a body as big as a dragonfly and has six legs. But he has a curious dull look in his face, and where his wings should be, there are only two short stumps.

He crawls very slowly up the stem till he comes out of the water into the air. Then a strange thing happens. (2) The skin of his back cracks, and out creeps a real dragonfly.

(3) First his head, then his body with its six legs and four soft, crumpled wings, and lastly his tail. He cannot fly yet. (4) He stands by his old empty skin, and slowly stretches out his wings to the sun. In a few hours, they are long and strong and hard. (5) Then he is ready to fly over the pond and feed.

This is how the dragonfly comes up to the air. You will not find him so easily under the water, but we will try next week with our net. We have seen so much at the top of the pond today that we have not had time to dredge in the mud below.

Outlines have a very specific form. For the first level, which is also the only level in a one-level outline, we number each main point with a capital Roman numeral as follows.

In the story, the main changes for the dragonfly are numbered 1-5. These are our main points.

    I. A six-legged insect crawls up the stem of a plant.

   II. The skin of his back cracks.

  III. The dragonfly creeps out—body, legs, wings, then tail.

  IV. He stretches his wings to dry in the sun.

   V. After a few hours, he is ready to fly.

Now you can write an outline detailing the life cycle of the humble bee from the last lesson. See the instructions on the next page.

The Father's Vineyard

Anonymous

As round their dying father's bed
His sons attend, the peasant said:
"Children, deep hid from prying eyes,
A treasure in my vineyard lies;
When you have laid me in the grave,
Dig, search-and your reward you'll have."

"Father," cries one, "but where's the spot?"
He sighs! He sinks! He answers not.

The tedious burial service over,
Home go his sons, and straight explore
Each corner of the vineyard round,
Dig up, beat, break, and sift the ground;
Yet though to search so well inclined,
Nor gold, nor treasure could they find;
But when the autumn next drew near,
A double vintage crowned the year.

"Now," quoth the peasant's wisest son,
"Our father's legacy is known,
In yon rich purple grapes 'tis seen,
Which, but for digging, never had been.
Then let us all reflect with pleasure.
That labor is the source of treasure."

Writing: Outline

Your new model story from the last lesson, "The Humble Bee's Nest," tells about the life cycle of the humble bee. Each stage is numbered, 1-4, within the story. Write an outline about this transformation. Make sure you write about each stage in your own words.

Exercise

Review memory work. Copy each sentence below. Double underline the predicate, and underline the subject. Label the part of speech of each word. Noun, N; Proper Noun, PN; Pronoun, PRO; Verb, V; Linking Verb, LV; Adjective, ADJ; Article, ART; Adverb, ADV; Conjunctions, CJ; Interjections, INJ. Diagram each sentence.

The wind had been very changeable.

Sometimes driver and horse must wait.

"Can't I do something?" [Hint: **something** is a pronoun.]

Commonplace Book

With your instructor's approval, add this part of today's poem to your commonplace book, or choose your own poem.

> As round their dying father's bed
> His sons attend, the peasant said:
> "Children, deep hid from prying eyes,
> A treasure in my vineyard lies;
> When you have laid me in the grave,
> Dig, search-and your reward you'll have."
>
> "Father," cries one, "but where's the spot?"
> He sighs! He sinks! He answers not.

Dictation

Good will is worth nothing unless it is accompanied by good acts.

At Claremont, Cape Province by Pieter Wenning

Picture Study

1. Read the title and the name of the artist. Study the picture for several minutes, then put the picture away.

2. Describe the picture.

3. Look at the picture again. Do you notice any details that you missed before? What do you like or dislike about this painting? Does it remind you of anything?

39. Literary Analysis

• Black Beauty, Chapter 46

Writing: Literary Analysis

Today you have another literary analysis assignment. Now that you have had some practice, this should be a written assignment, though it can be helpful to talk about your ideas before writing.

With your instructor's approval, choose *Black Beauty* or one of the other books you are currently reading, and answer the following questions. If you have already used *Black Beauty* twice for literary analysis, choose one of your other books.

What is the book about? Give a brief summary, just a few sentences. Do any of the characters change in the story? What causes them to change?

The Song in Camp

By Bayard Taylor

"Give us a song!" the soldiers cried,
  The outer trenches guarding,
When the heated guns of the camps allied
  Grew weary of bombarding.

The dark Redan, in silent scoff,
  Lay, grim and threatening, under;
And the tawny mound of the Malakoff
  No longer belched its thunder.

There was a pause. A guardsman said,
  "We storm the forts tomorrow;
Sing while we may, another day
  Will bring enough of sorrow."

They lay along the battery's side,
  Below the smoking cannon:
Brave hearts, from Severn and from Clyde,
  And from the banks of Shannon.

They sang of love, and not of fame;
  Forgot was Britain's glory:
Each heart recalled a different name,
  But all sang "Annie Laurie."

Voice after voice caught up the song,
  Until its tender passion
Rose like an anthem, rich and strong,—
  Their battle-eve confession.

Dear girl, her name he dared not speak,
  But, as the song grew louder,
Something upon the soldier's cheek
  Washed off the stains of powder.

Beyond the darkening ocean burned
  The bloody sunset's embers,
While the Crimean valleys learned
  How English love remembers.

And once again a fire of hell
  Rained on the Russian quarters,
With scream of shot, and burst of shell,
  And bellowing of the mortars!

And Irish Nora's eyes are dim
  For a singer, dumb and gory;
And English Mary mourns for him
  Who sang of "Annie Laurie."

Sleep, soldiers! Still in honored rest
  Your truth and valour wearing:
The bravest are the tenderest,—
  The loving are the daring.

To Lose an Elephant for the Sake of a Wren Is a Very Foolish Thing To Do

From *West African Folk-Tales* by William H. Barker

In the olden times there stood in the King's town a very great tree. This tree was so huge that it began to overshadow the neighboring fields. The King decided to have it cut down. He caused his servants to proclaim throughout the country that anyone who succeeded in cutting down the tree with a wooden axe should have an elephant in payment.

People thought it would be impossible to cut down such a great tree with an axe of wood. Spider, however, decided to try by cunning to gain the elephant. He accordingly presented himself before the King and expressed his readiness to get rid of the tree.

A servant was sent with him to keep watch and to see that he only used the wooden axe given him. Spider, however, had taken care to have another, made of steel, hidden in his bag.

He now began to fell the tree. In a very few minutes, he said to the servant, "See, yonder is a fine antelope. If you are quick, you will be able to hit it with a stone. Run!" The lad did as he was bid and ran a long way—but he could see no sign of the antelope. In his absence, Spider seized the sharp axe and hastened to cut as much of the tree as he could, carefully hiding the axe in his bag before the servant's return.

This trick he repeated several times till finally the tree was cut down. Spider went to the King to get the elephant, and he took the servant to prove that he had used only the wooden axe. He got his promised reward and started for home in great glee. On the way, however, he began to think over the matter. "Shall I take this animal home?" thought he. "That would be foolish, for then I would be obliged to share it with my family. No! I will hide it in the forest and eat it at my leisure. In that way I can have the whole of it for myself. Now what can I take home for the children's dinner?"

Thereupon he looked around and a little distance away saw a tiny wren sitting on a tree. "Exactly what I want," he said to himself. "That will be quite sufficient for them. I will tie my elephant to this tree while I catch the bird."

This he did, but when he tried to seize the bird, it flew off. He chased it for some time without success. "Well! Well!" said he. "My family will just have to go without dinner. I will now go back and get my elephant." He returned to the spot where he had left the animal, but to his dismay, the elephant had escaped. Spider was obliged to go home empty-handed, and he, as well as his family, went dinnerless that day.

Exercise

Review memory work. Copy each sentence below. Double underline the predicate, and underline the subject. Label the part of speech of each word. Noun, N; Proper Noun, PN; Pronoun, PRO; Verb, V; Linking Verb, LV; Adjective, ADJ; Article, ART; Adverb, ADV; Conjunctions, CJ; Interjections, INJ. Diagram each sentence.

Dolly was crying and kissed me too.

"Is it a heavy load?"

He was raising the whip again.

Commonplace Book

With your instructor's approval, add the passage below to your commonplace book, or choose your own passage from a work of non-fiction. This can be from religious scriptures, a biography, or one of your history or science books.

> The lady had walked along the footpath and now came across into the road. She stroked and patted my neck as I had not been patted for many a long day.

"You see, he was quite willing when you gave him the chance; I am sure he is a fine-tempered creature, and I daresay has known better days. You won't put that rein on again, will you?" For he was just going to hitch it up on the old plan.

Editing

- Did you meet the goal of this writing exercise?
- Look at your word choice. Is there a good mixture of nouns and pronouns? Is the antecedent of each pronoun clear?

40. The Paragraph

- Black Beauty, Chapters 47-48

Definition: A paragraph is a group of sentences on a single topic.

A paragraph must have a **topic**. The **topic** is what the paragraph is about. I like turtles. Every sentence should be related to this topic and to one another. Otherwise, the paragraph becomes confusing.

Did you catch the turtle sentence in the above paragraph? That was not on topic. Did it confuse you? Usually, an off-topic sentence won't be that obvious. What if I would started talking about punctuation instead? Then, I would still be talking about writing. But my topic was the paragraph and how it needs a topic, so it would have been just as out of place as the mention of turtles, which are very cool.

A topic can be **broad** or **narrow**. A **broad topic** is one which is very general. For example, a paragraph about the solar system would not be very detailed. You could mention what's in the solar system, but not much else. You could not tell about the atmosphere, terrain, temperature, and moons of all the planets, plus other features of the solar system, all in one paragraph. You would need more paragraphs to do that.

Perhaps you would decide to have a paragraph for a single planet instead. Now, your topic is much more **narrow**. You could make the topic even more narrow by writing about only the special features of the planet, such as the atmosphere. Do you want to make the topic more narrow still? Then you could write about what you can find in a corner of your own backyard.

After you read today's story, "The Ungrateful Man," look back at each paragraph and decide what the topic of the paragraph is.

Lovelocks

By Walter De La Mare

I watched the Lady Caroline
Bind up her dark and beauteous hair;
Her face was rosy in the glass,

And 'twixt the coils her hands would pass,
White in the candleshine.

Her bottles on the table lay,
Stoppered yet sweet of violet;
Her image in the mirror stooped
To view those locks as lightly looped
As cherry-boughs in May.

The snowy night lay dim without,
I heard the Waits their sweet song sing;
The window smouldered keen with frost;
Yet still she twisted, sleeked and tossed
Her beauteous hair about.

The Ungrateful Man

From *West African Folk-Tales* by William H. Barker

Part I

A hunter, who was terribly poor, was walking through the forest one day in search of food. Coming to a deep hole, he found there a leopard, a serpent, a rat, and a man. These had all fallen into the trap and were unable to get out again. Seeing the hunter, they begged him to help them out of the hole.

At first he did not wish to release any but the man. The leopard, he said, had often stolen his cattle and eaten them. The serpent very frequently bit men and caused their death. The rat did no good to anyone. He saw no use in setting them free.

However, these animals pleaded so hard for life that at last he helped them all out of the pit. Each, in turn, promised to reward him for his kindness—except the man. He, saying he was very poor, was taken home by the kind-hearted hunter and allowed to stay with him.

A short time after, Serpent came to the hunter and gave him a very powerful antidote for snake poison. "Keep it carefully," said Serpent. "You will find it very useful one day. When you are using it, be sure to ask for the blood of a traitor to mix with it." The hunter, having thanked Serpent very much, took great care of the powder and always carried it about with him.

The leopard also showed his gratitude by killing animals for the hunter and supplying him with food for many weeks.

Then, one day, the rat came to him and gave him a large bundle. "These," said he, "are some native cloths, gold dust, and ivory. They will make you rich." The hunter thanked the rat very heartily and took the bundle into his cottage.

After this, the hunter was able to live in great comfort. He built himself a fine new house and supplied it with everything needful. The man whom he had taken out of the pit still lived with him.

Writing: Copia

Take the following sentence and play with it. Remember that the point is not necessarily to make the sentence better. The point is to play with the sentence and make it different. Make a new sentence for each number, using at least one change from that category.

> The mother bee was very uneasy while we were looking at her nest.

1. Change the grammar.
   - Change the nouns from common to proper and vice versa.
   - Change the nouns from singular to plural and vice versa.
   - Change the sentence type.
   - Change the adjectives from articles to descriptive to possessive, etc.
   - Change a quotation from direct to indirect and vice versa.

2. Condense the sentence.
   - Remove details.
   - Remove modifiers.

3. Amplify the sentence.
   - Add details.
   - Add dialogue.
   - Add modifiers.

4. Use synonyms and antonyms.
   - Substitute synonyms.
   - Say the opposite thing using antonyms.

Exercise

Review memory work. Copy each sentence below. Double underline the predicate, and underline the subject. Label the part of speech of each word. Noun, N; Proper Noun, PN; Pronoun, PRO; Verb, V; Linking Verb, LV; Adjective, ADJ; Article, ART; Adverb, ADV; Conjunctions, CJ; Interjections, INJ. Diagram each sentence.

> He had black eyes and a hooked nose.

> "Can your horse do it?"

> "Do take a second cab."

Commonplace Book

With your instructor's approval, add the passage below to your commonplace book, or choose your own passage from a work of fiction. This can be from either school reading or free reading.

> My gentle friend had to obey, and box after box was dragged up and lodged on the top of the cab or settled by the side of the driver. At last all was ready, and with his usual jerk at the rein and slash of the whip, he drove out of the station.

Dictation

The boy was proud of his charge and undertook it in all seriousness. There was not a day when he did not pay me a visit, sometimes picking me out from among the other horses and giving me a bit of carrot or something good, or sometimes standing by me while I ate my oats. He always came with kind words and caresses, and of course I grew very fond of him. He called me Old Crony as I used to come to him in the field and follow him about.

41. Point of View

- Black Beauty, Chapter 49

> Definition: Point of view is the perspective from which
> a writer tells a story or presents information.

You have learned—and hopefully memorized—the personal pronouns. We use first person pronouns when we talk about ourselves.

The first person pronouns are I, me, my, mine, we, us, our, ours.

We use second person pronouns to refer to the person we are talking to. Singular and plural pronouns are the same in the second person.

The second person pronouns are you, your, yours.

We use third person pronouns to refer to people and things which we are talking about.

The third person pronouns are he, him, his, she, her, hers, it, its, they, them, their, theirs.

Writers must choose from which point of view to write. We describe different points of view based on which pronouns we would use. In your model story, "The Humble Bee's Nest," the author writes from the point of view of one of the group of children making observations. She is no mere spectator, observing the actions of the children. Instead, she is one of them. We know this because of the use of the first person pronouns.

> **We** used to find her dragging in little pieces of moss. But **we** did not look in, for fear she should go away. After a fortnight Paul said **we** might look, and hidden in the grass, **we** found a small round patch of moss lined with beeswax.

She could have chosen to write the story from the third person point of view. In this case, she would be an observer instead of one of the group.

They used to find her dragging in little pieces of moss. But **they** did not look in, for fear she should go away. After a fortnight Paul said **they** might look, and hidden in the grass, **they** found a small round patch of moss lined with beeswax.

The first person point of view makes the story feel more personal, and the third person makes the story feel more objective. Both points of view have merit, but they serve different purposes.

There was another first person point of view the author could have chosen—that of the bee!

"Look out, Peter," said one child. "That is a mother humble bee, who has been asleep all the winter. She must be making a nest." So the one called Peter followed **me**. **I** flew to a bank and went in among some tufts of grass. Peter put a large stick there, and they came to see **me** every day.

They used to find **me** dragging in little pieces of moss. But they did not look in, for fear **I** would go away. After a fortnight Paul said they might look, and hidden in the grass, they found **my** small round patch of moss lined with beeswax.

Each change in point of view gives the story a slightly different feel. It will also change some details. The children and the bee, for instance, experienced different events within the same narrative. Just as the bee had experiences that the children did not observe, the children had experiences about which the bee would know nothing.

Read today's story. From what point of view is the story written? Look back at each paragraph and decide what the topic of the paragraph is.

Good Enough
By C. J. Dennis

I do not think there ever was,
   Or ever will, or ever could be,
A little girl or little boy
   As good as she or as he should be.

But still, I think, you will agree,
   Though perfect very, very few are,
They're not so bad when "pretty good"—
   That's just about as good as you are.

The Ungrateful Man
From *West African Folk-Tales* by William H. Barker

Part II

This man, however, was of a very envious disposition. He was not at all pleased at his host's good fortune, and he only waited an opportunity to do him some harm. He very soon had a chance.

A proclamation was sounded throughout the country to say that some robbers had broken into the King's palace and stolen his jewels and many other valuables. The ungrateful man instantly hurried to the King and asked what the reward would be if he pointed out the thief. The King promised to give him half of the things which had been stolen. The wicked fellow thereupon falsely accused his host of the theft although he knew quite well that he was innocent.

The honest hunter was immediately thrown into prison. He was then brought into Court and asked to show how he had become so rich. He told them, faithfully, the source of his income, but no one believed him. He was condemned to die the following day at noon.

Next morning, while preparations were being made for his execution, word was brought to the prison that the King's eldest son had been bitten by a serpent and was dying. Anyone who could cure him was begged to come and do so.

The hunter immediately thought of the powder which his serpent friend had given him, and he asked to be allowed to use it. At first they were unwilling to let him try, but finally he received permission. The King asked him if there were anything he needed for it, and he replied, "A traitor's blood to mix it with."

His Majesty immediately pointed out the wicked fellow who had accused the hunter and said: "There stands the worst traitor, for he gave up the kind host who had saved his life." The man was at once beheaded, and the powder was mixed as the serpent had commanded. As soon as it was applied to the prince's wound, the young man was cured. In great delight, the King loaded the hunter with honors and sent him happily home.

Exercise

Review memory work. Copy each sentence below. Double underline the predicate, and underline the subject. Label the part of speech of each word. Noun, N; Proper Noun, PN; Pronoun, PRO; Verb, V; Linking Verb, LV; Adjective, ADJ; Article, ART; Adverb, ADV; Conjunctions, CJ; Interjections, INJ. Diagram each sentence.

The boy could hardly control his delight.

The groom cleaned and dressed me.

"Check his mouth."

Writing: Commonplace Book

Add the passage below from your model story to your commonplace book.

> The mother bee was very uneasy while we were looking at her nest. She sat down quite near. We could see how big and stout she was. She was so handsome. Her brown body was covered with soft yellow hairs, with stripes of black hairs between. Her wings were broad and shone so brightly in the sun. She did not sting us. Paul says that humble bees are very gentle. But she was afraid we would hurt the grubs, which were going to grow up into working bees.

Dictation

Use part of today's poem for dictation.

42. Point of View Narration:

The Humble Bee's Nest

- Ozma of Oz, Chapter 1

Today, write your narration on "The Humble Bee's Nest." Choose a point of view from which to write your narration. Are you the bee, one of the children, or an objective observer of the events? Use your outline to keep the life cycle of the bumble bee in the proper order. Pay attention to your pronouns as you write!

The Coming of the Great Bird

By Hilda Conkling

A boy was watching the water
As it came lapping the edge of fern.
Little ships passed him
As the moon came leaning across dark blue rays of light.
The spruce trees saw the white ships sailing away,
And the moon bending up the blue sky
Where stars were twinkling like fairy lamps;
The boy was looking toward foreign lands
As the ships passed,
Their white sails glittering in the moonlight.
He was thinking how he wished to see
Foreign lands, strange people,
When suddenly a bird came flying!
It swooped down upon the slope
And spoke to him:
"Do you want to go across the deep blue sea?
Get on my back; I will take you."
"Oh," cried the little boy, "who sent you?
Who knew my thoughts of foreign lands?"

Editing

- Did you meet the goal of this writing exercise?
- Look at your word choice. Is there a good mixture of nouns and pronouns? Is the antecedent of each pronoun clear?
- Look at your paragraphs. Are all the sentences related? Does each paragraph focus on a single topic?

43. Phrases and Clauses

• Ozma of Oz, Chapter 2

> Definition: A phrase is a group of related words
> which does not include a subject-predicate pair.
>
> Definition: A clause is a group of words
> which contains a subject-predicate pair.

You probably noticed that the two definitions above are almost identical. The defining characteristic of both phrases and clauses is whether or not they have a subject-predicate pair. A subject-predicate pair is simply a verb with its subject.

Phrases can be short or long. Some phrases have specific names based on the main word or usage of the phrase. A noun phrase consists of a noun and its modifiers. A verb phrase consists of the helping verbs, main verb, and any modifiers and objects which the verb has. Look at the following sentences from *Ozma of Oz*. The first has a noun phrase and the second has a verb phrase, both of which are large and bold.

The little girl was quite an experienced traveler.

He **had been working hard** on his Kansas farm.

Unlike a phrase, a clause must have a subject and a predicate. Look at these clauses. The predicate is double underlined, and the subject is underlined, in each clause.

when the wind began blowing

while he traveled far away to Australia

Dorothy had almost fallen asleep

Notice that some clauses express a complete thought. That makes them sentences. But some of the clauses do not express a complete thought. Why do you think that is? Which of the clauses above could be a sentence? What is different about it?

The last clause could be a complete sentence on its own. The other clauses begin with certain words that tell us that there is more to the thought. When a clause begins with a word like **when**, **while**, or **before**, it leaves us wondering, "And then what?" We need the rest of the information to have a complete thought expressed. Look at those clauses again, this time with that beginning word removed.

The <u>wind</u> <u>began</u> blowing.

<u>He</u> <u>traveled</u> far away to Australia.

When I took away that beginning word, I also took away the expectation for the rest of the story. Now these clauses can stand alone as complete sentences.

The Buckle

By Walter De La Mare

I had a silver buckle,
I sewed it on my shoe,
And 'neath a sprig of mistletoe
I danced the evening through!

I had a bunch of cowslips,
I hid 'em in a grot,
In case the elves should come by night
And me remember not.

I had a yellow riband,
I tied it in my hair,
That, walking in the garden,
The birds might see it there.

I had a secret laughter,
I laughed it near the wall:
Only the ivy and the wind
May tell of it at all.

Writing: Oral Narration

Read your new model story below, and then give your instructor an oral narration of it.

A Frog's Life

From *By Pond and River* by Arabella Buckley

Croak, croak, croak. We hear the frogs in the month of March. They make a great deal of noise in this month because they are just awake from their winter's sleep at the bottom of the pond.

(1) The mother frogs are laying their tiny dark eggs in the water. Each egg is not bigger than a grain of sand. But it has a coat of jelly, and this jelly swells and swells

in the water till it is as large as a pea, with a little black dot in the middle. The jelly lumps all cling together. You may see them in almost any pond, driven up to the side by the wind.

(2) Soon the dark speck lengthens. A head grows at one end and a tail at the other. The head has a mouth, but no eyes as yet. The tail has a fin all round it, and the tadpole wriggles about in its slimy bed.

(3) In about a week, it wriggles out of the jelly, and hangs by its mouth to the weeds. Then two curious tufts grow on each side of its head. It uses these tufts to breathe by taking air out of the water. You can see them if you dip a glass into the pond and catch a few tadpoles.

(4) By this time the tadpole has let go of the weed and is swimming about. A sharp beak has grown on to his mouth. He uses it to tear off pieces of weed to eat. Now he grows eyes, nose-holes, and flat ears. His tufts shrivel up, and a cover grows over them so that you cannot see them. They are now like the gills of a fish. He gulps water in at his mouth and sends it out through the cover. As it passes, the gills take the air out of it, and so the tadpole breathes.

(5) Soon two small lumps appear on each side of his body, behind the cover, just where it joins his tail. They grow larger and larger till at last two hind legs come out. These legs grow very long and strong, and he uses them to swim. Two front legs are growing as well, but you cannot see them because they are under the cover. In a few days these peep out, but they are short and stumpy.

Our tadpole has now four legs and a tail. He has four toes on the front feet and five toes on the hind feet, with a skin between the toes. So his hind legs are web-footed, and this helps him to swim.

He comes to the top of the water much more often than before and sends a bubble of air out of his mouth. What do you think has happened? The gills under his cover have closed up, and a small air-bag has grown inside him. So he comes up to breathe in the air through his mouth instead of taking it out of the water through his gills.

Now he likes to jump on a piece of weed and sit in the shade. He does not want his tail any longer, for he can swim quite well with his legs. So his tail is slowly sucked in to feed his body.

(6) There you have your little frog. If you look through the web of his foot at the sun, you will see that he has red blood now. But it is not warm blood like ours. He is always cold and clammy because his blood moves slowly.

He has a number of teeth in the top of his mouth and such a curious tongue. It is tied down to the front of his mouth, and the tip, which is very sticky, lies back down his throat. He does not eat weed now. He feeds on insects and slugs. He catches them by throwing out his tongue and drawing it back very quickly.

He lives chiefly on land during the summer if he is not eaten by ducks, rats, or snakes. Then he drops to the bottom of the pond to sleep in the mud all winter.

Exercise

Review memory work. Identify each group of words below as either a phrase or a clause. If it is a clause, double underline the predicate and underline the subject.

in his little sleeping-berth

the wind blew hard and joggled the water of the ocean

she sat down in a corner of the coop

Copy each sentence below. Double underline the predicate, and underline the subject. Label the part of speech of each word. Noun, N; Proper Noun, PN; Pronoun, PRO; Verb, V; Linking Verb, LV; Adjective, ADJ; Article, ART; Adverb, ADV; Conjunctions, CJ; Interjections, INJ. Diagram each sentence.

"Have you been here, too?"

"Do I speak quite properly?"

"You may have my egg."

Commonplace Book

With your instructor's approval, add the passage below to your commonplace book, or choose your own passage from a work of fiction. This can be from either school reading or free reading.

> "Very well, Billina. My name is Dorothy Gale—just Dorothy to my friends and Miss Gale to strangers. You may call me Dorothy, if you like. We're getting very near the shore. Do you suppose it is too deep for me to wade the rest of the way?"

Dictation

> "Why, as for that," answered the yellow hen thoughtfully, "I've clucked and cackled all my life, and never spoken a word before this morning, that I can remember. But when you asked a question, a minute ago, it seemed the most natural thing in the world to answer you. So I spoke, and I seem to keep on speaking, just as you and other human beings do. Strange, isn't it?"

44. Parts of Speech: Conjunctions

- Ozma of Oz, Chapter 3

Definition: A conjunction is a word that joins words and groups of words together. There are three types of conjunctions: coordinating, subordinating, and correlative.

Conjunctions join words and groups of words together. The most common conjunctions are the seven coordinating conjunctions.

The seven coordinating conjunctions are For, And, Nor, But, Or, Yet, and So. (FANBOYS)

The seven coordinating conjunctions can be easily remembered with the mnemonic FANBOYS: For, And, Nor, But, Or, Yet, and So.

And and **or** are two of the most common of the FANBOYS. They often join words to create compound subjects, predicates, and other compound structures. Look at these sentences from *Ozma of Oz*:

"Of course we'll have to stay in the cabin," she said to Uncle Henry **and** the other passengers.

"I do not know what I have said **or** done that leads you to insult me!"

In the first sentence, **and** joins the proper noun **Uncle Henry** to the noun phrase **the other passengers**. In the second sentence, **or** joins the verbs **have said** and **done**. The other FANBOYS are frequently seen joining clauses.

"When the coop blew away from the ship, I clung fast to this corner, with claws and beak, **for** I knew if I fell into the water, I'd surely be drowned."

He had sailed his ship through them in safety, **but** he knew that his passengers would be in danger if they tried to stay on deck.

But there were no houses to be seen **nor** any sign of people who might inhabit this unknown land.

As soon as she got there, the wind struck her so fiercely that it almost tore away the skirts of her dress, **yet** Dorothy felt a sort of joyous excitement in defying the storm.

Uncle Henry thought she would be good company and help cheer him up, **so** he decided to take her along.

The FANBOYS do not keep clauses from expressing a complete thought! Any of the above sentences could become two sentences quite easily by separating the two clauses with a period.

As soon as she got there, the wind struck her so fiercely that it almost tore away the skirts of her dress. **Yet** Dorothy felt a sort of joyous excitement in defying the storm.

Remember that the part of speech of a word is determined by the job it is performing in a sentence. **Soccer** is a noun when we are talking about the sport; **soccer** is an adjective when we are describing the type of ball. In the same way, **so** is a conjunction when it's joining words or groups of words together. **So** is an adverb when it shows to what extent.

A Life on the Ocean Wave

By Epes Sargent

A life on the ocean wave,
  A home on the rolling deep,
Where the scattered waters rave,
  And the winds their revels keep!
Like an eagle caged, I pine
  On this dull, unchanging shore:
Oh! Give me the flashing brine,
  The spray and the tempest's roar!

Once more on the deck I stand
  Of my own swift-gliding craft:
Set sail! Farewell to the land!
  The gale follows fair abaft.
We shoot through the sparkling foam
  Like an ocean-bird set free;—
Like the ocean-bird, our home
  We'll find far out on the sea.

The land is no longer in view,
  The clouds have begun to frown;
But with a stout vessel and crew,
  We'll say, Let the storm come down!
And the song of our hearts shall be,

While the winds and the waters rave,
A home on the rolling sea!
A life on the ocean wave!

The Omanhene Who Liked Riddles

From *West African Folk-Tales* by William H. Barker

Part I

The Omanhene is the chief of a village. A certain Omanhene had three sons who were very anxious to see the world. They went to their father and asked permission to travel. This permission he readily gave.

It was the turn of the eldest to go first. He was provided with a servant and with all he could possibly require for the journey.

After traveling for some time, he came to a town where lived an Omanhene who loved riddles. According to custom, strangers were brought by the people before the chief. The chief explained to the traveler that they had certain laws in their village. One law was that every stranger must best the Omanhene in answering riddles, or he would be beheaded. He must be prepared to begin the contest the following morning.

Next day he came to the Assembly Place and found the Omanhene there with all his attendants. The Omanhene asked many riddles. As the young man was unable to answer any of them, he was judged to have failed and was beheaded.

After some time the second son of the Omanhene started on his travels. By a strange chance he arrived at the same town where his brother had died. He also was asked many riddles and failed to answer them. Accordingly he too was put to death.

By and by the third brother announced his intention of traveling. His mother did all in her power to persuade him to stay at home. It was quite in vain.

She was sure that if he also reached the town where his brothers had died, the same thing would happen to him. Rather than allow this, she thought she would prefer him to die on the way.

She prepared for him a food called cankey—which she filled with poison. Having packed it away in his bag, he set off. Very soon he began to feel hungry. Knowing, however, that his mother had not wished him to leave home, and therefore might have put some poison in the food, he thought he would test it before eating it himself. Seeing a vulture nearby, he threw it half the cake.

The bird ate the cankey and immediately fell dead by the roadside. Three panthers came along and began to eat the vulture. They also fell dead.

The young man cut off some of the flesh of the panthers and roasted it. He then packed it carefully away in his bundle.

Writing: Outline

Your new model story from the last lesson, "A Frog's Life," tells of the transformation of a tadpole into a frog. Each stage is numbered, 1-6, within the story. Read the story today and write an outline about this transformation. Make sure you write about each stage in your own words.

Exercise

Review memory work. Identify each group of words below as either a phrase or a clause. If it is a clause, double underline the predicate and underline the subject.

while she was speaking

when Billina suddenly cried

upon all fours

Copy each sentence below. Double underline the predicate, and underline the subject. Label the part of speech of each word. Noun, N; Proper Noun, PN; Pronoun, PRO; Verb, V; Linking Verb, LV; Adjective, ADJ; Article, ART; Adverb, ADV; Conjunctions, CJ; Interjections, INJ. Diagram each sentence.

"Can I tell metal?"

"Run!"

The Wheeler gave a sharp, wild cry and chased her.

Commonplace Book

With your instructor's approval, add this part of today's poem to your commonplace book, or choose your own poem.

> A life on the ocean wave,
>   A home on the rolling deep,
> Where the scattered waters rave,
>   And the winds their revels keep!
> Like an eagle caged, I pine
>   On this dull, unchanging shore:
> Oh! Give me the flashing brine,
>   The spray and the tempest's roar!

Dictation

All work and no play makes Jack a dull boy.

Backyard, Malta Farm Observatory by Pieter Wenning

Picture Study

1. Read the title and the name of the artist. Study the picture for several minutes, then put the picture away.

2. Describe the picture.

3. Look at the picture again. Do you notice any details that you missed before? What do you like or dislike about this painting? Does it remind you of anything?

45. Descriptive Writing

• Ozma of Oz, Chapter 4

Writing: Descriptive Writing

In the last chapter of *Ozma of Oz*, Dorothy and Billina encounter the Wheelers. Read that passage below, paying close attention to the details that make a vivid picture in your mind, and then write a narration of it. Notice the words that L. Frank Baum uses to create a word picture. How does he describe the Wheelers? How does he describe Dorothy's and Billina's reactions to the Wheelers?

Add details if you wish. Remember, the point of this exercise is to write as descriptively as possible, not just to narrate the passage exactly.

Ozma of Oz

Dorothy turned quickly around and saw, coming out of a path that led from between the trees, the most peculiar person her eyes had ever beheld.

It had the form of a man, except that it walked, or rather rolled, upon all fours, and its legs were the same length as its arms, giving them the appearance of the four legs of a beast. Yet it was no beast that Dorothy had discovered, for the person was clothed most gorgeously in embroidered garments of many colors and wore a straw hat perched jauntily upon the side of its head. But it differed from human beings in this respect: instead of hands and feet, there grew at the end of its arms and legs round wheels, and by means of these wheels, it rolled very swiftly over the level ground. Afterward Dorothy found that these odd wheels were of the same hard substance that our fingernails and toenails are composed of, and she also learned that creatures of this strange race were born in this queer fashion. But when our little girl first caught sight of the first individual of a race that was destined to cause her a lot of trouble, she had an idea that the brilliantly-clothed personage was on roller-skates which were attached to his hands as well as to his feet.

"Run!" screamed the yellow hen, fluttering away in great fright. "It's a Wheeler!"

The Hare

By Walter De La Mare

In the black furrow of a field
I saw an old witch-hare this night;
And she cocked her lissome ear,
And she eyed the moon so bright,
And she nibbled o' the green;
And I whispered 'Whsst! witch-hare,'
Away like a ghostie o'er the field
She fled, and left the moonlight there.

The Omanhene Who Liked Riddles

From *West African Folk-Tales* by William H. Barker

Part II

A little farther on, he was attacked by seven highway robbers. They wanted to kill him at once. He told them that he had some good roast meat in his bundle and invited them to eat with him first. They agreed and divided up the food into eight parts.

While they were eating, the young man carefully hid his portion. Soon all the seven robbers fell ill and died. The young man then went on his way.

At last he reached the town where his brothers had died. Like them, he was summoned to the Assembly Place to answer the riddles of the Omanhene. For two days the contest proved equal. At the end of that time, the young man said, "I have only one riddle left. If you are able to answer that, you may put me to death." He then gave this riddle to the Omanhene:

> Half kills one—
> One kills three—
> Three kills seven.

The ruler failed to answer it that evening, so it was postponed till the next day.

During the night, the Omanhene disguised himself and went to the house where the stranger was staying. There he found the young man asleep in the hall.

Imagining that the man before him was the stranger's servant, and never dreaming that it was the stranger himself, he roused the sleeper and promised him a large reward if he would give him the solution to the riddle. The young man replied that he would tell the answer if the Omanhene would bring him the costume which he always wore at the Assembly.

The ruler was only too pleased to go and fetch it for him. When the young man had the garments quite safely, he explained the riddle fully to the crafty Omanhene. He said that as they were leaving home, the mother of his master made him cankey. In order to find out if the cankey was good, he gave half to a vulture which died. Three panthers which tasted the vulture also died. A little of the panther's roasted flesh killed seven robbers.

The Omanhene was delighted to have found out the answer. He warned the supposed servant not to tell his master what had happened.

In the morning all the villagers assembled together again. The Omanhene proudly gave the answer to the riddle as if he himself had found it out. But the young man asked him to produce his ceremonial dress, which he ought to be wearing in Assembly. This, of course, he was unable to do, as the young man had hidden it carefully away.

The stranger then told what had happened in the night and how the ruler had got the answer to the riddle by cheating.

The Assembly declared that the Omanhene had failed to find out the riddle and must die. Accordingly he was beheaded—and the young man was appointed Omanhene in his place.

Exercise

Review memory work. Identify each group of words below as either a phrase or a clause. If it is a clause, double underline the predicate and underline the subject.

> that crack in the rock

> so I think

> don't be frightened

Copy each sentence below. Double underline the predicate, and underline the subject. Label the part of speech of each word. Noun, N; Proper Noun, PN; Pronoun, PRO; Verb, V; Linking Verb, LV; Adjective, ADJ; Article, ART; Adverb, ADV; Conjunctions, CJ; Interjections, INJ. Diagram each sentence.

> "We could unlock it."

> "Try it and see."

> "Don't be frightened."

Commonplace Book

With your instructor's approval, add the passage below to your commonplace book, or choose your own passage from a work of non-fiction. This can be from religious scriptures, a biography, or one of your history or science books.

> Dorothy stepped inside the little room to get a back view of the copper man, and in this way, she discovered a printed card that hung between his shoulders, suspended from a small copper peg at the back of his neck. She unfastened this card and returned to the path, where the light was better, and sat herself down upon a slab of rock to read the printing.

46. Parts of Speech: Interjections; Nouns of Direct Address

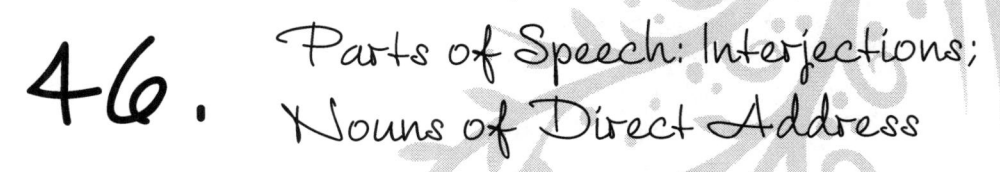

- Ozma of Oz, Chapter 5

Definition: An interjection is a word or group of words that shows sudden or strong feeling.

Oh, no! There is no set list of words that can be used as interjections. Aiee! However shall we find them?

Well, perhaps it will not be difficult afterall. Although the word **why** usually begins a question, it is also often used as an interjection at the beginning of a sentence, as are **yes**, **no**, and **indeed**. **Hello** is an interjection when it is used as a greeting or to express surprise. Look at the examples below from *Ozma of Oz*:

"**Dear me**!" said Dorothy, in a frightened tone. "What can the matter be?"

"**Oh**, I'm sure it was ripe," declared Dorothy.

"**No**, that can't be," answered the little girl.

Interjections can be one word or more than one word, and they are set apart from the rest of the sentence by commas or exclamation marks.

Definition: A noun of direct address is the name or other reference directly to the person being addressed.

We use nouns of direct address to refer directly to the person or persons we are talking to. This can be the person's name, but it can also be another word or phrase, such as **my friends**, **boys and girls**, or a title like **sir**. Below, the second sentence has both an interjection and a noun of direct address.

"So I don't believe there can be any automobiles, **Billina**."

"**Now**, **Tiktok**," said Dorothy, "the first thing to be done is to find a way for us to escape from these rocks."

What do interjections and nouns of direct address have in common that made me put them both in the same lesson?

Neither has any grammatical relationship to the rest of the sentence! In other words, we can take them out of a sentence without changing the meaning of the sentence at all. See for yourself by reading the sentences from above without the interjections and the noun of direct address:

"So I don't believe there can be any automobiles."

Dorothy said, "The first thing to be done is to find a way for us to escape from these rocks."

Interjections and nouns of direct address are also both diagrammed and punctuated exactly the same way. Both should be set apart from the rest of the sentence, usually with commas, but both are sometimes set apart with exclamation marks as well.

Because nouns of direct address have no grammatical relationship to the rest of the sentence, they will never be the subject of the sentence.

That last sentence is important. Nouns of direct address will never be the subject of the sentence. They also will not fill any other role, but they often look like the subject, especially when the real subject is the understood **you** of an imperative sentence.

"**Dorothy**, run!"

In the sentence above, **Dorothy** is the noun of direct address. The subject is the understood **you**. Does this sound like nonsense? Try removing the direct address from the sentence.

"Run!"

The sentence still makes sense. It still expresses a complete thought. The subject is an essential part of the sentence, even when it is the unstated, understood **you**. The direct address is never an essential part of the sentence, not in a grammatical sense.

Interjections and nouns of direct address are both diagrammed on a floating line above the rest of the diagram:

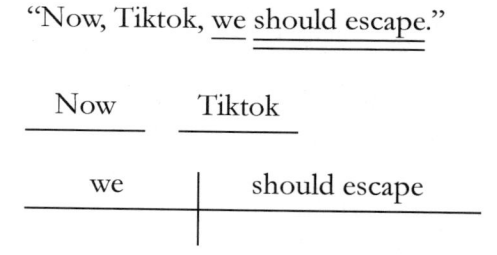

"Now, Tiktok, we should escape."

```
   Now        Tiktok
_____  _____

    we     |  should escape
_____|_____
           |
```

Tree-Toad

By Hilda Conkling

Tree-toad is a small gray person
With a silver voice.
Tree-toad is a leaf-gray shadow
That sings.
Tree-toad is never seen

Unless a star squeezes through the leaves,
Or a moth looks sharply at a gray branch.
How would it be, I wonder,
To sing patiently all night,
Never thinking that people are asleep?
Raindrops and mist, starriness over the trees,
The moon, the dew, the other little singers,
Cricket . . . toad . . . leaf rustling . . .
They would listen:
It would be music like weather
That gets into all the corners
Of out-of-doors.

Every night I see little shadows
I never saw before.
Every night I hear little voices
I never heard before.
When night comes trailing her starry cloak,
I start out for slumberland,
With tree-toads calling along the roadside.
Good-night, I say to one, Good-by, I say to another:
I hope to find you on the way
We have traveled before!
I hope to hear you singing on the Road of Dreams!

The Hunt of Lion and Jackal

From *South-African Folk-Tales* by James A. Honey

Lion and Jackal, it is said, were one day lying in wait for Eland. Lion shot with a bow and missed, but Jackal hit and sang out, "Hah! Hah!"

Lion said, "No, you did not shoot anything. It was I who hit."

Jackal answered, "Yea, my father, thou hast hit."

Then they went home in order to return when the eland was dead and cut it up. Jackal, however, turned back, unknown to Lion, hit his nose so that the blood ran on the spoor of the eland, and followed their track in order to cheat Lion. When he had gone some distance, he returned by another way to the dead eland and, creeping into its carcass, cut out all the fat.

Meanwhile Lion followed the blood-stained spoor of Jackal, thinking that it was eland blood, and only when he had gone some distance did he find out that he had been deceived. He then returned on Jackal's spoor and reached the dead eland, where he found Jackal in its carcass, and he seized Jackal by his tail and drew him out with a swing.

Lion upbraided Jackal with these words: "Why do you cheat me?"

Jackal answered: "No, my father, I do not cheat you; you may know it, I think. I prepared this fat for you, father."

Lion said: "Then take the fat and carry it to your mother, the lioness." And he gave him the lungs to take to his own wife and children.

When Jackal arrived, he did not give the fat to Lion's wife, but to his own wife and children; he gave the lungs to Lion's wife, and he pelted Lion's little children with the lungs, saying:

> "You children of the big-pawed one!
> You big-pawed ones!"

He said to Lioness, "I go to help my father, the lion." But he went far away with his wife and children.

Writing: Copia

Take the following sentence and play with it. Remember that the point is not necessarily to make the sentence better. The point is to play with the sentence and make it different. Make a new sentence for each number, using at least one change from that category.

> He comes to the top of the water much more often than before and sends a bubble of air out of his mouth.

1. Change the grammar.
   - Change the nouns from common to proper and vice versa.
   - Change the nouns from singular to plural and vice versa.
   - Change the sentence type.
   - Change the adjectives from articles to descriptive to possessive, etc.
   - Change a quotation from direct to indirect and vice versa.

2. Condense the sentence.
   - Remove details.
   - Remove modifiers.
   - Remove phrases or clauses.

3. Amplify the sentence.
   - Add details.
   - Add dialogue.
   - Add modifiers.
   - Add phrases or clauses.

4. Use synonyms and antonyms.
   - Substitute synonyms.
   - Say the opposite thing using antonyms.

5. Point of view.
   - Change the point of view.

Exercise

Review memory work. Identify each group of words below as either a phrase or a clause. If it is a clause, double underline the predicate and underline the subject.

until suddenly he became motionless

that low bow to you

she ran around the copper man

Copy each sentence below. Double underline the predicate, and underline the subject. Label the part of speech of each word. Noun, N; Proper Noun, PN; Pronoun, PRO; Verb, V; Linking Verb, LV; Adjective, ADJ; Article, ART; Conjunction, CJ; Interjection, INJ. Diagram each sentence.

"Haven't you a club?"

"He must have been a great loss." [Hint: **loss** has an article modifier. What part of speech does that make it?]

"The best thinker was a scarecrow."

Commonplace Book

With your instructor's approval, add the passage below to your commonplace book, or choose your own passage from a work of fiction. This can be from either school reading or free reading.

> He gave a sort of gurgle and stopped short, waving his hands frantically until suddenly he became motionless, with one arm in the air and the other held stiffly before him with all the copper fingers of the hand spread out like a fan.

Dictation

At once she wound up Tiktok's voice, taking care to give the key as many turns as it would go around. She found this quite a task, as you may imagine if you have ever tried to wind a clock, but the machine man's first words were to assure Dorothy that he would now run for at least twenty-four hours.

"You did not wind me much, at first," he calmly said, "and I told you that long story about King Evoldo; so it is no wonder that I ran down."

47. Appositives

• Ozma of Oz, Chapter 6

> Definition: An appositive is a noun, a noun phrase, or a
> noun clause that sits next to another noun and renames it.

An appositive is very like a predicate nominative in that it identifies or renames another noun. However, it does not need a linking verb to link the two words together. Instead, it sits beside the noun it identifies or renames. In fact, **apposition** means to be side by side. In *Ozma of Oz*, so far you have met:

> **Dorothy**, the little **girl** from Kansas,
> **Billina**, the yellow **hen**, and
> **Tiktok**, the machine **man**.

The appositive is the noun which renames the noun it sits beside. Each appositive above also has modifiers. The appositive of **Dorothy** is **girl**; the appositive of **Billina** is **hen**; and the appositive of **Tiktok** is **man**.

Look at the following sentence from *Ozma of Oz*. It has two appositives. Can you find them?

> "I was purchased from Smith & Tinker, my manufacturers, by a cruel King of Ev, Evoldo, who used to beat all his servants until they died."

In the above sentence, **Smith & Tinker** has the appositive **manufacturers**. **King of Ev** has the appositive **Evoldo**.

The appositive identifies or renames the noun it sits beside. We diagram an appositive by placing it beside the noun it identifies or renames and placing it in parentheses **( )**. When the appositive has a modifier, it goes on a slanted line under the appositive, just as always.

> Tiktok the machine man spoke.

```
          Tiktok  ( man  )  |  spoke
                  \the \machine
```

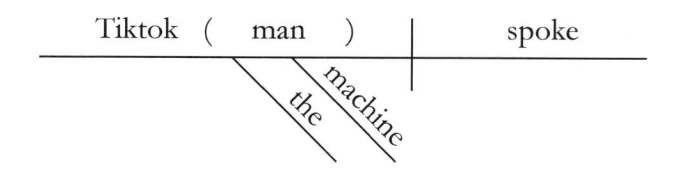

Evoldo, the cruel king, purchased Tiktok.

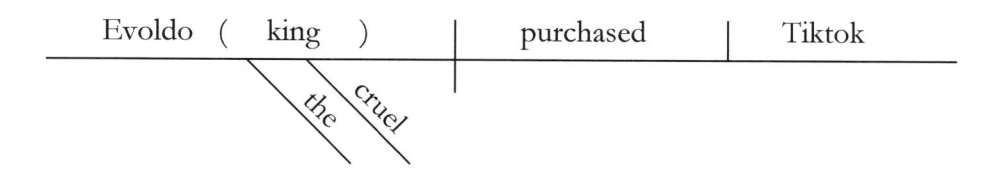

```
   Evoldo  ( king  )  |  purchased  |  Tiktok
            \the \cruel
```

Red-Cap Moss

By Hilda Conkling

Have you seen red-cap moss
In the woods?
Have you looked under the trembling caps
For faces?
Have you seen wonder on those faces
Because you are so big?

The Robber and the Old Man

From *West African Folk-Tales* by William H. Barker

In a big town lived a very rich gentleman. The fame of his wealth soon spread. A clever thief heard of it and determined to have some for himself.

He managed to hide himself in a dark corner of the gentleman's room—while the latter was counting his bags of money. As soon as the old gentleman left the room to fetch something, the thief caught up two of the bags and escaped.

The owner was astonished on his return a few minutes later to find two bags short. He could find no trace of the thief.

Next morning, however, he chanced to meet the robber just outside the house. The dishonest man looked so confused that the rich man at once suspected he was the thief. He could not, however, prove it, so took the case before the judge.

The thief was much alarmed when he heard this. He sought a man in the village and asked his advice. The wise man undertook to help him—if he would promise to pay him half the money when he got off. This the robber at once said he would do.

The old man then advised him to go home and dress in rags. He must ruffle his hair and beard and behave as if he were mad. If anyone asked a question he must answer, "Moo."

The thief did so. To every question asked by the judge he said, "Moo, moo." The judge at last grew angry and dismissed the court. The thief went home in great glee.

Next day, the wise man came to him for his half of the stolen money. But he could get no answer but, "Moo," from the thief, and at last, in despair, he had to go home without a penny. The ungrateful robber kept everything for himself. The wise man regretted very much that he had saved the thief from his just punishment, but it was now too late.

Exercise

Review memory work. Identify each group of words below as either a phrase or a clause. If it is a clause, double underline the predicate and underline the subject.

> from those ugly creatures

> and the copper fingers closed firmly over the stout handle

> the yellow hen gave a cackle of delight

Copy each sentence below. Double underline the predicate, and underline the subject. Label the part of speech of each word. Noun, N; Proper Noun, PN; Pronoun, PRO; Verb, V; Linking Verb, LV; Adjective, ADJ; Article, ART; Conjunction, CJ; Interjection, INJ. Diagram each sentence.

> "Will you exchange heads?"

> "Wind me up, quick."

> "You have company, Your Highness."

Writing: Commonplace Book

Add the passage below from your model story to your commonplace book.

> He comes to the top of the water much more often than before and sends a bubble of air out of his mouth. What do you think has happened? The gills under his cover have closed up, and a small air-bag has grown inside him. So he comes up to breathe in the air through his mouth instead of taking it out of the water through his gills.

Dictation

Use part of today's poem for dictation.

48. Point of View Narration: A Frog's Life

- Ozma of Oz, Chapter 7

Today, write your narration on "A Frog's Life." Choose a point of view from which to write your narration. Are you the frog, one of the children, or an objective observer of the events? Use your outline to keep the life cycle of the frog in the proper order. Pay attention to your pronouns as you write!

The Island

By Hilda Conkling

They flew as the night-wind flowed, very softly,
They heard sweet singing that the water sang,
They came to a place where the sea was shallow
And saw treasure hidden there.
There was one poplar tree
On the lonely island,
Swaying for sadness.
The clouds went over their heads
Like a fleet of drifting ships.
And there they sank down out of the air
Into the dream.

Editing

- Did you meet the goal of this writing exercise?
- Look at your word choice. Is there a good mixture of nouns and pronouns? Is the antecedent of each pronoun clear?
- Look at your paragraphs. Are all the sentences related? Does each paragraph focus on a single topic?

49. Commas in a Series

• Ozma of Oz, Chapter 8

Today we'll be talking about commas in a series. The word **series** means a number of things, people, or events which are similar or closely related and, for our purposes, listed together in a sentence. Items in lists of this sort can be joined with commas or conjunctions. When we are joining only two words or two groups of words, we only need a coordinating conjunction to do so.

"He is holding the Queen **and** her children prisoners."

"But you are wrong to think yourself terrible **or** fierce."

When we have more than two words or two groups of words, we can use commas to separate items in a series instead of using the word **and** every time.

Dorothy **and** the Tin Woodman **and** the Scarecrow were reunited.
Dorothy**,** the Tin Woodman**,** and the Scarecrow were reunited.

The little servant bowed **and** withdrew **and** went through several passages.
The little servant bowed**,** withdrew**,** and went through several passages.

Dorothy Gale **and** Billina **and** Tiktok saw the princess.
Dorothy Gale**,** Billina**,** and Tiktok saw the princess.

Note that each word in our list except for the last one is followed by a comma instead of the conjunction **and**. We only use the conjunction **and** before the last word in our list.

Our Cow

By C. J. Dennis

Down by the sliprails stands our cow
   Chewing, chewing, chewing,

She does not care what folks out there
   In the great, big world are doing.
She sees the small cloud-shadows pass
   And green grass shining under.
If she does think, what does she think
   About it all, I wonder?

She sees the swallows skimming by
   Above the sweet young clover,
The light reeds swaying in the wind
   And tall trees bending over.
Far down the track she hears the crack
   of bullock-whips, and raving
Of angry men where, in the sun,
   Her fellow-beasts are slaving.

Girls, we are told, can scratch and scold,
   And boys will fight and wrangle,
And big, grown men, just now and then,
   Fret o'er some fingle-fangle,
Vexing the earth with grief or mirth,
   Longing, rejoicing, rueing—
But by the sliprails stands our cow,
   Chewing.

Writing: Oral Narration

Read your new model story below, and then give your instructor an oral narration of it.

The Greedy Stranger

From *Wild Life in Woods and Fields* by Arabella B. Buckley

It was the middle of April this year when we first heard the cuckoo. We love to hear it, for it tells us that spring has come. This year we were very lucky. We saw a young cuckoo grow up in his nest.

This was how it happened.

We had heard the cuckoo for some time, cuck-oo, cuck-oo, and it seemed as if many cuckoos were singing. One day we heard such a funny noise, like kik-kik-kik. "Ah!" said Peggy. "Father says that is the cry of the mother cuckoo which lays the eggs. That is why there are so many cuckoos about. They are singing to her."

"Well then," said Peter, "if she stops here, perhaps we may find one of her eggs. I do so want to see a young cuckoo."

About a week after this, Peter found a titlark's nest. It was in a tuft of grass, on the bank near the wood. Two small dull-grey eggs, spotted with brown, were lying in the nest. The next day, as we went to school, there were three eggs. The next morning, there were four. But as we came back from school that afternoon, there were five eggs.

"The titlark cannot have laid two eggs in one day," said Peter. "I wonder if the cuckoo has brought one of her eggs here." For we know that the cuckoo lays her eggs on the ground and brings it in her wide beak to the nest of some other bird.

We looked every day for a fortnight. The little titlark was so used to our coming that she did not even fly off the nest. She was a pretty little bird, with brown spotted wings and a yellow throat and chin.

At the end of a fortnight, two little titlarks came out of their shells, and the next day, two more appeared. They opened their beaks for food, and the father titlark flew out to the field and brought flies and caterpillars to feed them. But the mother still sat on the fifth egg.

Two day later, the fifth bird came out. It had a curved beak and bent toes with short, sharp claws. Its toes were two in front and two at the back. Titlarks have straight beaks and flat toes, three in front and one at the back. So we knew our young cuckoo by his beak and toes.

We came next day to look. The little titlarks had quills on their wings where the feathers were growing, and their eyes were open. The cuckoo was naked and blind. But he had pushed two of the titlarks out of the nest, and they lay on the bank, quite dead.

The cuckoo had grown bigger even in one day, and the old titlarks kept feeding him with insects as he sat with his beak wide open. While we were looking at him, the cuckoo pushed about in the nest and shoved another little titlark over the edge onto the bank. We put it back in the nest, and then we had to go on to school. When we came back, the cuckoo sat in the nest alone. All the four little titlarks were dead on the bank. He had pushed them all out.

The old birds did not seem to see their dead children. They were so busy feeding the big hungry stranger. They fed him for five or six weeks, even after he could come out of the nest.

It was so funny to see! The cuckoo was larger than a thrush, and the titlarks were not bigger than a sparrow. Yet the big bird sat on a branch with his beak open and let these little birds carry all his food.

At last he flew away. We heard a cuckoo singing in August, when we knew the old birds were all gone. We wondered if it was our young "greedy stranger."

Exercise

Review memory work. Punctuate the following sentence.

> Dorothy was guided to the chicken house by a loud cackling crowing and distracting hubbub of sounds

Identify each group of words below as either a phrase or a clause. If it is a clause, double underline the predicate and underline the subject.

> as cowardly as ever

> but suddenly the bunch of feathers stopped whirling

> which Dorothy unlatched

Copy each sentence below. Double underline the predicate, and underline the subject. Label the part of speech of each word. Noun, N; Proper Noun, PN; Pronoun,

PRO; Verb, V; Linking Verb, LV; Adjective, ADJ; Article, ART; Conjunction, CJ; Interjection, INJ. Diagram each sentence.

> "Why, Billina! Have you been fighting?"

> The Cowardly Lion introduced his friend, the Hungry Tiger.

> "Don't worry."

Commonplace Book

With your instructor's approval, add the passage below to your commonplace book, or choose your own passage from a work of fiction. This can be from either school reading or free reading.

> Then Dorothy carried her pet into the drawing-room of the palace, where Tiktok, being invited to do so by Ozma, had seated himself between the Scarecrow and the Tin Woodman. Opposite to them sat Ozma herself and the Princess Langwidere, and beside them there was a vacant chair for Dorothy.

Dictation

> "They are, all except one," answered the Tin Woodman. "I have in my Army eight Generals, six Colonels, seven Majors, and five Captains, besides one private for them to command. I'd like to promote the private, for I believe no private should ever be in public life; and I've also noticed that officers usually fight better and are more reliable than common soldiers. Besides, the officers are more important looking and lend dignity to our army."

50. Writing an Outline

- Ozma of Oz, Chapter 9

So far, you have created outlines from just a small portion of your model story. Today, you will learn how to write an outline of the whole model story.

When you learned how to write a summary, you learned to include only the most important parts of the story. You learned to identify the beginning, the middle, and the end of the story.

To write an outline of the whole story, you do the same thing. The first Roman numeral will have the story's beginning. The last Roman numeral will have the story's ending. And then you will include a Roman numeral, or perhaps more than one, to list the events in the middle of the story.

Read the following story.

King Chameleon and the Animals

From *West African Folk-Tales* by William H. Barker

In the olden days, all the animals of the world lived together in friendship. They had no one to rule over them and judge them. In consequence, many very wicked deeds were constantly being done as no one needed to fear any punishment.

At last they all met together to discuss this bad state of affairs, and as a result, they decided to choose a king. The great difficulty was how to choose him.

Lion was the first animal suggested. But all opposed him because, they said, he was too fierce. Wolf was next named. But the sheep and goats refused to have him because he was their foe. They knew they would have bad treatment if he were chosen.

As it was impossible to please everyone by choice, they decided in another way. Two miles away was a great stool, placed under a very ancient tree which they believed to be the abode of some of their gods. They would have a great race. The animal which reached and sat down first on the stool should be chosen king.

The day of the race arrived. All animals, great and small, prepared to take part in it. After the signal was given, they started off. The hare—being a very fine runner—speedily outdistanced the others. He reached the stool quite five hundred yards ahead of the next animal. You may judge of his annoyance when, just as he was going to sit down, a voice came from the stool saying, "Take care, Mr. Hare, take care. I was here first." This was the chameleon. He, being able to change his color to suit his surroundings, had seized Mr. Hare's tail just as the race began. Since he had made his color match the hare's, no one had noticed him. He had held on very tightly, and when the hare turned round to take his seat, Chameleon dropped off and landed on the stool.

The hare saw how he had been tricked and was very angry. The other animals, however, arrived before he could harm the chameleon. According to the agreement they had made, they had no choice but to make Chameleon king.

But none of the animals were satisfied with the choice. So as soon as the meeting was over, all scattered in every direction and left Chameleon quite alone.

He was so ashamed that he went and made his home at the top of a very high tree on a mountain. In the dead of night you may hear him calling his attendants to come and stay with him. But he is left quite alone. "A king without subjects is no king."

What are the main events in the story? Each main event will be a point in the outline. Remember that outlines have a very specific form. Each main point has a Roman numeral before it.

I. The animals have no ruler, so the wicked were never punished.

II. The animals decided to have a race to choose a king.

III. The Chameleon cheated and became the king, but the animals were unhappy about this and left him alone.

IV. The ashamed Chameleon made his home at the top of a high tree on a mountain, and sometimes at night he calls for his attendants.

The one-level outline includes only the most important parts of the story, just like the summary. The main difference between a summary and an outline is the form that the outline takes. Today, you will write an outline of your new model story which you read in the last lesson.

Lochinvar

By Sir Walter Scott

Oh, young Lochinvar is come out of the west.
Through all the wide Border his steed was the best,
And save his good broadsword he weapons had none;
He rode all unarmed, and he rode all alone.
So faithful in love, and so dauntless in war,
There never was knight like the young Lochinvar.

He stayed not for brake, and he stopped not for stone,
He swam the Eske River where ford there was none;
But ere he alighted at Netherby gate
The bride had consented, the gallant came late:

For a laggard in love, and a dastard in war
Was to wed the fair Ellen of brave Lochinvar.

So boldly he entered the Netherby Hall,
Among bridesmen and kinsmen and brothers and all:
Then spoke the bride's father, his hand on his sword
(For the poor craven bridegroom said never a word),
 "Oh, come ye in peace here, or come ye in war,
Or to dance at our bridal, young Lord Lochinvar?"

 "I long woo'd your daughter, my suit you denied;—
Love swells like the Solway, but ebbs like its tide—
And now am I come, with this lost love of mine,
To lead but one measure, drink one cup of wine.
There are maidens in Scotland more lovely by far,
That would gladly be bride to the young Lochinvar."

The bride kissed the goblet; the knight took it up;
He quaffed of the wine, and he threw down the cup.
She looked down to blush, and she looked up to sigh,
With a smile on her lips and a tear in her eye.
He took her soft hand ere her mother could bar,—
 "Now tread we a measure!" said young Lochinvar.

So stately his form, and so lovely her face,
That never a hall such a galliard did grace;
While her mother did fret, and her father did fume,
And the bridegroom stood dangling his bonnet and plume,
And the bridemaidens whispered, "'Twere better by far
To have matched our fair cousin with young Lochinvar."

One touch to her hand, and one word in her ear,
When they reached the hall door, and the charger stood near;
So light to the croupe the fair lady he swung,
So light to the saddle before her he sprung!
 "She is won! We are gone, over bank, bush, and scaur;
They'll have fleet steeds that follow," quoth young Lochinvar.

There was mounting 'mong Græmes of the Netherby clan;
Forsters, Fenwicks, and Musgraves, they rode and they ran:
There was racing and chasing, on Cannobie Lee,
But the lost bride of Netherby ne'er did they see.
So daring in love, and so dauntless in war,
Have ye e'er heard of gallant like young Lochinvar?

Writing: Outline

 Write or type an outline of the new model story which you read in the last lesson.

Exercise

Review memory work. Punctuate the following sentence.

> Please get me about thirty pounds of tenderloin steak a peck of boiled potatoes and five gallons of ice-cream for dessert

Identify each group of words below as either a phrase or a clause. If it is a clause, double underline the predicate and underline the subject.

> a queen mother and her ten children

> for the sake of the poor prisoners

> I will now retire to my cabinet

Copy each sentence below. Double underline the predicate, and underline the subject. Label the part of speech of each word. Noun, N; Proper Noun, PN; Pronoun, PRO; Verb, V; Linking Verb, LV; Adjective, ADJ; Article, ART; Conjunction, CJ; Interjection, INJ. Diagram each sentence.

> "Are you so very hungry?"

> He bowed politely and blinked his eyes.

> "My uncle, Evoldo, was a very wicked man."

Commonplace Book

With your instructor's approval, add this part of today's poem to your commonplace book, or choose your own poem.

> Oh, young Lochinvar is come out of the west.
> Through all the wide Border his steed was the best,
> And save his good broadsword he weapons had none;
> He rode all unarmed, and he rode all alone.
> So faithful in love, and so dauntless in war,
> There never was knight like the young Lochinvar.

> He stayed not for brake, and he stopped not for stone,
> He swam the Eske River where ford there was none;
> But ere he alighted at Netherby gate
> The bride had consented, the gallant came late:
> For a laggard in love, and a dastard in war
> Was to wed the fair Ellen of brave Lochinvar.

Dictation

All's fair in love and war.

Clouds, Pretoria by Pieter Wenning

Picture Study

1. Read the title and the name of the artist. Study the picture for several minutes, then put the picture away.

2. Describe the picture.

3. Look at the picture again. Do you notice any details that you missed before? What do you like or dislike about this painting? Does it remind you of anything?

51. Literary Analysis

- Ozma of Oz, Chapter 10

Writing: Literary Analysis

Today you have another literary analysis assignment. Now that you have had some practice, this should be a written assignment, though it can be helpful to talk about your ideas before writing.

With your instructor's approval, choose *Ozma of Oz* or one of the other books you are currently reading, and answer the following questions.

What is the book about? Give a brief summary, just a few sentences. Has any part of the book made you laugh so far? Has any part of the book made you sad? Has any part of the book made you bored?

To a Mouse

By Robert Burns

Wee, sleekit, cow'rin', tim'rous beastie,
Oh, what a panic's in thy breastie!
Thou needna start awa' sae hasty,
  Wi' bickering brattle!
I wad be laith to rin and chase thee,
  Wi' murd'ring pattle!

I'm truly sorry man's dominion
Has broken Nature's social union,
And justifies that ill opinion,
  Which makes thee startle
At me, thy poor earth-born companion
  And fellow-mortal!

I doubtna, whiles, but thou may thieve;
What then? poor beastie, thou maun live!

A daimen icker in a thrave
  'S a sma' request:
I'll get a blessin' wi' the lave,
  And never miss 't!

Thy wee bit housie, too, in ruin!
Its silly wa's the win's are strewin'!
And naething now to big a new ane
  O' foggage green,
And bleak December's winds ensuin',
  Baith snell and keen!

Thou saw the fields laid bare and waste,
And weary winter comin' fast,
And cozie here, beneath the blast,
  Thou thought to dwell,
Till, crash! The cruel coulter passed
  Out through thy cell.

That wee bit heap o' leaves and stibble
Has cost thee monie a weary nibble!
Now thou's turned out for a' thy trouble,
  But house or hald,
To thole the winter's sleety dribble,
  And cranreuch cauld!

But, Mousie, thou art no thy lane,
In proving foresight may be vain:
The best-laid schemes o' mice and men
  Gang aft a-gley,
And lea'e us naught but grief and pain,
  For promised joy.

Still thou art blest, compared wi' me!
The present only toucheth thee:
But, och! I backward cast my e'e
  On prospects drear!
And forward, though I canna see,
  I guess and fear.

The Lioness and the Ostrich

From *South-African Folk-Tales* by James A. Honey

It is said that once when a lioness roared, the ostrich also roared. The lioness went toward the place where the ostrich was. They met. The lioness said to the ostrich, "Please to roar." The ostrich roared. Then the lioness roared. The voices were equal. The lioness said to the ostrich, "You are my match."

Then the lioness said to the ostrich, "Let us hunt game together." They saw eland and made toward it. The lioness caught only one; the ostrich killed a great many by striking them with the claw which was on his leg; but the lioness killed only one. When they had met after the hunting, they went to the game, and the lioness saw that the ostrich had killed a great deal.

Now, the lioness also had young cubs. They went to the shade to rest themselves. The lioness said to the ostrich, "Get up and rip open; let us eat." Said the ostrich, "Go and rip open; I shall eat the blood." The lioness stood up, and ripped open, and ate with the cubs. And when she had eaten, the ostrich got up and ate the blood. They went to sleep.

The cubs played about. While they were playing, they went to the ostrich, who was asleep. When he went to sleep, he also opened his mouth. The young lions saw that the ostrich had no teeth. They went to their mother and said, "This fellow, who says he is your equal, has no teeth. He is insulting you."

Then the lioness went to wake the ostrich and said, "Get up. Let us fight." And they fought.

And the ostrich said, "Go to that side of the anthill, and I will go to this side of it." The ostrich struck the anthill and sent it toward the lioness. But the second time, he struck the lioness in a vulnerable spot, near the liver, and killed her.

Exercise

Review memory work. Identify each group of words below as either a phrase or a clause. If it is a clause, double underline the predicate and underline the subject.

she lays one every morning

about this time

although all were restless and anxious [Hint: **all** is a pronoun.]

Copy each sentence below. Double underline the predicate, and underline the subject. Label the part of speech of each word. Noun, N; Proper Noun, PN; Pronoun, PRO; Verb, V; Linking Verb, LV; Adjective, ADJ; Article, ART; Conjunction, CJ; Interjection, INJ. Diagram each sentence.

"Why, Billina is laying her egg."

"Billina won't be long." [Hint: **long** tells when.]

The Cowardly Lion was dreadfully nervous.

Commonplace Book

With your instructor's approval, add the passage below to your commonplace book, or choose your own passage from a work of non-fiction. This can be from religious scriptures, a biography, or one of your history or science books.

> "I'll get it," said the Scarecrow; and at his command, the Sawhorse pranced into the bushes. The straw man soon found the egg, which he placed in his jacket pocket. The cavalcade, having moved rapidly on, was even then far in advance; but it did not take the Sawhorse long to catch up with it, and presently the Scarecrow was riding in his accustomed place behind Ozma's chariot.

52. Homonyms

• Ozma of Oz, Chapter 11

Definition: Homophones are words that sound
the same, but are spelled differently.

Definition: Homographs are words that are spelled
the same, but have different origins and meanings.

The prefix **homo** is from the Greek language. It means **the same**. **Phono** means **sound**, so **homophone** means **same sound**. You can remember this by thinking of words like tele**phone**; we use telephones to transfer sound. **Homophones** sound the same, but they do not mean the same thing, and they are spelled differently. The words listed below are all homophones:

dear and **deer**

to, **two**, and **too**

blew and **blue**

Graph means **drawn** or **written**. So **homograph** means **same writing**. You can remember this by thinking of photographs; photo**graphs** are light drawings. **Homographs** look the same, but they do not mean the same thing, and they may sound different; homographs may also have different origins or etymologies. Since homographs look the same, we can only tell which word a homograph is by looking at the **context**—the other words in the sentence. The large, bold words in these sentences are homographs:

I **live**, and once I saw a **live** bear.

The **wind**-up toy blew about in the **wind**.

The word **homonyms** is a word which means a homophone or a homograph. Look at the following sentence from *Ozma of Oz*. Look at the homonyms. Are they homophones, **same sound,** or homographs, **same writing**?

There were **no** birds.

They were now **close** to the Nome King's dominions.

There is a homophone. **There** is an adverb; **their** is a possessive pronoun; and **they're** is a contraction for **they are**.

No is a homophone. It expresses a negative, while **know** is the verb which means to understand or to have information.

Close is a homograph. Here, it means near. **Close** can also be the verb which means to shut.

To a Mountain Daisy

By Robert Burns

Wee, modest, crimson-tipped flower,
Thou's met me in an evil hour;
For I maun crush amang the stoure
  Thy slender stem:
To spare thee now is past my power,
  Thou bonny gem.

Alas! It's no thy neebor sweet,
The bonny lark, companion meet,
Bending thee 'mang the dewy weet,
  Wi' speckled breast,
When upward-springing, blithe, to greet
  The purpling east!

Cauld blew the bitter biting north
Upon thy early, humble birth;
Yet cheerfully thou glinted forth
  Amid the storm,
Scarce reared above the parent earth
  Thy tender form.

The flaunting flowers our gardens yield,
High sheltering woods and wa's maun shield,
But thou, beneath the random bield
  O' clod or stane,
Adorns the histie stibble-field,
  Unseen, alane.

There, in thy scanty mantle clad,
Thy snawie bosom sunward spread,
Thou lifts thy unassuming head
  In humble guise;

But now the share uptears thy bed,
  And low thou lies!

Such is the fate of artless maid,
Sweet floweret of the rural shade!
By love's simplicity betrayed,
  And guileless trust,
Till she, like thee, all soiled, is laid
  Low i' the dust.

Such is the fate of simple bard,
On life's rough ocean luckless starr'd!
Unskilful he to note the card
  Of prudent lore,
Till billows rage, and gales blow hard,
  And whelm him o'er!

Such fate to suffering worth is given,
Who long with wants and woes has striven,
By human pride or cunning driven
  To misery's brink,
Till wrenched of every stay but Heaven,
  He, ruined, sink!

Even thou who mourn'st the Daisy's fate,
That fate is thine—no distant date;
Stern Ruin's plowshare drives, elate,
  Full on thy bloom,
Till crushed beneath the furrow's weight
  Shall be thy doom.

The Lost Message

From *South-African Folk-Tales* by James A. Honey

    The ant has had from time immemorial many enemies, and because he is small and destructive, there have been a great many slaughters among them. Not only were most of the birds their enemies, but Anteater lived almost wholly from them, and Centipede beset them every time and at all places when he had the chance.

    So now there were a few among them who thought it would be well to hold council together and see if they could not come to some arrangement whereby they could retreat to some place of safety when attacked by robber birds and animals.

    But at the gathering, their opinions were most discordant, and they could come to no decision.

    There was Red-ant, Rice-ant, Black-ant, Wagtail-ant, Gray-ant, Shining-ant, and many other varieties. The discussion was a true babel of diversity, which continued for a long time and came to nothing.

    A part desired that they should all go into a small hole in the ground and live there; another part wanted to have a large and strong dwelling built on the ground, where nobody could enter but an ant; still another wanted to dwell in trees, so as to get rid of

Anteater, forgetting entirely that there they would be the prey of birds; another part seemed inclined to have wings and fly.

And, as has already been said, this deliberation amounted to nothing, and each party resolved to go to work in its own way and on its own responsibility.

Greater unity than that which existed in each separate faction could be seen nowhere in the world. Each had his appointed task; each did his work regularly and well. And all worked together in the same way. From among them, they chose a king— that is to say, some of the groups did—and they divided the labor so that all went as smoothly as it possibly could.

But each group did it in its own way, and not one of them thought of protecting themselves against the onslaught of birds or Anteater.

The Red-ants built their house on the ground and lived under it, but Anteater leveled to the ground in a minute what had cost them many days of precious labor. The Rice-ants lived under the ground, and with them it went no better. For whenever they came out, Anteater visited them and took them out sack and pack. The Wagtail-ants fled to the trees, but there on many occasions sat Centipede waiting for them, or the birds gobbled them up. The Gray-ants had intended to save themselves from extermination by taking to flight, but this also availed them nothing because the Lizard, the Hunting-spider, and the birds went a great deal faster than they.

When the Insect-king heard that they could come to no agreement, he sent them the secret of unity and the message of Work-together. But unfortunately, he chose for his messenger the Beetle, and he has never yet arrived at the Ants, so they are still today the embodiment of discord and consequently the prey of enemies.

Writing: Copia

Take the following sentence and play with it. Remember that the point is not necessarily to make the sentence better. The point is to play with the sentence and make it different. Make a new sentence for each number, using at least one change from that category.

> "I wonder if the cuckoo has brought one of her eggs here."

1. Change the grammar.
   - Change the nouns from common to proper and vice versa.
   - Change the nouns from singular to plural and vice versa.
   - Change the sentence type.
   - Change the adjectives from articles to descriptive to possessive, etc.
   - Change a quotation from direct to indirect and vice versa.

2. Condense the sentence.
   - Remove details.
   - Remove modifiers.
   - Remove phrases or clauses.

3. Amplify the sentence.
   - Add details.
   - Add dialogue.
   - Add modifiers.
   - Add phrases or clauses.

4. Use synonyms and antonyms.
   - Substitute synonyms.
   - Say the opposite thing using antonyms.

5. Point of view.
   - Change the point of view.

Exercise

Review memory work. In the following sentences, label homographs GR and homophones PH.

> Ozma and Dorothy were a little awed by the silence.

> We will dig him out of his hole, like a fox.

Copy each sentence below. Double underline the predicate, and underline the subject. Label the part of speech of each word. Noun, N; Proper Noun, PN; Pronoun, PRO; Verb, V; Linking Verb, LV; Adjective, ADJ; Article, ART; Conjunction, CJ; Interjection, INJ. Diagram each sentence.

> "Please Mr. Nome King, come here and see us."

> "Isn't it a trick?"

> The Nome King, the underground monarch, answered.

Commonplace Book

With your instructor's approval, add the passage below to your commonplace book, or choose your own passage from a work of fiction. This can be from either school reading or free reading.

> So Ozma led the way, hand in hand with Dorothy, and they passed through the arched doorway of rock and entered a long passage which was lighted by jewels set in the walls and having lamps behind them. There was no one to escort them or to show them the way, but all the party pressed through the passage until they came to a round, domed cavern that was grandly furnished.

Dictation

> This important monarch of the Underground World was a little fat man clothed in gray-brown garments that were the exact color of the rock throne in which he was seated. His bushy hair and flowing beard were also colored like the rocks, and so was his face. He wore no crown of any sort, and his only ornament was a broad, jewel-studded belt that encircled his fat little body.

53. Parts of Speech: Prepositions

• Ozma of Oz, Chapter 12

> Definition: A preposition is a word that shows
> the relationship between a noun or a pronoun
> and another word in the sentence.

Look at the following sentences from *Ozma of Oz*:

Ozma went **into** the royal palace.

The Nome King had left her **at** the entrance.

The King climbed down **with** some difficulty.

In the sentences above, the big, bold words are prepositions which show the relationship between a noun or pronoun and another word in the sentence. In the first sentence, **into** shows the relationship between **palace** and **went**; it tells where Ozma went. In the second sentence, **at** shows the relationship between **entrance** and **left**; it tells where he left Ozma. In the third sentence, **with** shows the relationship between **difficulty** and **climbed**. It tells how he climbed.

There are many prepositions, around one hundred and fifty. Here is a list of some of the most common prepositions:

aboard, about, above, across, after, against, along, among, around, at,
before, behind, below, beneath, beside, between, beyond, by,
down, during, except, for, from, in, inside, into, like, near, of, off,
on, onto, outside, over, past, round, since, through, throughout, till,
to, toward, under, underneath, until, up, upon, with, within, without

One clue for finding prepositions is to remember prePOSITION. Prepositions often tell the position of nouns and pronouns. Prepositions can show the position in space—the physical world—as well as the position in time. Look at the following sentence:

After her acceptance, Ozma went **into** the palace.

Her position in space was **into the palace**. Her position in time was **after her acceptance**.

Another way to find prepositions is to think of anywhere a rabbit can hop. You can use this sentence as a test: The rabbit hopped _____ the hat(s).

The rabbit hopped **over** the hat. The rabbit hopped **past** the hat. The rabbit hopped **between** the hats. The rabbit hopped **with** the hat. The rabbit hopped **through** the hat.

Not all prepositions will fit into that sentence, though we can still use our rabbit theme. A rabbit hops **according to** his nature, **since** the beginning, **during** his lifetime, and **until** bedtime. The rabbit hopped high **like** his father, high **as** a bird. Each preposition shows the relationship between its **object** and another word in the sentence. A preposition needs an object to be complete. We will talk about the object of the preposition in another lesson.

The Stranger

By Walter De La Mare

In the nook of a wood where a pool freshed with dew
Glassed, daybreak till evening, blue sky glimpsing through
Then a star; or a slip of May-moon silver-white,
Thridding softly aloof the quiet of night,
Was a thicket of flowers.
Willow herb, mint, pale speedwell and rattle
Water hemlock and sundew—to the wind's tittle-tattle
They nodded, dreamed, swayed in jocund delight,
In beauty and sweetness arrayed, still and bright.
By turn scampered rabbit; trotted fox; bee and bird
Paused droning, sang shrill, and the fair water stirred.
Plashed green frog, or some brisk little flickering fish—
Gudgeon, stickleback, minnow—set the ripples a-swish.
A lone pool, a pool grass-fringed, crystal-clear:
Deep, placid, and cool in the sweet of the year;
Edge-parched when the sun to the Dog Days drew near;
And with winter's bleak rime hard as glass, robed in snow,
The whole wild-wood sleeping, and nothing a-blow
But the wind from the North—bringing snow.
That is all. Save that one long, sweet, June night-tide straying,
The harsh hemlock's pale umbelliferous bloom
Tenting nook, dense with fragrance and secret with gloom,
In a beaming of moon-colored light faintly raying,
On buds orbed with dew phosphorescently playing,
Came a Stranger—still-footed, feat-fingered, clear face
Unhumanly lovely: ... and supped in that place.

Why Tigers Never Attack Men Unless They Are Provoked

From *West African Folk-Tales* by William H. Barker

A man, hunting one day in the forest, met a tiger. At first each was afraid of the other; but after some talking they became quite friendly. They agreed to live together for a little time. First the man would live with the tiger in his forest home for two weeks. Then the tiger would come and live in the man's home.

The tiger behaved so well to the man during his visit that the man felt he had never been so well treated in all his life. Then came the time for the tiger to return home with the man. As they were going, the tiger was somewhat afraid. He asked the man if he really thought he would be safe. "What if your friends do not like my face and kill me?" he asked.

"You need fear nothing," said his host. "No one will touch you while I am there." The tiger therefore came to the man's house and stayed with him three weeks. He had brought his male cub with him, and the young tiger became very friendly with the man's son.

Some months later, the man's father died. When Tiger heard of his friend's great loss, he and his cub set out at once to see and condole with him. They brought a large sum of money to help the man.

As Tiger was going home again, two of the man's friends lay in hiding for him and shot him. Fortunately, he was not killed, but he was very much grieved lest these men had shot him at his friend's wish. He determined to find out if the man had known anything at all about the shot.

Accordingly he went to the place in the forest where he had first met his friend. There he lay down as if he were dead, after telling his cub to watch and see what would happen.

By and by the man came along. When he saw the tiger lying, as he thought, dead, he was terribly troubled. He began to cry and mourn for his friend and sat there all night long with Tiger's cub, to watch that no harm should befall the body.

When morning came and Tiger was quite assured that his friend had had nothing at all to do with the shot, he was very glad. He got up, then, to the man's great astonishment, and explained why he had pretended to be dead.

"Go home," said Tiger, "and remember me always. In future, for your sake, I will never touch a man unless he first meddles with me."

Exercise

Review memory work. Punctuate the following sentence.

> Dorothy the Scarecrow and the Tin Woodman each gave a start of dismay and stared into one another's eyes

In the following sentences, label homographs GR and homophones PH.

> "Surely I ought to guess one object in eleven correctly."

> "It would be weak and cowardly in us to abandon the adventure."

Copy each sentence below. Double underline the predicate, and underline the subject. Label the part of speech of each word. Noun, N; Proper Noun, PN; Pronoun, PRO; Verb, V; Linking Verb, LV; Adjective, ADJ; Article, ART; Conjunction, CJ; Interjection, INJ. Diagram each sentence.

Ozma the pretty grasshopper was an emerald.

"Has she failed?"

The Nome King suddenly looked up and smiled.

Writing: Commonplace Book

Add the passage below from your model story to your commonplace book.

> For we know that the cuckoo lays her eggs on the ground and brings it in her wide beak to the nest of some other bird. We looked every day for a fortnight. The little titlark was so used to our coming that she did not even fly off the nest. She was a pretty little bird, with brown spotted wings and a yellow throat and chin.

Dictation

Use part of today's poem for dictation.

54. Point of View Narration: The Greedy Stranger

- Ozma of Oz, Chapter 13

Today, use your outline to write your narration on "The Greedy Stranger." Choose a point of view from which to write your narration. Are you the cuckoo, one of the children, or an objective observer of the events? Pay attention to your pronouns as you write!

Bunches of Grapes

By Walter De La Mare

'Bunches of grapes,' says Timothy;
'Pomegranates pink,' says Elaine;
'A junket of cream and a cranberry tart
For me,' says Jane.

'Love-in-a-mist,' says Timothy;
'Primroses pale,' says Elaine;
'A nosegay of pinks and mignonette
For me,' says Jane.

'Chariots of gold,' says Timothy;
'Silvery wings,' says Elaine;
'A bumpity ride in a wagon of hay
For me,' says Jane.

Editing

- Did you meet the goal of this writing exercise?
- Look at your word choice. Is there a good mixture of nouns and pronouns? Is the antecedent of each pronoun clear?

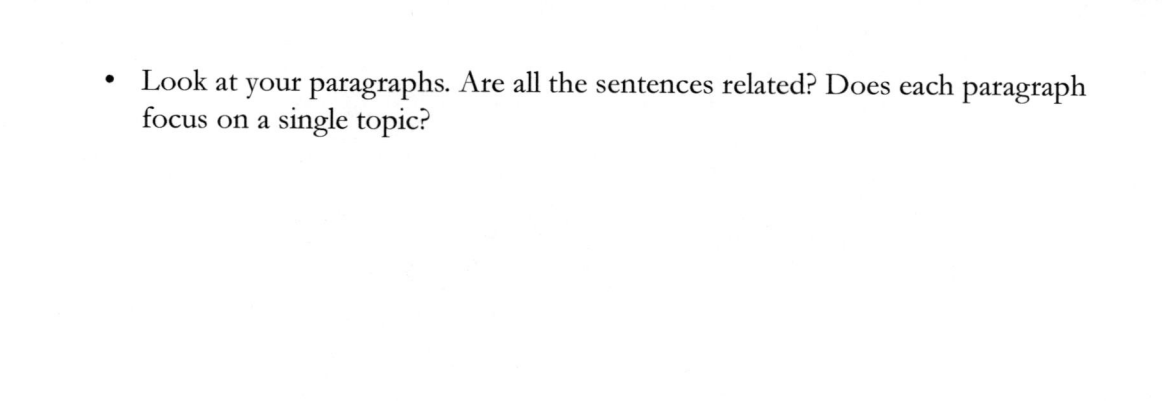

- Look at your paragraphs. Are all the sentences related? Does each paragraph focus on a single topic?

55. Object of the Preposition

• Ozma of Oz, Chapter 14

> Definition: The object of the preposition is a noun or pronoun which teams up with the preposition and completes its meaning.

Here is a list of some of the most common prepositions:

> aboard, about, above, across, after, against, along, among, around, at, before, behind, below, beneath, beside, between, beyond, by, down, during, except, for, from, in, inside, into, like, near, of, off, on, onto, outside, over, past, round, since, through, throughout, till, to, toward, under, underneath, until, up, upon, with, within, without

One clue for finding prepositions is to remember prePOSITION. Prepositions often tell the position of nouns and pronouns. Prepositions can show the position in space—the physical world—as well as the position in time.

A preposition shows the relationship between a **noun or a pronoun** and another word in the sentence. We call that noun or pronoun the **object of the preposition**. A preposition needs an object in order to make sense. The object of the preposition answers the question **what** or **whom**. We call the preposition, its object, and any modifiers of the object the **prepositional phrase**.

Look at the following sentence from *Ozma of Oz*. The prepositional phrase is in brackets, which is how you will mark them in your exercises.

> Meantime the Chief Steward had returned [to the throne room].

Above, the preposition shows the Chief Steward's position in the physical world. He had returned where? To the throne room. The word **room** is the object of the preposition **to**. It completes the meaning of the preposition. The prepositional phrase is **to the throne room**. Without the object of the preposition, the sentence reads:

> Meantime the Chief Steward had returned to.

To **what**? The preposition no longer makes sense. It must have its object to complete its meaning.

"But there are no other purple ornaments [in the palace] ."

Above, the preposition shows position of the purple ornaments in the physical world. There were no other purple ornaments where? In the palace. The word **palace** is the object of the preposition **in**. It completes the meaning of the preposition. The prepositional phrase is **in the palace**. Without the object of the preposition, the sentence reads:

"But there are no other purple ornaments in."

In **what**? The preposition no longer makes sense. It must have its object to complete its meaning.

"So we do not care much what becomes [of us] ."

Above, the word **us** is the object of the preposition **of**. It completes the meaning of the preposition. The prepositional phrase is **of us**. Without the object of the preposition, the sentence reads:

"So we do not care much what becomes of."

Of **whom**? The preposition no longer makes sense. It must have its object to complete its meaning.

Be careful not to depend upon a list to determine the part of speech of any word. While the above words all can be prepositions, some of them are not always prepositions. For instance, **but** and **for** are on the list. You have learned another list—coordinating conjunctions—that included both words.

But and **for** are conjunctions when they join words or groups of words together. When **for** is a conjunction, it means **because.**

"I shall have nothing to do **but** admire my new ornaments."

Now follow me to my chamber, **for** I am going to bed.

But and **for** are prepositions when one shows a relationship between its object and another word in the sentence. When **but** is a preposition, it shows an exception, meaning **other than.**

None knew the secret **but** Billina.

"It serves to keep me amused **for** a long time."

When you understand the functions of the different parts of speech, you can more easily tell the difference in sentences.

John Mouldy
By Walter De La Mare

I spied John Mouldy in his cellar,
Deep down twenty steps of stone;

In the dusk he sat a-smiling,
Smiling there alone.

He read no book, he snuffed no candle;
The rats ran in, the rats ran out;
And far and near, the drip of water
Went whisp'ring about.

The dusk was still, with dew a-falling,
I saw the Dog-star bleak and grim,
I saw a slim brown rat of Norway
Creep over him.

I spied John Mouldy in his cellar,
Deep down twenty steps of stone;
In the dusk he sat a-smiling,
Smiling there alone.

Writing: Oral Narration

Read your new model story below, and then give your instructor an oral narration of it.

The Ants and the Grasshopper

From *The Aesop for Children* illustrated by Milo Winter

One bright day in late autumn, a family of Ants was bustling about in the warm sunshine, drying out the grain they had stored up during the summer, when a starving Grasshopper, his fiddle under his arm, came up and humbly begged for a bite to eat.

"What!" cried the Ants in surprise. "Haven't you stored anything away for the winter? What in the world were you doing all last summer?"

"I didn't have time to store up any food," whined the Grasshopper. "I was so busy making music that before I knew it, the summer was gone."

The Ants shrugged their shoulders in disgust.

"Making music, were you?" they cried. "Very well; now dance!" And they turned their backs on the Grasshopper and went on with their work.

There's a time for work and a time for play.

Exercise

Review memory work. Punctuate the following sentence.

> Dorothy the Lion and Tiger were given their breakfast in their rooms

Identify each group of words below as either a phrase or a clause. If it is a clause, double underline the predicate and underline the subject.

> where he said to the King

> in so enraged a voice

squatting under the throne

Copy each sentence below. Double underline the predicate, and underline the subject. Put brackets around any prepositional phrases. Label the part of speech of each word. Noun, N; Proper Noun, PN; Pronoun, PRO; Verb, V; Linking Verb, LV; Adjective, ADJ; Article, ART; Adverb, ADV; Conjunctions, CJ; Prepositions, Prep; Interjections, INJ. Diagram each sentence.

Had Billina listened carefully?

"Your Majesty, you are a fool."

"Oh, cease your tiresome chatter!"

Commonplace Book

With your instructor's approval, add the passage below to your commonplace book, or choose your own passage from a work of fiction. This can be from either school reading or free reading.

> So Dorothy, trying to be brave in spite of her fears, passed through the doorway into the gorgeous rooms of the palace. The stillness of the place awed her at first, and the child drew short breaths, and pressed her hand to her heart, and looked all around with wondering eyes.

Dictation

> Dorothy begged to be allowed to go first into the palace, but Tiktok firmly maintained that the slave should face danger before the mistress. The Scarecrow agreed with him in that, so the Nome King opened the door for the machine man, who tramped into the palace to meet his fate. Then his Majesty returned to his throne and puffed his pipe so contentedly that a small cloud of smoke formed above his head.

56. Diagramming Prepositions

- Ozma of Oz, Chapter 15

Prepositional phrases are modifiers. Sometimes, they are **adjective phrases** and modify nouns or pronouns. Other times, they are **adverb phrases** and modify verbs. Like other modifiers, several prepositional phrases can modify the same word. Adjective prepositional phrases can even modify the object of another preposition.

Occasionally, it can be difficult to determine which word a prepositional phrase modifies. **Remember**: Just like adjectives, an adjective prepositional phrase will stay with the noun or pronoun which it modifies. Adjectives normally come before the noun or pronoun, while adjective prepositional phrases come after.

She touched a **bowl** [of alabaster].

What kind of bowl? An alabaster bowl. **Of alabaster** modifies **bowl** by telling **what kind**.

And just like adverbs which modify the verb, an adverb prepositional phrase can often be moved around in the sentence without changing the meaning.

Billina laid her egg [under the Nome King's throne].
Under the Nome King's throne, Billina laid her egg.
Billina, under the Nome King's throne, laid her egg.

Notice that while some of those sentences above sound better than others, they all make sense. This is because the prepositional phrase modifies the verb. Try doing that with the adjective prepositional phrase in the first sentence above. Can you move it and have it still make sense?

No! The adjective prepositional phrase becomes nonsense when separated from the noun or pronoun which it modifies.

Remember that **adjectives** tell what kind, how many, which one, and whose; **adverbs** tell how, when, where, how often, and to what extent. This information will tell you whether the prepositional phrase is an adjective or an adverb, which will in turn point towards the word it modifies. Knowing this information is imperative. If you do not know the difference between what adjectives tell and what adverbs tell, you will struggle with knowing which word a prepositional phrase modifies. Use these words as questions when evaluating a prepositional phrase: Does it tell which one? Where? How many?

Like other modifiers, prepositional phrases are diagrammed on a slanted line under the word the prepositional phrase modifies. The entire prepositional phrase is diagrammed like this:

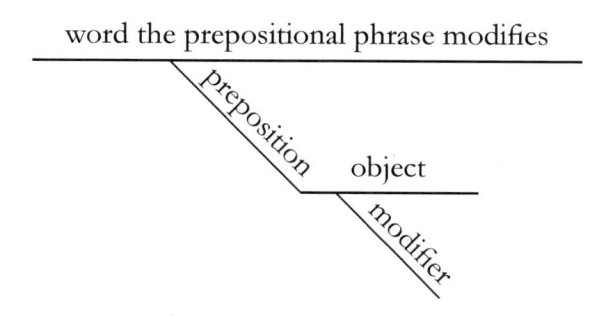

```
word the prepositional phrase modifies
         \
    preposition   object
              \
           modifier
```

Follow this procedure for analyzing sentences.

Put brackets around prepositional phrases.

What is the predicate? The main verb is often easier to find than its subject, so find it first. Double underline it. Is it an action verb or a linking verb?

What is the subject? Underline it once.

For action verbs, is there a direct object which receives the action of the verb by answering the question **whom** or **what**?

For linking verbs, is there a subject complement—a predicate nominative or a predicate adjective—which renames or modifies the subject?

The object of a prepositional phrase will never be the subject of a sentence, a predicate nominative, or a direct object, so marking them from the beginning simplifies the process.

His little friend would suffer the fate [of Ozma].

Whose fate? Ozma's fate. A prepositional phrase which tells **whose** can often be replaced with the possessive form of the object of the preposition. The prepositional phrase modifies **fate**.

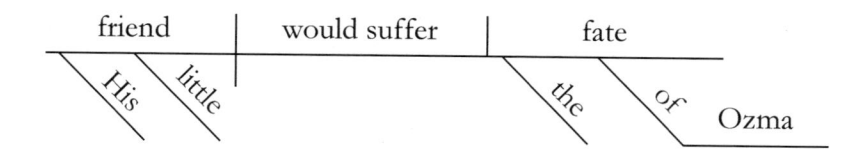

```
friend | would suffer | fate
  \  \                   \  \
  His little             the  of
                              Ozma
```

He placed the egg [in another pocket] [of his jacket].

He placed the egg **where**? In another pocket. **What kind** of pocket? The pocket of his jacket. The first prepositional phrase modifies **egg**. The second prepositional phrase modifies **pocket**.

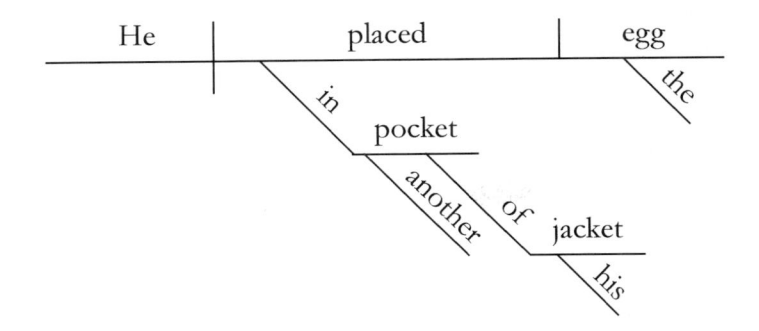

[Diagram: He | placed | egg, with "in pocket" and "of jacket" modifiers, plus "the", "another", "his"]

If you think a prepositional phrase modifies a word other than the verb, remove that word from the sentence. Does the prepositional phrase still make since? If it does, then it's not modifying the word you removed. Consider the sentence from the beginning of the lesson.

She touched a bowl [of alabaster].

Imagine that you cannot decide whether **of alabaster** modifies the verb **touched** or the noun **bowl**. Try taking the words **a bowl** out of the sentence. Does the sentence still make sense?

She touched of alabaster.

The sentence no longer makes sense because of alabaster has nothing to modify!

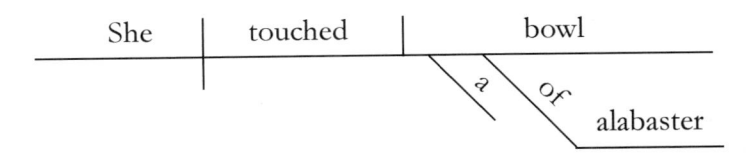

[Diagram: She | touched | bowl, with "a" and "of alabaster" modifiers]

Notice that in the next sentence, the word **two** acts as a pronoun, meaning the two individuals.

The two sat [in moody silence] [for several minutes].

They sat **how**? In moody silence. They sat **when**? For several minutes. Both of these prepositional phrases are adverbs which modify the verb **sat**.

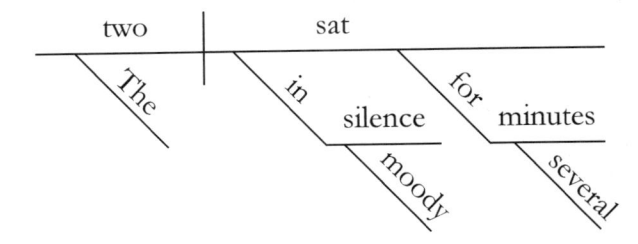

[Diagram: two | sat, with "The", "in silence" (moody), "for minutes" (several) modifiers]

Does the prepositional phrase tell what kind, how many, which one, or whose? Does it tell how, when, where, how often, or to what extent? Sometimes, these descriptions fit in a way that feels rather odd. However, only one will work, and that will tell you whether the prepositional phrase is an adjective or an adverb.

A Dream

By William Blake

Once a dream did wave a shade
O'er my angel-guarded bed,
That an emmet lost its way
When on grass methought I lay.

Troubled, 'wildered, and forlorn,
Dark, benighted, travel-worn,
Over many a tangled spray,
All heart-broke, I heard her say:

"Oh, my children! Do they cry?
Do they hear their father sigh?
Now they look abroad to see.
Now return and weep for me."

Pitying, I dropped a tear;
But I saw a glow-worm near,
Who replied, "What wailing wight
Calls the watchman of the night?

"I am set to light the ground
While the beetle goes his round.
Follow now the beetle's hum—
Little wanderer, hie thee home!"

Jackal's Bride

From *South-African Folk-Tales* by James A. Honey

Jackal, it is said, married Hyena and carried off a cow belonging to the ants to slaughter her for the wedding; and when he had slaughtered her, he put the cowskin over his bride; and when he had fixed a pole on which to hang the flesh, he placed on the top of the pole (which was forked) the hearth for the cooking, in order to cook upon it all sorts of delicious food. There came also Lion, who wished to go up. Jackal, therefore, asked his little daughter for a thong with which he could pull Lion up; and he began to pull him up; and when his face came near to the cooking-pot, he cut the thong in two so that Lion tumbled down. Then Jackal upbraided his little daughter with these words: "Why do you give me such an old thong?" And he added, "Give me a fresh thong." She gave him a new thong, and he pulled Lion up again, and when his face came near the pot, which stood on the fire, he said, "Open your mouth." Then he put into his mouth a hot piece of quartz which had been boiled together with the fat, and the stone went down, burning his throat. Thus died Lion.

There came also the ants running after the cow, and when Jackal saw them, he fled. Then they beat the bride in her brookaross dress. Hyena, believing that it was Jackal, said: "You tawny rogue! Have you not played at beating long enough? Have you no more loving game than this?"

But when she had bitten a hole through the cowskin, she saw that they were other people; then she fled, falling here and there, yet made her escape.

Writing: Outline

Write or type an outline of the new model story which you read in the last lesson.

Exercise

Review memory work. Punctuate the following sentences.

> The Scarecrow Billina and the Nome King were in the throne room

> Why it's Billina

In the following sentences, label homographs GR and homophones PH.

> "I've got a right to cackle, I guess."

> "Well, you'll have to bear this one around."

Copy each sentence below. Double underline the predicate, and underline the subject. Put brackets around any prepositional phrases. Label the part of speech of each word. Noun, N; Proper Noun, PN; Pronoun, PRO; Verb, V; Linking Verb, LV; Adjective, ADJ; Article, ART; Adverb, ADV; Conjunctions, CJ; Prepositions, Prep; Interjections, INJ. Diagram each sentence.

> "Take it away at once!" [Hint: **once** is usually an adverb, but it is a noun in this sentence.]

> "Will she now return to us in safety?"

> Dorothy led the little Prince Evring by the hand.

Commonplace Book

With your instructor's approval, add this part of today's poem to your commonplace book, or choose your own poem.

> Pitying, I dropped a tear;
> But I saw a glow-worm near,
> Who replied, "What wailing wight
> Calls the watchman of the night?
>
> "I am set to light the ground
> While the beetle goes his round.
> Follow now the beetle's hum—
> Little wanderer, hie thee home!"

Dictation

> The road to hell is paved with good intentions.

Landscape, Bishops Court by Pieter Wenning

Picture Study

1. Read the title and the name of the artist. Study the picture for several minutes, then put the picture away.

2. Describe the picture.

3. Look at the picture again. Do you notice any details that you missed before? What do you like or dislike about this painting? Does it remind you of anything?

57. Descriptive Writing

• Ozma of Oz, Chapter 16

Writing: Descriptive Writing

In the last chapter of *Ozma of Oz*, Billina and the Nome King had a discussion on the propriety of laying eggs in the throne room. Read that passage below, paying close attention to the details that make a vivid picture in your mind, and then write a narration of it. Both Billina and the Nome King get rather emotional during this discussion. How does the L. Frank Baum let us know what they're feeling and how they're expressing these emotions?

Add details if you wish. Remember, the point of this exercise is to write as descriptively as possible, not just to narrate the passage exactly.

Ozma of Oz

"I've got a right to cackle, I guess," replied Billina. "I've just laid my egg."

"What! Laid an egg! In my throne room! How dare you do such a thing?" asked the King, in a voice of fury.

"I lay eggs wherever I happen to be," said the hen, ruffling her feathers and then shaking them into place.

"But—thunderation! Don't you know that eggs are poison?" roared the King while his rock-colored eyes stuck out in great terror.

"Poison! Well, I declare," said Billina, indignantly. "I'll have you know all my eggs are warranted strictly fresh and up to date. Poison, indeed!"

"You don't understand," retorted the little monarch, nervously. "Eggs belong only to the outside world—to the world on the earth's surface, where you came from. Here, in my underground kingdom, they are rank poison, as I said, and we Nomes can't bear them around."

"Well, you'll have to bear this one around," declared Billina, "for I've laid it."

"Where?" asked the King.

"Under your throne," said the hen.

The King jumped three feet into the air, so anxious was he to get away from the throne.

"Take it away! Take it away at once!" he shouted.

253

Tea Talk

By C. J. Dennis

'Excuse me if I sit on you,' the cup said to the saucer.
   'I fear I've been here all the afternoon.'
'Spare excuses,' said the saucer; 'you have sat on me before, sir.'
   'Oh, I'll stir him up directly,' said the spoon.
'Stop your clatter! Stop your clatter!' cried the bread-and-butter platter
   'Tittle-tattle!' sneered the tea-pot, with a shrug;
'Now, the most important question is my chronic indigestion.'
   'Ah, you've taken too much tannin,' jeered the jug.
'Hey, hey, hey!' sang the silver-plated tray,
'It's time you had your faces washed. I've come to clear away!'

The Monkey's Fiddle

From *South-African Folk-Tales* by James A. Honey

Part I

   Hunger and want forced Monkey one day to forsake his land and to seek elsewhere among strangers for much-needed work. Bulbs, earth beans, scorpions, insects, and such things were completely exhausted in his own land. But fortunately he received, for the time being, shelter with a great uncle of his, Orang Outang, who lived in another part of the country.

   When he had worked for quite a while, he wanted to return home, and as recompense, his great uncle gave him a fiddle and a bow and arrow and told him that with the bow and arrow, he could hit and kill anything he desired, and with the fiddle, he could force anything to dance.

   The first he met upon his return to his own land was Brer Wolf. This old fellow told him all the news and also that he had since early morning been attempting to stalk a deer, but all in vain.

   Then Monkey laid before him all the wonders of the bow and arrow that he carried on his back and assured him if he could but see the deer, he would bring it down for him. When Wolf showed him the deer, Monkey was ready, and down fell the deer.

   They made a good meal together, but instead of Wolf being thankful, jealousy overmastered him, and he begged for the bow and arrow. When Monkey refused to give it to him, he thereupon began to threaten him with his greater strength, and so when Jackal passed by, Wolf told him that Monkey had stolen his bow and arrow. After Jackal had heard both of them, he declared himself unqualified to settle the case alone, and he proposed that they bring the matter to the court of Lion, Tiger, and the other animals. In the meantime, he declared he would take possession of what had been the cause of their quarrel so that it would be safe, as he said. But he immediately brought to earth all that was eatable, so there was a long time of slaughter before Monkey and Wolf agreed to have the affair in court.

   Monkey's evidence was weak, and to make it worse, Jackal's testimony was against him. Jackal thought that in this way it would be easier to obtain the bow and arrow from Wolf for himself.

And so fell the sentence against Monkey. Theft was looked upon as a great wrong; he must hang.

Exercise

Review memory work. Identify each group of words below as either a phrase or a clause. If it is a clause, double underline the predicate and underline the subject.

    with an air of vast importance

    then I thank you for the gracious favor

    don't worry

Copy each sentence below. Double underline the predicate, and underline the subject. Put brackets around any prepositional phrases. Label the part of speech of each word. Noun, N; Proper Noun, PN; Pronoun, PRO; Verb, V; Linking Verb, LV; Adjective, ADJ; Article, ART; Adverb, ADV; Conjunctions, CJ; Prepositions, Prep; Interjections, INJ. Diagram each sentence.

    "Why, my name is Bill, by rights."

    "Am I a good guesser, Mr. Nome King?"

    Evanna, a sweet-faced girl, stood beside them.

Commonplace Book

With your instructor's approval, add the passage below to your commonplace book, or choose your own passage from a work of non-fiction. This can be from religious scriptures, a biography, or one of your history or science books.

> Then she disenchanted another girl, whom the Queen addressed as Evrose, and afterwards a boy named Evardo, who was older than his brother Evring. Indeed, the yellow hen kept the good Queen exclaiming and embracing for some time until five Princesses and four Princes, all looking very much alike except for the difference in size, stood in a row beside their happy mother.

58. Prepositions and Adverbs

• Ozma of Oz, Chapter 17

Here is a list of some of the most common prepositions:

aboard, about, above, across, after, against, along, among, around, at,
before, behind, below, beneath, beside, between, beyond, by,
down, during, except, for, from, in, inside, into, like, near, of, off,
on, onto, outside, over, past, round, since, through, throughout, till,
to, toward, under, underneath, until, up, upon, with, within, without

An important thing to remember about this list is that some of the words on it are not always prepositions. Many of these words can also be adverbs. How can you tell the difference?

A preposition must have an object. An adverb never has an object. Look at these sentences closely. Does the prep-adverb have an object?

The boy wants to color **outside** with his siblings.

The boy wants to color **outside** the lines.

To determine whether the prep-adverb has an object, we can ask the question **what** or **whom**. In the first sentence, the boy wants to color outside **what**? Well, just **outside**. We do not have another answer to that. There is no object.

In the second sentence, the boy wants to color outside **what**? The lines; he wants to color **outside the lines**. The object of the preposition outside is **lines**, and the prepositional phrase is **outside the lines**.

In the first sentence, **outside** is an adverb. It does not have an object. In the second sentence, **outside** is a preposition with **lines** as the object.

Look at the sentences below from *Ozma of Oz*. Which of the large, bold words are adverbs, and which are prepositions?

"Ah, I'd forgotten that," said the King, getting **up**.

The ten men in the first row fell **over** like so many toy soldiers.

The warriors fairly tumbled **over** one another.

In the first sentence, **up** is an adverb. It has no object. In the second sentence, **over** is an adverb. It has no object. In the third sentence, however, **over** is a preposition. They tumbled over **what**? One another. **Another** is the object of the prepositional phrase **over one another**.

The direct object can never be the object of a preposition. If you have a phrase which follows a prep-adverb, you have to decide if it is part of a prepositional phrase or if it is receiving the action of the verb by answering the question **whom** or **what**, as in the sentences at the beginning of this lesson.

The Dream

By Hilda Conkling

When I slept, I thought I was upon the mountain-tops,
And this is my dream.
I saw the little people come out into the night,
I saw their wings glittering under the stars.
Crickets played all the tunes they knew.
It was so comfortable with light . . .
Stars, a rainbow, the moon!
The fairies had shiny crowns
On their bright hair.
The bottoms of their little gowns were roses!
It was musical in the moony light,
And the fairy queen,
Oh, it was all golden where she came
With tiny pages on her trail.
She walked slowly to her high throne,
Slowly, slowly to music,
And watched the dancing that went on
All night long in star-glitter
On the mountain-tops.

The Monkey's Fiddle

From *South-African Folk-Tales* by James A. Honey

Part II

The fiddle was still at his side, and he received as a last favor from the court the right to play a tune on it.

He was a master player of his time, and in addition to this came the wonderful power of his charmed fiddle. Thus, when he struck the first note of "Cockcrow" upon it, the court began at once to show an unusual and spontaneous liveliness, and before he came to the first waltzing turn of the old tune, the whole court was dancing like a whirlwind.

Over and over, quicker and quicker, sounded the tune of "Cockcrow" on the charmed fiddle until some of the dancers, exhausted, fell down, although still keeping their feet in motion. But Monkey, musician as he was, heard and saw nothing of what had happened around him. With his head placed lovingly against the instrument, and his eyes half closed, he played on, keeping time ever with his foot.

Wolf was the first to cry out in pleading tones, breathlessly, "Please stop, Cousin Monkey! For love's sake, please stop!"

But Monkey did not even hear him. Over and over sounded the resistless waltz of "Cockcrow."

After a while Lion showed signs of fatigue, and when he had gone the round once more with his young lion wife, he growled as he passed Monkey, "My whole kingdom is yours, ape, if you just stop playing."

"I do not want it," answered Monkey, "but withdraw the sentence and give me my bow and arrow, and you, Wolf, acknowledge that you stole it from me."

"I acknowledge, I acknowledge!" cried Wolf while Lion cried, at the same instant, that he withdrew the sentence.

Monkey gave them just a few more turns of the "Cockcrow," gathered up his bow and arrow, and seated himself high up in the nearest camel thorn tree.

The court and other animals were so afraid that he might begin again that they hastily disbanded to new parts of the world.

Writing: Copia

Take the following sentence and play with it. Remember that the point is not necessarily to make the sentence better. The point is to play with the sentence and make it different. Make a new sentence for each number, using at least one change from that category.

> "I was so busy making music that before I knew it, the summer was gone."

1. Change the grammar.
   - Change the nouns from common to proper and vice versa.
   - Change the nouns from singular to plural and vice versa.
   - Change the sentence type.
   - Change the adjectives from articles to descriptive to possessive, etc.
   - Change a quotation from direct to indirect and vice versa.

2. Condense the sentence.
   - Remove details.
   - Remove modifiers.
   - Remove phrases or clauses.

3. Amplify the sentence.
   - Add details.
   - Add dialogue.
   - Add modifiers.
   - Add phrases or clauses.

4. Use synonyms and antonyms.
   - Substitute synonyms.
   - Say the opposite thing using antonyms.

5. Point of view.
   - Change the point of view.

Exercise

Review memory work. Punctuate the following sentence.

> The generals the colonels the majors and the captains all commanded Forward, march

In the following sentences, label homographs GR and homophones PH.

> "The creature is made of wood."

> At once the army filed out in great numbers, led by their captain.

Copy each sentence below. Double underline the predicate, and underline the subject. Put brackets around any prepositional phrases. Label the part of speech of each word. Noun, N; Proper Noun, PN; Pronoun, PRO; Verb, V; Linking Verb, LV; Adjective, ADJ; Article, ART; Adverb, ADV; Conjunctions, CJ; Prepositions, Prep; Interjections, INJ. Diagram each sentence.

> "The creature is made of wood."

> "Don't mind them!"

> "Do you surrender?"

Commonplace Book

With your instructor's approval, add the passage below to your commonplace book, or choose your own passage from a work of fiction. This can be from either school reading or free reading.

> But in spite of the magic, the Sawhorse moved; and he moved so quickly toward the King that the fat little man could not get out of his way. Thump—BANG!—came the wooden heels, right against his round body, and the King flew into the air and fell upon the head of his captain, who let him drop flat upon the ground.

Dictation

> The captain of the Nomes was so surprised by this sudden onslaught that he forgot to command his warriors to fight, so the ten men in the first row, who stood in front of the private's spear, fell over like so many toy soldiers. The spear could not go through their steel armor, however, so the warriors scrambled to their feet again, and by that time, the private had knocked over another row of them.

59. Slant Narratives

• Ozma of Oz, Chapter 18

Many stories are told in the third person, which means that the narrator tells a story told about the characters instead of the narrator being one of the participants in the story. That means that we do not always know what the characters are thinking. The person telling the tale is different from the characters experiencing the tale.

Often, the story would read much differently if one of the people involved in the story were to tell the tale. Have you ever had to tell your side of a story when you have been in an argument with someone, or have you heard another tell his side of a story? What does it mean for a story to have "sides"? Your side of the story is your version, the way you remember it. Even if you do not mean to, the story you tell will usually favor yourself over the other person. We call this a **slant**. When something is slanted, it is tipped to one side.

Read "The Cat and the Birds" below. And then read the same story, first from the Cat's point of view, and then from the point of view of the Birds.

The Cat and the Birds

From *The Aesop for Children* illustrated by Milo Winter

A Cat was growing very thin. As you have guessed, he did not get enough to eat. One day he heard that some Birds in the neighborhood were ailing and needed a doctor. So he put on a pair of spectacles and, with a leather box in his hand, knocked at the door of the Birds' home.

The Birds peeped out, and Dr. Cat, with much solicitude, asked how they were. He would be very happy to give them some medicine.

"Tweet, tweet," laughed the Birds. "Very smart, aren't you? We are very well, thank you, and more so, if you only keep away from here."

Be wise and shun the quack.

The Cat's Point of View

Once, during a sad time in my life, I was growing thin from lack of food. I was in desperate need of work, so when I heard that some Birds needed a doctor, I put on my spectacles, grabbed my leather box, and went to their home to offer my services.

When they answered, I asked how they were. I offered both my services and my medicines.

The Birds laughed at me! They said that they would stay very well indeed, if only I would keep away.

The Birds' Point of View

Some of us birds were ailing once and needed a doctor. One day during this time, a knock sounded at the door. We opened the door to find a skinny cat standing there, wearing spectacles and carrying a leather box! He asked how we were and offered us medicine.

How we laughed! We told him that we'd stay very well indeed, as long as he should stay away. As if we didn't know that his only medicine was in his belly.

Crossing the Bar

By Alfred Tennyson

Sunset and evening star,
  And one clear call for me!
And may there be no moaning of the bar,
  When I put out to sea,

But such a tide as moving seems asleep,
  Too full for sound and foam,
When that which drew from out the boundless deep
  Turns again home.

Twilight and evening bell,
  And after that the dark!
And may there be no sadness of farewell,
  When I embark;

For tho' from out our bourne of Time and Place
  The flood may bear me far,
I hope to see my Pilot face to face
  When I have cross'd the bar.

The Tiger, the Ram, and the Jackal

From *South-African Folk-Tales* by James A. Honey

Tiger (Leopard) was returning home from hunting on one occasion when he lighted on the kraal of Ram. Now, Tiger had never seen Ram before, and accordingly, approaching submissively, he said, "Good day, friend! What may your name be?"

The other, in his gruff voice and striking his breast with his forefoot, said, "I am Ram. Who are you?"

"Tiger," answered the other, more dead than alive, and then, taking leave of Ram, he ran home as fast as he could.

Jackal lived at the same place as Tiger did, and Tiger went to him and said, "Friend Jackal, I am quite out of breath and am half dead with fright, for I have just seen a terrible looking fellow, with a large and thick head, and on my asking him what his name was, he answered, 'I am Ram.'"

"What a foolish fellow you are," cried Jackal, "to let such a nice piece of flesh stand! Why did you do so? But we shall go tomorrow and eat it together."

Next day the two set off for the kraal of Ram, and as they appeared over a hill, Ram, who had turned out to look about him and was calculating where he should that day crop a tender salad, saw them, and he immediately went to his wife and said, "I fear this is our last day, for Jackal and Tiger are both coming against us. What shall we do?"

"Don't be afraid," said the wife. "But take up the child in your arms, go out with it, and pinch it to make it cry as if it were hungry." Ram did so as the confederates came on.

No sooner did Tiger cast his eyes on Ram than fear again took possession of him, and he wished to turn back. Jackal had provided against this, and made Tiger fasten himself to Jackal with a leathern thong, and said, "Come on."

Pinching his child at the same time, Ram cried in a loud voice, "You have done well, Friend Jackal, to have brought us Tiger to eat, for you hear how my child is crying for food."

On these dreadful words, notwithstanding the entreaties of Jackal to let him go, to let him loose, Tiger set off in the greatest alarm, and dragged Jackal after him, over hill and valley, through bushes and over rocks, and never stopped to look behind him till he brought back himself and half-dead Jackal to his place again. And so Ram escaped.

Exercise

Review memory work. Identify each group of words below as either a phrase or a clause. If it is a clause, double underline the predicate and underline the subject.

although I wonder why

so the King stopped and looked at them in surprise

where the king jeered at Dorothy

Copy each sentence below. Double underline the predicate, and underline the subject. Put brackets around any prepositional phrases. Label the part of speech of each word. Noun, N; Proper Noun, PN; Pronoun, PRO; Verb, V; Linking Verb, LV; Adjective, ADJ; Article, ART; Adverb, ADV; Conjunctions, CJ; Prepositions, Prep; Interjections, INJ. Diagram each sentence.

"Why, you are not wearing your magic belt."

Dorothy welcomed back Ozma and the Queen of Ev.
[Hint: **what kind** of queen.]

The others went with Dorothy.

Writing: Commonplace Book

Add the passage below from your model story to your commonplace book.

> One bright day in late autumn, a family of Ants were bustling about in the warm sunshine, drying out the grain they had stored up during the summer, when a starving Grasshopper, his fiddle under his arm, came up and humbly begged for a bite to eat.
> "What!" cried the Ants in surprise. "Haven't you stored anything away for the winter? What in the world were you doing all last summer?"

Dictation

Use part of today's poem for dictation.

60. Slant Narrative: The Ants and the Grasshopper

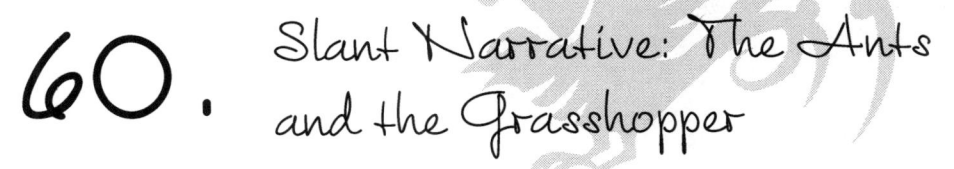

- Ozma of Oz, Chapter 19

Today, use your outline to write "The Ants and the Grasshopper" as a slant narrative. Write it in the first person. Who are you—the grasshopper or one of the ants? Remember to watch your pronouns. And do not be objective! Cast blame, make accusations, and show how **you** were not at fault!

The Chambered Nautilus

By Oliver Wendell Holmes

This is the ship of pearl, which, poets feign,
  Sailed the unshadowed main,—
  The venturous bark that flings
On the sweet summer wind its purpled wings
In gulfs enchanted, where the Siren sings,
  And coral reefs lie bare,
Where the cold sea-maids rise to sun their streaming hair.

Its webs of living gauze no more unfurl;
  Wrecked is the ship of pearl!
  And every chambered cell,
Where its dim dreaming life was wont to dwell,
As the frail tenant shaped his growing shell,
  Before thee lies revealed,—
Its irised ceiling rent, its sunless crypt unsealed!

Year after year beheld the silent toil
  That spread his lustrous coil;
  Still, as the spiral grew,
He left the past year's dwelling for the new,
Stole with soft step its shining archway through,
  Built up its idle door,
Stretched in his last-found home, and knew the old no more.

Thanks for the heavenly message brought by thee,
  Child of the wandering sea,
  Cast from her lap, forlorn!
From thy dead lips a clearer note is born
Than ever Triton blew from wreathed horn!
  While on mine ear it rings,
Through the deep caves of thought I hear a voice that sings:—

Build thee more stately mansions, O my soul,
  As the swift seasons roll!
  Leave thy low-vaulted past!
Let each new temple, nobler than the last,
Shut thee from heaven with a dome more vast,
  Till thou at length art free,
Leaving thine outgrown shell by life's unresting sea!

Editing

- Did you meet the goal of this writing exercise?

- Look at your word choice. Is there a good mixture of nouns and pronouns? Is the antecedent of each pronoun clear?

- Look at your paragraphs. Are all the sentences related? Does each paragraph focus on a single topic?

61. Noun and Pronouns Cases

• Ozma of Oz, Chapter 20

Definition: Cases are changes in form based on a noun or pronoun's job in the sentence.

	Nominative/Subjective	Objective	Possessive
1st Person Singular	I	me	my, mine
1st Person Plural	we	us	our, ours
2nd Person	you	you	your, yours
3rd Person Singular	he, she, it	him, her, it	his, her, hers, its
3rd Person Plural	they	them	their, theirs

English has twenty-six personal pronouns—the first person, second person, and third person pronouns which you have learned. We need so many because we use different pronouns for different jobs. You would not say, "My going to my room." Babies often talk like that while they are learning, but as you learned to speak proper English, you learned to say, "I am going to my room."

The word **cases** is just a way to talk about the different jobs that nouns and pronouns perform. In English, the cases are **nominative/subjective, objective,** and **possessive**. Although pronouns have different forms for all three cases, English nouns only change for possessive case.

Nominative case is also called **subjective case**. We use nominative/subjective case for the subject of a verb and for predicate nominatives. Subject does not have to mean the main subject of the sentence. In this case, it simply means the subject of a verb. Look at the following sentences from *Ozma of Oz*:

"He will know better next time, I am sure."

Afterward they sat down to a splendid feast.

Objective case is used for objects. That can mean a direct object, an indirect object, or the object of a preposition.

"I promote **you** to be Captain General."

The army caught sight [of **him**] and set up a cheer.

Possessive case is also called **genitive case**. Possessive case shows relationship or ownership. Possessive case nouns and pronouns always acts as adjectives, and this is how you should mark them for your lesson exercises.

adj
"Where is **your** husband?"

adj
She sat in **Ozma's** private room.

The Lotos-Eaters

By Alfred Tennyson

"Courage!" he said, and pointed toward the land,
"This mounting wave will roll us shoreward soon."
In the afternoon they came unto a land
In which it seemed always afternoon.
All round the coast the languid air did swoon,
Breathing like one that hath a weary dream.
Full-faced above the valley stood the moon;
And like a downward smoke, the slender stream
Along the cliff to fall and pause and fall did seem.

A land of streams! Some, like a downward smoke,
Slow-dropping veils of thinnest lawn, did go;
And some thro' wavering lights and shadows broke,
Rolling a slumbrous sheet of foam below.
They saw the gleaming river seaward flow
From the inner land: far off, three mountain-tops,
Three silent pinnacles of aged snow,
Stood sunset-flush'd: and, dew'd with showery drops,
Up-clomb the shadowy pine above the woven copse.

The charmed sunset linger'd low adown
In the red West: thro' mountain clefts the dale
Was seen far inland, and the yellow down
Border'd with palm, and many a winding vale
And meadow, set with slender galingale;
A land where all things always seem'd the same!
And round about the keel with faces pale,
Dark faces pale against that rosy flame,
The mild-eyed melancholy Lotos-eaters came.

Branches they bore of that enchanted stem,
Laden with flower and fruit, whereof they gave
To each, but whoso did receive of them,
And taste, to him the gushing of the wave
Far, far away did seem to mourn and rave
On alien shores; and if his fellow spake,
His voice was thin, as voices from the grave;
And deep-asleep he seem'd, yet all awake,
And music in his ears his beating heart did make.

They sat them down upon the yellow sand,
Between the sun and moon upon the shore;
And sweet it was to dream of Fatherland,
Of child, and wife, and slave; but evermore
Most weary seem'd the sea, weary the oar,
Weary the wandering fields of barren foam.
Then someone said, "We will return no more;"
And all at once they sang, "Our island home
Is far beyond the wave; we will no longer roam."

Writing: Oral Narration

Read your new model story below, and then give your instructor an oral narration of it.

The Town Mouse and the Country Mouse

From *The Aesop for Children* illustrated by Milo Winter

A Town Mouse once visited a relative who lived in the country. For lunch the Country Mouse served wheat stalks, roots, and acorns, with a dash of cold water for drink. The Town Mouse ate very sparingly, nibbling a little of this and a little of that, and by her manner making it very plain that she ate the simple food only to be polite.

After the meal the friends had a long talk, or rather, the Town Mouse talked about her life in the city while the Country Mouse listened. They then went to bed in a cozy nest in the hedgerow and slept in quiet and comfort until morning. In her sleep the Country Mouse dreamed she was a Town Mouse with all the luxuries and delights of city life that her friend had described for her. So the next day when the Town Mouse asked the Country Mouse to go home with her to the city, she gladly said yes.

When they reached the mansion in which the Town Mouse lived, they found on the table in the dining room the leavings of a very fine banquet. There were sweetmeats and jellies, pastries, delicious cheeses—indeed, the most tempting foods that a Mouse can imagine. But just as the Country Mouse was about to nibble a dainty bit of pastry, she heard a Cat mew loudly and scratch at the door. In great fear, the Mice scurried to a hiding place where they lay quite still for a long time, hardly daring to breathe. When at last they ventured back to the feast, the door opened suddenly, and in came the servants to clear the table, followed by the House Dog.

The Country Mouse stopped in the Town Mouse's den only long enough to pick up her carpet bag and umbrella.

"You may have luxuries and dainties that I have not," she said as she hurried away, "but I prefer my plain food and simple life in the country with the peace and security that go with it."

Poverty with security is better than plenty in the midst of fear and uncertainty.

Exercise

Review memory work. Punctuate the following sentence.

> For Ozma of Oz ruled the King of the Munchkins the King of the Winkies the King of the Quadlings and the King of the Gillikins

In the following sentences, label homographs GR and homophones PH.

> She lives in the Emerald City, which is in the exact center of the four kingdoms of the Land of Oz.

> "Now I am happy and contented and willing to lead a quiet life and mind my own business."

Copy each sentence below. Double underline the predicate, and underline the subject. Put brackets around any prepositional phrases. Label the part of speech of each word. Noun, N; Proper Noun, PN; Pronoun, PRO; Verb, V; Linking Verb, LV; Adjective, ADJ; Article, ART; Adverb, ADV; Conjunctions, CJ; Prepositions, Prep; Interjections, INJ. Diagram each sentence.

> "Have we any other privates in the armies?"

> "Omby Amby, I promote you."

> Ozma, the Ruler of Oz, returned to the Emerald City.

Commonplace Book

With your instructor's approval, add the passage below to your commonplace book, or choose your own passage from a work of fiction. This can be from either school reading or free reading.

> That evening there was a grand reception in the royal palace, attended by the most important persons of Oz, and Jack Pumpkinhead, who was a little overripe but still active, read an address congratulating Ozma of Oz

upon the success of her generous mission to rescue the royal family of a neighboring kingdom.

Dictation

Then magnificent gold medals set with precious stones were presented to each of the twenty-six officers; and the Tin Woodman was given a new axe studded with diamonds; and the Scarecrow received a silver jar of complexion powder. Dorothy was presented with a pretty coronet and made a Princess of Oz, and Tiktok received two bracelets set with eight rows of very clear and sparkling emeralds.

62. Pronoun Cases: Correct Usage

• Ozma of Oz, Chapter 21

When you use a noun and a pronoun together, it can be difficult to determine whether to use the nominative/subjective case or objective case pronoun. It is sometimes helpful to think of it as two sentences instead of one.

> The King said goodbye. She said goodbye.
> The King and she said goodbye.

> The feast was for Ozma. The feast was for them.
> The feast was for Ozma and them.

> You read the chapter. I read the chapter.
> You and I read the chapter.

You can do the same thing, of course, by determining what part of the sentence the pronoun is and which case that part needs. However, this can be quicker, especially when speaking.

Many of the sentences below have linking verbs and predicate nominatives. A predicate nominative is always in the nominative/subjective case. Nowadays, it is common to hear these sentences spoken incorrectly.

> It is I.
> This is he.
> This is she.
> It is we.
> It was I.
> It was not I; it was she.
> I think it was he.
> I am sure it is she.
> It was we.
> It might have been they.
> It was he and I.
> It was they.

No, it is not she.
Yes, it is he.
Did you call her?
Did you call me?
Did you call him and me?
Mother bought a ball for you.
Mother bought a ball for me.
Mother bought a ball for you and me.
Between you and me, I wanted a dinosaur.

The Overland-Mail

By Rudyard Kipling

In the name of the Empress of India, make way,
O Lords of the Jungle wherever you roam,
The woods are astir at the close of the day—
We exiles are waiting for letters from Home—
Let the robber retreat; let the tiger turn tail,
In the name of the Empress the Overland-Mail!

With a jingle of bells as the dusk gathers in,
He turns to the foot-path that leads up the hill—
The bags on his back, and a cloth round his chin,
And, tucked in his belt, the Post-Office bill;—
   "Despatched on this date, as received by the rail,
Per runner, two bags of the Overland-Mail."

Is the torrent in spate? He must ford it or swim.
Has the rain wrecked the road? He must climb by the cliff.
Does the tempest cry "Halt"? What are tempests to him?
The service admits not a "but" or an "if";
While the breath's in his mouth, he must bear without fail,
In the name of the Empress the Overland-Mail.

From aloe to rose-oak, from rose-oak to fir,
From level to upland, from upland to crest,
From rice-field to rock-ridge, from rock-ridge to spur,
Fly the soft-sandaled feet, strains the brawny brown chest.
From rail to ravine—to the peak from the vale—
Up, up through the night goes the Overland-Mail.

There's a speck on the hillside, a dot on the road—
A jingle of bells on the foot-path below—
There's a scuffle above in the monkeys' abode—
The world is awake, and the clouds are aglow—
For the great Sun himself must attend to the hail;—
In the name of the Empress the Overland-Mail.

Tink-Tinkje

From *South-African Folk-Tales* by James A. Honey

The birds wanted a king. Men have a king, so have animals, and why shouldn't they? All had assembled.

"The Ostrich, because he is the largest," one called out.

"No, he can't fly."

"Eagle, on account of his strength."

"Not he, he is too ugly."

"Vulture, because he can fly the highest."

"No, Vulture is too dirty; his odor is terrible."

"Peacock, he is so beautiful."

"His feet are too ugly, and also his voice."

"Owl, because he can see well."

"Not Owl; he is ashamed of the light."

And so they got no further. Then one shouted aloud, "He who can fly the highest will be king."

"Yes, yes," they all screamed, and at a given signal, they all ascended straight up into the sky.

Vulture flew for three whole days without stopping, straight toward the sun. Then he cried aloud, "I am the highest, I am king."

"T-sie, t-sie, t-sie," he heard above him. There Tink-tinkje was flying. He had held fast to one of the great wing feathers of Vulture and had never been felt, he was so light. "T-sie, t-sie, t-sie. I am the highest. I am king," piped Tink-tinkje.

Vulture flew for another day still ascending. "I am highest. I am king."

"T-sie, t-sie, t-sie. I am the highest. I am king," Tink-tinkje mocked. There he was again, having crept out from under the wing of Vulture.

Vulture flew on the fifth day straight up in the air. "I am the highest. I am king," he called.

"T-sie, t-sie, t-sie," piped the little fellow above him. "I am the highest. I am king."

Vulture was tired and now flew direct to earth. The other birds were mad through and through. Tink-tinkje must die because he had taken advantage of Vulture's feathers and there hidden himself. All flew after him, and he had to take refuge in a mouse hole. But how were they to get him out? Someone must stand guard to seize him the moment he put out his head.

"Owl must keep guard; he has the largest eyes; he can see well," they exclaimed.

Owl went and took up his position before the hole. The sun was warm, and soon Owl became sleepy, and presently he was fast asleep.

Tink-tinkje peeped, saw that Owl was asleep, and—z-zip—away he went. Shortly afterwards the other birds came to see if Tink-tinkje were still in the hole. "T-sie, t-sie," they heard in a tree; and there the little vagabond was sitting.

White-crow, perfectly disgusted, turned around and exclaimed, "Now I won't say a single word more." And from that day to this White-crow has never spoken. Even though you strike him, he makes no sound and utters no cry.

Writing: Outline

Write or type an outline of the new model story which you read in the last lesson.

Exercise

Review memory work. Punctuate the following sentence.

> The belt has magical powers only while it is in some fairy country my little friend

Copy each sentence below. Double underline the predicate, and underline the subject. Put brackets around any prepositional phrases. Label the part of speech of each word. Noun, N; Proper Noun, PN; Pronoun, PRO; Verb, V; Linking Verb, LV; Adjective, ADJ; Article, ART; Adverb, ADV; Conjunctions, CJ; Prepositions, Prep; Interjections, INJ. Diagram each sentence.

> Uncle Henry was seated in an easy chair.

> Instantly the farmhouse appeared in the picture.

> Dorothy, the little Kansas girl, might visit.

Commonplace Book

With your instructor's approval, add this part of today's poem to your commonplace book, or choose your own poem.

> In the name of the Empress of India, make way,
> O Lords of the Jungle wherever you roam,
> The woods are astir at the close of the day—
> We exiles are waiting for letters from Home—
> Let the robber retreat; let the tiger turn tail,
> In the name of the Empress the Overland-Mail!

> With a jingle of bells as the dusk gathers in,
> He turns to the foot-path that leads up the hill—
> The bags on his back, and a cloth round his chin,
> And, tucked in his belt, the Post-Office bill;—
>   "Despatched on this date, as received by the rail,
> Per runner, two bags of the Overland-Mail."

Dictation

Early to bed and early to rise makes a man healthy, wealthy, and wise.

Still Life by Pieter Wenning

Picture Study

1. Read the title and the name of the artist. Study the picture for several minutes, then put the picture away.

2. Describe the picture.

3. Look at the picture again. Do you notice any details that you missed before? What do you like or dislike about this painting? Does it remind you of anything?

63. Literary Analysis

• The Reluctant Dragon, approximately 10 pages (1/5 of the story)

Writing: Literary Analysis

Today you have another literary analysis assignment. Now that you have had some practice, this should be a written assignment, though it can be helpful to talk about your ideas before writing.

With your instructor's approval, choose *Ozma of Oz*, or one of the other books you have finished reading, and answer the following questions.

What is the book about? Give a brief summary, just a few sentences. Did you hope the book would end another way? If so, how? If not, what did you like about the ending?

The Fly

By Walter De La Mare

How large unto the tiny fly
Must little things appear!—
A rosebud like a feather bed,
Its prickle like a spear;
A dewdrop like a looking-glass,
A hair like golden wire;
The smallest grain of mustard-seed
As fierce as coals of fire;
A loaf of bread, a lofty hill;
A wasp, a cruel leopard;
And specks of salt as bright to see
As lambkins to a shepherd.

Cloud-Eating

From *South-African Folk-Tales* by James A. Honey

Jackal and Hyena were together, it is said, when a white cloud rose. Jackal descended upon it and ate of the cloud as if it were fat.

When he wanted to come down, he said to Hyena, "My sister, as I am going to divide with thee, catch me well." So she caught him and broke his fall. Then she also went up and ate there, high up on the top of the cloud.

When she was satisfied, she said, "My greyish brother, now catch me well." The greyish rogue said to his friend, "My sister, I shall catch thee well. Come therefore down."

He held up his hands, and she came down from the cloud, and when she was near, Jackal cried out while painfully jumping to one side, "My sister, do not take it ill. Oh me! Oh me! A thorn has pricked me and sticks in me." Thus she fell down from above and was sadly hurt.

Since that day, it is said that Hyena's hind feet have been shorter and smaller than the front ones.

Exercise

Review memory work. Copy each sentence below. Double underline the predicate, and underline the subject. Put brackets around any prepositional phrases. Label the part of speech of each word. Noun, N; Proper Noun, PN; Pronoun, PRO; Verb, V; Linking Verb, LV; Adjective, ADJ; Article, ART; Adverb, ADV; Conjunctions, CJ; Prepositions, Prep; Interjections, INJ. Diagram each sentence.

"Oh, yes, he was a peaceable sort of beast."

"Tell us about it first." [Hint: **first** tells when in this sentence.]

His parents were very fond of him.

Commonplace Book

With your instructor's approval, add the passage below to your commonplace book, or choose your own passage from a work of non-fiction. This can be from religious scriptures, a biography, or one of your history or science books.

Long ago—might have been hundreds of years ago—in a cottage halfway between this village and yonder shoulder of the Downs up there, a shepherd lived with his wife and their little son. Now the shepherd spent his days—and at certain times of the year his nights too—up on the wide ocean-bosom of the Downs, with only the sun and the stars and the sheep for company and the friendly, chattering world of men and women far out of sight and hearing.

64. Interrogative Adverbs

• The Reluctant Dragon, approximately 10 pages (1/5 of the story)

The interrogative adverbs are when, where, why, and how.

Interrogative adverbs introduce questions. They do not always introduce questions, though, and not all questions need them. They are only called interrogative adverbs when they are performing the task of introducing a question.

You already know that some adverbs answer the questions how, when, and where.

"Going to make a long stay here?" he asked, politely.

He asked how? Politely. When? Now. Where? Here, at the dragon's cave.

The words how, when, and where are adverbs themselves, and so is why. They are diagrammed just like other adverbs even when they introduce questions.

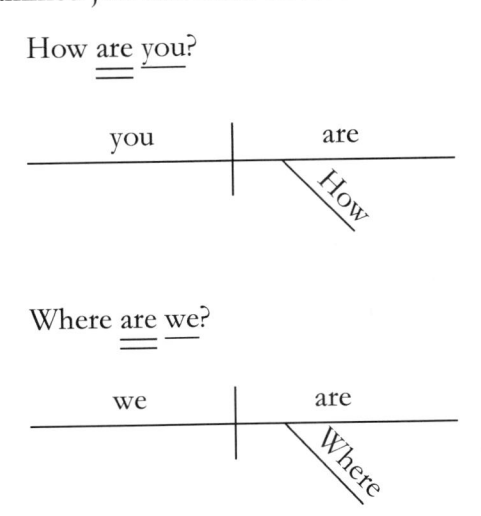

How are you?

```
    you    |   are
                \
                 How
```

Where are we?

```
    we     |   are
                \
                 Where
```

Notice that when we diagram interrogative adverbs, which introduce questions, we have to turn the sentence around, just as we have to do with other questions.

Where are we?   →   We are where?

An adverb cannot be the subject of the sentence. When we rearrange the sentence, we can more clearly see the subject. Adverbs that tell how, when, where, and how often modify verbs, so these interrogative adverbs modify the verb.

Now look at this sentence from "The Reluctant Dragon." What is **why** in this sentence?

"Why, St. George, of course," replied his friend.

In the above sentence, why is not an interrogative adverb. It is an interjection! You are learning many lists of words, but do not let those lists take the place of your brain. Compare the following two diagrams:

Why, is he St. George?

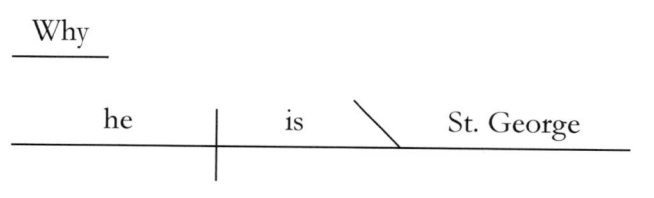

```
Why
―――

―――――― ――――― ――――――――
  he   |  is  \  St. George
       |
```

Why is St. George coming?

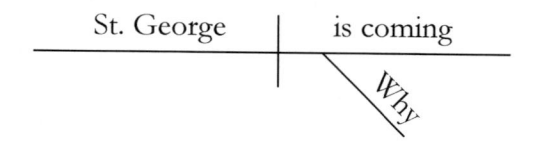

```
――――――――――― ――――――――――
 St. George |  is coming
            |
             \Why
```

In the first sentence, **why** is an interjection. In the second sentence, however, **why** is an interrogative adjective introducing a question.

How Sleep the Brave
By William Collins

How sleep the brave, who sink to rest
By all their country's wishes blest!
When Spring, with dewy fingers cold,
Returns to deck their hallow'd mould,
She there shall dress a sweeter sod
Than Fancy's feet have ever trod.

By fairy hands their knell is rung,
By forms unseen their dirge is sung:
There Honor comes, a pilgrim gray,
To bless the turf that wraps their clay;
And Freedom shall a while repair
To dwell a weeping hermit there!

The Lion and Jackal

From *South-African Folk-Tales* by James A. Honey

Lion had now caught a large eland which lay dead on the top of a high bank. Lion was thirsty and wanted to go and drink water. "Jackal, look after my eland. I am going to get a drink. Don't you eat any."

"Very well, Uncle Lion."

Lion went to the river, and Jackal quietly removed a stone on which Lion had to step to reach the bank on his return. After that Jackal and his wife ate heartily of the eland. Lion returned, but could not scale the bank. "Jackal, help me," he shouted.

"Yes, Uncle Lion, I will let down a rope, and then you can climb up."

Jackal whispered to his wife, "Give me one of the old, thin hide ropes." And then aloud he added, "Wife, give me one of the strong, buffalo ropes, so Uncle Lion won't fall."

His wife gave him an old rotten rope. Jackal and his wife first ate ravenously of the meat then gradually let the rope down. Lion seized it and struggled up. When he neared the brink, Jackal gave the rope a jerk. It broke and down Lion began to roll. He rolled the whole way down and finally lay at the foot near the river.

Jackal began to beat a dry hide that lay there as he howled, cried, and shouted: "Wife, why did you give me such a bad rope that caused Uncle Lion to fall?"

Lion heard the row and roared, "Jackal, stop beating your wife. I will hurt you if you don't cease. Help me to climb up."

"Uncle Lion, I will give you a rope." Whispering again to his wife, "Give me one of the old, thin hide ropes," and shouting aloud again, "Give me a strong, buffalo rope, wife, that will not break again with Lion."

Jackal gave out the rope, and when Lion had nearly reached the top, he cut the rope through. Snap! And Lion began to roll to the bottom. Jackal again beat on the hide and shouted, "Wife, why did you give me such a rotten rope? Didn't I tell you to give me a strong one?"

Lion roared, "Jackal, stop beating your wife at once. Help me instantly or you will be sorry."

"Wife," Jackal said aloud, "give me now the strongest rope you have," and aside to her, "Give me the worst rope of the lot."

Jackal again let down a rope, but just as Lion reached the top, Jackal gave a strong tug and broke the rope. Poor old Lion rolled down the side of the hill and lay there roaring from pain. He had been fatally hurt.

Jackal inquired, "Uncle Lion, have you hurt yourself? Have you much pain? Wait a while; I am coming directly to help you." Jackal and his wife slowly walked away.

Writing: Copia

Take the following sentence and play with it. Remember that the point is not necessarily to make the sentence better. The point is to play with the sentence and make it different. Make a new sentence for each number, using at least one change from that category.

> "I prefer my plain food and simple life in the country with the peace and security that go with it."

1. Change the grammar.
    - Change the nouns from common to proper and vice versa.
    - Change the nouns from singular to plural and vice versa.
    - Change the sentence type.
    - Change the adjectives from articles to descriptive to possessive, etc.
    - Change a quotation from direct to indirect and vice versa.

2. Condense the sentence.
    - Remove details.
    - Remove modifiers.
    - Remove phrases or clauses.

3. Amplify the sentence.
    - Add details.
    - Add dialogue.
    - Add modifiers.
    - Add phrases or clauses.

4. Use synonyms and antonyms.
    - Substitute synonyms.
    - Say the opposite thing using antonyms.

5. Point of view.
    - Change the point of view.
    - Slant the sentence.

Exercise

Review memory work. Copy each sentence below. Double underline the predicate, and underline the subject. Put brackets around any prepositional phrases. Label the part of speech of each word. Noun, N; Proper Noun, PN; Pronoun, PRO; Verb, V; Linking Verb, LV; Adjective, ADJ; Article, ART; Adverb, ADV; Conjunctions, CJ; Prepositions, Prep; Interjections, INJ. Diagram each sentence.

"Now don't hit me."

Where did he see the dragon?

A cool breeze played over the surface of the grass.

Commonplace Book

With your instructor's approval, add the passage below to your commonplace book, or choose your own passage from a work of fiction. This can be from either school reading or free reading.

"Hullo, dragon!" said the Boy, quietly, when he had got up to him.

The dragon, on hearing the approaching footsteps, made the beginning of a courteous effort to rise. But when he saw it was a Boy, he set his eyebrows severely.

"Now don't you hit me," he said, "or bung stones, or squirt water, or anything. I won't have it, I tell you!"

Dictation

"It's the sad truth," the dragon went on, settling down between his paws and evidently delighted to have found a listener at last. "And I fancy that's really how I came to be here. You see, all the other fellows were so active and earnest and all that sort of thing—always rampaging, and skirmishing, and scouring the desert sands, and pacing the margin of the sea, and chasing knights all over the place, and devouring damsels, and going on generally—whereas I liked to get my meals regular, and then to prop my back against a bit of rock and snooze a bit, and wake up, and think of things going on and how they kept going on just the same, you know!"

65. The Principal Parts of the Verb

- The Reluctant Dragon, approximately 10 pages (1/5 of the story)

The five principal parts of the verb are the
infinitive, the present tense, the present participle,
the past tense, and the past participle.

Verbs have five principal parts. You have used all of these parts before and even diagrammed most of them.

The first part is the infinitive. The infinitive is formed by using the word **to** in front of the simplest form of the verb. **To walk** is the infinitive form of **walk**.

"You'll be able **to arrange** something."

The second part is the present tense, simplest form of the verb. **Tense** means time, so the present tense tells us that the action is happening in the present rather than in the past or in the future.

"Oh, I **think** not," said the dragon.

The third part is called the present participle. It is formed by adding the ending *-ing* to the base form. If the verb ends in silent final *e*, drop the *e* before adding *-ing*. In the sentence below, notice that to use the present participle as a verb, it needs a helping verb.

The dragon was **licking** his scales.

The fourth part is called the past tense form. Regular verbs form the past tense by adding the ending *-ed*.

"It's all up, dragon!" he **shouted**.

The fifth part is called the past participle. For regular verbs, it is the same as the past tense form. To use the past participle as a verb, it needs a helping verb.

The dreadful beast must be **exterminated**.

So we have:

287

To bake, I bake, I am baking, I baked, I have baked.
To cry, I cry, I am crying, I cried, I have cried.
To try, I try, I am trying, I tried, I have tried.
To play, I play, I am playing, I played, I have played.
To obey, I obey, I am obeying, I obeyed, I have obeyed.
To crack, I crack, I am cracking, I cracked, I have cracked.

Infinitive	Simple Present	Present Participle	Simple Past	Past Participle
to bake	bake	baking	baked	baked
to cry	cry	crying	cried	cried
to try	try	trying	tried	tried
to play	play	playing	played	played
to obey	obey	obeying	obeyed	obeyed
to crack	crack	cracking	cracked	cracked

The Flag Goes By

By Henry Holcomb Bennett

Hats off!
Along the street there comes
A blare of bugles, a ruffle of drums,
A flash of color beneath the sky:
Hats off!
The flag is passing by!

Blue and crimson and white it shines
Over the steel-tipped, ordered lines.
Hats off!
The colors before us fly;
But more than the flag is passing by.

Sea-fights and land-fights, grim and great,
Fought to make and to save the State:
Weary marches and sinking ships;
Cheers of victory on dying lips;

Days of plenty and years of peace;
March of a strong land's swift increase;

Equal justice, right, and law,
Stately honor and reverend awe;

Sign of a nation, great and strong
Toward her people from foreign wrong:
Pride and glory and honor,—all
Live in the colors to stand or fall.

Hats off!
Along the street there comes
A blare of bugles, a ruffle of drums;
And loyal hearts are beating high:
Hats off!
The flag is passing by!

The Lion, the Jackal, and the Man

From *South-African Folk-Tales* by James A. Honey

It so happened one day that Lion and Jackal came together to converse on affairs of land and state. Jackal, let me say, was the most important adviser to the king of the forest, and after they had spoken about these matters for quite a while, the conversation took a more personal turn.

Lion began to boast and talk big about his strength. Jackal had, perhaps, given him cause for it because by nature, he was a flatterer. But now that Lion began to assume so many airs, said he, "See here, Lion, I will show you an animal that is still more powerful than you are."

They walked along, Jackal leading the way, and met first a little boy.

"Is this the strong man?" asked Lion.

"No," answered Jackal. "He must still become a man, O king."

After a while they found an old man walking with bowed head, supporting his bent figure with a stick.

"Is this the wonderful strong man?" asked Lion.

"Not yet, O king," was Jackal's answer. "He has been a man."

Continuing their walk a short distance farther, they came across a young hunter in the prime of youth, accompanied by some of his dogs.

"There you have him now, O king," said Jackal. "Pit your strength against his, and if you win, then truly you are the strength of the earth."

Then Jackal made tracks to one side toward a little rocky kopje from which he would be able to see the meeting.

Growling, growling, Lion strode forward to meet the man, but when he came close, the dogs beset him. However, he paid but little attention to the dogs. He pushed and separated them on all sides with a few sweeps of his front paws. They howled aloud, beating a hasty retreat toward the man.

Thereupon the man fired a charge of shot, hitting him behind the shoulder, but even to this Lion paid but little attention. Thereupon the hunter pulled out his steel knife and gave him a few good jabs. Lion retreated, followed by the flying bullets of the hunter.

"Well, are you strongest now?" was Jackal's first question when Lion arrived at his side.

"No, Jackal," answered Lion. "Let that fellow there keep the name and welcome. Such as he I have never before seen. In the first place he had about ten of his bodyguard storm me. I really did not bother myself much about them, but when I attempted to turn him to chaff, he spat and blew fire at me, mostly into my face, that burned just a little but not very badly. And when I again endeavored to pull him to the ground, he jerked out from his body one of his ribs with which he gave me some very ugly wounds, so bad that I had to make chips fly, and as a parting, he sent some warm bullets after me. No, Jackal, give him the name."

Exercise

Review memory work. Name the parts of the verb marked in the following sentences.

I **hear** so much of it, and it's monotonous and makes me tired.

I began to think it would be fun **to work** my way upstairs.

Copy each sentence below. Double underline the predicate, and underline the subject. Put brackets around any prepositional phrases. Label the part of speech of each word. Noun, N; Proper Noun, PN; Pronoun, PRO; Verb, V; Linking Verb, LV; Adjective, ADJ; Article, ART; Adverb, ADV; Conjunctions, CJ; Prepositions, Prep; Interjections, INJ. Diagram each sentence.

Where is St. George?

"My dear little man, just understand."

The Boy jumped round in sheer delight.

Writing: Commonplace Book

Add the passage below from your model story to your commonplace book.

A Town Mouse once visited a relative who lived in the country. For lunch the Country Mouse served wheat stalks, roots, and acorns, with a dash of cold water for drink. The Town Mouse ate very sparingly, nibbling a little of this and a little of that, and by her manner making it very plain that she ate the simple food only to be polite.

Dictation

Use part of today's poem for dictation.

66. Slant Narrative: The Town Mouse and the Country Mouse

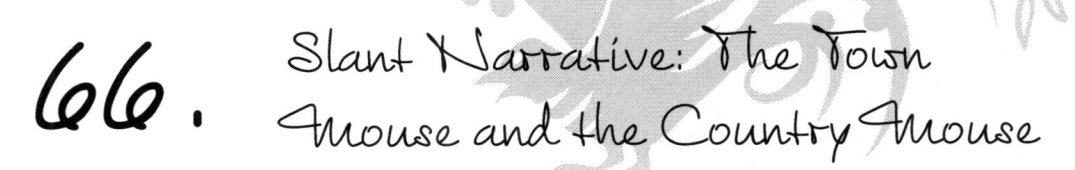

- The Reluctant Dragon, approximately 10 pages (1/5 of the story)

Today, use your outline to write "The Town Mouse and the Country Mouse" as a slant narrative. Write it in the first person. Who are you—the town mouse or the country mouse? Remember to watch your pronouns. And do not be objective! Cast blame, make accusations, and show how *you* were not at fault!

Song

By Walter De La Mare

O for a moon to light me home!
O for a lanthorn green!
For those sweet stars the Pleiades,
That glitter in the twilight trees;
O for a lovelorn taper! O
For a lanthorn green!

O for a frock of tartan!
O for clear, wild, grey eyes!
For fingers light as violets,
'Neath branches that the blackbird frets;
O for a thistly meadow! O
For clear, wild grey eyes!

O for a heart like almond boughs!
O for sweet thoughts like rain!
O for first-love like fields of grey,
Shut April-buds at break of day!
O for a sleep like music!
For still dreams like rain!

Editing

- Did you meet the goal of this writing exercise?
- Look at your word choice. Is there a good mixture of nouns and pronouns? Is the antecedent of each pronoun clear?
- Look at your paragraphs. Are all the sentences related? Does each paragraph focus on a single topic?

67. The Infinitive; Verb Properties: Person

- The Reluctant Dragon, approximately 10 pages (1/5 of the story)

The five properties of verbs are person,
number, tense, voice, mood.

To use the infinitive **to walk** as a verb, we need to **conjugate** it. We conjugate a verb by changing its form depending on who is or who is doing the action (person), how many are or are doing the action (number), and when they are or are doing the action (tense). These are called properties of the verb.

to walk	Singular	Plural
1st Person	I walk	we walk
2nd Person	you walk	you walk
3rd Person	he, she, or it walks	they walk

Verbs have five properties. We will be learning about three of them in this book. The first one is that verbs have person. Does that sound familiar? (Hint: Look at the chart above.) Person tells us the identity of the subject—first person, second person, or third person. Look at the following sentences from "The Reluctant Dragon." Notice how the verb changes depending on the property of person.

"I take a cast round by the cave, quietly."

He takes to the road like any tame civilized tax-payer.

They take his word without a murmur.

Reverie

By Walter De La Mare

When slim Sophia mounts her horse
And paces down the avenue,
It seems an inward melody
She paces to.
Each narrow hoof is lifted high
Beneath the dark enclust'ring pines,
A silver ray within his bit
And bridle shines.
His eye burns deep, his tail is arched,
And streams upon the shadowy air,
The daylight sleeks his jetty flanks,
His mistress' hair.
Her habit flows in darkness down,
Upon the stirrup rests her foot,
Her brow is lifted, as if earth
She heeded not.
'Tis silent in the avenue,
The sombre pines are mute of song,
The blue is dark, there moves no breeze
The boughs among.
When slim Sophia mounts her horse
And paces down the avenue,
It seems an inward melody
She paces to.

Writing: Oral Narration

Read your new model story below, and then give your instructor an oral narration of it.

The Hare and the Tortoise

From *The Aesop for Children* illustrated by Milo Winter

A Hare was making fun of the Tortoise one day for being so slow. "Do you ever get anywhere?" he asked with a mocking laugh.

"Yes," replied the Tortoise. "And I get there sooner than you think. I'll run you a race and prove it."

The Hare was much amused at the idea of running a race with the Tortoise, but for the fun of the thing, he agreed. So the Fox, who had consented to act as judge, marked the distance and started the runners off.

The Hare was soon far out of sight, and to make the Tortoise feel very deeply how ridiculous it was for him to try a race with a Hare, he lay down beside the course to take a nap until the Tortoise should catch up.

The Tortoise, meanwhile, kept going slowly but steadily and, after a time, passed the place where the Hare was sleeping. But the Hare slept on very peacefully; and when at last he did wake up, the Tortoise was near the goal. The Hare now ran his swiftest, but he could not overtake the Tortoise in time.

The race is not always to the swift.

Exercise

Review memory work. Name the part of the verb marked in the following sentences.

"Are you going **to make** a long stay here?"

"I **am going** off home."

Copy each sentence below. Double underline the predicate, and underline the subject. Put brackets around any prepositional phrases. Label the part of speech of each word. Noun, N; Proper Noun, PN; Pronoun, PRO; Verb, V; Linking Verb, LV; Adjective, ADJ; Article, ART; Adverb, ADV; Conjunctions, CJ; Prepositions, Prep; Interjections, INJ. Diagram each sentence.

The Boy had secured a good front place.

"Boy, can't you arrange a Princess?"

When did St. George the dragon slayer arrive?

Commonplace Book

With your instructor's approval, add the passage below to your commonplace book, or choose your own passage from a work of fiction. This can be from either school reading or free reading.

> It all seemed so genuine that the Boy ran in breathlessly, hoping the dear old dragon wasn't really hurt. As he approached, the dragon lifted one large eyelid, winked solemnly, and collapsed again. He was held fast to earth by the neck, but the Saint had hit him in the spare place agreed upon, and it didn't even seem to tickle.

Dictation

> "Oh, it's this great lumbering pig of a dragon!" sobbed the Boy. "First he makes me promise to see him home, and then he says I'd better do it and goes to sleep! Might as well try to see a haystack home! And I'm so tired, and mother's—" here he broke down again.
> "Now don't take on," said St. George. "I'll stand by you, and we'll both see him home. Wake up, dragon!" he said sharply, shaking the beast by the elbow.

68. Verb Properties: Number

- Heidi, Chapter 1

The second property of verbs that we are talking about is **number**. Verbs have number. That means that verbs change form depending on how many are or are doing. Look at the chart again. One column is singular, and the other is plural.

to walk	Singular	Plural
1st Person	I walk	we walk
2nd Person	you walk	you walk
3rd Person	he, she, or it walks	they walk

Most verbs are **regular**. That means that they all change the same way. Notice that all of the verb forms above are the same except the third person singular, which has an **ending**. Its ending is *-s*. Now conjugate **to move**. Look at the chart above to remember the order if necessary.

Did you notice that **to move** is exactly the same? Only the third person singular has an ending, and that ending is *-s*. Most verbs are regular. The exact same thing happens when you conjugate **to bake, to ask, to joke,** or **to squeeze**.

Look at the following sentences from *Heidi*. Notice how the verb changes depending on the property of number.

She climbs up the mountain.

They climb up the mountain.

Heidi is tired.

<u>They <u>are</u> tired.</u>

I Saw Three Witches

By Walter De La Mare

I saw three witches
That bowed down like barley,
And took to their brooms 'neath a louring sky,
And, mounting a storm-cloud,
Aloft on its margin,
Stood black in the silver as up they did fly.

I saw three witches
That mocked the poor sparrows
They carried in cages of wicker along,
Till a hawk from his eyrie
Swooped down like an arrow,
And smote on the cages, and ended their song.

I saw three witches
That sailed in a shallop,
All turning their heads with a truculent smile,
Till a bank of green osiers
Concealed their grim faces,
Though I heard them lamenting for many a mile.

I saw three witches
Asleep in a valley,
Their heads in a row, like stones in a flood,
Till the moon, creeping upward,
Looked white through the valley,
And turned them to bushes in bright scarlet bud.

Story of Lion and Little Jackal

From *South-African Folk-Tales* by James A. Honey

Part I

Little Jackal one day went out hunting, and he met Lion. Lion proposed that they should hunt together, on condition that if a small antelope was killed, it was to be Little Jackal's, and if a large one was killed, it was to be Lion's. Little Jackal agreed to this.

The first animal killed was a large eland. Lion was very glad and said to Little Jackal: "I will continue hunting while you go to my house and call my children to carry the meat home."

Little Jackal replied: "Yes, I agree to that."

Lion went away to hunt. When he had gone, Little Jackal went to his own house and called his own children to carry away the meat. He said: "Lion takes me for a fool if he thinks I will call his children while my own are dying with hunger."

So Little Jackal's children carried the meat to their home on the top of a high rock, where the only way to get to their house was by means of a rope.

Lion caught nothing more, and after a time he went home and asked his wife where the meat was. She told him there was no meat. He said: "Did not Little Jackal bring a message to my children to carry meat?"

His wife replied: "No, he was not here. We are still dying with hunger."

Lion then went to Little Jackal's house, but he could not get up the rock to it. So he sat down by the water, waiting. After a time Little Jackal went to get some water. He was close to the water when he saw Lion. He at once ran away, and Lion ran after him. He ran into a hole under a tree, but Lion caught his tail before he got far in. He said to him: "That is not my tail you have hold of; it is a root of the tree. If you do not believe me, take a stone and strike it, and see if any blood comes."

Lion let go the tail and went for a stone to prove what it was. While he was gone for the stone, Little Jackal went far into the hole. When Lion returned, he could not be found. Lion lay down by the hole and waited. After a long time, Little Jackal wanted to come out. He went to the entrance and looked round, but he could not see Lion. To make sure, he said: "Ho, I see you, my master, although you are in hiding."

Lion did not move from the place where he lay concealed. Then Little Jackal went out, and Lion pursued him, but he got away.

Lion watched for him, and one day, when Little Jackal was out hunting, he came upon him in a place where he could not escape. Lion was just about to spring upon him when Little Jackal said softly: "Be still, do you not see that bushbuck on the other side of the rock? I am glad you have come to help me. Just remain here while I run round and drive him toward you."

Lion did so, and Little Jackal made his escape.

Writing: Outline

Write or type an outline of the new model story which you read in the last lesson.

Exercise

Review memory work. Name the part of the verb marked in the following sentences.

Then she **looked** around to see that the child was not close.

"I **have** often **noticed** that and I am glad for her."

Copy each sentence below. Double underline the predicate, and underline the subject. Put brackets around any prepositional phrases. Label the part of speech of each word. Noun, N; Proper Noun, PN; Pronoun, PRO; Verb, V; Linking Verb, LV; Adjective, ADJ; Article, ART; Adverb, ADV; Conjunctions, CJ; Prepositions, Prep; Interjections, INJ. Diagram each sentence.

"Where are you taking the child, Deta?"

"Why are his eyes so fierce?"

"She is climbing up with the goatherd Peter."

Commonplace Book

With your instructor's approval, add this part of today's poem to your commonplace book, or choose your own poem.

> I saw three witches
> Asleep in a valley,
> Their heads in a row, like stones in a flood,
> Till the moon, creeping upward,
> Looked white through the valley,
> And turned them to bushes in bright scarlet bud.

Dictation

No news is good news.

The Bridge, Rondebosch by Pieter Wenning

Picture Study

1. Read the title and the name of the artist. Study the picture for several minutes, then put the picture away.

2. Describe the picture.

3. Look at the picture again. Do you notice any details that you missed before? What do you like or dislike about this painting? Does it remind you of anything?

69. Descriptive Writing

• Heidi, Chapter 2

Writing: Descriptive Writing

Remember that the purpose of descriptive writing is to describe a person, place, thing, or event so well that an image forms in the mind of the reader.

Your last six picture studies have been on paintings by Pieter Wenning. Today, choose one of his paintings, either one from this book or one from another source, and write a description of it. Imagine that you are describing the picture to someone who has never seen it before. Get creative if you wish. Write a description for a museum catalog or as part of a police report describing stolen merchandise. Or get really creative. Imagine that the painting is a window to another dimension, and you have just been pulled in. Describe the environment in which you find yourself. Or, write a story about the picture or about your experiences within it. Be as creative as you want. Just do not forget to describe the picture!

Old Folks at Home

By Stephen Collins Foster

Way down upon de Swanee Ribber,
  Far, far away,
Dere's wha my heart is turning ebber,
  Dere's wha de old folks stay.
All up and down de whole creation
  Sadly I roam,
Still longing for de old plantation,
  And for de old folks at home.

All de world am sad and dreary,
  Eberywhere I roam;
Oh, darkeys, how my heart grows weary,
  Far from de old folks at home!

All round de little farm I wandered
  When I was young,
Den many happy days I squandered,
  Many de songs I sung.
When I was playing wid my brudder
  Happy was I;
Oh, take me to my kind old mudder!
  Dere let me live and die.

One little hut among de bushes,
  One dat I love,
Still sadly to my memory rushes,
  No matter where I rove.
When will I see de bees a-humming
  All round de comb?
When will I hear de banjo tumming,
  Down in my good old home?

All de world am sad and dreary,
  Eberywhere I roam;
Oh, darkeys, how my heart grows weary,
  Far from de old folks at home!

Story of Lion and Little Jackal

From *South-African Folk-Tales* by James A. Honey

Part II

At another time there was a meeting of the animals, and Lion was the chief at the meeting. Little Jackal wanted to attend, but there was a law made that no one should be present unless he had horns. So Little Jackal took wax out of a nest of bees and made horns for himself with it. He fastened the horns on his head and went to the meeting. Lion did not know him on account of the horns. But Little Jackal sat near the fire and went to sleep, and the horns melted.

Lion looked at him and saw who it was. He immediately tried to catch him, but Little Jackal was quick in springing away. He ran under an overhanging rock and sang out: "Help! Help! This rock is falling upon me!"

Lion went for a pole to prop up the rock that he might get at Little Jackal. While he was away, Little Jackal escaped.

After that they became companions again and went hunting another time. They killed an ox. Lion said: "I will watch it while you carry the pieces away."

Lion gave him the breast and said: "Take this to my wife."

Little Jackal took it to his own wife. When he returned, Lion gave him a shin, and said: "Take this to your wife."

Little Jackal took the shin to Lion's house. Lion's wife said: "I cannot take this because it should not come here."

Little Jackal thereupon struck Lion's wife in the face and went back to the place where the ox was killed. Lion gave him a large piece of meat and said: "Take this to my wife."

Little Jackal took it to his own wife. This continued till the ox was finished. Then they both went home. When Lion arrived at his house, he found there was weeping in his family.

His wife said: "Is it you who sent Little Jackal to beat me and my children, and is it you who sent this shin? Did I ever eat a shin?"

When Lion heard this, he was very angry and at once went to Little Jackal's house. When he reached the rock, Little Jackal looked down and said: "Who are you, and what is your name, and whose son are you, and where are you from, and where are you going to, and whom do you want, and what do you want him for?"

Lion replied: "I have merely come to see you. I wish you to let down the rope."

Little Jackal let down a rope made of mouse skins, and when Lion climbed a little way up, the rope broke, and he fell and was hurt. He then went home.

Exercise

Review memory work. Identify each group of words below as either a phrase or a clause. If it is a clause, double underline the predicate and underline the subject.

after looking around attentively in the room

Heidi followed him into a fairly spacious room

when he opened it

Copy each sentence below. Double underline the predicate, and underline the subject. Put brackets around any prepositional phrases. Label the part of speech of each word. Noun, N; Proper Noun, PN; Pronoun, PRO; Verb, V; Linking Verb, LV; Adjective, ADJ; Article, ART; Adverb, ADV; Conjunctions, CJ; Prepositions, Prep; Interjections, INJ. Diagram each sentence.

"Why don't you need them?"

"Come then."

Beside the old man's bed she saw a ladder.

Commonplace Book

With your instructor's approval, add the passage below to your commonplace book, or choose your own passage from a work of non-fiction. This can be from religious scriptures, a biography, or one of your history or science books.

> "All right, you can; but fetch the things, and we'll put them in the cupboard." The child obeyed the command. The old man now opened the door, and Heidi followed him into a fairly spacious room, which took in the entire expanse of the hut. In one corner stood a table and a chair, and in another the grandfather's bed.

70. Verb Properties: Tense

• Heidi, Chapter 3

The third property of verbs that we are talking about is tense. Tense means time. Today we will be talking about the simple forms of the three basic tenses: past, present, and future. The first chart shows just the first person singular so that you can see the forms of all three tenses.

Infinitive	Past Simple	Present Simple	Future Simple
to ask	I asked	I ask	I will ask
to move	I moved	I move	I will move
to bake	I baked	I bake	I will bake
to hurry	I hurried	I hurry	I will hurry

Notice that the past tense has an **ending**, **-ed**. Regular verbs form the past tense by adding **-ed**. Look at this sentence from *Heidi*:

She **remembered** how she had come up the mountain the day before.

Notice the helping verb **will** in the future tense. Verbs form the future tense by using the helping verb **will**.

"For the sun **will laugh** at you if he sees how dirty you are."

The next two charts show the conjugation of the past tense and the future tense. Notice that the verb does not change.

307

Past Tense

to walk	Singular	Plural
1st Person	I walked	we walked
2nd Person	you walked	you walked
3rd Person	he, she, or it walked	they walked

Future Tense

to walk	Singular	Plural
1st Person	I will walk	we will walk
2nd Person	you will walk	you will walk
3rd Person	he, she, or it will walk	they will walk

Look at the following sentences from *Heidi*. Notice how the tense changes.

"Yes," cried Heidi.

"I am sure the old man will show you the door."

You may notice that you have seen other ways to speak about the past, present, and future which are not listed on these charts. That is because English actually has twelve tenses. Today, you only learned the simple forms.

Butterfly

By Hilda Conkling

Butterfly,
I like the way you wear your wings.
Show me their colors,
For the light is going.
Spread out their edges of gold,

Before the Sandman puts me to sleep
And evening murmurs by.

The Story of a Dam

From *South-African Folk-Tales* by James A. Honey

Part I

There was a great drought in the land; and Lion called together a number of animals so that they might devise a plan for retaining water when the rains fell.

The animals which attended at Lion's summons were Baboon, Leopard, Hyena, Jackal, Hare, and Mountain Tortoise.

It was agreed that they should scratch a large hole in some suitable place to hold water; and the next day they all began to work, with the exception of Jackal, who continually hovered about in that locality and was overheard to mutter that he was not going to scratch his nails off in making water holes.

When the dam was finished, the rains fell, and it was soon filled with water, to the great delight of those who had worked so hard at it. The first one, however, to come and drink there was Jackal, who not only drank, but filled his clay pot with water and then proceeded to swim in the rest of the water, making it as muddy and dirty as he could.

This was brought to the knowledge of Lion, who was very angry and ordered Baboon to guard the water the next day, armed with a huge knobkirrie. Baboon was concealed in a bush close to the water; but Jackal soon became aware of his presence there and guessed its cause. Knowing the fondness of baboons for honey, Jackal at once hit upon a plan and, marching to and fro, every now and then dipped his fingers into his clay pot and licked them with an expression of intense relish, saying, in a low voice to himself, "I don't want any of their dirty water when I have a pot full of delicious honey." This was too much for poor Baboon, whose mouth began to water. He soon began to beg Jackal to give him a little honey, as he had been watching for several hours and was very hungry and tired.

After taking no notice of Baboon at first, Jackal looked round and said, in a patronizing manner, that he pitied such an unfortunate creature and would give him some honey on certain conditions—that Baboon should give up his knobkirrie and allow himself to be bound by Jackal. He foolishly agreed and was soon tied in such a manner that he could not move hand or foot.

Jackal now proceeded to drink of the water, to fill his pot, and to swim in the sight of Baboon, from time to time telling him what a foolish fellow he had been to be so easily duped, and that he (Jackal) had no honey or anything else to give him, excepting a good blow on the head every now and then with his own knobkirrie.

The animals soon appeared and found poor Baboon in this sorry plight, looking the picture of misery. Lion was so exasperated that he caused Baboon to be severely punished and to be denounced as a fool.

Tortoise hereupon stepped forward and offered his services for the capture of Jackal. It was at first thought that he was merely joking; but when he explained in what manner he proposed to catch him, his plan was considered so feasible that his offer was accepted. He proposed that a thick coating of "bijenwerk" (a kind of sticky black substance found on beehives) should be spread all over him and that he should then go and stand at the entrance of the dam, on the water level, so that Jackal might tread upon him and stick fast. This was accordingly done, and Tortoise posted there.

Writing: Copia

Take the following sentence and play with it. Remember that the point is not necessarily to make the sentence better. The point is to play with the sentence and make it different. Make a new sentence for each number, using at least one change from that category.

A Hare was making fun of the Tortoise one day for being so slow.

1. Change the grammar.
   - Change the nouns from common to proper and vice versa.
   - Change the nouns from singular to plural and vice versa.
   - Change the sentence type.
   - Change the adjectives from articles to descriptive to possessive, etc.
   - Change a quotation from direct to indirect and vice versa.
   - Change the verb tense.

2. Condense the sentence.
   - Remove details.
   - Remove modifiers.
   - Remove phrases or clauses.

3. Amplify the sentence.
   - Add details.
   - Add dialogue.
   - Add modifiers.
   - Add phrases or clauses.

4. Use synonyms and antonyms.
   - Substitute synonyms.
   - Say the opposite thing using antonyms.

5. Point of view.
   - Change the point of view.
   - Slant the sentence.

Exercise

Review memory work. Name the part of the verb marked in the following sentences.

Peter now begins **to call** loudly and to whistle.

Heidi, knowing that something **had happened**, followed him.

Copy each sentence below. Double underline the predicate, and underline the subject. Put brackets around any prepositional phrases. Label the part of speech of each word. Noun, N; Proper Noun, PN; Pronoun, PRO; Verb, V; Linking Verb, LV; Adjective, ADJ; Article, ART; Adverb, ADV; Conjunctions, CJ; Prepositions, Prep; Interjections, INJ. Diagram each sentence.

"Oh, does it really live there?

"Where is her grandmother?"

Heidi at last went to the little thing again.

Commonplace Book

With your instructor's approval, add the passage below to your commonplace book, or choose your own passage from a work of fiction. This can be from either school reading or free reading.

> Not taking Heidi in earnest, he hesitated till she put the things on his knees. Then he saw she really meant it, and he seized his prize. Nodding his thanks to her, he ate the most luxurious meal he had ever had in all his life. Heidi was watching the goats in the meantime and asked Peter for their names.

Dictation

Heidi at last went to the little thing again, and throwing her arms around its head, she asked, "What is the matter with you, Snowhopper? Why do you always cry for help?" The little goat pressed close to Heidi's side and became perfectly quiet. Peter was still eating, but between the swallows he called to Heidi: "She is so unhappy because the old goat has left us. She was sold to somebody in Mayenfeld two days ago."

71. Properties of Nouns and Pronouns

• Heidi, Chapter 4

Nouns and pronouns have four properties. They are **number, gender, person,** and **case**.

- **Number** simply means that nouns and pronouns are either singular or plural.

- **Gender** means that nouns and pronouns can be either masculine—having to do with males; feminine—having to do with females; or neuter—neither male nor female.

- **Person** tells us the identity of the subject—first person, second person, or third person.

- **Case** is the change in form based on a noun or pronoun's job in a sentence. You had a lesson on noun and pronoun cases and learned that different pronouns are used for nominative/subjective case, possessive case, and objective case. Nouns keep the same form for nominative/subjective case and objective case, but they change form for possessive case by adding *'s*.

Sometimes when speaking or writing, we don't know whether the subject is male or female. Think of the word **someone**. We know **someone** is singular, but the word could refer to either a male or a female person. So how do we add a possessive pronoun to this sentence?

Someone left _____ book.

The traditional way is to use the masculine pronoun when gender is not known, so the sentence could read:

Someone left his book.

But nowadays, the feminine pronoun can also be used, so the sentence could read:

Someone left her book.

Some people prefer to say:

Someone left <u>his or her</u> book.

Sometimes, we can avoid the whole issue by saying it in a different way.

Someone left <u>a</u> book.

That will not always work, though, so you should ask your instructor which form you should use.

<u>Pronouns</u> and <u>their</u> antecedents must agree in number, gender, and person. This helps the reader understand to which noun a pronoun refers.

Evening

By Hilda Conkling

Now it is dusky,
And the hermit thrush and the black and white warbler
Are singing and answering together.
There is sweetness in the tree,
And fireflies are counting the leaves.

I like this country,
I like the way it has,
But I cannot forget my dream I had of the sea,
The gulls swinging and calling,
And the foamy towers of the waves.

The Story of a Dam

From *South-African Folk-Tales* by James A. Honey

Part II

The next day, when Jackal came, he approached the water very cautiously and wondered to find no one there. He then ventured to the entrance of the water and remarked how kind they had been in placing there a large black stepping-stone for him. However, as soon as he trod upon the supposed stone, he stuck fast and saw that he had been tricked; for Tortoise now put his head out and began to move. Jackal's hind feet being still free, he threatened to smash Tortoise with them if he did not let him go. Tortoise merely answered, "Do as you like."

Jackal thereupon made a violent jump and found, with horror, that his hind feet were now also fast. "Tortoise," said he, "I have still my mouth and teeth left, and I will eat you alive if you do not let me go."

"Do as you like," Tortoise again replied. Jackal, in his endeavors to free himself, at last made a desperate bite at Tortoise and found himself fixed, both head and feet. Tortoise, feeling proud of his successful capture, now marched quietly up to the top of the bank with Jackal on his back so that he could easily be seen by the animals as they came to the water.

They were indeed astonished to find how cleverly the crafty Jackal had been caught; and Tortoise was much praised while the unhappy Baboon was again reminded of his misconduct when set to guard the water.

Jackal was at once condemned to death by Lion; and Hyena was to execute the sentence. Jackal pleaded hard for mercy, but finding this useless, he made a last request to Lion—always, as he said, so fair and just in his dealings—that he should not have to suffer a lingering death.

Lion inquired of him in what manner he wished to die; and he asked that his tail might be shaved and rubbed with a little fat, and that Hyena might then swing him round twice and dash his brains out upon a stone. This, being considered sufficiently fair by Lion, was ordered by him to be carried out in his presence.

When Jackal's tail had been shaved and greased, Hyena caught hold of him with great force, and before he had fairly lifted him from the ground, the cunning Jackal had slipped away from Hyena's grasp and was running for his life, pursued by all the animals.

Lion was the foremost pursuer, and after a great chase, Jackal got under an overhanging precipice and, standing on his hind legs with his shoulders pressed against the rock, called loudly to Lion to help him as the rock was falling and would crush them both. Lion put his shoulders to the rock and exerted himself to the utmost. After some little time Jackal proposed that he should creep slowly out and fetch a large pole to prop up the rock so that Lion could get out and save his life. Jackal did creep out, and left Lion there to starve and die.

Exercise

Review memory work. Copy each sentence below. Double underline the predicate, and underline the subject. Put brackets around any prepositional phrases. Label the part of speech of each word. Noun, N; Proper Noun, PN; Pronoun, PRO; Verb, V; Linking Verb, LV; Adjective, ADJ; Article, ART; Adverb, ADV; Conjunctions, CJ; Prepositions, Prep; Interjections, INJ. Diagram each sentence.

"How is it possible?"

"Why, grandmother, can't you see the shutter?"

Heidi would talk about her life.

Writing: Commonplace Book

Add the passage below from your model story to your commonplace book.

> The Tortoise meanwhile kept going, slowly but steadily, and after a time, passed the place where the Hare was sleeping. But the Hare slept on very peacefully; and when at last he did wake up, the Tortoise was near the goal. The Hare now ran his swiftest, but he could not overtake the Tortoise in time.

Dictation

Use part of today's poem for dictation.

72. Slant Narrative: The Hare and the Tortoise

- Heidi, Chapter 5

Today, use your outline to write "The Hare and the Tortoise" as a slant narrative. Write it in the first person. Who are you—the tortoise or the hare? Remember to watch your pronouns. And do not be objective! Cast blame, make accusations, and show how *you* were not at fault!

Upon the Road to Rockabout

By C. J. Dennis

Upon the road to Rockabout
I came upon some sheep—
A large and woolly flock about
As wide as it was deep.

I was about to turn about
To ask the man to tell
Some things I wished to learn about
Both sheep and wool as well,

When I beheld a rouseabout
Who lay upon his back
Beside a little house about
A furlong from the track.

I had a lot to talk about,
And said to him "Good day."
But he got up to walk about,
And so I went away—

Editing

- Did you meet the goal of this writing exercise?

- Look at your word choice. Is there a good mixture of nouns and pronouns? Is the antecedent of each pronoun clear?

- Look at your paragraphs. Are all the sentences related? Does each paragraph focus on a single topic?

73. Collective Nouns

• Heidi, Chapter 6

> Definition: A collective noun is a noun which refers to a group of individuals. Collective nouns are usually treated as singular nouns in American English.

A collective noun is a group of nouns. **Family, team,** and **orchestra** are all collective nouns. Each is made up of a group of people.

Although there can be many members of a group, the group itself is singular in nature. This leads to an important question: Do we use singular or plural verbs and pronouns with collective nouns?

In American English, we generally treat collective nouns as singular.

Heidi's family lives in the mountain region.

They live in the mountain region.

In the first sentence, **family** is a collective noun. Though the family is made up of more than one person, since family is a singular group, it takes a singular verb. The same rule tells whether to use singular or plural pronouns.

Clara's household has **its** own set of rules.

They have **their** own set of rules.

Household is a group made up of everyone who lives in a house, but since it is a singular group, it uses a singular pronoun since pronouns and their antecedents must agree in number.

Some other common collective nouns are army, audience, board, cabinet, committee, company, corporation, council, department, faculty, firm, group, jury, majority, minority, navy, public, school, senate, society.

John Anderson
By Robert Burns

John Anderson, my jo, John,
When we were first acquent
Your locks were like the raven,
Your bonnie brow was brent;
But now your brow is bald, John,
Your locks are like the snow;
But blessings on your frosty pow,
John Anderson, my jo.

John Anderson, my jo, John,
We clamb the hill thegither,
And mony a canty day, John,
We've had wi' ane anither;
Now we maun totter down, John,
But hand in hand we'll go,
And sleep thegither at the foot,
John Anderson, my jo.

Writing: Oral Narration

Read your new model story below, and then give your instructor an oral narration of it.

Snow

From *The Secret of Everyday Things* by Jean Henri Fabre

"Snow has the same origin as rain: it comes from vapor in the atmosphere, especially from vapor rising from the surface of the sea. When a sudden cooling-off takes place in clouds at a high elevation, the condensation of vapor is immediately followed by freezing, which turns water into ice.

"I have already told you that cirrus clouds, which are the highest of all clouds and hence more exposed to cold than the others, are composed of extremely fine needles of ice. Lower clouds, too, if subjected to a sufficient degree of cold, undergo the same transformation. Then there follows a symmetrical grouping of adjacent needles in delicate six-pointed stars which, in greater or less numbers and heaped together at random, make a snowflake. Soon afterward, when it has grown too heavy to float in the air, the flake falls to the ground.

"Examine attentively one that has just fallen on the dark background of your sleeve or cap. You will see a mass of beautiful little starry crystals so graceful in form, so delicate in structure, that the most skilful fingers could never hope to make anything like them. These exquisite formations, which put to shame our poor human artistry, have nevertheless sprung from the haphazard mingling of cloud-masses.

"Such then is the nature of snow, the schoolboy's favorite plaything. From a somber and silent sky, it falls softly, almost perpendicularly. The eye follows it in its fall. Above, in the gray depths, it looks like the confused whirling of a swarm of white insects; below it resembles a shower of down, each flake turning round and round and reaching the ground only after considerable hesitation. If the snowfall continues thus for a little while, everything will be hidden under a sheet of dazzling whiteness.

"Now is the time for dusting the back of a schoolmate with a well-directed snowball, which will bring a prompt reply. Now is the time for rolling up an immense snowball which, turning over and over and creaking as it grows, at last becomes too large to move even under our united efforts. On top of this ball, a similar one will be hoisted, then another still smaller on that, and the whole will be shaped into a grotesque giant having for mustache two large turkey feathers and for arms an old broomstick. But look out for the hands in modeling this masterpiece! More than one young sculptor will hasten to thrust them, aching with cold, into his pockets. But, though inactive himself, he will none the less give the others plenty of advice on how to finish off the colossus.

"Oh, how glorious is a holiday when there is snow on the ground! If I were to let myself go, how eloquent I could be on the subject! But, after all, what could I say that would be new to you? You know better than I all about the games appropriate to the occasion. You belong to the present, and I to the past; you make the snowman now and here; I only tell about it from memory. We shall do better to go on with our modest studies, in which I can be of some help to you.

"From snow to hail is a short step, both being nothing but atmospheric vapor turned to ice by cold. But while snow is in delicate flakes, hail takes the form of hard pellets of ice called hailstones. These vary greatly in size, from that of a tiny pinhead to that of a pea, a plum, a pigeon's egg, and larger.

"Hail often does much harm. The icy pellets, hard as stone, in falling from the clouds gain speed enough to make them break windowpanes, bruise the unfortunate person not under cover, and cut to pieces in a few minutes harvests, vineyards, and fruit-crops. It is nearly always in warm weather that hail falls, and as necessary conditions, there must be a violent storm with flashes of lightning and peals of thunder.

"If on the one hand a hailstorm is to be regarded as a disaster, on the other a fall of snow if often to be welcomed as a blessing. Snow slowly saturates the earth with moisture that is of more lasting benefit than a rainfall. It also covers the fields with a mantle that affords protection from severe frost so that the young shoots from seeds recently sown remain green and vigorous instead of being exposed to the deadly sting of the north wind.

"Snow plays still another part, and a very important one, a part having to do with the very existence of our streams. On account of the cold in high regions, it snows more often on the mountains than in the plains. In our latitude, peaks three thousand meters high, or more, are unvisited by rain. Every cloud borne to them by the wind deposits, instead of a shower of rain, a mantle of snow, and that in all seasons of the year, summer as well as winter.

"Driven by the wind or sliding down the steep slopes, this snow from the mountaintops, renewed almost daily, collects in the neighboring valleys and piles up there in drifts hundreds of meters deep, which finally turn to ice as hard and clear as that of the pond where we go skating. In this way there are formed and maintained those masses of moving ice known as glaciers, immense reservoirs of frozen water which abound in all the larger mountain systems.

"In its upper reaches, where the mountain peaks pierce the sky, the glacier is continually receiving fresh snow that comes sliding down the neighboring slopes, while in its lower course, farther down the valley, where the warmth is sufficient, the ice melts and gives rise to a stream which is soon added to by others from neighboring glaciers. In this way the largest rivers are started on their courses.

"From the soil saturated with rain-water and snow-water come springs and brooks and larger streams, each but a slender thread at first, a few drops trickling slowly, a tiny streamlet that one could stop with the hand. But, collecting drop by drop from all around, trickling down the mountainside, a little here and a little there, one thimbleful added to another, one tiny streamlet uniting with its neighbor, at last we have, first, the little brook babbling over its smooth pebbles, then the larger brook that drives the mill-wheel, then the stream on which rides the rowboat, and finally the majestic river carrying to the sea all the drainage of an immense watershed.

"Every drop of water that irrigates the soil comes from the sea, and every drop returns to the sea. The heat of the sun draws the water up in the form of vapor; this vapor goes to make clouds, which the wind scatters in all directions; from these clouds fall rain and snow; and from this rain and snow are formed rivers and other streams which all combine to return to the sea the water thus distributed.

"The water of every spring, well, fountain, lake, pond, marsh, and ditch—all, absolutely all, even to the tiniest mud-puddle and the moisture that bedews a sprig of moss—comes from the sea and returns to it.

"If water cannot run because it is held back in the hollow of some rock, or in a depression in the ground, or in a leaf that has drunk its fill of sap, no matter: the great journey will be accomplished all the same. The sun will turn it to vapor, which will be dissipated in the atmosphere; and, having once started on this broad highway that leads everywhere, sooner or later it must return to the sea.

"I hope now you are beginning to understand all this, except one puzzling detail that must certainly have occurred to you. You wonder how it can be that, sea-water being so salt and so disagreeable to drink, rain-water, snow-water, spring-water, river-water, and so on, should be so tasteless. The answer is easy. Recall to mind the experiment of the plate of salt water placed in the sun. The part that disappears, evaporated by the heat, is pure water and nothing more. What remains in the plate is the salt that water contained, a substance on which evaporation has no hold.

"The same process of evaporation is constantly going on over all the broad expanse of the sea: the water alone is reduced to vapor; the salt remains. From this vapor, purged of all that made the sea-water so disagreeable to the taste, only tasteless water can result."

Exercise

Review memory work. Name the part of the verb marked in the following sentences.

She **is sitting** in a comfortable rolling-chair.

"That's not my business," **grumbled** the coachman.

Copy each sentence below. Double underline the predicate, and underline the subject. Put brackets around any prepositional phrases. Label the part of speech of each word. Noun, N; Proper Noun, PN; Pronoun, PRO; Verb, V; Linking Verb, LV; Adjective, ADJ; Article, ART; Adverb, ADV; Conjunctions, CJ; Prepositions, Prep; Interjections, INJ. Diagram each sentence.

Sebastian, the butler, soon stood before her.

"Miss Deta, how could you bring this child?"

"I have never heard the name before."

Commonplace Book

With your instructor's approval, add the passage below to your commonplace book, or choose your own passage from a work of fiction. This can be from either school reading or free reading.

> "What a curious child you are," said Clara. "You have come to Frankfurt to stay with me, don't you know that? We shall have our lessons together, and I think it will be great fun when you learn to read. Generally the morning seems to have no end, for Mr. Candidate comes at ten and stays till two."

Dictation

When Miss Rottenmeier found that she was unable to recall Deta, she came back to the children. She was in a very excited mood, for she felt responsible for Heidi's coming and did not know how to cancel this unfortunate step. She soon got up again to go to the dining room, criticizing the butler and giving orders to the maid. Sebastian, not daring to show his rage otherwise, noisily opened the folding doors. When he went up to Clara's chair, he saw Heidi watching him intently. At last she said, "You look like Peter."

74. Subject-Verb Agreement

- Heidi, Chapter 7

Nouns, pronouns, and verbs all possess the property **number**.

Sentences can have more than one verb, and each verb has a subject. Each subject must agree with its verb in number. You have probably already noticed this. In your Copia exercises, you may have tried to change the number of a noun or verb and found that you had to change other words in the sentence, too.

Look at the following sentences from *Heidi*. Change the subject's number without changing the verb's, and see how that sounds. Change the verb's number without changing the subject's, and see how that sounds.

> She was sitting in a comfortable rolling-chair.

> Clara's father leaves the management of the house to this lady.

Subjects and verbs must agree in number.

Each subject must agree with its verb in number. In most cases, this is somewhat automatic for native speakers of a language. However, four situations can cause confusion. We will talk about two of these situations today. In all cases, the solution is to determine the subject of the verb.

The first situation occurs when the subject is separated from the verb by modifiers. Look at these sentences:

> Heidi, Clara, and Mr. Candidate were in the study.

> The group was in the study.

> The group of people was in the study.

In the first sentence, we have a compound subject. This plural subject requires a plural verb, so we use **were**. In the second sentence, the subject is **group**. **Group** is a **collective noun**. While there may be many in a group, the group is singular. This singular subject requires a singular verb, so we use **was**.

In the last sentence, the subject and the verb are divided by a prepositional phrase, and the object of the preposition is plural. Remember, though, that the verb must agree with its subject, and the subject of that sentence is still **group**, a singular noun.

A second situation occurs with conjunctions. When **and** joins two or more subjects, the subject combines to be more than one and needs a plural verb. However, when **or** or **nor** join singular subjects, the subject is not combining. Instead, the conjunction shows a choice, one **or** the other. The subject remains singular, and the sentence needs a singular verb. These rules make perfect sense when you think about it.

Both Heidi and Clara were in the study.

Neither Heidi nor Clara was in the kitchen.

The God of Music
By Edith M. Thomas

The God of Music dwelleth out of doors.
All seasons through his minstrelsy we meet,
Breathing by field and covert haunting-sweet
From organ-lofts in forests old he pours:
A solemn harmony: on leafy floors
To smooth autumnal pipes he moves his feet,
Or with the tingling plectrum of the sleet
In winter keen beats out his thrilling scores.
Leave me the reed unplucked beside the stream.
And he will stoop and fill it with the breeze;
Leave me the viol's frame in secret trees,
Unwrought, and it shall wake a druid theme;
Leave me the whispering shell on Nereid shores.
The God of Music dwelleth out of doors.

Lion's Illness

From *South-African Folk-Tales* by James A. Honey

Lion, it is said, was ill, and they all went to see him in his suffering. But Jackal did not go because the traces of the people who went to see him did not turn back. Thereupon, he was accused by Hyena, who said, "Though I go to look, yet Jackal does not want to come and look at the man's sufferings."

Then Lion let Hyena go, in order that she might catch Jackal; and she did so and brought him.

Lion asked Jackal: "Why did you not come here to see me?"

Jackal said, "Oh, no! When I heard that my uncle was so very ill, I went to the witch (doctor) to consult him, whether and what medicine would be good for my uncle against the pain. The doctor said to me, 'Go and tell your uncle to take hold of Hyena, and draw off her skin, and put it on while it is still warm. Then he will recover.' Hyena is one who does not care for my uncle's sufferings."

Lion followed his advice, got hold of Hyena, drew the skin over her ears while she howled with all her might, and put it on.

Writing: Outline

Write or type an outline of the new model story which you read in the last lesson.

Exercise

Review memory work. Name the part of the verb marked in the following sentences.

"This child **brings** nothing but misfortunes on us."

"I **hear** the fir trees rustle."

Copy each sentence below. Double underline the predicate, and underline the subject. Put brackets around any prepositional phrases. Label the part of speech of each word. Noun, N; Proper Noun, PN; Pronoun, PRO; Verb, V; Linking Verb, LV; Adjective, ADJ; Article, ART; Adverb, ADV; Conjunctions, CJ; Prepositions, Prep; Interjections, INJ. Diagram each sentence.

Where has she gone?

"Where is the tower with the golden dome?"

"Can you open a window for me?"

Commonplace Book

With your instructor's approval, add this part of today's poem to your commonplace book, or choose your own poem.

> The God of Music dwelleth out of doors.
> All seasons through his minstrelsy we meet,
> Breathing by field and covert haunting-sweet
> From organ-lofts in forests old he pours:
> A solemn harmony: on leafy floors
> To smooth autumnal pipes he moves his feet,
> Or with the tingling plectrum of the sleet
> In winter keen beats out his thrilling scores.

Dictation

No man can serve two masters.

Street of the Bavolle at Honfleur by Claude Monet

Picture Study

1. Read the title and the name of the artist. Study the picture for several minutes, then put the picture away.

2. Describe the picture.

3. Look at the picture again. Do you notice any details that you missed before? What do you like or dislike about this painting? Does it remind you of anything?

75. Literary Analysis

• Heidi, Chapter 8

Writing: Literary Analysis

Today you have another literary analysis assignment. Now that you have had some practice, this should be a written assignment, though it can be helpful to talk about your ideas before writing.

With your instructor's approval, choose *Heidi* or one of the other books you are currently reading, and answer the following questions.

What is the book about? Give a brief summary, just a few sentences. Has any part of the book seemed particularly real or particularly unlikely?

A Musical Instrument

By Elizabeth Barrett Browning

"The great god sighed for the cost and the pain."

What was he doing, the great god Pan,
  Down in the reeds by the river?
Spreading ruin and scattering ban,
Splashing and paddling with hoofs of a goat,
And breaking the golden lilies afloat
  With the dragonfly on the river.

He tore out a reed, the great god Pan,
  From the deep cool bed of the river:
The limpid water turbidly ran,
And the broken lilies a-dying lay,
And the dragonfly had fled away,
  Ere he brought it out of the river.

High on the shore sat the great god Pan,
  While turbidly flow'd the river;
And hack'd and hew'd as a great god can,
With his hard bleak steel at the patient reed,
Till there was not a sign of a leaf indeed
  To prove it fresh from the river.

He cut it short, did the great god Pan
  (How tall it stood in the river!),
Then drew the pith, like the heart of a man,
Steadily from the outside ring,
And notched the poor dry empty thing
  In holes, as he sat by the river.

  "This is the way," laugh'd the great god Pan
  (Laugh'd while he sat by the river),
  "The only way, since gods began
To make sweet music, they could succeed."
Then, dropping his mouth to a hole in the reed
  He blew in power by the river.

Sweet, sweet, sweet, O Pan!
  Piercing sweet by the river!
Blinding sweet, O great god Pan!
The sun on the hill forgot to die,
And the lilies reviv'd, and the dragonfly
  Came back to dream on the river.

Yet half a beast is the great god Pan,
  To laugh as he sits by the river,
Making a poet out of a man:
The true gods sigh for the cost and pain,—
For the reed which grows nevermore again
  As a reed with the reeds in the river.

The Man and Snake

From *South-African Folk-Tales* by James A. Honey

  A Dutchman was walking by himself and saw Snake lying under a large stone. Snake implored his help; but when she had become free, she said, "Now I shall eat you."
  The Man answered, "That is not right. Let us first go to Hare."
  When Hare had heard the affair, he said, "It is right."
  "No," said the Man. "Let us ask Hyena."
  Hyena declared the same, saying, "It is right."
  "Now let us ask Jackal," said the Man in his despair.
  Jackal answered very slowly and considerately, doubting the whole affair, and demanding to see first the place, and whether the Man was able to lift the stone. Snake lay down, and the Man, to prove the truth of his account, put the stone again over her.
  When she was fast, Jackal said, "Now let her lie there."

Exercise

Review memory work. Punctuate the following sentence.

Oh please Mr. Candidate can't we just peep in

Identify each group of words below as either a phrase or a clause. If it is a clause, double underline the predicate and underline the subject. Remember to find the verb first! Then ask who or what did the action.

the furious lady proceeded

whispered the frightened child

for mercy's sake

Copy each sentence below. Double underline the predicate, and underline the subject. Put brackets around any prepositional phrases. Label the part of speech of each word. Noun, N; Proper Noun, PN; Pronoun, PRO; Verb, V; Linking Verb, LV; Adjective, ADJ; Article, ART; Adverb, ADV; Conjunctions, CJ; Prepositions, Prep; Interjections, INJ. Diagram each sentence.

Sebastian obediently pulled the boy after him.

Clara, on the contrary, enjoyed her companion's society.

"Bring the unlucky child up!"

Commonplace Book

With your instructor's approval, add the passage below to your commonplace book, or choose your own passage from a work of non-fiction. This can be from religious scriptures, a biography, or one of your history or science books.

> "Stop! Stop!" she called, but in vain, for the music drowned her voice. Suddenly she made a big jump, for there, between her feet, crawled a black turtle. Only when she shrieked for Sebastian could her voice be heard. The butler came straight in, for he had seen everything behind the door, and a great scene it had been!

76. Comparatives

• Heidi, Chapter 9

Definition: Comparative adjectives and adverbs compare two things.

We use **comparative adjectives** to compare two nouns and **comparative adverbs** to compare two adjectives or verbs.

To make comparatives of one-syllable words, we add the ending *-er*. Look at the following examples:

Adjectives: cold, colder; hot, hotter

The wind was **cold**, but the ice was **colder**.

Adverbs: hard, harder; fast, faster

That boy ran **fast**, but the other boy ran **faster**.

In two-syllable adjectives which end in *y*, we add *-er* after changing the *y* to *i*.

Adjectives: wavy, wavier; dry, drier; happy, happier

We are so **happy** that we cannot imagine being any **happier**.

Adverbs: early, earlier

The **early** bird wanted the worm, but the **earlier** bird got it.

For other words with two or more syllables, adjectives and adverbs, we don't change the form. Instead, we add the word **more**.

Adjectives: radiant, more radiant; comfortable, more comfortable

I am **comfortable** now, but I was **more comfortable** then.

Adverbs: carefully, more carefully; horribly, more horribly

She moved the boxes **carefully** and the eggs even **more carefully**.

Look at the examples of comparatives in the following sentences from *Heidi*:

They will be much **softer** than those stale ones you have kept.

The grandmother exclaimed every time **more joyfully**.

But the teacher had **more serious** troubles still.

The Harp That Once Through Tara's Halls

By Thomas Moore

The harp that once through Tara's halls
  The soul of music shed,
Now hangs as mute on Tara's walls
  As if that soul were fled.
So sleeps the pride of former days,
  So glory's thrill is o'er,
And hearts, that once beat high for praise,
  Now feel that pulse no more.

No more to chiefs and ladies bright
  The harp of Tara swells;
The chord alone, that breaks at night,
  Its tale of ruin tells.
Thus Freedom now so seldom wakes,
  The only throb she gives
Is when some heart indignant breaks,
  To show that still she lives.

Lion's Share

From *South-African Folk-Tales* by James A. Honey

Part I

    Lion and Jackal went together a-hunting. They shot with arrows. Lion shot first, but his arrow fell short of its aim; but Jackal hit the game and joyfully cried out, "It has hit."
    Lion looked at him with his two large eyes; Jackal, however, did not lose his countenance, but said, "No, uncle, I mean to say that you have hit." Then they followed the game, and Jackal passed the arrow of Lion without drawing the latter's

attention to it. When they arrived at a crossway, Jackal said: "Dear uncle, you are old and tired; stay here." Jackal went then on a wrong track, beat his nose, and in returning, let the blood drop from it like traces of game. "I could not find anything," he said, "but I met with traces of blood. You had better go yourself to look for it. In the meantime I shall go this other way."

Jackal soon found the killed animal, crept inside of it, and devoured the best portion; but his tail remained outside, and when Lion arrived, he got hold of it, pulled Jackal out, and threw him on the ground with these words: "You rascal!"

Jackal rose quickly again, complained of the rough handling, and asked, "What have I now done, dear uncle? I was busy cutting out the best part."

"Now let us go and fetch our wives," said Lion, but Jackal entreated his dear uncle to remain at the place because he was old. Jackal then went away, taking with him two portions of the flesh, one for his own wife, but the best part for the wife of Lion. When Jackal arrived with the flesh, the children of Lion, seeing him, began to jump, and clapping their hands, cried out: "There comes cousin with flesh!" Jackal threw, grumbling, the worst portion to them, and said, "There, you brood of the big-eyed one!" Then he went to his own house and told his wife immediately to break up the house and to go where the killed game was. Lioness wished to do the same, but he forbade her and said that Lion would himself come to fetch her.

Writing: Copia

Take the following sentence and play with it. Remember that the point is not necessarily to make the sentence better. The point is to play with the sentence and make it different. Make a new sentence for each number, using at least one change from that category.

> "Snow has the same origin as rain: it comes from vapor in the atmosphere, especially from vapor rising from the surface of the sea."

1. Change the grammar.
    - Change the nouns from common to proper and vice versa.
    - Change the nouns from singular to plural and vice versa.
    - Change the sentence type.
    - Change the adjectives from articles to descriptive to possessive, etc.
    - Change a quotation from direct to indirect and vice versa.
    - Change the verb tense.

2. Condense the sentence.
    - Remove details.
    - Remove modifiers.
    - Remove phrases or clauses.

3. Amplify the sentence.
    - Add details.
    - Add dialogue.
    - Add modifiers.
    - Add phrases or clauses.

4. Use synonyms and antonyms.
    - Substitute synonyms.
    - Say the opposite thing using antonyms.

5. Point of view.
   - Change the point of view.
   - Slant the sentence.

Exercise

Review memory work. Copy each sentence below. Double underline the predicate, and underline the subject. Put brackets around any prepositional phrases. Label the part of speech of each word. Noun, N; Proper Noun, PN; Pronoun, PRO; Verb, V; Linking Verb, LV; Adjective, ADJ; Article, ART; Adverb, ADV; Conjunctions, CJ; Prepositions, Prep; Interjections, INJ. Diagram each sentence.

"How do you mean?"

"Oh, Mr. Sesemann, we have been terribly disappointed."

"I thought of this Swiss child."

Commonplace Book

With your instructor's approval, add the passage below to your commonplace book, or choose your own passage from a work of fiction. This can be from either school reading or free reading.

> Clara now began to relate to her father all the incidents with the kittens and the turtle and explained Heidi's speeches that had so frightened the lady. Mr. Sesemann laughed heartily and asked Clara if she wished Heidi to remain.

Dictation

But this was impossible for Mr. Candidate, who had to greet Mr. Sesemann first. Then he began to reassure his host about the child, pointing out to him that her education had been neglected till then, and so on. But poor Mr. Sesemann, unfortunately, did not get his answer and had to listen to very long-winded explanations of the child's character. At last Mr. Sesemann got up, saying: "Excuse me, Mr. Candidate, but I must go over to Clara now."

77. Superlatives

• Heidi, Chapter 10

Definition: Superlative adjectives and adverbs
compare three or more things.

We use **superlative adjectives** to compare three or more nouns and **superlative adverbs** to compare three or more adjectives or verbs.

To make superlatives of one-syllable words, we add the ending *-est*. Look at the following examples:

Adjectives: cold, colder, coldest; hot, hotter, hottest

The wind was **cold**; the water was **colder**; and the ice was **coldest**.

Adverbs: hard, harder, hardest; fast, faster, fastest

That boy ran **fast**; the other boy ran **faster**; but the girl ran **fastest**.

In two-syllable adjectives which end in *y*, we add *-est* after changing the *y* to *i*.

Adjectives: wavy, wavier, waviest; dry, drier, driest; happy, happier, happiest

We were so **happy** that we could imagine being any **happier**, yet today we are the **happiest** of all.

Adverbs: early, earlier, earliest

The **early** bird wanted the worm, and so did the **earlier** bird, but the **earliest** bird of all got the prize.

For other words with two or more syllables, adjectives and adverbs, we don't change the form. Instead, we add the word **most**.

Adjectives: radiant, more radiant, most radiant; comfortable, more comfortable, most comfortable

That chair is **comfortable**, and the other chair is **more comfortable**, but this chair is the **most comfortable** of all.

Adverbs: carefully, more carefully, most carefully; horribly, more horribly, most horribly

She moved the boxes **carefully**, the eggs even **more carefully**, and the dynamite the **most carefully** of all.

Some adjectives and adverbs are **irregular**, meaning they do not follow the normal form. Here are a few irregular adjectives:

Adjective	Comparative	Superlative
good	better	best
bad	worse	worst
little	less	least
many	more	most

And here are a few irregular adverbs:

Adverb	Comparative	Superlative
well	better	best
badly	worse	worst
much	more	most

Look at the examples of superlatives in the following sentences from *Heidi*:

He found Miss Rottenmeier surveying the table with a **most tragic** face.

"This child has brought the **most frightful** animals into the house."

"She has not the **slightest** desire to do something useful."

Thunder Shower

By Hilda Conkling

The dark cloud raged.
Gone was the morning light.
The big drops darted down:
The storm stood tall on the rose-trees:

And the bees that were getting honey
Out of wet roses,
The hiding bees would not come out of the flowers
Into the rain.

Lion's Share

From *South-African Folk-Tales* by James A. Honey

Part II

When Jackal, with his wife and children, arrived in the neighborhood of the killed animal, he ran into a thorn bush, scratched his face so that it bled, and thus made his appearance before Lion, to whom he said, "Ah! What a wife you have got. Look here, how she scratched my face when I told her that she should come with us. You must fetch her yourself; I cannot bring her." Lion went home very angry. Then Jackal said, "Quick, let us build a tower." They heaped stone upon stone, stone upon stone, stone upon stone; and when it was high enough, everything was carried to the top of it. When Jackal saw Lion approaching with his wife and children, he cried out to him:

"Uncle, while you were away, we have built a tower, in order to be better able to see game."

"All right," said Lion. "But let me come up to you."

"Certainly, dear uncle; but how will you manage to come up? We must let down a thong for you."

Lion tied the thong around his body, and Jackal began drawing him up, but when he was nearly to the top, Jackal cried to Lion, "My, uncle, how heavy you are!" Then, unseen by Lion, he cut the thong. Lion fell to the ground while Jackal began loudly and angrily to scold his wife, and then said, "Go, wife, fetch me a new thong"—"an old one," he said aside to her.

Lion again tied himself to the thong, and just as he was near the top, Jackal cut the thong as before; Lion fell heavily to the bottom, groaning aloud, as he had been seriously hurt.

"No," said Jackal, "that will never do: you must, however, manage to come up high enough so that you may get a mouthful at least." Then aloud he ordered his wife to prepare a good piece, but aside he told her to make a stone hot and to cover it with fat. Then he drew Lion up once more and, complaining how heavy he was to hold, told him to open his mouth, and thereupon threw the hot stone down his throat. Lion fell to the ground and lay there pleading for water while Jackal climbed down and made his escape.

Exercise

Review memory work. Name the part of the verb marked in the following sentences.

"What **have** you **learned**, child, tell me?"

"I **am going** to tell you something, Heidi."

Copy each sentence below. Double underline the predicate, and underline the subject. Put brackets around any prepositional phrases. Label the part of speech of each word. Noun, N; Proper Noun, PN; Pronoun, PRO; Verb, V; Linking Verb, LV; Adjective, ADJ; Article, ART; Adverb, ADV; Conjunctions, CJ; Prepositions, Prep; Interjections, INJ. Diagram each sentence.

"Rottenmeier, where is the child?"

"When I am going home?" [Hint: **home** tells where.]

Heidi was looking with wondering eyes at the splendid pictures.

Writing: Commonplace Book

Add the passage below from your model story to your commonplace book.

"I have already told you that cirrus clouds, which are the highest of all clouds and hence more exposed to cold than the others, are composed of extremely fine needles of ice. Lower clouds, too, if subjected to a sufficient degree of cold, undergo the same transformation. Then there follows a symmetrical grouping of adjacent needles in delicate six-pointed stars which, in greater or less numbers and heaped together at random, make a snowflake."

Dictation

Use part of today's poem for dictation.

78. Scientific Narration: Snow

• Heidi, Chapter 11

Your next three narrations will be on scientific topics. The model stories are from Jean Henri Fabre's *The Secret of Everyday Things*. In his book, the character of Uncle Paul is explaining these scientific concepts to a group of children. The stories are written in the first person with frequent use of the second person as he speaks directly to the children.

Use your outline to write a narration on this topic. Do not include references to the children or Uncle Paul; just write about the topic. Your narration should be in the third person. You may use other sources for more details if desired. You will need to decide which details are important to your narration and which ones should be left out.

Red Cross Song
By Hilda Conkling

When I heard the bees humming in the hive,
They were so busy about their honey,
I said to my mother,
What can I give,
What can I give to help the Red Cross?
And Mother said to me:
You can give honey too!
Honey of smiles!
Honey of love!

Editing

- Did you meet the goal of this writing exercise?

- Look at your word choice. Is there a good mixture of nouns and pronouns? Is the antecedent of each pronoun clear?

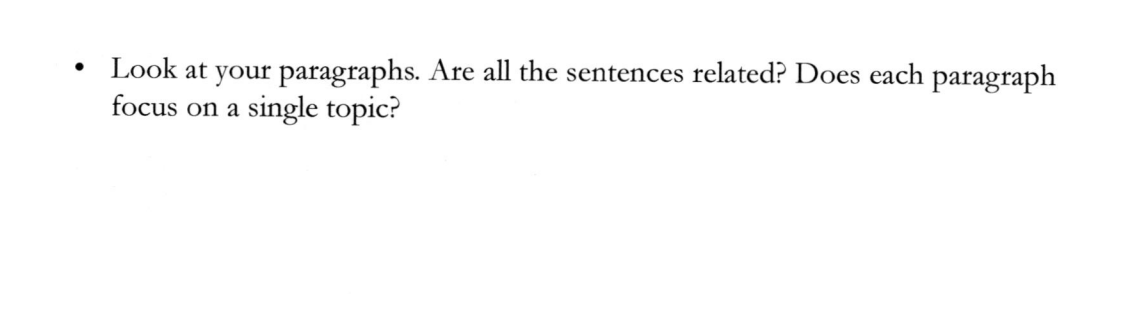

- Look at your paragraphs. Are all the sentences related? Does each paragraph focus on a single topic?

79. Irregular Verbs

• Heidi, Chapter 12

Many common verbs are irregular. Irregular verbs do not have principal parts which follow the normal pattern, and they sometimes have irregular conjugations.

Participle just means a word formed from a verb. Participles can act as other parts of speech. To act as a verb, a participle requires a helping verb.

"Something secret and horrible has happened in this house."

"Tell me honestly if you have played the ghost for Miss Rottenmeier's pastime?"

With regular verbs, the past participle is made up of the past tense form. You will see it used without a helping verb. It is the past tense then, not the past participle.

When the doctor laughed, Mr. Sesemann continued.

This becomes more important with irregular verbs. Irregular verbs have irregular past participles, and some of these words are never used as verbs without a helping verb, such as **gone**, **done**, and **seen**.

I have gone; she has done; they have seen.

"It went up and was gone in a moment," gasped John.

"Come with me now to see what you have done."

They went upstairs to report to the housekeeper what they had seen.

See the chart on the next page which shows the principal parts of some irregular verbs.

Infinitive	Present	Present Participle	Past	Past Participle
to go	go	going	went	gone
to do	do	doing	did	done
to see	see	seeing	saw	seen
to come	come	coming	came	come
to have	have	having	had	had

Contentment

By Edward Dyer

My mind to me a kingdom is;
  Such perfect joy therein I find
As far excels all earthly bliss
  That God or Nature hath assigned;
Though much I want that most would have,
Yet still my mind forbids to crave.

Content I live; this is my stay,—
  I seek no more than may suffice.
I press to bear no haughty sway;
  Look, what I lack my mind supplies.
Lo, thus I triumph like a king,
Content with that my mind doth bring.

I laugh not at another's loss,
  I grudge not at another's gain;
No worldly wave my mind can toss;
  I brook that is another's bane.
I fear no foe, nor fawn on friend;
I loathe not life, nor dread mine end.

My wealth is health and perfect ease;
  My conscience clear my chief defense;
I never seek by bribes to please
  Nor by desert to give offense.
Thus do I live, thus will I die;
Would all did so as well as I!

Writing: Oral Narration

Read your new model story below, and then give your instructor an oral narration of it.

Silk

From *The Secret of Everyday Things* by Jean Henri Fabre

The culture of the silkworm having been explained by Uncle Paul in one of his previous talks, he now confined himself chiefly to the structure of the cocoon and the unwinding of the delicate silk thread composing it.

"The cocoon of the silkworm," he began, "is composed of two envelopes: an outer one of very coarse gauze and an inner one of very fine fabric. This latter is the cocoon properly so called, and from it alone is obtained the silk thread so highly valued in manufacture and commerce, whereas the other, owing to its irregular structure, cannot be unwound and furnishes only an inferior grade of silk suitable for carding.

"The outer envelope is fastened by some of its threads to the little twigs amid which the worm has taken its position and forms merely a sort of scaffolding or openwork hammock wherein the worm seeks seclusion and establishes itself for the serious and delicate task of spinning its inner envelope. When, accordingly, the hammock is ready, the worm fixes its hind feet in the threads and proceeds to raise and bend its body, carrying its head from one side to the other and emitting from its spinneret as it does so a tiny thread which, by its sticky quality, immediately adheres to the points touched. Without change of position, the caterpillar thus lays one thickness of its web over that portion of the enclosure which it faces. Then it turns to another part and carpets that in the same manner. After the entire enclosure has thus been lined, other layers are added, to the number of five or six or even more. In fact, the process goes on until the store of silk-making material is exhausted and the thickness of the wall is sufficient for the security of the future chrysalis.

"From the way the caterpillar works, you will see that the thread of silk is not wound in circles, as it is in a ball of cotton, but is arranged in a series of zigzags, back and forth, and to right and left. Yet in spite of these abrupt changes in direction and notwithstanding the length of the thread—from three hundred to five hundred meters—there is never any break in its continuity. The silkworm gives it forth uninterruptedly without suspending for a moment the work of its spinneret until the cocoon is finished. This cocoon has an average weight of a decigram and a half, and it would take only fifteen or twenty kilograms of the silk thread to extend ten thousand leagues, or once around the earth.

"Examined under the microscope, the thread is seen to be an exceedingly fine tube, flattened and with an irregular surface, and composed of three distinct concentric layers, of which the innermost one is pure silk. Over this is laid a varnish that resists the action of warm water, but dissolves in a weak alkaline solution. Finally, on the outside there is a gummy coating which serves to bind the zigzag courses firmly together and thus to make of them a substantial envelope.

"As soon as the caterpillars have completed their tasks, the cocoons are gathered from the sprigs of heather. A few of these cocoons, selected from those that show the best condition, are set aside and left for the completion of the metamorphosis. The resulting butterflies furnish the eggs or 'seeds' whence, next year, will come the new litter of worms. The rest of the cocoons are immediately subjected to the action of very hot steam, which kills the chrysalis in each just when the tender flesh is beginning slowly to take form. Without this precaution, the butterfly would break through the cocoon, which, no longer capable of being unwound, because of its broken strands, would lose all its value.

"The cocoons are unwound in workrooms fitted up for the purpose. First the cocoons are put into a pan of boiling water to dissolve the gum which holds together the several courses of thread. An operator equipped with a small broom of heather twigs stirs the cocoons in the water in order to find and seize the end of the thread, which is then attached to a reel in motion. Under the tension thus exerted by the machine, the thread of the silk unwinds while the cocoon jumps up and down in the warm water like a ball of worsted when you pull at the loose end of the yarn. In the heart of the unwound cocoon there remains a chrysalis, inert, killed by the steam.

"Since a single strand would not be strong enough for the purpose of weaving, it is usual to unwind all at once a number of cocoons, from three to fifteen and even more, according to the thickness of the fabric for which the silk is destined; and these united strands are used later as one thread in the weaving machines.

"As it comes from the pan, the raw silk of the cocoon is found to have shed its coating of gum, which has become dissolved in the hot water; but it is still coated with its natural varnish, which gives it its firmness, its elasticity, its color, often of a golden yellow. In this state it is called raw silk and has a yellow or white appearance according to the color of the cocoons from which it came. In order to take in the dye that is to enhance its brilliance and add to its value, the silk must first be cleansed of its varnish by a gentle washing in a solution of lye and soap in warm water. This process causes it to lose about a quarter of its weight and to become a beautiful white, whatever may have been its original color. After this purifying process, it is called washed silk or finished silk. Finally, if perfect whiteness is desired, the silk is exposed to the action of sulphur, as I will explain to you when we come to the subject of wool.

"Cocoons that have been punctured by the butterfly, together with all scraps and remnants that cannot be disentangled and straightened out, are carded and thus reduced to a sort of fluff known as floss-silk, which is spun on the distaff or the spinning-wheel very much as wool is treated; but even with the utmost pains, the thread thus obtained never has the beautiful regularity and the soft fineness of that which is furnished by unwinding the cocoon. It is used for fabrics of inferior quality, for stockings, shoelaces, and corset-laces.

"The silkworm and the tree that feeds it, the mulberry, are indigenous to China, where silk weaving has been practiced for some four or five thousand years. Today, when the highly prized caterpillar is dying out in our part of the world, China and its neighbor Japan are called upon to furnish healthy silkworm eggs. Silk-culture was introduced into Europe from Asia in the year 555 by two monks who came to Constantinople with mulberry plants and silkworm eggs concealed in a hollow cane; for it was strictly forbidden to disseminate abroad an industry that yielded such immense riches."

Exercise

Review memory work. Name the part of the verb marked in the following sentences.

"I want **to speak** to him alone."

"Come here, Sebastian, and tell me honestly, if you **have played** the ghost for Miss Rottenmeier's pastime?"

Copy each sentence below. Double underline the predicate, and underline the subject. Put brackets around any prepositional phrases. Label the part of speech of each word. Noun, N; Proper Noun, PN; Pronoun, PRO; Verb, V; Linking Verb, LV; Adjective, ADJ; Article, ART; Adverb, ADV; Conjunctions, CJ; Prepositions, Prep; Interjections, INJ. Diagram each sentence.

His eyes were lively and kind.

"Have patience, my old friend."

A few bottles of wine stood on the table.

Commonplace Book

With your instructor's approval, add the passage below to your commonplace book, or choose your own passage from a work of fiction. This can be from either school reading or free reading.

"Who is there?" thundered the doctor, approaching the figure. It turned and uttered a low shriek. There stood Heidi, with bare feet and in her white nightgown, looking bewildered at the bright light and the weapons. She was shaking with fear, while the two men were looking at her in amazement.

Dictation

"Really! Tell me, what did you dream?"
"Oh, I have the same dream every night. I always think I am with my grandfather again and can hear the fir trees roar. I always think how beautiful the stars must be, and then I open the door of the hut, and oh, it is so wonderful! But when I wake up I am always in Frankfurt." Heidi had to fight the sobs that were rising in her throat.

80. Tenses: Negatives and Questions

- Heidi, Chapter 13

The simple past tense is formed by adding **-ed** to regular verbs. The simple future tense is formed by adding the word **will** to the base verb.

The helping verb **will** makes it easy to form negatives and questions in the future tense. Look at the following sentence from *Heidi*.

"If you show my card, they will give you good accommodations."

We can easily change it to a negative by adding the word **not**:

"If you show my card, they will not give you good accommodations."

And we can easily change it into a question by changing the word order:

"If you show my card, will they give you good accommodations?"

But how can we form negatives and questions from sentences in the past tense like this one?

He stepped into the cottage.

We use the helping verb **did** and drop the **-ed** ending. It allows us to form negatives in the past tense:

He did not step into the cottage.

And we can ask questions in the past tense like this one:

Did he step into the cottage?

The Old Oaken Bucket

By Samuel Woodworth

How dear to this heart are the scenes of my childhood,
  When fond recollection presents them to view!

The orchard, the meadow, the deep-tangled wild-wood,
  And every loved spot which my infancy knew!
The wide-spreading pond, and the mill that stood by it,
  The bridge, and the rock where the cataract fell,
The cot of my father, the dairy-house nigh it,
  And e'en the rude bucket that hung in the well—
The old oaken bucket, the iron-bound bucket,
The moss-covered bucket which hung in the well.

That moss-covered vessel I hailed as a treasure,
  For often at noon, when returned from the field,
I found it the source of an exquisite pleasure,
  The purest and sweetest that nature can yield.
How ardent I seized it, with hands that were glowing,
  And quick to the white-pebbled bottom it fell;
Then soon, with the emblem of truth overflowing,
  And dripping with coolness, it rose from the well—
The old oaken bucket, the iron-bound bucket,
The moss-covered bucket arose from the well.

How sweet from the green mossy brim to receive it
  As poised on the curb it inclined to my lips!
Not a full blushing goblet could tempt me to leave it,
  The brightest that beauty or revelry sips.
And now, far removed from the loved habitation,
  The tear of regret will intrusively swell.
As fancy reverts to my father's plantation,
  And sighs for the bucket that hangs in the well—
The old oaken bucket, the iron-bound bucket,
The moss-covered bucket that hangs in the well!

Elephant and Tortoise

From *South-African Folk-Tales* by James A. Honey

  Two powers, Elephant and Rain, had a dispute.
  Elephant said, "If you say that you nourish me, in what way is it that you say so?"
  Rain answered, "If you say that I do not nourish you, when I go away, will you not die?" And Rain then departed.
  Elephant said, "Vulture! Cast lots to make rain for me."
  Vulture said, "I will not cast lots."
  Then Elephant said to Crow, "Cast lots!"
  Crow answered, "Give the things with which I may cast lots." Crow cast lots and rain fell. It rained at the lagoons, but they dried up, and only one lagoon remained.
  Elephant went a-hunting. There was, however, Tortoise, to whom Elephant said, "Tortoise, remain at the water!" Thus Tortoise was left behind when Elephant went a-hunting.
  There came Giraffe, who said to Tortoise, "Give me water!"
  Tortoise answered, "The water belongs to Elephant."
  There came Zebra, who said to Tortoise, "Give me water!"

Tortoise answered, "The water belongs to Elephant."
There came Gemsbok, who said to Tortoise, "Give me water!"
Tortoise answered, "The water belongs to Elephant."
There came Wildebeest, who said, "Give me water!"
Tortoise said, "The water belongs to Elephant."
There came Roodebok, who said to Tortoise, "Give me water!"
Tortoise answered, "The water belongs to Elephant."
There came Springbok, who said to Tortoise, "Give me water!"
Tortoise said, "The water belongs to Elephant."
There came Jackal, who said to Tortoise, "Give me water!"
Tortoise said, "The water belongs to Elephant."
There came Lion, who said, "Little Tortoise, give me water!"

When little Tortoise was about to say something, Lion got hold of him and beat him; Lion drank of the water, and since then the animals drink water.

When Elephant came back from the hunting, he said, "Little Tortoise, is there water?"

Tortoise answered, "The animals have drunk the water."

Elephant asked, "Little Tortoise, shall I chew you or swallow you down?"

Little Tortoise said, "Swallow me, if you please!" And Elephant swallowed him whole.

After Elephant had swallowed Little Tortoise, and he had entered his body, he tore off his liver, heart, and kidneys. Elephant said, "Little Tortoise, you kill me."

So Elephant died; but little Tortoise came out of his dead body, and went wherever he liked.

Writing: Outline

Write or type an outline of the new model story which you read in the last lesson.

Exercise

Review memory work. Name the part of the verb marked in the following sentences.

Mr. Sesemann **called** her now.

Sebastian **is feeling** ashamed.

Copy each sentence below. Double underline the predicate, and underline the subject. Put brackets around any prepositional phrases. Label the part of speech of each word. Noun, N; Proper Noun, PN; Pronoun, PRO; Verb, V; Linking Verb, LV; Adjective, ADJ; Article, ART; Adverb, ADV; Conjunctions, CJ; Prepositions, Prep; Interjections, INJ. Diagram each sentence.

Heidi looked up to him in amazement. [Hint: **up to** is a two word preposition.]

Heidi was dressed in her Sunday frock.

"Why don't you give it to me?"

Commonplace Book

With your instructor's approval, add this part of today's poem to your commonplace book, or choose your own poem.

> How dear to this heart are the scenes of my childhood,
>   When fond recollection presents them to view!
> The orchard, the meadow, the deep-tangled wild-wood,
>   And every loved spot which my infancy knew!
> The wide-spreading pond, and the mill that stood by it,
>   The bridge, and the rock where the cataract fell,
> The cot of my father, the dairy-house nigh it,
>   And e'en the rude bucket that hung in the well—
> The old oaken bucket, the iron-bound bucket,
> The moss-covered bucket which hung in the well.

Dictation

No man is an island.

A Farmyard in Normandy by Claude Monet

Picture Study

1. Read the title and the name of the artist. Study the picture for several minutes, then put the picture away.

2. Describe the picture.

3. Look at the picture again. Do you notice any details that you missed before? What do you like or dislike about this painting? Does it remind you of anything?

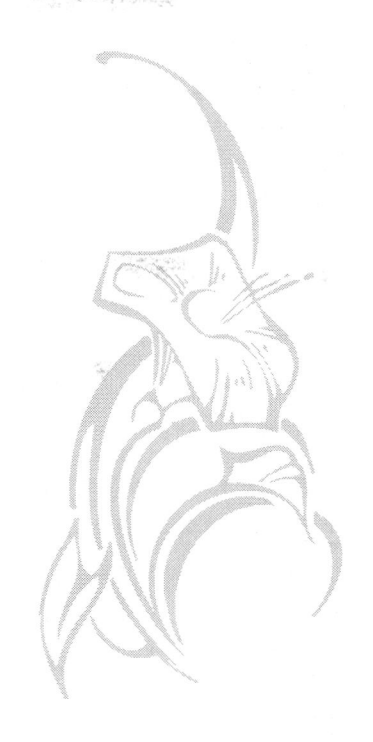

81. Descriptive Writing

• Heidi, Chapter 14

Writing: Descriptive Writing

In the first chapter of *Heidi*, we are given a brief description of the town of Mayenfeld and the footpath that leads up the Alps, of Heidi, and of Deta taking Heidi to her grandfather. Read the opening paragraphs below, paying close attention to the details that make a vivid picture in your mind, and then write a narration of it. What is the landscape like? How is Heidi described? What is the weather like, and how does it affect the little girl?

Add details if you wish. Remember, the point of this exercise is to write as descriptively as possible, not just to narrate the passage exactly.

Heidi

The little old town of Mayenfeld is charmingly situated. From it a footpath leads through green, well-wooded stretches to the foot of the heights which look down imposingly upon the valley. Where the footpath begins to go steeply and abruptly up the Alps, the heath, with its short grass and pungent herbage, at once sends out its soft perfume to meet the wayfarer.

One bright sunny morning in June, a tall, vigorous maiden of the mountain region climbed up the narrow path, leading a little girl by the hand. The youngster's cheeks were in such a glow that it showed even through her sun-browned skin. Small wonder though! For in spite of the heat, the little one, who was scarcely five years old, was bundled up as if she had to brave a bitter frost. Her shape was difficult to distinguish, for she wore two dresses, if not three, and around her shoulders a large red cotton shawl. With her feet encased in heavy hob-nailed boots, this hot and shapeless little person toiled up the mountain.

The pair had been climbing for about an hour when they reached a hamlet halfway up the great mountain named the Alm. This hamlet was called "Im Dörfli" or "The Little Village." It was the elder girl's home town, and therefore she was greeted from nearly every house; people called to her from windows, and doors, and very often from the road. But, answering questions and calls as she went by, the girl did not loiter on her way and only stood still when she reached the end of the hamlet. There a few cottages lay scattered about, from the furthest of which a voice called out to her through an open door: "Deta, please wait one moment! I am coming with you, if you are going further up."

The Skylark

By Thomas Hogg

Bird of the wilderness,
Blithesome and cumberless,
Sweet be thy matin o'er moorland and lea!
Emblem of happiness,
Blest is thy dwelling-place—
Oh, to abide in the desert with thee!

Wild is thy lay and loud,
Far in the downy cloud,
Love gives it energy, love gave it birth.
Where, on thy dewy wing,
Where art thou journeying?
Thy lay is in heaven, thy love is on earth.

O'er fell and fountain sheen,
O'er moor and mountain green,
O'er the red streamer that heralds the day,
Over the cloudlet dim,
Over the rainbow's rim,
Musical cherub, soar, singing, away!

Then, when the gloaming comes,
Low in the heather blooms
Sweet will thy welcome and bed of love be!
Emblem of happiness,
Blest is thy dwelling-place—
Oh, to abide in the desert with thee!

The Jackal and the Wolf

From *South-African Folk-Tales* by James A. Honey

Once on a time Jackal, who lived on the borders of the colony, saw a wagon returning from the seaside laden with fish; he tried to get into the wagon from behind, but he could not; he then ran on before and lay in the road as if dead. The wagon came up to him, and the leader cried to the driver, "Here is a fine kaross for your wife!"

"Throw it into the wagon," said the driver, and Jackal was thrown in.

The wagon traveled on, through a moonlight night, and all the while Jackal was throwing out the fish into the road; he then jumped out himself and secured a great prize. But stupid old Wolf (hyena), coming by, ate more than his share, for which Jackal owed him a grudge, and he said to him, "You can get plenty of fish, too, if you lie in the way of a wagon as I did and keep quite still whatever happens."

"So!" mumbled Wolf.

Accordingly, when the next wagon came from the sea, Wolf stretched himself out in the road. "What ugly thing is this?" cried the leader as he kicked Wolf. He then took a stick and thrashed him within an inch of his life. Wolf, according to the directions of Jackal, lay quiet as long as he could; he then got up and hobbled off to tell his misfortune to Jackal, who pretended to comfort him.

"What a pity," said Wolf. "I have not got such a handsome skin as you have!"

Exercise

Review memory work. Identify each group of words below as either a phrase or a clause. If it is a clause, double underline the predicate and underline the subject.

    to mar the happiness of the child

    after she had carefully wiped it off

    shall I read you a song from your book now

Copy each sentence below. Double underline the predicate, and underline the subject. Put brackets around any prepositional phrases. Label the part of speech of each word. Noun, N; Proper Noun, PN; Pronoun, PRO; Verb, V; Linking Verb, LV; Adjective, ADJ; Article, ART; Adverb, ADV; Conjunctions, CJ; Prepositions, Prep; Interjections, INJ. Diagram each sentence.

    "Have you come again, child?"

    Grandmother's face changed to a joyous expression.

Commonplace Book

With your instructor's approval, add the passage below to your commonplace book, or choose your own passage from a work of non-fiction. This can be from religious scriptures, a biography, or one of your history or science books.

> Heidi's face suddenly shone. "Oh, grandmother, I have an awful lot of money," she cried. "Now I know what I'll do with it. Every day you must have a fresh roll and two on Sundays. Peter can bring them up from the village."
>
> "No, no, child," the grandmother implored. "That must not be. You must give it to grandfather, and he'll tell you what to do with it."

82. To Be

• Heidi, Chapter 15

The verb **to be** is the basic verb form of the state of being verbs. It is one of the most common irregular verbs. These are the principal parts of **to be**:

Infinitive	Simple Present	Present Participle	Simple Past	Past Participle
to be	am/are/is	being	was/were	been

In the simple present, we conjugate **to be** like this:

to be	Singular	Plural
1st Person	I am	we are
2nd Person	you are	you are
3rd Person	he, she, or it is	they are

To be is an irregular verb in all of its tenses, and it has an irregular past participle. The future tense is just **will be**. I will be, you will be, he will be, etc., like this:

to be (future tense)	Singular	Plural
1st Person	I will be	we will be
2nd Person	you will be	you will be
3rd Person	he, she, or it will be	they will be

Its past tense form, however, must be conjugated, like this:

to be (past tense)	Singular	Plural
1st Person	I was	we were
2nd Person	you were	you were
3rd Person	he, she, or it was	they were

Now that you can conjugate **to be**, it's probably obvious why **be, being,** and **been** are also part of our state of being verbs. These are also forms of the verb **to be**.

Remember that when we use **to be** as a linking verb, it can include helping verbs. Look at the following sentences from *Heidi*:

The blooming girl had been his only joy.

"That would have been ungrateful."

All of the above verb forms are linking verbs because they end in a form of **to be**; **to be** is the main verb. What does that make the nouns and adjectives which follow the linking verbs?

Subject complements follow the linking verbs. The nouns are predicate nominatives, and the adjectives are predicate adjectives.

The Englishman

By Walter De La Mare

I met a sailor in the woods,
A silver ring wore he,
His hair hung black, his eyes shone blue,
And thus he said to me:—

'What country, say, of this round earth,
What shore of what salt sea,
Be this, my son, I wander in,
And looks so strange to me?'

Says I, 'O foreign sailorman,
In England now you be,
This is her wood, and this her sky,
And that her roaring sea.'

He lifts his voice yet louder,
'What smell be this,' says he,
'My nose on the sharp morning air
Snuffs up so greedily?'

Says I, 'It is wild roses
Do smell so winsomely,
And winy briar too,' says I,
'That in these thickets be.'

'And oh!' says he, 'what leetle bird
Is singing in yon high tree,
So every shrill and long-drawn note
Like bubbles breaks in me?'

Says I, 'It is the mavis
That perches in the tree,
And sings so shrill, and sings so sweet,
When dawn comes up the sea.'

At which he fell a-musing,
And fixed his eye on me,
As one alone 'twixt light and dark
A spirit thinks to see.

'England!' he whispers soft and harsh,
'England!' repeated he,
'And briar, and rose, and mavis,
A-singing in yon high tree.

'Ye speak me true, my leetle son,
So—so, it came to me,
A-drifting landwards on a spar,
And grey dawn on the sea.

'Ay, ay, I could not be mistook;
I knew them leafy trees,
I knew that land so witcherie sweet,
And that old noise of seas.

'Though here I've sailed a score of years,
And heard 'em, dream or wake,

Lap small and hollow 'gainst my cheek,
On sand and coral break;

"'Yet now, my leetle son," says I,
A-drifting on the wave,
"That land I see so safe and green
Is England, I believe.

"'And that there wood is English wood,
And this here cruel sea,
The selfsame old blue ocean
Years gone remembers me,

"A-sitting with my bread and butter
Down ahind yon chitterin' mill;
And this same Marinere"—(that's me),
"Is that same leetle Will!—

"That very same wee leetle Will
Eating his bread and butter there,
A-looking on the broad blue sea
Betwixt his yaller hair!"

'And here be I, my son, throwed up
Like corpses from the sea,
Ships, stars, winds, tempests, pirates past,
Yet leetle Will I be!'

He said no more, that sailorman,
But in a reverie
Stared like the figure of a ship
With painted eyes to sea.

The Judgment of Baboon

From *South-African Folk-Tales* by James A. Honey

One day, it is said, the following story happened:

Mouse had torn the clothes of Itkler (the tailor), who then went to Baboon and accused Mouse with these words:

"In this manner I come to thee: Mouse has torn my clothes, but will not know anything of it, and accuses Cat; Cat protests likewise her innocence and says, 'Dog must have done it'; but Dog denies it also and declares Wood has done it; and Wood throws the blame on Fire and says, 'Fire did it'; Fire says, 'I have not; Water did it'; Water says, 'Elephant tore the clothes'; and Elephant says, 'Ant tore them.' Thus a dispute has arisen among them. Therefore, I, Itkler, come to thee with this proposition: Assemble the people and try them in order that I may get satisfaction."

Thus he spake, and Baboon assembled them for trial. Then they made the same excuses which had been mentioned by Itkler, each one putting the blame upon the other.

So Baboon did not see any other way of punishing them save through making them punish each other; he therefore said, "Mouse, give Itkler satisfaction."

Mouse, however, pleaded not guilty. But Baboon said, "Cat, bite Mouse." She did so.

He then put the same question to Cat, and when she exculpated herself, Baboon called to Dog, "Here, bite Cat."

In this manner Baboon questioned them all, one after the other, but they each denied the charge. Then he addressed the following words to them, and said,

"Wood, beat Dog.

Fire, burn Wood.

Water, quench Fire.

Elephant, drink Water.

Ant, bite Elephant in his most tender parts."

They did so, and since that day they cannot any longer agree with each other.

Ant enters into Elephant's most tender parts and bites him.

Elephant swallows Water.

Water quenches Fire.

Fire consumes Wood.

Wood beats Dog.

Dog bites Cat.

And Cat bites Mouse.

Through this judgment Itkler got satisfaction and addressed Baboon in the following manner: "Yes! Now I am content since I have received satisfaction, and with all my heart I thank thee, Baboon, because thou hast exercised justice on my behalf and given me redress."

Then Baboon said, "From today I will not any longer be called Jan, but Baboon shall be my name."

Since that time Baboon walks on all fours, having probably lost the privilege of walking erect through this foolish judgment.

Writing: Copia

Take the following sentence and play with it. Remember that the point is not necessarily to make the sentence better. The point is to play with the sentence and make it different. Make a new sentence for each number, using at least one change from that category.

> "The cocoon of the silkworm," he began, "is composed of two envelopes: an outer one of very coarse gauze and an inner one of very fine fabric."

1. Change the grammar.
   - Change the nouns from common to proper and vice versa.
   - Change the nouns from singular to plural and vice versa.
   - Change the sentence type.
   - Change the adjectives from articles to descriptive to possessive, etc.
   - Change a quotation from direct to indirect and vice versa.
   - Change the verb tense.

2. Condense the sentence.
   - Remove details.
   - Remove modifiers.
   - Remove phrases or clauses.

3. Amplify the sentence.
   - Add details.
   - Add dialogue.
   - Add modifiers.
   - Add phrases or clauses.

4. Use synonyms and antonyms.
   - Substitute synonyms.
   - Say the opposite thing using antonyms.

5. Point of view.
   - Change the point of view.
   - Slant the sentence.

Exercise

Review memory work. Copy each sentence below. Double underline the predicate, and underline the subject. Put brackets around any prepositional phrases. Label the part of speech of each word. Noun, N; Proper Noun, PN; Pronoun, PRO; Verb, V; Linking Verb, LV; Adjective, ADJ; Article, ART; Adverb, ADV; Conjunctions, CJ; Prepositions, Prep; Interjections, INJ. Diagram each sentence.

> "Oh please, doctor, do go to Heidi."

> With shrugging shoulders the doctor replied.

> Clara's eyes had filled with tears.

Commonplace Book

With your instructor's approval, add the passage below to your commonplace book, or choose your own passage from a work of fiction. This can be from either school reading or free reading.

> "Oh please, doctor, do go to Heidi; then you can tell me all about her and can describe her grandfather to me, and Peter, with his goats—I seem to know them all so well. Then you can take all the things to her that I had planned to take myself. Oh, please doctor, go, and then I'll be good and take as much cod-liver oil as ever you want me to."

Dictation

> The doctor had to laugh. "Why don't you chide me for being here still? I shall go as quickly as I can, Sesemann."
> Clara gave many messages to him for Heidi. She also told him to be sure to observe everything closely so that he would be able to tell her all about it when he came back. The things for Heidi were to be sent to him later, for Miss

Rottenmeier, who had to pack them, was out on one of her lengthy wanderings about town.

83. To Do and To Go

• Heidi, Chapter 16

These are the principal parts of **to do**:

Infinitive	Simple Present	Present Participle	Simple Past	Past Participle
to do	do/does	doing	did	done

In the simple present, we conjugate **to do** like this:

to do	Singular	Plural
1st Person	I do	we do
2nd Person	you do	you do
3rd Person	he, she, or it does	they do

To do is an irregular verb in both its present and simple past tenses, and it has an irregular past participle. The future tense is just **will do**. I will do, you will do, he will do, etc. Its past tense form is simply **did**: I did, you did, he did, etc. Look at these sentences from *Heidi*:

"That will do," he interrupted.

"How happy I am to be able to thank you for what you have done, uncle!"

She did many things that had never occurred to her before.

Our next irregular verb is **to go**. These are the principal parts of **to go**:

Infinitive	Simple Present	Present Participle	Simple Past	Past Participle
to go	go/goes	going	went	gone

In the simple present, we conjugate **to go** like this:

to go	Singular	Plural
1st Person	I go	we go
2nd Person	you go	you go
3rd Person	he, she, or it goes	they go

To go is an irregular verb in both its present and simple past tenses, and it has an irregular past participle. The future tense is just **will go**: I will go, you will go, he will go, etc. Its past tense form is simply **went**: I went, you went, he went, etc.

"Who do you think will go way down there to fetch those things up again?"

Since she had gone from him, the ever-cheerful doctor was bowed down with grief.

For the doctor made friends wherever he went.

Remember that the past participle is never used as a verb without a helping verb, and the past participles of **to do** and **to go** are irregular. You should never use their past participles, **done** and **gone**, without a helping verb.

The Dwarf

By Walter De La Mare

'Now, Jinnie, my dear, to the dwarf be off,
That lives in Barberry Wood,
And fetch me some honey, but be sure you don't laugh,—
He hates little girls that are rude, are rude,
He hates little girls that are rude.'

Jane tapped at the door of the house in the wood,
And the dwarf looked over the wall,
He eyed her so queer, 'twas as much as she could

To keep from laughing at all, at all,
To keep from laughing at all.

His shoes down the passage came clod, clod, clod,
And when he opened the door,
He croaked so harsh, 'twas as much as she could
To keep from laughing the more, the more,
To keep from laughing the more.

As there, with his bushy red beard, he stood,
Pricked out to double its size,
He squinted so cross, 'twas as much as she could
To keep the tears out of her eyes, her eyes,
To keep the tears out of her eyes.

He slammed the door, and went clod, clod, clod,
But while in the porch she bides,
He squealed so fierce, 'twas as much as she could
To keep from cracking her sides, her sides,
To keep from cracking her sides.

He threw a pumpkin over the wall,
And melons and apples beside,
So thick in the air, that to see 'em all fall,
She laughed, and laughed, till she cried, cried, cried,
Jane laughed and laughed till she cried.

Down fell her teardrops a pit-apat-pat,
And red as a rose she grew;—
'Kah! Kah!' said the dwarf, 'is it crying you're at?
It's the very worst thing you could do, do, do,
It's the very worst thing you could do.'

He slipped like a monkey up into a tree,
He shook her down cherries like rain;
'See now,' says he, cheeping, 'a blackbird I be,
Laugh, laugh, little Jinnie, again-gain-gain,
Laugh, laugh, little Jinnie, again.'

Ah me! What a strange, what a gladsome duet
From a house i' the deeps of a wood!
Such shrill and such harsh voices never met yet
A-laughing as loud as they could-could-could,
A-laughing as loud as they could.

Come Jinnie, come dwarf, cocksparrow, and bee,
There's a ring gaudy-green in the dell,
Sing, sing, ye sweet cherubs, that flit in the tree;
La! Who can draw tears from a well-well-well,
Who ever drew tears from a well!

The Zebra Stallion

From *South-African Folk-Tales* by James A. Honey

The Baboons, it is said, used to disturb the Zebra Mares in drinking. But one of the Mares became the mother of a foal. The others then helped her to suckle the young stallion so that he might soon grow up.

When he was grown up and they were in want of water, he brought them to the water. The Baboons, seeing this, came, as they formerly were used to do, into their way, and kept them from the water.

While the Mares stood thus, the Stallion stepped forward and spoke to one of the Baboons, "Thou gum-eater's child!"

The Baboon said to the Stallion, "Please open thy mouth that I may see what thou livest on." The Stallion opened his mouth, and it was milky.

Then the Stallion said to the Baboon, "Please open thy mouth also, that I may see." The Baboon did so, and there was some gum in it. But the Baboon quickly licked some milk off the Stallion's tongue. The Stallion on this became angry, took the Baboon by his shoulders, and pressed him upon a hot, flat rock. Since that day the Baboon has a bald place on his back.

The Baboon said, lamenting, "I, my mother's child, I, the gum-eater, am outdone by this milk-eater!"

Exercise

Review memory work. Name the part of the verb marked in the following sentences.

When Heidi at last **reached** her old friend, he held out his hand.

She **caressed** them tenderly.

Copy each sentence below. Double underline the predicate, and underline the subject. Put brackets around any prepositional phrases. Label the part of speech of each word. Noun, N; Proper Noun, PN; Pronoun, PRO; Verb, V; Linking Verb, LV; Adjective, ADJ; Article, ART; Adverb, ADV; Conjunctions, CJ; Prepositions, Prep; Interjections, INJ. Diagram each sentence.

"Are your eyes bright already?"

With an old rag she would rub the chairs and table.

The grandfather had been busy in his little shop.

Writing: Commonplace Book

Add the passage below from your model story to your commonplace book.

"The cocoon of the silkworm," he began, "is composed of two envelopes: an outer one of very coarse gauze and an inner one of very fine fabric. This latter is the cocoon properly so called, and from it alone is obtained the silk thread so highly valued in manufacture and commerce, whereas the other, owing to its irregular structure, cannot be unwound and furnishes only an inferior grade of silk suitable for carding.

Dictation

Use part of today's poem for dictation.

84. Scientific Narration: Silk

• Heidi, Chapter 17

Your model story, "Silk," is from Jean Henri Fabre's *The Secret of Everyday Things*. In his book, the character of Uncle Paul is explaining these scientific concepts to a group of children. The stories are written in the first person with frequent use of the second person as he speaks directly to the children.

Use your outline to write a narration on this topic. Do not include references to the children or Uncle Paul; just write about the topic. Your narration should be in the third person. You may use other sources for more details if desired. You will need to decide which details are important to your narration and which ones should be left out.

Purple Asters

By Hilda Conkling

It isn't alone the asters
In my garden,
It is the butterflies gleaming
Like crowns of kings and queens!
It isn't alone purple
And blue on the edge of purple,
It is what the sun does,
And the air moving clearly,
The petals moving and the wings,
In my queer little garden!

Editing

- Did you meet the goal of this writing exercise?

- Look at your word choice. Is there a good mixture of nouns and pronouns? Is the antecedent of each pronoun clear?

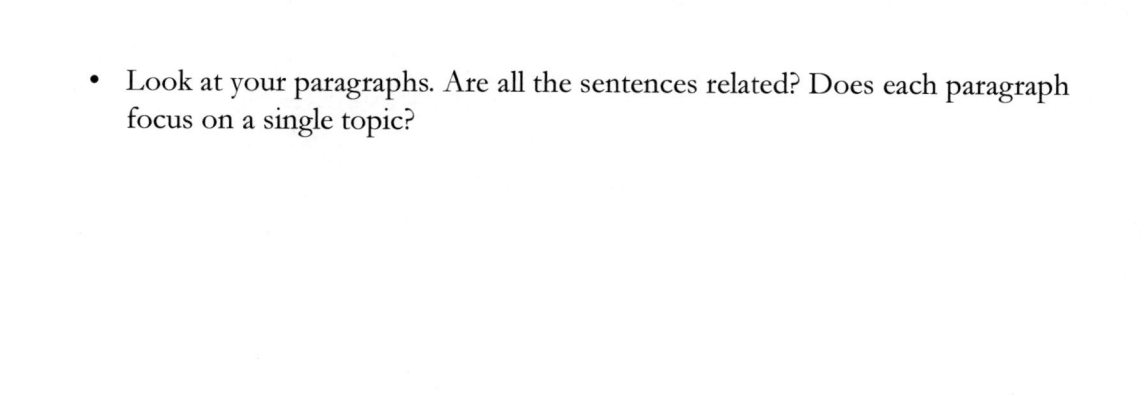

- Look at your paragraphs. Are all the sentences related? Does each paragraph focus on a single topic?

85. To See and To Come

• Heidi, Chapter 18

These are the principal parts of **to see**:

Infinitive	Simple Present	Present Participle	Simple Past	Past Participle
to see	see(s)	seeing	saw	seen

In the simple present, we conjugate **to see** like this:

to see	Singular	Plural
1st Person	I see	we see
2nd Person	you see	you see
3rd Person	he, she, or it sees	they see

To do is an irregular verb in simple past tense, and it has an irregular past participle. The future tense is just **will see**. I will see, you will see, he will see, etc. Its past tense form is simply **saw**: I saw, you saw, he saw, etc. Look at these sentences from *Heidi*:

"Maybe your eyes will see again, too, when you are strong and well."

On one side the remains of a chapel could be seen.

Heidi saw the doctor.

375

Our next irregular verb is **to come**. These are the principal parts of **to come**:

Infinitive	Simple Present	Present Participle	Simple Past	Past Participle
to come	come(s)	coming	came	come

In the simple present, we conjugate **to come** like this:

to come	Singular	Plural
1st Person	I come	we come
2nd Person	you come	you come
3rd Person	he, she, or it comes	they come

To come is an irregular verb in its simple past tense, and it has an irregular past participle. The future tense is just **will come**: I will come, you will come, he will come, etc. Its past tense form is simply **came**: I came, you came, he came, etc. Look at these sentences from *Heidi*:

"Oh, it won't last long till spring comes again; then they will come for sure."

The time had come for him to go back to Frankfurt.

A large hall came next.

Remember that the past participle is never used as a verb without a helping verb. This means that you should never use the word **seen** without a helping verb. Notice, however, that the past participle for **to come** is the same as its simple present.

Rambler Rose

By Hilda Conkling

Rambler Rose in great clusters,
Looking at me, at my mother with me
Under this apple-tree,
Your faces watch us from outside the shade.
The wind blows on you,
The rain drops on you,
The sun shines on you,
You are brighter than before.
You turn your faces to the wind
And watch my mother and me,

Thinking of things I cannot mention
Outside of my mind.
Rambler Rose in the shining wind,
You smile at me,
Smile at my mother!

Writing: Oral Narration

Read your new model story below, and then give your instructor an oral narration of it.

Sound

From *The Secret of Everyday Things* by Jean Henri Fabre

"Give a light blow to a wineglass. The glass will ring, giving forth a sound, weaker or stronger, lower or higher, according to the quality and size of the glass. The sound lasts but a moment and then ceases. Strike the glass once more, and while it is still ringing, touch the rim with your finger. Instantly all is still again; not a sound from the glass. Why does it ring when struck, and why does it stop ringing at the touch of a finger? Before replying let us experiment with other resonant objects.

"A violin string twangs on being scraped by the bow or plucked with the finger, and while it thus gives forth its note, it is seen to vibrate rapidly. So rapid, indeed, is its vibration that it appears to fill the entire space between its extreme positions, with the result that it presents a swollen appearance in the middle, after the manner of a spindle. With the cessation of its vibration, it becomes silent. It also falls silent immediately at the touch of a finger.

"A bell rings on being struck by its clapper, and if observed closely, the substance of the bell will be seen to tremble in an unmistakable manner. Place your hand on the bronze, and you will experience a disagreeable sensation almost amounting to pain, due to the vibration of the metal. Finally, if your hand continues to rest on the bell, the vibration will cease and with it, the sound.

"Let us try something still more remarkable. Take a pin by its pointed end and bring the head very close to a ringing wineglass or bell. You will hear a rapid succession of little taps. Whence do they come? From the glass or the bell metal striking the pin a series of quick blows as long as the ringing continues. They come from the lively trembling of the sonorous object.

"It is unnecessary to cite other examples; these three will suffice. They show that, in order to give forth sound, a wineglass or a bell or a violin string—in short, any object whatever—must be made to tremble or vibrate with great rapidity. The sound is heard as long as the vibration continues and ceases when the vibrating object returns to a state of rest. That explains why the wineglass and the violin string stop sounding at the touch of a finger and why the bell will not ring if you rest your hand against it. The finger in the one instance, the hand in the other, stop the resonant trembling, and in so doing, arrest the sound. Motion causes the sound; rest brings silence.

"To this rapid motion back and forth is given the name I have already used, vibration. An object from which comes a sound is in vibration; it vibrates. Each of its backward and forward movements, too rapid for the eye to follow, is a vibration; and the quicker these vibrations, the higher the note sounded; the slower they are, the lower the note. In a word, sound is motion, and its place in the scale measures the rapidity of that motion.

"In order to be heard, this sound—this motion—must reach us. The hand detects it in its own way when, resting on the vibrating bell, it experiences a very disagreeable thrill; the finger becomes conscious of it in a peculiar manner when, touching the violin string, it feels a ticking sensation. But how does the ear contrive to receive the sound when it is at a distance from the resonant object and apparently in no sort of communication with it?

"At this point let me invite you to join me in a sport very familiar to you all. We will take a big stone and drop it into a calm sheet of water. Around the place where the stone struck the water, there is instantly formed a circle, then another and another, and so on indefinitely; and all these circles, described about the same center and as regular as if drawn with a pair of compasses, grow larger and larger, in successive rings, until they die out at a long distance from their common center—if the sheet of water is large enough.

"Now, do those circles really chase one another over the water's surface as they appear to? One would certainly think so. You remember how fast they go, one ring after another, each in apparent haste to catch up with its predecessor. But the pursued always keep clear of the pursuers, and the distance between the rings remains the same. And so the fact is they are not really chasing one another; they are not, in fact, moving at all; but they have that deceptive appearance, and it will not be hard for us to understand why.

"Let us drop a straw or a dry leaf upon the surface of the water. When one of these concentric circles passes like a wave, the straw or leaf is lifted up, after which the wave goes on and leaves it, and it sinks down again, remaining exactly where it was in the first place. Thus it is proved that the water does not move forward at all, for if it did, it would carry with it the straw or leaf on its surface.

"What, then, are those waves? Mere palpitations of the water as, without changing its place, it gently rises and falls, thus producing a succession of alternate billows and furrows which appear to go chasing after one another. Watch a field of wheat when the wind blows. Its surface undulates in waves that seem to move forward although the wheat stalks remain firmly rooted in the ground. Of like sort is the apparent movement of a sheet of smooth water when disturbed by the fall of a stone.

"The circles of the water and the undulations of the wheat field explain to us the nature of sound. Every object emitting a sound is in rapid vibration, and each of these vibrations causing a shock to the surrounding air and producing a wave which spreads out in all directions, immediately followed by a second, a third, and countless others, all resulting from as many successive vibrations.

"In the air thus shocked by the vibrating body, there takes place exactly what we see in the sheet of smooth water disturbed by a falling stone and in the wheat field ruffled by the wind. Without changing its place, the air undergoes an undulatory movement which is transmitted to great distances. In other words, airwaves are formed which propagate themselves in every direction at once through the atmosphere, thus taking the form, not of circles, but rather of hollow spheres, all having a common center.

"These airwaves are not visible to us because air itself is invisible; but they are none the less real, just as real as waves of water and undulations of a wheat field. If the eye cannot see them, the ear can hear them, for it is from them that sound comes. Hence they are called sound waves. The ear hears when sound waves reach it from any vibrating object."

Exercise

Review memory work. Punctuate the following sentence.

Oh grandfather I have found my bedroom

Copy each sentence below. Double underline the predicate, and underline the subject. Put brackets around any prepositional phrases. Label the part of speech of each word. Noun, N; Proper Noun, PN; Pronoun, PRO; Verb, V; Linking Verb, LV; Adjective, ADJ; Article, ART; Adverb, ADV; Conjunctions, CJ; Prepositions, Prep; Interjections, INJ. Diagram each sentence.

"Now come and look at mine."

Heidi slept very well in her chimney corner.

Was she away from home? [Hint: **away from** is a two word preposition.]

Commonplace Book

With your instructor's approval, add the passage below to your commonplace book, or choose your own passage from a work of fiction. This can be from either school reading or free reading.

> But the grandfather shook his head and said, "You can't go yet, child. The snow is fathoms deep up there and is still falling. Peter can hardly get through. A little girl like you would be snowed up and lost in no time. Wait a while till it freezes, and then you can walk on top of the crust."

Dictation

> With that the grandfather led her into his bedroom. From there a door led into the hugest kitchen Heidi had ever seen. With a great deal of trouble, the grandfather had fitted up this place. Many boards were nailed across the walls, and the door had been fastened with heavy wires, for beyond, the building lay in ruins. Thick underbrush was growing there, sheltering thousands of insects and lizards. Heidi was delighted with her new home, and when Peter arrived next day, she did not rest till he had seen every nook and corner of the curious dwelling place.

86. To Have

• Heidi, Chapter 19

These are the principal parts of **to have**:

Infinitive	Simple Present	Present Participle	Simple Past	Past Participle
to have	have/has	having	had	had

In the simple present, we conjugate **to have** like this:

to see	Singular	Plural
1st Person	I have	we have
2nd Person	you have	you have
3rd Person	he, she, or it has	they have

To have is an irregular verb in simple past tense, and it has an irregular past participle. The future tense is just **will have**. I will have, you will have, he will have, etc. Its past tense form is simply **had**: I had, you had, he had, etc.

"Thank you for your kindness, but you will have to wait in vain."

She must have had a happy dream.

He soon had but three letters left.

Remember that the past participle is never used as a verb without a helping verb. Notice, however, that the past participle for **to have** is **had**, the same as its simple past.

I Remember, I Remember

By Thomas Hood

I remember, I remember
The house where I was born,
The little window where the sun
Came peeping in at morn;
He never came a wink too soon
Nor brought too long a day;
But now, I often wish the night
Had borne my breath away.

I remember, I remember
The roses, red and white,
The violets, and the lily-cups—
Those flowers made of light!
The lilacs where the robin built,
And where my brother set
The laburnum on his birthday,—
The tree is living yet!

I remember, I remember
Where I was used to swing,
And thought the air must rush as fresh
To swallows on the wing;
My spirit flew in feathers then
That is so heavy now,
And summer pools could hardly cool
The fever on my brow.

I remember, I remember
The fir trees dark and high;
I used to think their slender tops
Were close against the sky:
It was a childish ignorance,
But now 'tis little joy
To know I'm farther off from Heaven
Than when I was a boy.

Lion Who Thought Himself Wiser Than His Mother

From *South-African Folk-Tales* by James A. Honey

It is said that when Lion and Gurikhoisip (the Only man), together with Baboon, Buffalo, and other friends, were playing one day at a certain game, there was a thunderstorm and rain at Aroxaams. Lion and Gurikhoisip began to quarrel. "I shall run to the rain field," said Lion.

Gurikhoisip said also, "I shall run to the rain field." As neither would concede this to the other, they separated angrily. After they had parted, Lion went to tell his Mother those things which they had both said.

His Mother said to him, "My son! That Man whose head is in a line with his shoulders and breast, who has pinching weapons, who keeps white dogs, who goes about wearing the tuft of a tiger's tail, beware of him!"

Lion, however, said, "Why need I be on my guard against those whom I know?"

Lioness answered, "My Son, take care of him who has pinching weapons!"

But Lion would not follow his Mother's advice, and the same morning, when it was still pitch dark, he went to Aroxaams and laid himself in ambush. Gurikhoisip went also that morning to the same place. When he had arrived, he let his dogs drink and then bathe. After they had finished, they wallowed. Then also Man drank; and, when he had done drinking, Lion came out of the bush. Dogs surrounded him as his Mother had foretold, and he was speared by Gurikhoisip. Just as he became aware that he was speared, the Dogs drew him down again. In this manner he grew faint.

While he was in this state, Gurikhoisip said to the Dogs, "Let him alone now so that he may go and be taught by his Mother."

So the Dogs let him go. They left him and went home as he lay there. The same night he walked towards home, but while he was on the way, his strength failed him, and he lamented:

> "Mother! Take me up!
> Grandmother! Take me up! Oh me! Alas!"

At the dawn of day, his Mother heard his wailing and said—

> "My Son, this is the thing which I have told thee:
> 'Beware of the one who has pinching weapons,
> Who wears a tuft of tiger's tail,
> Of him who has white dogs!
> Alas! Thou son of her who is short-eared,
> Thou, my short-eared child!
> Son of her who eats raw flesh,
> Thou flesh-devourer;
> Son of her whose nostrils are red from the prey,
> Thou with blood-stained nostrils!
> Son of her who drinks pit-water,
> Thou water-drinker!'"

Writing: Outline

Write or type an outline of the new model story which you read in the last lesson.

Exercise

Review memory work. Name the part of the verb marked in the following sentences.

Peter **began** and read three lines without stopping.

383

"I shall not say **to read**, but to stammer through a line?"

Copy each sentence below. Double underline the predicate, and underline the subject. Put brackets around any prepositional phrases. Label the part of speech of each word. Noun, N; Proper Noun, PN; Pronoun, PRO; Verb, V; Linking Verb, LV; Adjective, ADJ; Article, ART; Adverb, ADV; Conjunctions, CJ; Prepositions, Prep; Interjections, INJ. Diagram each sentence.

"Hurry and learn the three letters."

He came daily to her for his lesson.

"What, is it possible?"

Commonplace Book

With your instructor's approval, add this part of today's poem to your commonplace book, or choose your own poem.

> I remember, I remember
> The house where I was born,
> The little window where the sun
> Came peeping in at morn;
> He never came a wink too soon
> Nor brought too long a day;
> But now, I often wish the night
> Had borne my breath away.
>
> I remember, I remember
> The roses, red and white,
> The violets, and the lily-cups—
> Those flowers made of light!
> The lilacs where the robin built,
> And where my brother set
> The laburnum on his birthday,—
> The tree is living yet!

Dictation

Never look a gift horse in the mouth.

Garden at Sainte Adresse by Claude Monet

Picture Study

1. Read the title and the name of the artist. Study the picture for several minutes, then put the picture away.

2. Describe the picture.

3. Look at the picture again. Do you notice any details that you missed before? What do you like or dislike about this painting? Does it remind you of anything?

87. Literary Analysis

• Heidi, Chapter 20

Writing: Literary Analysis

Today you have another literary analysis assignment. Now that you have had some practice, this should be a written assignment, though it can be helpful to talk about your ideas before writing.

With your instructor's approval, choose *Heidi* or one of the other books you are currently reading, and answer the following questions.

What is the book about? Give a brief summary, just a few sentences. Who is this book about? What does she want? Who or what prevents her from getting it?

A Modest Wit

By Selleck Osborne

A supercilious nabob of the East—
  Haughty, being great—purse-proud, being rich—
A governor, or general, at the least,
  I have forgotten which—
Had in his family a humble youth,
  Who went from England in his patron's suit,
An unassuming boy, in truth
  A lad of decent parts, and good repute.

This youth had sense and spirit;
  But yet with all his sense,
    Excessive diffidence
Obscured his merit.

One day, at table, flushed with pride and wine,
  His honor, proudly free, severely merry,

Conceived it would be vastly fine
    To crack a joke upon his secretary.

    "Young man," he said, "by what art, craft, or trade,
    Did your good father gain a livelihood?"—
    "He was a saddler, sir," Modestus said,
  "And in his time was reckon'd good."

    "A saddler, eh! And taught you Greek,
      Instead of teaching you to sew!
  Pray, why did not your father make
      A saddler, sir, of you?"

  Each parasite, then, as in duty bound,
  The joke applauded, and the laugh went round.
    At length Modestus, bowing low,
  Said (craving pardon, if too free he made),
    "Sir, by your leave, I fain would know
  Your father's trade!"

    "My father's trade! By heaven, that's too bad!
  My father's trade? Why, blockhead, are you mad?
  My father, sir, did never stoop so low—
  He was a gentleman, I'd have you know."

    "Excuse the liberty I take,"
    Modestus said, with archness on his brow,
      "Pray, why did not your father make
    A gentleman of you?"

Rooster and Jackal

From *South-African Folk-Tales* by James A. Honey

Rooster, it is said, was once overtaken by Jackal and caught. Rooster said to Jackal, "Please, pray first before you kill me, as the man does."

Jackal asked, "In what manner does he pray? Tell me."

"He folds his hands in praying," said Rooster. Jackal folded his hands and prayed. Then Rooster spoke again. "You ought not to look about you as you do. You had better shut your eyes." He did so; and Rooster flew away, upbraiding at the same time Jackal with these words, "You rogue! Do you also pray?"

There sat Jackal, speechless, because he had been outdone.

Exercise

Review memory work. Identify each group of words below as either a phrase or a clause. If it is a clause, double underline the predicate and underline the subject.

  thoughtfully looking at the backless chairs

  what the grandfather had meant

but not with us

Copy each sentence below. Double underline the predicate, and underline the subject. Put brackets around any prepositional phrases. Label the part of speech of each word. Noun, N; Proper Noun, PN; Pronoun, PRO; Verb, V; Linking Verb, LV; Adjective, ADJ; Article, ART; Adverb, ADV; Conjunctions, CJ; Prepositions, Prep; Interjections, INJ. Diagram each sentence.

"Did you get a letter for me on the pasture?"

The letter had been given to Peter.

Clara, her true friend, wrote a letter.

Commonplace Book

With your instructor's approval, add the passage below to your commonplace book, or choose your own passage from a work of non-fiction. This can be from religious scriptures, a biography, or one of your history or science books.

>Heidi visited the grandmother next day, for she had to tell her the good news. Sitting up in her corner, the old woman was spinning as usual. Her face looked sad, for Peter had already announced the near visit of Heidi's friends, and she dreaded the result.
>After having poured out her full heart, Heidi looked at the old woman. "What is it, grandmother?" said the child. "Are you not glad?"

88. Other Irregular Verbs

- Heidi, Chapter 21

Regular verbs form the simple past with the ending *-ed*. The past participle is the same as the simple past and uses a helping verb when it acts as a verb.

"I have often wished that I should never have to eat."

"Grandfather has promised to let us come up with you once."

Irregular verbs do not follow this pattern. The simple past and past participles of irregular verbs can end in a variety of ways, following no pattern at all. But just as with regular verbs, the simple past tense has just one part while the past participle must have a helping verb when acting as a verb.

"All my life I have only eaten because I had to."

Clara had many things to relate of all the people that Heidi knew.

But the uncle had known how to help himself.

In her dreams Clara saw before her a field that was thickly strewn with light-blue flowers.

In truth she had never seen them before.

The chart on the following page contains many common irregular verbs. A longer chart with more examples appears in the appendices so that you can refer to it easily. But when in doubt, use the dictionary. It will list the various forms of the verb.

Infinitive	Simple Present	Present Participle	Simple Past	Past Participle
to arise	arise(s)	arising	arose	arisen
to be	am, is, are	being	was, were	been
to beat	beat(s)	beating	beat	beaten
to become	become(s)	becoming	became	become
to begin	begin(s)	beginning	began	begun
to blow	blow(s)	blowing	blew	blown
to break	break(s)	breaking	broke	broken
to choose	choose(s)	choosing	chose	chosen
to come	come(s)	coming	came	come
to do	do(es)	doing	did	done
to draw	draw(s)	drawing	drew	drawn
to eat	eat(s)	eating	ate	eaten
to fall	fall(s)	falling	fell	fallen
to fly	flies, fly	flying	flew	flown
to forbid	forbid(s)	forbidding	forbade	forbidden
to freeze	freeze(s)	freezing	froze	frozen
to give	give(s)	giving	gave	given
to go	go(es)	going	went	gone
to have	has, have	having	had	had
to lead	lead(s)	leading	led	led
to ride	ride(s)	riding	rode	ridden
to ring	ring(s)	ringing	rang	rung
to rise	rise(s)	rising	rose	risen
to run	run(s)	running	ran	run
to see	see(s)	seeing	saw	seen
to shake	shake(s)	shaking	shook	shaken
to shrink	shrink(s)	shrinking	shrank	shrunk
to sing	sing(s)	singing	sang	sung
to sink	sink(s)	sinking	sank or sunk	sunk
to speak	speak(s)	speaking	spoke	spoken
to steal	steal(s)	stealing	stole	stolen
to swim	swim(s)	swimming	swam	swum
to take	take(s)	taking	took	taken
to tear	tear(s)	tearing	tore	torn
to throw	throw(s)	throwing	threw	thrown
to wear	wear(s)	wearing	wore	worn
to write	write(s)	writing	wrote	written

The Burial of Sir John Moore
By C. Wolfe

Not a drum was heard, not a funeral note,
  As his corse to the rampart we hurried;
Not a soldier discharged his farewell shot
  O'er the grave where our hero we buried.

We buried him darkly at dead of night,
  The sods with our bayonets turning;
By the struggling moonbeam's misty light,
  And the lantern dimly burning.

No useless coffin enclosed his breast,
  Not in sheet nor in shroud we wound him;
But he lay like a warrior taking his rest,
  With his martial cloak around him.

Few and short were the prayers we said,
  And we spoke not a word of sorrow;
But we steadfastly gazed on the face that was dead,
  And we bitterly thought of the morrow.

We thought, as we hollowed his narrow bed,
  And smoothed down his lonely pillow,
That the foe and the stranger would tread o'er his head,
  And we far away on the billow!

Lightly they'll talk of the spirit that's gone,
  And o'er his cold ashes upbraid him,—
But little he'll reck, if they let him sleep on
  In the grave where a Briton has laid him.

But half of our heavy task was done
  When the clock struck the hour for retiring;
And we heard the distant and random gun
  That the foe was sullenly firing.

Slowly and sadly we laid him down,
  From the field of his fame fresh and gory;
We carved not a line, and we raised not a stone—
  But we left him alone with his glory!

Why Has Jackal a Long Black Stripe On His Back?
From *South-African Folk-Tales* by James A. Honey

    The Sun, it is said, was one day on earth, and the men who were traveling saw him sitting by the wayside, but passed him without notice. Jackal, however, who came after them and saw him also sitting, went to him and said, "Such a fine little child is left behind by the men." He then took Sun up and put it into his awa-skin (on his back). When it burnt him, he said, "Get down," and shook himself; but Sun stuck fast to his back and burned Jackal's back black from that day.

Writing: Copia

Take the following sentence and play with it. Remember that the point is not necessarily to make the sentence better. The point is to play with the sentence and make it different. Make a new sentence for each number, using at least one change from that category.

> The sound lasts but a moment and then ceases.

1. Change the grammar.
   - Change the nouns from common to proper and vice versa.
   - Change the nouns from singular to plural and vice versa.
   - Change the sentence type.
   - Change the adjectives from articles to descriptive to possessive, etc.
   - Change a quotation from direct to indirect and vice versa.
   - Change the verb tense.

2. Condense the sentence.
   - Remove details.
   - Remove modifiers.
   - Remove phrases or clauses.

3. Amplify the sentence.
   - Add details.
   - Add dialogue.
   - Add modifiers.
   - Add phrases or clauses.

4. Use synonyms and antonyms.
   - Substitute synonyms.
   - Say the opposite thing using antonyms.

5. Point of view.
   - Change the point of view.
   - Slant the sentence.

Exercise

Review memory work. Punctuate the following sentence.

> The grandfather Heidi and Clara were all in the mountain home

Copy each sentence below. Double underline the predicate, and underline the subject. Put brackets around any prepositional phrases. Label the part of speech of each word. Noun, N; Proper Noun, PN; Pronoun, PRO; Verb, V; Linking Verb, LV; Adjective, ADJ; Article, ART; Adverb, ADV; Conjunctions, CJ; Prepositions, Prep; Interjections, INJ. Diagram each sentence.

"How did you sleep?"

The grandfather was just coming out of the shed with two full bowls of milk. [Hint: **out of** is a two word preposition.]

Heidi merrily came running with her message.

Commonplace Book

With your instructor's approval, add the passage below to your commonplace book, or choose your own passage from a work of fiction. This can be from either school reading or free reading.

> The children had just resolved to stay awake all night to talk about the coming day when their conversation suddenly ceased and they were both peacefully slumbering. In her dreams, Clara saw before her a field that was thickly strewn with light-blue flowers, while Heidi heard the eagle scream to her from above, "Come! Come! Come!"

Dictation

This evening, Clara fell asleep the moment she lay down. Two or three days passed in this pleasant way. The next brought a surprise. Two strong porters came up the Alp, each carrying on his back a fresh, white bed. They also brought a letter from grandmama, in which she thanked the children for their faithful writing and told them that the beds were meant for them. When they went to sleep that night, they found their new beds in exactly the same position as their former ones had been.

89. Subordinate Conjunctions

• Heidi, Chapter 22

The subordinate conjunctions are **after, although, as, because, before, even if, even though, if, in order that, once, provided that, rather than, since, so that, than, that, though, unless, until, when, whenever, where, whereas, wherever, whether, while.**

Some clauses express a complete thought and stand alone as sentences. But some clauses do not express a complete thought, even though they have both a subject and a predicate. Certain words which can begin clauses prevent them from being complete sentences. When a clause begins with a word like **when, while,** or **before,** it leaves us wondering, "And then what?" We need more information to have a complete thought expressed.

One type of word which prevents clauses from being complete sentences is the **subordinate conjunction**. A list of subordinate conjunctions is above. This is an important list to memorize.

Consider the following clauses from *Heidi*:

when, arriving on top, they saw Peter already lying on the ground

when dinner-time had come

Even though the sentences above each have a subject and a predicate, they are not complete sentences because of the subordinate conjunction which begins each clause. Look at those same clauses without the subordinate conjunctions:

Arriving on top, they saw Peter already lying on the ground.

Dinner-time had come.

When I took away that beginning word, I also took away the expectation for the rest of the story. Now these clauses can stand alone as complete sentences.

A clause which can stand alone as a complete sentence is called an **independent clause**. A clause which cannot stand as a complete sentence is a **dependent clause** because it **depends** on another clause to express a complete thought. Subordinate conjunctions make clauses dependent. We call a clause which begins with a subordinate conjunction a **subordinate clause**.

The Lamplighter

By Walter De La Mare

When the light of day declineth,
And a swift angel through the sky
Kindleth God's tapers clear,
With ashen staff the lamplighter
Passeth along the darkling streets
To light our earthly lamps;
Lest, prowling in the darkness,
The thief should haunt with quiet tread,
Or men on evil errands set;
Or wayfarers be benighted;
Or neighbors bent from house to house
Should need a guiding torch.

He is like a needlewoman
Who deftly on a sable hem
Stitches in gleaming jewels;
Or, haply, he is like a hero,
Whose bright deeds on the long journey
Are beacons on our way.
And when in the East cometh morning,
And the broad splendor of the sun,
Then, with the tune of little birds
Ringing on high, the lamplighter
Passeth by each quiet house,
And putteth out the lamps.

Horse Cursed by Sun

From *South-African Folk-Tales* by James A. Honey

It is said that once Sun was on earth and caught Horse to ride it. But it was unable to bear his weight, and therefore Ox took the place of Horse and carried Sun on its back. Since that time Horse is cursed in these words, because it could not carry Sun's weight:

> "From today thou shalt have a certain time of dying.
> This is thy curse, that thou hast a certain time of dying.
> And day and night shalt thou eat,
> But the desire of thy heart shall not be at rest,
> Though thou grazest till morning and again until sunset.
> Behold, this is the judgment which I pass upon thee."

So said Sun. Since that day Horse's certain time of dying commenced.

Exercise

Review memory work. Punctuate the following sentence.

Grandfather the wind has done it exclaimed Heidi eagerly

Copy each sentence below. Double underline the predicate, and underline the subject. Put brackets around any prepositional phrases. Label the part of speech of each word. Noun, N; Proper Noun, PN; Pronoun, PRO; Verb, V; Linking Verb, LV; Adjective, ADJ; Article, ART; Adverb, ADV; Conjunctions, CJ; Prepositions, Prep; Interjections, INJ. Diagram each sentence.

Heidi had told Clara of the flowers on the pasture.

"Have you seen the chair?"

"Oh, Clara, would you be angry?"

Writing: Commonplace Book

Add the passage below from your model story to your commonplace book.

> "Give a light blow to a wineglass. The glass will ring, giving forth a sound, weaker or stronger, lower or higher, according to the quality and size of the glass. The sound lasts but a moment and then ceases. Strike the glass once more, and while it is still ringing, touch the rim with your finger. Instantly all is still again; not a sound from the glass. Why does it ring when struck, and why does it stop ringing at the touch of a finger? Before replying let us experiment with other resonant objects.

Dictation

Use part of today's poem for dictation.

90. Scientific Narration: Sound

- Heidi, Chapter 23

Your model story, "Sound," is from Jean Henri Fabre's *The Secret of Everyday Things*. In his book, the character of Uncle Paul is explaining these scientific concepts to a group of children. The stories are written in the first person with frequent use of the second person as he speaks directly to the children.

Use your outline to write a narration on this topic. Do not include references to the children or Uncle Paul; just write about the topic. Your narration should be in the third person. You may use other sources for more details if desired. You will need to decide which details are important to your narration and which ones should be left out.

The Planting of the Apple-Tree
By William Cullen Bryant

  Come, let us plant the apple-tree.
Cleave the tough greensward with the spade;
Wide let its hollow bed be made;
There gently lay the roots, and there
Sift the dark mould with kindly care,
  And press it o'er them tenderly,
As round the sleeping infant's feet
We softly fold the cradle sheet;
  So plant we the apple-tree.

  What plant we in this apple-tree?
Buds, which the breath of summer days
Shall lengthen into leafy sprays;
Boughs where the thrush, with crimson breast,
Shall haunt, and sing, and hide her nest;
  We plant, upon the sunny lea,
A shadow for the noontide hour,
A shelter from the summer shower,
  When we plant the apple-tree.

What plant we in this apple-tree?
Sweets for a hundred flowery springs,
To load the May wind's restless wings,
When, from the orchard row, he pours
Its fragrance through our open doors;
　A world of blossoms for the bee,
Flowers for the sick girl's silent room,
For the glad infant sprigs of bloom,
　We plant with the apple-tree.

What plant we in this apple-tree?
Fruits that shall swell in sunny June,
And redden in the August noon,
And drop, when gentle airs come by,
That fan the blue September sky,
　While children come, with cries of glee,
And seek them where the fragrant grass
Betrays their bed to those who pass,
　At the foot of the apple-tree.

　And when, above this apple-tree,
The winter stars are quivering bright,
The winds go howling through the night,
Girls, whose eyes o'erflow with mirth,
Shall peel its fruit by cottage hearth,
　And guests in prouder homes shall see,
Heaped with the grape of Cintra's vine,
And golden orange of the line,
　The fruit of the apple-tree.

　The fruitage of this apple-tree,
Winds and our flag of stripe and star
Shall bear to coasts that lie afar,
Where men shall wonder at the view,
And ask in what fair groves they grew;
　And sojourners beyond the sea
Shall think of childhood's careless day,
And long, long hours of summer play,
　In the shade of the apple-tree.

　Each year shall give this apple-tree
A broader flush of roseate bloom,
A deeper maze of verdurous gloom,
And loosen, when the frost-clouds lower,
The crisp brown leaves in thicker shower.
　The years shall come and pass, but we
Shall hear no longer, where we lie,
The summer's songs, the autumn's sigh,
　In the boughs of the apple-tree.

And time shall waste this apple-tree.
Oh, when its aged branches throw
Thin shadows on the ground below,
Shall fraud and force and iron will
Oppress the weak and helpless still!
  What shall the tasks of mercy be,
Amid the toils, the strifes, the tears
Of those who live when length of years
    Is wasting this apple-tree?

"Who planted this old apple-tree?"
The children of that distant day
Thus to some aged man shall say;
And, gazing on its mossy stem,
The gray-haired man shall answer them:
"A poet of the land was he,
Born in the rude but good old times;
   'Tis said he made some quaint old rhymes
    On planting the apple-tree."

Editing

- Did you meet the goal of this writing exercise?
- Look at your word choice. Is there a good mixture of nouns and pronouns? Is the antecedent of each pronoun clear?
- Look at your paragraphs. Are all the sentences related? Does each paragraph focus on a single topic?

91. Compound Sentences

- **This Week:** Tanglewood Tales, The Minotaur

In grammar, we use the word **compound** to show that we have two or more of something. A compound subject is two or more subjects. A compound predicate is two or more predicates. What do you think a **compound sentence** is?

A **compound sentence** is one which has two or more independent clauses. Consider this sentence from "The Minotaur."

"Be patient, and we shall see."

Notice that the sentence above has two subject-predicate pairs, which means two clauses. The first clause is a command, so it has the understood **you** as its subject. Both clauses are independent. Remember that an independent clause is one which can stand alone as a complete sentence.

Three ways exist to correctly punctuate between two independent clauses. When proper punctuation is not used, it creates a **run-on sentence**. These are known as run-on sentences because they continue running on even when they should have stopped. In the following examples from *Tanglewood Tales*, I've taken liberties with Hawthorne's writing to produce a **fused sentence** and a **comma splice**.

A **fused sentence** occurs when two or more independent clauses are joined with no punctuation at all. Have you ever known someone who talked really fast and never seemed to pause for breath? That is what a fused sentence is like. Here is an example of a fused sentence:

X   "Be patient we shall see."

A **comma splice** occurs when two or more independent clauses are joined with only a comma, like this:

X   "Be patient, we shall see."

In the example above, the clauses seem to go together. They seem to be part of the same thought. However, each is an independent clause, so they need more than just a comma between them.

Each independent clause can stand as a sentence in its own right. Therefore, the first way to punctuate two or more independent clauses is to allow them to do precisely that. This method of punctuation produces two separate simple sentences.

"Be patient**.** We shall see."

No wonder he could not move it**.** It would have taken all the force of a very strong man to lift it out of its earthy bed.

The other ways to punctuate between independent clauses result in compound sentences.

The second way to punctuate two or more independent clauses is to use a comma with a coordinating conjunction. When we join two or more independent clauses with a coordinating conjunction, the FANBOYS, both the comma and the coordinating conjunction are required. Only using a comma would produce a comma splice, and only using a conjunction would produce a run-on sentence.

"Be patient**, and** we shall see."

No wonder he could not move it**, for** it would have taken all the force of a very strong man to lift it out of its earthy bed.

The third way to punctuate two or more independent clauses is to use a semicolon. The semicolon can be used alone. Since it does not end the sentence, the word following the semicolon is not capitalized unless it is a proper noun or adjective.

"Be patient**;** we shall see."

No wonder he could not move it**;** it would have taken all the force of a very strong man to lift it out of its earthy bed.

Some people mistakenly believe that run-on sentences are about the length of a sentence, but that is not so! Run-on sentences are errors of punctuation. Sentences can be quite long as long as they are properly punctuated.

The Sleeping Beauty

By Walter De La Mare

The scent of bramble sweets the air,
Amid her folded sheets she lies,
The gold of evening in her hair,
The blue of morn shut in her eyes.
How many a changing moon hath lit
The unchanging roses of her face!

Her mirror ever broods on it
In silver stillness of the days.
Oft flits the moth on filmy wings
Into his solitary lair;
Shrill evensong the cricket sings

From some still shadow in her hair.
In heat, in snow, in wind, in flood,
She sleeps in lovely loneliness,
Half folded like an April bud
On winter-haunted trees.

Writing: Oral Narration

Read your new model story below, and then give your instructor an oral narration of it.

Hieroglyphics

From *The Story of Mankind* by Hendrik Van Loon

These earliest ancestors of ours who lived in the great European wilderness were rapidly learning many new things. It is safe to say that in due course of time, they would have developed a civilization of their own. But suddenly there came an end to their isolation. They were discovered.

A traveler from an unknown southern land who had dared to cross the sea and the high mountain passes had found his way to the wild people of the European continent. He came from Africa. His home was in Egypt.

The valley of the Nile had developed a high stage of civilization thousands of years before the people of the west had dreamed of the possibilities of a fork or a wheel or a house. And we shall therefore leave our great-great-grandfathers in their caves while we visit the southern and eastern shores of the Mediterranean, where stood the earliest school of the human race.

The Egyptians have taught us many things. They were excellent farmers. They knew all about irrigation. They built temples which were afterwards copied by the Greeks and which served as the earliest models for the churches in which people worship nowadays. They had invented a calendar which proved such a useful instrument for the purpose of measuring time that it has survived with a few changes until today. But most important of all, the Egyptians had learned how to preserve speech for the benefit of future generations. They had invented the art of writing.

In the first century before our era, when the Romans came to Egypt, they found the valley full of strange little pictures which seemed to have something to do with the history of the country. But the Romans were not interested in anything foreign and did not inquire into the origin of these queer figures which covered the walls of the temples and the walls of the palaces and endless reams of flat sheets made out of the papyrus reed. The last of the Egyptian priests who had understood the holy art of making such pictures had died several years before. Egypt, deprived of its independence, had become a storehouse filled with important historical documents which no one could decipher and which were of no earthly use to either man or beast.

Seventeen centuries went by, and Egypt remained a land of mystery. But in the year 1798, a French general by the name of Bonaparte happened to visit eastern Africa to prepare for an attack upon the British Indian Colonies. He did not get beyond the Nile, and his campaign was a failure. But, quite accidentally, the famous French expedition solved the problem of the ancient Egyptian picture language.

One day a young French officer, much bored by the dreary life of his little fortress on the Rosetta river—a mouth of the Nile—decided to spend a few idle hours rummaging among the ruins of the Nile Delta. And behold! He found a stone which greatly puzzled him. Like everything else in Egypt, it was covered with little figures. But this particular slab of black basalt was different from anything that had ever been discovered. It carried three inscriptions. One of these was in Greek. The Greek language was known. "All that is necessary," so he reasoned, "is to compare the Greek text with the Egyptian figures, and they will at once tell their secrets."

The plan sounded simple enough, but it took more than twenty years to solve the riddle. In the year 1802, a French professor by the name of Champollion began to compare the Greek and the Egyptian texts of the famous Rosetta stone. In the year 1823, he announced that he had discovered the meaning of fourteen little figures. A short time later, he died, but the main principles of Egyptian writing had become known. Today the story of the valley of the Nile is better known to us than the story of the Mississippi River. We possess a written record which covers four thousand years of chronicled history.

As the ancient Egyptian hieroglyphics, which means "sacred writing," have played such a very great role in history—a few of them in modified form have even found their way into our own alphabet—you ought to know something about the ingenious system which was used fifty centuries ago to preserve the spoken word for the benefit of the coming generations.

Of course, you know what a sign language is. Every Indian story of our western plains has a chapter devoted to strange messages written in the form of little pictures which tell how many buffaloes were killed and how many hunters there were in a certain party. As a rule it is not difficult to understand the meaning of such messages.

Ancient Egyptian, however, was not a sign language. The clever people of the Nile had passed beyond that stage long before. Their pictures meant a great deal more than the object which they represented, as I shall try to explain to you now.

Suppose that you were Champollion and that you were examining a stack of papyrus sheets, all covered with hieroglyphics. Suddenly you came across a picture of a man with a saw. "Very well," you would say, "that means of course that a farmer went out to cut down a tree." Then you take another papyrus. It tells the story of a queen who had died at the age of eighty-two. In the midst of a sentence appears the picture of the man with the saw. Queens of eighty-two do not handle saws. The picture therefore must mean something else. But what?

That is the riddle which the Frenchman finally solved. He discovered that the Egyptians were the first to use what we now call phonetic writing—a system of characters which reproduce the sound, or phone, of the spoken word and which make it possible for us to translate all our spoken words into a written form, with the help of only a few dots and dashes and pothooks.

Let us return for a moment to the little fellow with the saw. The word **saw** either means a certain tool which you will find in a carpenter's shop, or it means the past tense of the verb **to see**.

This is what had happened to the word during the course of centuries.

First of all it had meant only the particular tool which it represented. Then that meaning had been lost, and it had become the past participle of a verb. After several hundred years, the Egyptians lost sight of both these meanings, and the picture came to stand for a single letter, the letter *s*. A short sentence will show you what I mean. Here is a modern English sentence as it would have been written in hieroglyphics:

This either means one of these two round objects in your head, which allow you to see, or it means **I**, the person who is talking.

This is either an insect which gathers honey, or it represents the verb **to be** which means to exist. Again, it may be the first part of a verb like **be-come** or **be-have**. In this particular instance it is followed by

which means a **leaf** or **leave** or **lieve** (the sound of all three words is the same).

The **eye** you know all about.

Finally you get this last picture. It is a giraffe. It is part of the old sign language out of which the hieroglyphics developed.

You can now read that sentence without much difficulty.

"I believe I saw a giraffe."

Having invented this system, the Egyptians developed it during thousands of years until they could write anything they wanted, and they used these canned words to send messages to friends, to keep business accounts, and to keep a record of the history of their country so that future generations might benefit by the mistakes of the past.

Exercise

Review memory work. Below are two independent clauses. Show the three ways to join them.

> she began to be conscious that her son was no longer a child

> she must soon send him forth among the perils and troubles of the world

Copy each sentence below. Double underline the predicate, and underline the subject. Put brackets around any prepositional phrases. Label the part of speech of each word. Noun, N; Proper Noun, PN; Pronoun, PRO; Verb, V; Linking Verb, LV; Adjective, ADJ; Article, ART; Adverb, ADV; Conjunctions, CJ; Prepositions, Prep; Interjections, INJ. Diagram each sentence.

> "Be patient and see."

> "Why can not I go to this famous city of Athens?"

> The eyes of Theseus glowed with enthusiasm.

Commonplace Book

With your instructor's approval, add the passage below to your commonplace book, or choose your own passage from a work of fiction. This can be from either school reading or free reading.

> Often and often, after this, did Theseus ask his mother whether it was yet time for him to go to Athens; and still his mother pointed to the rock and told him that, for years to come, he could not be strong enough to move it. And again and again the rosy-cheeked and curly-headed boy would tug and strain at the huge mass of stone, striving, child as he was, to do what a giant could hardly have done without taking both of his great hands to the task.

Dictation

> Meanwhile, the rock seemed to be sinking farther and farther into the ground. The moss grew over it thicker and thicker until at last it looked almost like a soft green seat, with only a few gray knobs of granite peeping out. The overhanging trees, also, shed their brown leaves upon it as often as the autumn came; and at its base grew ferns and wild flowers, some of which crept quite over its surface. To all appearance, the rock was as firmly fastened as any other portion of the earth's substance.

92. Review: Phrases and Clauses

- This Week: Tanglewood Tales, The Minotaur

> Definition: A phrase is a group of related words which does not include a subject-predicate pair.

> Definition: A clause is a group of words which contains a subject-predicate pair.

A subject-predicate pair is simply a verb and its subject. Remember that the defining characteristic of both phrases and clauses is whether or not they have a subject-predicate pair. Phrases never have a subject-predicate pair, but clauses must have a subject-predicate pair.

Phrases can be short or long. Some phrases have specific names based on the main word or usage of the phrase. A noun phrase consists of a noun and its modifiers. A verb phrase consists of the helping verbs, main verb, and any modifiers and objects which the verb has. A prepositional phrase consists of the preposition, its object, and any modifiers of the object.

Look at the following sentences from "The Minotaur." The first has a noun phrase and a prepositional phrase, both of which are large and bold. The second has a verb phrase which includes the main verb, helping verbs, and a direct object with its modifiers.

"Only admit **this evil-minded young man to your presence**."

He **must have had a very sorrowful dream**.

Unlike a phrase, a clause must have a subject and a predicate. Look at these clauses. The predicate is double underlined and the subject is underlined in each clause.

when the king asked what he should do with Theseus

this naughty woman had an answer ready at her tongue's end

> because he might thus arrive within fifteen miles of Athens

> unless his sinews were made of brass

Some clauses express a complete thought. That makes them independent clauses. Independent clauses express a complete thought and can therefore stand alone as complete sentences. In the above list, only one clause is independent. Which one is it?

The independent clause in the previous list is this one:

> This naughty woman had an answer ready at her tongue's end.

Because it is an independent clause, it can stand as a complete sentence. The others are **subordinate clauses** because they begin with **subordinate conjunctions**.

Some clauses do not express a complete thought even though they possess both a subject and a predicate. That is because certain words which can begin clauses set up the expectation for more information. These words that tell us that the thought needs more information to be complete. When a clause begins with a subordinate conjunction, a word like **when, while,** or **before**, it leaves us wondering, "And then what?" We need more information to have a complete thought expressed. Look at those clauses again, this time with the subordinate conjunction removed.

> The king asked what he should do with Theseus.

> He might thus arrive within fifteen miles of Athens.

> His sinews were made of brass.

When I took away the subordinate conjunction at the beginning of each clause, I also took away the expectation for the rest of the story. Now these clauses can stand alone as complete, if sometimes rather odd, sentences.

Remember that coordinating conjunctions, the FANBOYS, do *not* make clauses dependent. They can still stand as complete sentences.

> But the king asked what he should do with Theseus.

> And he might thus arrive within fifteen miles of Athens.

Song for a Play
By Hilda Conkling

Soldier drop that golden spear!
Wait till the fires arise!
Wait till the sky drops down and touches the spear,
Crystal and mother-of-pearl!
The sunlight droops forward
Like wings.
The birds sing songs of sun-drops.
The sky leans down where the spear stands upward. . .

I hear music . . .
It is the end . . .

Lion's Defeat

From *South-African Folk-Tales* by James A. Honey

The wild animals, it is said, were once assembled at Lion's. When Lion was asleep, Jackal persuaded Little Fox to twist a rope of ostrich sinews in order to play Lion a trick. They took ostrich sinews, twisted them, and fastened the rope to Lion's tail and tied the other end of the rope to a shrub. When Lion awoke and saw that he was tied up, he became angry and called the animals together. When they had assembled, Lion said:

> "What child of his mother and father's love,
> Whose mother and father's love has tied me?"

Then answered the animal to whom the question was first put:

> "I, child of my mother and father's love,
> I, mother and father's love, I have not done it."

All answered the same; but when he asked Little Fox, Little Fox said:

> "I, child of my mother and father's love,
> I, mother and father's love, have tied thee!"

Then Lion tore the rope made of sinews and ran after Little Fox.
But Jackal said, "My boy, thou son of lean Mrs. Fox, thou wilt never be caught."
Truly Lion was thus beaten in running by Little Fox.

Writing: Outline

Write or type an outline of the new model story which you read in the last lesson.

Exercise

Review memory work. Below are two independent clauses. Show the three ways to join them.

> it was not more than a year afterwards

> they were again sitting on the moss-covered stone.

Copy each sentence below. Double underline the predicate, and underline the subject. Put brackets around any prepositional phrases. Label the part of speech of each word. Noun, N; Proper Noun, PN; Pronoun, PRO; Verb, V; Linking Verb, LV; Adjective, ADJ; Article, ART; Adverb, ADV; Conjunctions, CJ; Prepositions, Prep; Interjections, INJ. Diagram each sentence.

> Theseus had done many valiant deeds with his father's golden-hilted sword.

"Admit Theseus, this evil-minded young man, to your presence."

"Why, he must be a very wicked young fellow indeed!" [Hint: **indeed** tells **to what extent** he is a wicked young fellow.]

Commonplace Book

With your instructor's approval, add this part of today's poem to your commonplace book, or choose your own poem.

> Soldier drop that golden spear!
> Wait till the fires arise!
> Wait till the sky drops down and touches the spear,
> Crystal and mother-of-pearl!
> The sunlight droops forward
> Like wings.
> The birds sing songs of sun-drops.
> The sky leans down where the spear stands upward. . .
> I hear music . . .
> It is the end . . .

Dictation

Nothing is certain but death and taxes.

Hauling a Boat Ashore at Honfleur by Claude Monet

Picture Study

1. Read the title and the name of the artist. Study the picture for several minutes, then put the picture away.

2. Describe the picture.

3. Look at the picture again. Do you notice any details that you missed before? What do you like or dislike about this painting? Does it remind you of anything?

93. Descriptive Writing

- This Week: Tanglewood Tales, The Minotaur

Writing: Descriptive Writing

The purpose of descriptive writing is to describe a person, place, thing, or event so well that an image forms in the mind of the reader.

In "The Minotaur," Theseus travels through the labyrinth to discover the Minotaur. Read that passage below, paying close attention to the details that make a vivid picture in your mind, and then write a narration of it. What did the Minotaur look like? How did it behave? What helped to give Theseus courage?

Add details if you wish. Remember, the point of this exercise is to write as descriptively as possible, not just to narrate the passage exactly.

The Minotaur

He followed the dreadful roar of the Minotaur, which now grew louder and louder, and finally so very loud that Theseus fully expected to come close upon him, at every new zigzag and wriggle of the path. And at last, in an open space, at the very center of the labyrinth, he did discern the hideous creature.

Sure enough, what an ugly monster it was! Only his horned head belonged to a bull; and yet, somehow or other, he looked like a bull all over, preposterously waddling on his hind legs; or, if you happened to view him in another way, he seemed wholly a man, and all the more monstrous for being so. And there he was, the wretched thing, with no society, no companion, no kind of a mate, living only to do mischief, and incapable of knowing what affection means. Theseus hated him, and shuddered at him, and yet could not but be sensible of some sort of pity; and all the more, the uglier and more detestable the creature was. For he kept striding to and fro in a solitary frenzy of rage, continually emitting a hoarse roar, which was oddly mixed up with half-shaped words; and, after listening awhile, Theseus understood that the Minotaur was saying to himself how miserable he was, and how hungry, and how he hated everybody, and how he longed to eat up the human race alive.

Ah, the bull-headed villain! And O, my good little people, you will perhaps see, one of these days, as I do now, that every human being who suffers anything evil to get into his nature, or to remain there, is a kind of Minotaur, an enemy of his fellow-creatures and separated from all good companionship, as this poor monster was.

Was Theseus afraid? By no means, my dear auditors. What! A hero like Theseus afraid! Not had the Minotaur had twenty bull heads instead of one. Bold as he was, however, I rather fancy that it strengthened his valiant heart, just at this crisis, to feel a tremulous twitch at the silken cord, which he was still holding in his left hand. It was as if Ariadne were giving him all her might and courage; and, much as he already had, and little as she had to give, it made his own seem twice as much. And to confess the honest truth, he needed the whole; for now the Minotaur, turning suddenly about, caught sight of Theseus and instantly lowered his horribly sharp horns, exactly as a mad bull does when he means to rush against an enemy. At the same time, he belched forth a tremendous roar, in which there was something like the words of human language, but all disjointed and shaken-to pieces by passing through the gullet of a miserably enraged brute.

Lullaby

By Walter De La Mare

Sleep, sleep, lovely white soul!
The singing mouse sings plaintively,
The sweet night-bird in the chesnut-tree—
They sing together, bird and mouse,
In starlight, in darkness, lonely, sweet,
The wild notes and the faint notes meet—
Sleep, sleep, lovely white soul!

Sleep, sleep, lovely white soul!
Amid the lilies floats the moth,
The mole along his galleries goeth
In the dark earth; the summer moon
Looks like a shepherd through the pane
Seeking his feeble lamb again—
Sleep, sleep, lovely white soul!

Sleep, sleep, lovely white soul!
Time comes to keep night-watch with thee
Nodding with roses; and the sea
Saith 'Peace! Peace!' amid his foam
White as thy night-clothes; 'O be still!'
The wind cries up the whisp'ring hill—
Sleep, sleep, lovely white soul!

Tortoises Hunting Ostriches

From *South-African Folk-Tales* by James A. Honey

One day, it is said, the Tortoises held a council how they might hunt Ostriches, and they said, "Let us, on both sides, stand in rows near each other, and let one go to hunt the Ostriches so that they must flee along through the midst of us." They did so, and as they were many, the Ostriches were obliged to run along through the midst of them. During this they did not move, but, remaining always in the same places, called each to the other, "Are you there?" and each one answered, "I am here." The Ostriches, hearing this, ran so tremendously that they quite exhausted their strength and fell down. Then the Tortoises assembled by-and-by at the place where the Ostriches had fallen and devoured them.

Exercise

Review memory work. Below are two independent clauses. Show the three ways to join them.

> do but let me put a single drop into the goblet

> let the young man taste it

Copy each sentence below. Double underline the predicate, and underline the subject. Put brackets around any prepositional phrases. Label the part of speech of each word. Noun, N; Proper Noun, PN; Pronoun, PRO; Verb, V; Linking Verb, LV; Adjective, ADJ; Article, ART; Adverb, ADV; Conjunctions, CJ; Prepositions, Prep; Interjections, INJ. Diagram each sentence.

> "How came you by it?"

> He drew back the goblet.

> His eyes had fallen on the gold-hilted sword.

Commonplace Book

With your instructor's approval, add the passage below to your commonplace book, or choose your own passage from a work of non-fiction. This can be from religious scriptures, a biography, or one of your history or science books.

> I have quite forgotten what became of the king's nephews. But when the wicked Medea saw this new turn of affairs, she hurried out of the room and, going to her private chamber, lost no time in setting her enchantments at work. In a few moments, she heard a great noise of hissing snakes outside of the chamber window; and, behold! There was her fiery chariot and four huge winged serpents, wriggling and twisting in the air, flourishing their tails higher than the top of the palace, and all ready to set off on an aerial journey.

Editing

- Did you meet the goal of this writing exercise?
- Look at your word choice. Is there a good mixture of nouns and pronouns? Is the antecedent of each pronoun clear?
- Look at your paragraphs. Are all the sentences related? Does each paragraph focus on a single topic?

94. Complex Sentences

- This Week: Tanglewood Tales, The Pygmies

The subordinate conjunctions are after, although, as, because, before, even if, even though, if, in order that, once, provided that, rather than, since, so that, than, that, though, unless, until, when, whenever, where, whereas, wherever, whether, while.

You have learned that clauses can be either dependent or independent. One way to make a clause dependent is to begin it with a subordinate conjunction. This creates a **subordinate clause**. I hope you have been memorizing this list because it's an important one to know.

Definition: A complex sentence is a sentence with one independent clause and at least one dependent clause.

An independent clause is one which can stand alone as a complete sentence. A dependent clause needs more information to express a complete thought. Where do we get this additional information?

A dependent clause needs an independent clause! It relies on the independent clause to make sense. Without the independent clause, the reader is left wondering, "And then what?" The independent clause works with the dependent clause by answering that question.

Look at these sentences from "The Pygmies." Notice that each sentence is made up of at least two clauses. These are **complex sentences**. Complex sentences have one independent clause and at least one dependent clause.

Dependent / Independent
When the world was full of wonders, Antæus the Giant lived.

Independent / Dependent
The very breath of his life would depart from him **unless** the Giant touched Mother Earth as often as once in five minutes.

Look closely at the punctuation in those sentences. Punctuating a complex sentence is simple and straightforward. When the subordinate clause comes first, use a comma to separate it from the main clause. However, when the subordinate clause comes after the main clause, no comma is necessary. Below are the same sentences, but I've switched the order of the clauses. Notice how the punctuation changed.

Antæus the Giant lived **when** the world was full of wonders.

Unless the Giant touched Mother Earth as often as once in five minutes, the very breath of his life would depart from him.

June

By James Russell Lowell

What is so rare as a day in June?
Then, if ever, come perfect days;
Then Heaven tries the earth if it be in tune,
  And over it softly her warm ear lays:
Whether we look, or whether we listen,
We hear life murmur, or see it glisten;
Every clod feels a stir of might,
  An instinct within it that reaches and towers,
And, groping blindly above it for light,
  Climbs to a soul in grass and flowers;
The flush of life may well be seen
  Thrilling back over hills and valleys;
The cowslip startles in meadows green.
  The buttercup catches the sun in its chalice,
And there's never a leaf nor a blade too mean
  To be some happy creature's palace;
The little bird sits at his door in the sun,
  Atilt like a blossom among the leaves,
And lets his illumined being o'errun
  With the deluge of summer it receives;
His mate feels the eggs beneath her wings,
And the heart in her dumb breast flutters and sings;
He sings to the wide world, and she to her nest,—
In the nice ear of Nature which song is the best?

Farmer Mybrow and the Fairies

From *West African Folk-Tales* by William H. Barker

Part I

Farmer Mybrow was one day looking about for a suitable piece of land to convert into a field. He wished to grow corn and yams. He discovered a fine spot close to a great forest—which later was the home of some fairies. He set to work at once to prepare the field.

Having sharpened his great knife, he began to cut down the bushes. No sooner had he touched one than he heard a voice say, "Who is there, cutting down the bushes?"

Mybrow was too much astonished to answer. The question was repeated. This time the farmer realized that it must be one of the fairies, and so he replied, "I am Mybrow, come to prepare a field."

Fortunately for him, the fairies were in great good humor. He heard one say, "Let us all help Farmer Mybrow to cut down the bushes." The rest agreed. To Mybrow's great delight, the bushes were all rapidly cut down with very little trouble on his part. He returned home, exceedingly well pleased with his day's work, having resolved to keep the field a secret even from his wife.

Early in January, when it was time to burn the dry bush, he set off to his field one afternoon with the means of making a fire. Hoping to have the fairies' assistance once more, he intentionally struck the trunk of a tree as he passed. Immediately came the question, "Who is there, striking the stumps?"

He promptly replied, "I am Mybrow, come to burn down the bush." Accordingly, the dried bushes were all burned down and the field left clear in less time that it takes to tell it.

Next day the same thing happened. Mybrow came to chop up the stumps for firewood and clear the field for digging. In a very short time, his bundles of sticks and firewood were piled ready while the field was bare.

So it went on. The field was divided into two parts—one for maize and one for yams. In all the preparations—digging, sowing, planting—the fairies gave great assistance. Still, the farmer had managed to keep the whereabouts of his field a secret from his wife and neighbors.

Since the soil had been so carefully prepared, the crops promised to do exceedingly well. Mybrow visited them from time to time and congratulated himself on the splendid harvest he would have.

Writing: Copia

Take the following sentence and play with it. Remember that the point is not necessarily to make the sentence better. The point is to play with the sentence and make it different. Make a new sentence for each number, using at least one change from that category.

> In the first century before our era, when the Romans came to Egypt, they found the valley full of strange little pictures which seemed to have something to do with the history of the country.

1. Change the grammar.
   - Change the nouns from common to proper and vice versa.
   - Change the nouns from singular to plural and vice versa.
   - Change the sentence type.
   - Change the adjectives from articles to descriptive to possessive, etc.
   - Change a quotation from direct to indirect and vice versa.
   - Change the verb tense.

2. Condense the sentence.
   - Remove details.
   - Remove modifiers.
   - Remove phrases or clauses.

3. Amplify the sentence.
   - Add details.
   - Add dialogue.
   - Add modifiers.
   - Add phrases or clauses.

4. Use synonyms and antonyms.
   - Substitute synonyms.
   - Say the opposite thing using antonyms.

5. Point of view.
   - Change the point of view.
   - Slant the sentence.

Exercise

Review memory work. Below are two clauses, one dependent and one independent. Show the two ways to join them.

I shall probably have to teach you a little civility

before we part

Copy each sentence below. Double underline the predicate, and underline the subject. Put brackets around any prepositional phrases. Label the part of speech of each word. Noun, N; Proper Noun, PN; Pronoun, PRO; Verb, V; Linking Verb, LV; Adjective, ADJ; Article, ART; Adverb, ADV; Conjunctions, CJ; Prepositions, Prep; Interjections, INJ. Diagram each sentence.

Here the Pygmies planted wheat and other kinds of grain.

These funny Pygmies had a Giant for their neighbor.

"How are you, my good fellow?"

Commonplace Book

With your instructor's approval, add the passage below to your commonplace book, or choose your own passage from a work of fiction. This can be from either school reading or free reading.

Among the Pygmies, I suppose, if one of them grew to the height of six or eight inches, he was reckoned a prodigiously tall man. It must have been very pretty to behold their little cities, with streets two or three feet wide, paved with the smallest pebbles, and bordered by habitations about as big as a squirrel's cage. The king's palace attained to the stupendous magnitude of Periwinkle's baby-house and stood in the center of a spacious square, which could hardly have been covered by our hearth-rug.

Dictation

Their principal temple, or cathedral, was as lofty as yonder bureau and was looked upon as a wonderfully sublime and magnificent edifice. All these structures were built neither of stone nor wood. They were neatly plastered together by the Pygmy workmen, pretty much like bird's nests, out of straw, feathers, eggshells, and other small bits of stuff, with stiff clay instead of mortar; and when the hot sun had dried them, they were just as snug and comfortable as a Pygmy could desire.

95. Indirect Objects

- This Week: Tanglewood Tales, The Pygmies

A transitive verb is one which has a direct object. Intransitive verbs do not have direct objects. Occasionally, transitive verbs have an additional type of object.

> Definition: An indirect object is a noun or pronoun that tells TO or FOR whom/what the action of the verb is performed.

The direct object receives the action of the verb. It answers the question **whom** or **what** following a transitive verb. Sometimes, a transitive verb is performed for someone or something.

> He wrote a letter.

He wrote what? A **letter**. Letter is the direct object. But **to whom** did he write a letter?

> He wrote me a letter.

Now, the sentence tells **to whom** he wrote the letter: **me**. **Me** is the **indirect object**. Notice the position of the indirect object. It sits between the verb and the direct object. To have an indirect object, a sentence must have a direct object, and the indirect object will be between it and the verb. You will find indirect objects with verbs such as build, buy, do, get, give, make, read, save, send, show, and tell.

The indirect object answers the question **to whom or what**, or **for whom or what**, the action of the verb is performed.

Look at the following sentence from "The Pygmies":

> His one vast eye gave the whole **nation** a friendly wink.

The transitive verb **gave** has a direct object, **wink**. His eye gave a wink to whom? To the whole **nation**. **Nation** is the indirect object.

Note that the indirect object always tells us **TO or FOR whom/what** the action of the verb is performed. **To** and **for** are both prepositions, and this information can also appear as part of a prepositional phrase using the preposition **to** or **for**.

> His one vast eye gave a friendly wink **to the whole nation**.

With the preposition, the indirect object **nation** is the object of the preposition **to**; the prepositional phrase modifies **gave**, telling where the wink was given. In either case, the purpose is the same: to identify the recipient of the direct object. In other words, the indirect object tells who or what gets the direct object. But consider this: when the preposition is not there, it is understood—we know that the eye gave the wink **TO** the whole nation even when **to** is not stated.

His one vast <u>eye</u> <u>gave</u> **(to)** the whole nation a friendly wink.

Look at the diagrams below. Regardless of whether or not the preposition is missing from the sentence, this information will modify the verb, in this case **gave**. In the first diagram below, the pronoun **nation** is diagrammed as the object of the preposition **to**. In the second diagram, the pronoun **nation** is diagrammed with the preposition **to** missing from the sentence, so we put **(x)** on the diagram where the preposition would be if it were stated. Notice that the word **nation** is in the same place on the diagram regardless of whether or not a preposition is present in the sentence because it gives precisely the same information.

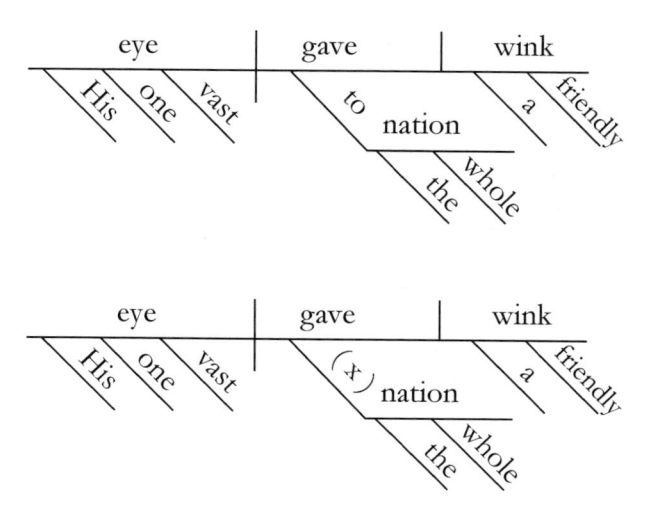

Remember that only a sentence which has a direct object can have an indirect object. Follow this procedure for analyzing sentences.

Put brackets around prepositional phrases.

What is the predicate? The main verb is often easier to find than its subject, so find it first. Double underline it. Is it an action verb or a linking verb?

What is the subject? Underline it once.

For action verbs, is there a direct object which receives the action of the verb by answering the question **whom** or **what**? IF THERE IS A DIRECT OBJECT, is there an indirect object between the DO and the verb which identifies the recipient of the direct object by answering the question **to whom or what**, or **for whom or what**, the action of the verb is performed?

For linking verbs, is there a subject complement—a predicate nominative or a predicate adjective—which renames or modifies the subject?

You can also have a compound indirect object.

He wrote mother and me a letter.

He wrote what? A **letter**; **letter** is the direct object. Who receives the letter? **Mother** and **me**. **Mother** and **me** is the compound indirect object.

A compound indirect object is diagrammed like this:

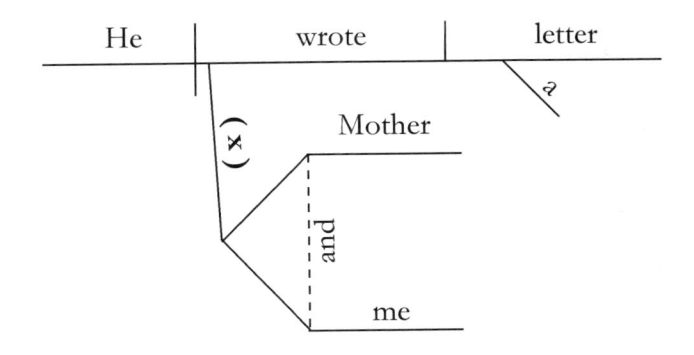

Barnacles

By Sidney Lanier

My soul is sailing through the sea,
But the Past is heavy and hindereth me.
The Past hath crusted cumbrous shells
That hold the flesh of cold sea-mells
About my soul.
The huge waves wash, the high waves roll,
Each barnacle clingeth and worketh dole
And hindereth me from sailing!

Old Past, let go, and drop i' the sea
Till fathomless waters cover thee!
For I am living, but thou art dead;
Thou drawest back, I strive ahead
The Day to find.
Thy shells unbind! Night comes behind;
I needs must hurry with the wind
And trim me best for sailing.

Farmer Mybrow and the Fairies

From *West African Folk-Tales* by William H. Barker

Part II

One day, while maize and yams were still in their green and milky state, Mybrow's wife came to him. She wished to know where his field lay so that she might go and fetch some of the firewood from it. At first he refused to tell her. Being very persistent, however, she finally succeeded in obtaining the information—but on one condition. She must not answer any question that should be asked her. This she readily promised and set off for the field.

When she arrived there, she was utterly amazed at the wealth of the corn and yam. She had never seen such magnificent crops. The maize looked most tempting—being still in the milky state—so she plucked an ear. While doing so, she heard a voice say, "Who is there, breaking the corn?"

"Who dares ask me such a question?" she replied angrily—quite forgetting her husband's command.

Going to the field of yams she plucked one of them also. "Who is there, picking the yams?" came the question again.

"It is I, Mybrow's wife. This is my husband's field, and I have a right to pick." Out came the fairies.

"Let us all help Mybrow's wife to pluck her corn and yams," said they. Before the frightened woman could say a word, the fairies had all set to work with a will, and the corn and yams lay useless on the ground. Being all green and unripe, the harvest was now utterly spoiled. The farmer's wife wept bitterly, but to no purpose. She returned slowly home, not knowing what to say to her husband about such a terrible catastrophe. She decided to keep silence about the matter.

Accordingly, next day the poor man set off gleefully to his field to see how his fine crops were going on. His anger and dismay may be imagined when he saw his field a complete ruin. All his work and foresight had been absolutely ruined through his wife's forgetfulness of her promise.

Exercise

Review memory work. Below are two clauses, one dependent and one independent. Show the two ways to join them.

> the figure looked all the more terrible

> because it carried an enormous brass club on its shoulder

Copy each sentence below. Double underline the predicate, and underline the subject. Put brackets around any prepositional phrases. Label the part of speech of each word. Noun, N; Proper Noun, PN; Pronoun, PRO; Verb, V; Linking Verb, LV; Adjective, ADJ; Article, ART; Adverb, ADV; Conjunctions, CJ; Prepositions, Prep; Interjections, INJ. Diagram each sentence.

The Giant gave them his brotherly kindness.

He gave the Pygmies a breeze with his breath.

The Pymies built themselves structures of clay.

Writing: Commonplace Book

Add the passage below from your model story to your commonplace book.

In the first century before our era, when the Romans came to Egypt, they found the valley full of strange little pictures which seemed to have something to do with the history of the country. But the Romans were not interested in anything foreign and did not inquire into the origin of these queer figures which covered the walls of the temples and the walls of the palaces and endless reams of flat sheets made out of the papyrus reed. The last of the Egyptian priests who had understood the holy art of making such pictures had died several years before.

Dictation

Use part of today's poem for dictation.

96. Historical Narration: Hieroglyphics

• This Week: Tanglewood Tales, The Pygmies

Your next three narrations will be on history topics. When you write about fictional stories, it's acceptable to get creative with the story, adding details and perhaps even new characters and events. However, with a historical topic, you should report the facts without making up new content.

Use your outline to write a narration on this topic. The **purpose** of your paper is what you wish to accomplish with your writing. Your purpose is to **inform** your reader about this topic.

Home, Sweet Home

By John Howard Payne

'Mid pleasures and palaces though we may roam,
Be it ever so humble, there's no place like home;
A charm from the sky seems to hallow us there,
Which, seek through the world, is ne'er met with elsewhere.
  Home! Home! Sweet, sweet Home!
There's no place like Home! There's no place like Home!

An exile from Home, splendor dazzles in vain;
O, give me my lowly thatched cottage again!
The birds singing gaily, that came at my call,—
Give me them,—and the peace of mind, dearer than all!
  Home! Home! Sweet, sweet Home!
There's no place like Home! There's no place like Home!

How sweet 'tis to sit 'neath a fond father's smile,
And the cares of a mother to soothe and beguile!
Let others delight 'mid new pleasures to roam,
But give me, oh, give me, the pleasures of Home!
  Home! Home! Sweet, sweet Home!
There's no place like Home! There's no place like Home!

To thee I'll return, overburdened with care;
The heart's dearest solace will smile on me there;
No more from that cottage again will I roam;
Be it ever so humble, there's no place like Home.
   Home! Home! Sweet, sweet Home!
There's no place like Home! There's no place like Home!

Editing

- Did you meet the goal of this writing exercise?

- Look at your word choice. Is there a good mixture of nouns and pronouns? Is the antecedent of each pronoun clear?

- Look at your paragraphs. Are all the sentences related? Does each paragraph focus on a single topic?

97. Review: Compound and Complex Sentences

• **This Week:** Tanglewood Tales, The Dragon's Teeth

Remember that we use the word **compound** to show that we have two or more of something. A compound subject is two or more subjects. A compound predicate is two or more predicates. A compound sentence is one which has two or more independent clauses. Consider this sentence from "The Dragon's Teeth":

> Europa screamed with delight, **and** Phœnix, Cilix, and Cadmus gaped at their sister mounted on a white bull.

The sentence above has two subject-predicate pairs, which means it has two clauses. Both clauses are independent. Remember that an independent clause is one which can stand alone as a complete sentence. This means that three correct ways to punctuate this sentence exist. Above, the two clauses are joined with a comma and a coordinating conjunction.

The next way to join the two clauses is to let them stand alone as two separate sentences.

> Europa screamed with delight. Phœnix, Cilix, and Cadmus gaped at their sister mounted on a white bull.

The final way to join the two clauses is to separate them with a semicolon.

> Europa screamed with delight; Phœnix, Cilix, and Cadmus gaped at their sister mounted on a white bull.

These are the only three correct ways to join independent clauses. When proper punctuation is not used, it creates a run-on sentence. These are known as run-on sentences because they continue running on even when they should have stopped.

A **fused sentence** occurs when two or more independent clauses are joined with no punctuation at all, like a person who never seems to pause for breath.

> **X** Europa screamed with delight Phœnix, Cilix, and Cadmus gaped at their sister mounted on a white bull.

A **comma splice** occurs when two or more independent clauses are joined with only a comma. The sentences are **spliced** together with a comma.

 X Europa screamed with delight**,** Phœnix, Cilix, and Cadmus gaped at their sister mounted on a white bull.

> Definition: A complex sentence is a sentence with one independent clause and at least one dependent clause.

Independent   Dependent
"You shall never see my face again **unless** you bring me back my little Europa."

Dependent   Independent
When they reached the margin of the sand**,** the treacherous animal was already far away in the wide blue sea.

Remember, punctuating a complex sentence is simple and straightforward. When the subordinate clause comes first, use a comma to separate it from the main clause. However, when the subordinate clause comes after the main clause, no comma is necessary. Below are the same sentences, but I've switched the order of the clauses. Notice how the punctuation changed in each sentence.

"**Unless** you bring me back my little Europa**,** you shall never see my face again."

The treacherous animal was already far away in the wide blue sea **when** they reached the margin of the sand.

A Happy Life
By Sir Henry Wotton

How happy is he born and taught
 That serveth not another's will;
Whose armour is his honest thought,
 And simple truth his utmost skill!

Whose passions not his master's are,
 Whose soul is still prepared for death,
Not tied unto the world with care
 Of public fame, or private breath.
Writing: Oral Narration

Read your new model story below, and then give your instructor an oral narration of it.

The Nile Valley

From *The Story of Mankind* by Hendrik Van Loon

The history of man is the record of a hungry creature in search of food. Wherever food was plentiful, there man has traveled to make his home.

The fame of the Valley of the Nile must have spread at an early date. From the interior of Africa and from the desert of Arabia and from the western part of Asia, people had flocked to Egypt to claim their share of the rich farms. Together these invaders had formed a new race which called itself "Remi" or "the Men." They had good reason to be grateful to a Fate which had carried them to this narrow strip of land. In the summer of each year, the Nile turned the valley into a shallow lake, and when the waters receded, all the grainfields and the pastures were covered with several inches of the most fertile clay.

In Egypt a kindly river did the work of a million men and made it possible to feed the teeming population of the first large cities of which we have any record. It is true that all the arable land was not in the valley. But a complicated system of small canals and well-sweeps carried water from the river level to the top of the highest banks, and an even more intricate system of irrigation trenches spread it throughout the land.

The Egyptian peasant or the inhabitant of the Egyptian city found himself possessed of a certain leisure. He used this spare time to make himself many things that were merely ornamental and not in the least bit useful.

More than that. One day he discovered that his brain was capable of thinking all kinds of thoughts which had nothing to do with the problems of eating and sleeping and finding a home for the children. The Egyptian began to speculate upon many strange problems that confronted him. Where did the stars come from? Who made the noise of the thunder which frightened him so terribly? Who made the River Nile rise with such regularity that it was possible to base the calendar upon the appearance and the disappearance of the annual floods? Who was he, himself, a strange little creature surrounded on all sides by death and sickness and yet happy and full of laughter?

He asked these many questions, and certain people obligingly stepped forward to answer these inquiries to the best of their ability. The Egyptians called them priests, and they became the guardians of his thoughts and gained great respect in the community. They were highly learned men who were entrusted with the sacred task of keeping the written records. They understood that it is not good for man to think only of his immediate advantage in this world, and they drew his attention to the days of the future when his soul would dwell beyond the mountains of the west and must give an account of his deeds to Osiris, the mighty god who was the Ruler of the Living and the Dead and who judged the acts of men according to their merits. Indeed, the priests made so much of that future day in the realm of Isis and Osiris that the Egyptians began to regard life merely as a short preparation for the Hereafter and turned the teeming valley of the Nile into a land devoted to the Dead.

In a strange way, the Egyptians had come to believe that no soul could enter the realm of Osiris without the possession of the body which had been its place of residence in this world. Therefore, as soon as a man was dead, his relatives took his corpse and had it embalmed. For weeks it was soaked in a solution of natron, and then it was filled with pitch. The Persian word for pitch was "Mumiai," and the embalmed body was called a "Mummy." It was wrapped in yards and yards of specially prepared linen, and it was placed in a specially prepared coffin ready to be removed to its final home. But an Egyptian grave was a real home where the body was surrounded by pieces of furniture and musical instruments—to while away the dreary hours of waiting—and by little statues of cooks and bakers and barbers so that the occupant of this dark home might be decently provided with food and need not go about unshaven.

Originally these graves had been dug into the rocks of the western mountains but as the Egyptians moved northward they were obliged to build their cemeteries in the desert. The desert, however, is full of wild animals and equally wild robbers, and they broke into the graves and disturbed the mummy or stole the jewelry that had been buried with the body. To prevent such unholy desecration, the Egyptians used to build small mounds of stones on top of the graves. These little mounds gradually grew in size because the rich people built higher mounds than the poor, and there was a good deal of competition to see who could make the highest hill of stones.

The record was made by King Khufu, whom the Greeks called Cheops and who lived thirty centuries before our era. His mound, which the Greeks called a pyramid, was over five hundred feet high. It covered more than thirteen acres of desert.

During twenty years, over a hundred thousand men were busy carrying the necessary stones from the other side of the river—ferrying them across the Nile—how they ever managed to do this, we do not understand—dragging them in many instances a long distance across the desert and finally hoisting them into their correct position. But so well did the King's architects and engineers perform their task that the narrow passageway which leads to the royal tomb in the heart of the stone monster has never yet been pushed out of shape by the weight of those thousands of tons of stone which press upon it from all sides.

Exercise

Review memory work. Below are two clauses, one dependent and one independent. Show the two ways to join them.

he ate them out of her hand

because he wanted to be friends with the child

Copy each sentence below. Double underline the predicate, and underline the subject. Put brackets around any prepositional phrases. Label the part of speech of each word. Noun, N; Proper Noun, PN; Pronoun, PRO; Verb, V; Linking Verb, LV; Adjective, ADJ; Article, ART; Adverb, ADV; Conjunctions, CJ; Prepositions, Prep; Interjections, INJ. Diagram each sentence.

"Where are you?"

"Come back, pretty creature!"

"Bring me back my little Europa."

Commonplace Book

With your instructor's approval, add the passage below to your commonplace book, or choose your own passage from a work of fiction. This can be from either school reading or free reading.

Never before did a bull have such bright and tender eyes and such smooth horns of ivory as this one. And the bull ran little races and capered sportively around the child so that she quite forgot how big and strong he was and, from the gentleness and playfulness of his actions, soon came to consider him as innocent a creature as a pet lamb.

Dictation

Nevertheless, it was the suddenness with which she had perceived the bull, rather than anything frightful in his appearance, that caused Europa so much alarm. On looking at him more attentively, she began to see that he was a beautiful animal and even fancied a particularly amiable expression in his face. As for his breath—the breath of cattle, you know, is always sweet—it was as fragrant as if he had been grazing on no other food than rosebuds or, at least, the most delicate of clover blossoms.

98. Commas After Introductory Elements

- This Week: Tanglewood Tales, The Dragon's Teeth

Phrases and clauses which introduce sentences often need commas to separate them from the rest of the sentence. These elements include several which you have already learned to punctuate, such as nouns of direct address:

"**Dear child,** let me give you a ride on my back."

Interjections:

"**Alas,** that is only another reason why I should go with you."

And even the speaker tag, the small clause which identifies the speaker of a quotation:

Thasus answered, "Never! Never! Never! Never!"

These elements need commas because they disturb the flow of the main part of the sentence. At the beginning of the sentence, they are known as introductory elements.

Other types of words, phrases, and clauses can also be introductory elements in sentences, including prepositional phrases and adverbs. These elements need to be separated from the rest of the sentence by commas when they create a strong break from the rest of the sentence. Look at the following sentences from "The Dragon's Teeth." In the first sentence, the introductory element is an adverb:

Indeed, his motion was as light as if he were flying through the air.

In this next sentence, the introductory element is a series of prepositional phrases:

At the first thought of such a thing, Europa drew back.

An introductory element can also be a participle phrase, which is a phrase which begins with either a past or present participle:

Frightened as she at first was, you might by and by have seen Europa stroking the bull's forehead with her small white hand.

Using commas after introductory elements can make writing more clear by separating the introductory material from the main thought in the sentence.

A-Tishoo

By Walter De La Mare

"Sneeze, Pretty, sneeze, Dainty,
Else the Elves will have you sure,
Sneeze, Light-of-Seven-Bright-Candles,
See they're tippeting at the door;
Their wee feet in measure falling,
All their little voices calling,
Calling, calling, calling, calling—
Sneeze, or never come no more!"
"A-tishoo!"

Giraffe and Tortoise

From *South-African Folk-Tales* by James A. Honey

Giraffe and Tortoise, they say, met one day. Giraffe said to Tortoise, "At once I could trample you to death." Tortoise, being afraid, remained silent. Then Giraffe said, "At once I could swallow you."

Tortoise said, in answer to this, "Well, I just belong to the family of those whom it has always been customary to swallow."

Then Giraffe swallowed Tortoise; but when the latter was being gulped down, he stuck in Giraffe's throat, and as the latter could not get it down, he was choked to death.

When Giraffe was dead, Tortoise crawled out and went to Crab, who is considered as the mother of Tortoise, and told her what had happened.

Then Crab said:

"The little Crab! I could sprinkle it under its arm with Boochoo,
The crooked-legged little one, I could sprinkle under its arm."

Tortoise answered its mother and said:

"Have you not always sprinkled me,
That you want to sprinkle me now?"

Then they went and fed for a whole year on the remains of Giraffe.

Writing: Outline

Write or type an outline of the new model story which you read in the last lesson.

Exercise

Review memory work. Below are two independent clauses. Show the three ways to join them.

it was delightful to witness the gratitude of this amiable bull

he capered higher than ever

Copy each sentence below. Double underline the predicate, and underline the subject. Put brackets around any prepositional phrases. Label the part of speech of each word. Noun, N; Proper Noun, PN; Pronoun, PRO; Verb, V; Linking Verb, LV; Adjective, ADJ; Article, ART; Adverb, ADV; Conjunctions, CJ; Prepositions, Prep; Interjections, INJ. Diagram each sentence.

"Come and drive away this bull!"

Where did the bull take Europa?

King Agenor, Europa's father, said this. [Hint: **this** is a pronoun in this sentence.]

Commonplace Book

With your instructor's approval, add this part of today's poem to your commonplace book, or choose your own poem.

> "Sneeze, Pretty, sneeze, Dainty,
> Else the Elves will have you sure,
> Sneeze, Light-of-Seven-Bright-Candles,
> See they're tippeting at the door;
> Their wee feet in measure falling,
> All their little voices calling,
> Calling, calling, calling, calling—
> Sneeze, or never come no more!"
> "A-tishoo!"

Dictation

Never say never.

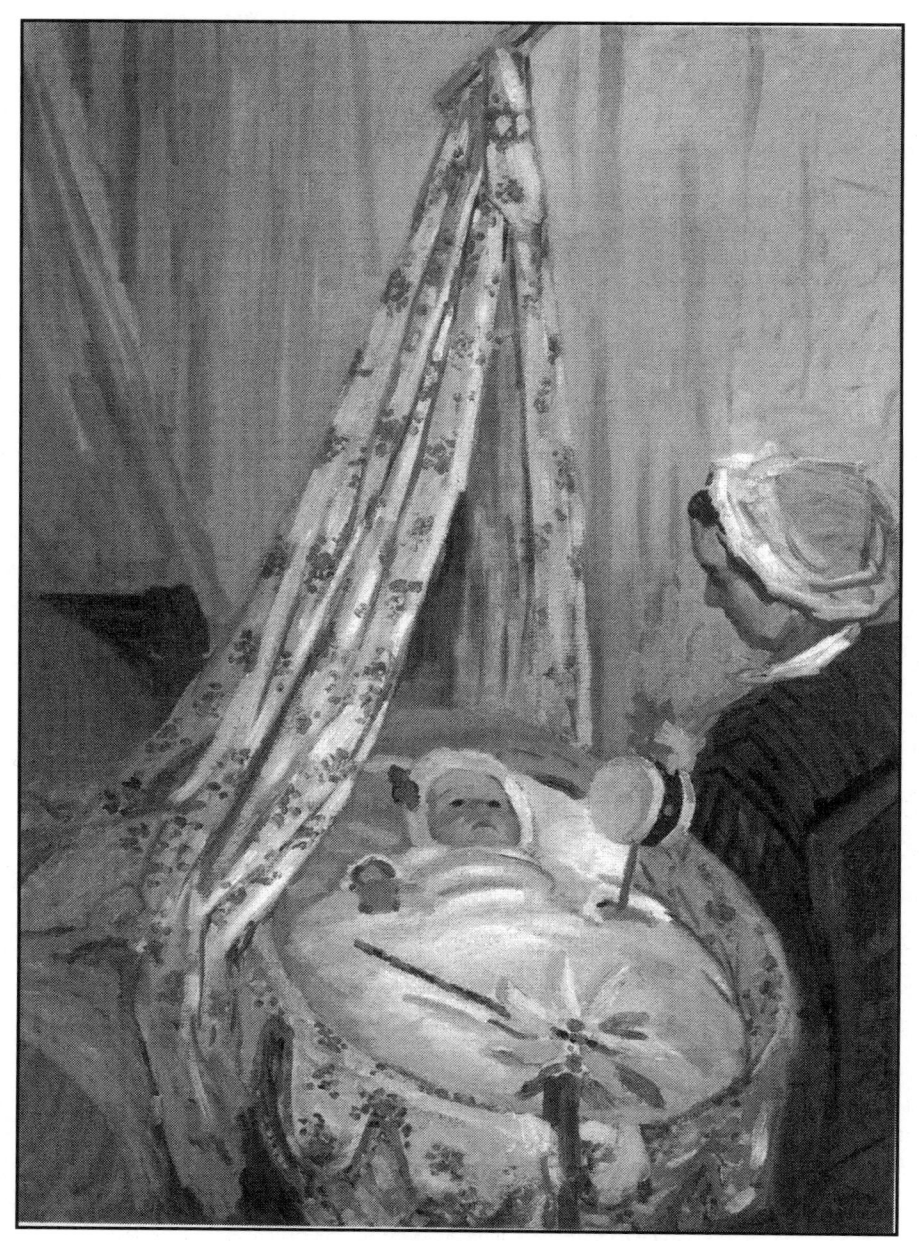

Jean Monet in the Cradle by Claude Monet

Picture Study

1. Read the title and the name of the artist. Study the picture for several minutes, then put the picture away.

2. Describe the picture.

3. Look at the picture again. Do you notice any details that you missed before? What do you like or dislike about this painting? Does it remind you of anything?

99. Literary Analysis

• This Week: Tanglewood Tales, The Dragon's Teeth

Writing: Literary Analysis

Today you have another literary analysis assignment. Now that you have had some practice, this should be a written assignment, though it can be helpful to talk about your ideas before writing.

With your instructor's approval, choose a story from *Tanglewood Tales* or one of the other books you are currently reading, and answer the following questions.

What is the story about? Give a brief summary, just a few sentences. Was there a character that you didn't like? Why? If you liked all the characters, choose one and tell what you liked about him. Give examples from the story.

Annie Laurie

By William Douglas

Maxwelton braes are bonnie
Where early fa's the dew,
And it's there that Annie Laurie
Gie'd me her promise true—
Gie'd me her promise true,
Which ne'er forgot will be;
And for bonnie Annie Laurie
I'd lay me doune and dee.

Her brow is like the snawdrift,
Her throat is like the swan,
Her face it is the fairest
That e'er the sun shone on—
That e'er the sun shone on;
And dark blue is her e'e;

And for bonnie Annie Laurie
I'd lay me doune and dee.

Like dew on the gowan lying
Is the fa' o' her fairy feet;
Like the winds in summer sighing,
Her voice is low and sweet—
Her voice is low and sweet;
And she's a' the world to me;
And for bonnie Annie Laurie
I'd lay me doune and dee.

Lion and Baboon

From *South-African Folk-Tales* by James A. Honey

Baboon, it is said, once worked bamboos, sitting on the edge of a precipice, and Lion stole upon him. Baboon, however, had fixed some round, glistening, eye-like plates on the back of his head. Therefore, when Lion crept upon him, and Baboon was looking at him, he thought that he sat with his back towards him, and he crept with all his might upon him. When, however, Baboon turned his back towards him, Lion thought that he was seen and hid himself. Thus, when Baboon looked at him, he crept upon him. When he was near him, Baboon looked up, and Lion continued to creep upon him. Baboon said aside, "While I am looking at him, he steals upon me while my hollow eyes are on him."

When at last Lion sprung at him, he lay quickly down upon his face, and Lion jumped over him, falling down the precipice, and was dashed to pieces.

Exercise

Review memory work. Below are two clauses, one dependent and one independent. Show the two ways to join them.

> Telephassa threw away her crown
>
> because it chafed her forehead

Copy each sentence below. Double underline the predicate, and underline the subject. Put brackets around any prepositional phrases. Label the part of speech of each word. Noun, N; Proper Noun, PN; Pronoun, PRO; Verb, V; Linking Verb, LV; Adjective, ADJ; Article, ART; Adverb, ADV; Conjunctions, CJ; Prepositions, Prep; Interjections, INJ. Diagram each sentence.

> "Do not seek her!"

> "Stop, my good cow."

> "I am pretty well acquainted with the ways of cattle."
> [Hint: **pretty** shows **to what extent**.]

Commonplace Book

With your instructor's approval, add the passage below to your commonplace book, or choose your own passage from a work of non-fiction. This can be from religious scriptures, a biography, or one of your history or science books.

> Then what a scream of terror did the poor child send forth! The three brothers screamed manfully, likewise, and ran to the shore as fast as their legs would carry them, with Cadmus at their head. But it was too late. When they reached the margin of the sand, the treacherous animal was already far away in the wide blue sea, with only his snowy head and tail emerging, and poor little Europa between them, stretching out one hand towards her dear brothers while she grasped the bull's ivory horn with the other.

Editing

- Did you meet the goal of this writing exercise?

- Look at your word choice. Is there a good mixture of nouns and pronouns? Is the antecedent of each pronoun clear?

- Look at your paragraphs. Are all the sentences related? Does each paragraph focus on a single topic?

100. Relative Pronouns

- **This Week:** Tanglewood Tales, Circe's Palace

You have learned that dependent clauses can begin with subordinate conjunctions. We call these clauses **subordinate clauses**.

Dependent clauses can also begin with **relative pronouns**. Clauses which begin with relative pronouns are called **relative clauses**.

> The relative pronouns are that, which, who.
> (Memorize these three and you can spot the others
> easily. The full list includes: that, which, whichever, who,
> whoever, whom, whomever, whose, whosever.)

Just like clauses which begin with subordinate conjunctions, seeing a relative pronoun at the beginning of a clause is a signal that the clause cannot stand alone as a complete sentence. Alone, it does not express a complete thought.

The function of conjunctions, including subordinate conjunctions, is to join words and groups of words together. Pronouns, on the other hand, stand in for nouns (he, she, we) or they modify nouns (his, her, our). When a relative pronoun begins a dependent clause, the relative pronoun will either be the subject of the clause or it will modify the subject of the clause.

> This misfortune was entirely owing to the foolish curiosity of his shipmates who had untied some very bulky leathern bags.

> It was the same pretty little bird **whose** behavior had so much surprised Ulysses.

In the first sentence above, **who** is the subject of the relative clause. In the second sentence, **whose** is an adjective which modifies behavior.

Now, consider this sentence:

> Who sent you hither?

In this sentence, **who** is an interrogative pronoun because it introduces a question. Do not confuse relative pronouns with interrogative pronouns! Although most of the words are the same, the purpose is different. Interrogative pronouns introduce a question. Relative pronouns introduce a dependent clause, not a question.

The Ship of State

By Henry Wadsworth Longfellow

Sail on, sail on, O Ship of State!
Sail on, O Union, strong and great!
Humanity, with all its fears,
With all the hopes of future years,
Is hanging breathless on thy fate!
We know what Master laid thy keel,
What Workmen wrought thy ribs of steel,
Who made each mast, and sail, and rope;
What anvils rang, what hammers beat,
In what a forge and what a heat
Were forged the anchors of thy hope!
Fear not each sudden sound and shock—
   'Tis of the wave, and not the rock;
   'Tis but the flapping of the sail,
And not a rent made by the gale!
In spite of rock, and tempest roar,
In spite of false lights on the shore,
Sail on, nor fear to breast the sea!
Our hearts, our hopes, are all with thee.
Our hearts, our hopes, our prayers, our tears,
Our faith, triumphant o'er our fears,
Are all with thee, are all with thee!

The Grinding-Stone That Ground Flour by Itself

From *West African Folk-Tales* by William H. Barker

Part I

There had been another great famine throughout the land. The villagers looked thin and pale for lack of food. Only one family appeared healthy and well. This was the household of Anansi's cousin.

Anansi was unable to understand this and felt sure his cousin was getting food in some way. The greedy fellow determined to find out the secret.

What had happened was this: Spider's cousin, while hunting one morning, had discovered a wonderful stone. The stone lay on the grass in the forest and ground flour of its own accord. Near by ran a stream of honey. Kofi was delighted. He sat down and had a good meal. Not being a greedy man, he took away with him only enough for his family's needs.

Each morning he returned to the stone and got sufficient food for that day. In this manner, he and his family kept well and plump while the surrounding villagers were starved and miserable-looking.

Anansi gave him no peace till he promised to show him the stone. This he was most unwilling to do—knowing his cousin's wicked ways. He felt sure that when Anansi saw the stone, he would not be content to take only what he needed. However, Anansi troubled him so much with questions that at last he promised. He told Anansi that they would start next morning as soon as the women set about their work. Anansi was too impatient to wait. In the middle of the night, he bade his children get up and make a noise with the pots as if they were the women at work. Spider at once ran and wakened his cousin, saying, "Quick! It is time to start." His cousin, however, saw he had been tricked and went back to bed again, saying he would not start till the women were sweeping. No sooner was he asleep again than Spider made his children take brooms and begin to sweep very noisily. He roused Kofi once more, saying, "It is time we had started." Once more his cousin refused to set off, saying it was only another trick of Spider's. He again returned to bed and to sleep. This time Spider slipped into his cousin's room and cut a hole in the bottom of his bag, which he then filled with ashes. After that he went off and left Kofi in peace.

Writing: Copia

Take the following sentence and play with it. Remember that the point is not necessarily to make the sentence better. The point is to play with the sentence and make it different. Make a new sentence for each number, using at least one change from that category.

> The Egyptian began to speculate upon many strange problems that confronted him.

1. Change the grammar.
   - Change the nouns from common to proper and vice versa.
   - Change the nouns from singular to plural and vice versa.
   - Change the sentence type.
   - Change the adjectives from articles to descriptive to possessive, etc.
   - Change a quotation from direct to indirect and vice versa.
   - Change the verb tense.

2. Condense the sentence.
   - Remove details.
   - Remove modifiers.
   - Remove phrases or clauses.

3. Amplify the sentence.
   - Add details.
   - Add dialogue.
   - Add modifiers.
   - Add phrases or clauses.

4. Use synonyms and antonyms.
   - Substitute synonyms.
   - Say the opposite thing using antonyms.

5. Point of view.
   - Change the point of view.
   - Slant the sentence.

Exercise

Review memory work. Below are two clauses, one dependent and one independent. Show the two ways to join them.

> when they bade him farewell

> Phoenix shed tears

Copy each sentence below. Double underline the predicate, and underline the subject. Put brackets around any prepositional phrases. Label the part of speech of each word. Noun, N; Proper Noun, PN; Pronoun, PRO; Verb, V; Linking Verb, LV; Adjective, ADJ; Article, ART; Adverb, ADV; Conjunctions, CJ; Prepositions, Prep; Interjections, INJ. Diagram each sentence.

> "That smoke comes from the kitchen!"

> A gush of smoke came from a chimney.

> The palace kitchen was now very perceptible.

Commonplace Book

With your instructor's approval, add the passage below to your commonplace book, or choose your own passage from a work of fiction. This can be from either school reading or free reading.

> At length they came within full sight of the palace, which proved to be very large and lofty, with a great number of airy pinnacles upon its roof. Though it was now midday, and the sun shone brightly over the marble front, yet its snowy whiteness and its fantastic style of architecture made it look unreal, like the frost work on a windowpane, or like the shapes of castles which one sees among the clouds by moonlight.

Dictation

> But, just then, a puff of wind brought down the smoke of the kitchen chimney among them and caused each man to smell the odor of the dish that he liked best; and after scenting it, they thought everything else moonshine, and nothing was real save this palace and save the banquet that was evidently ready to be served up in it.

101. Rhythm in Poetry

- **This Week: Tanglewood Tales, Circe's Palace**

A poem is a writing—a composition—that is a little like speech and a little like song. Poems tell about experiences, ideas, and feelings in an imaginative way. Poems are very descriptive. They have a distinct rhythm and, often, rhyme.

Unlike most writing, poems have a limited number of words or syllables on each line. Sometimes, part of the lines are indented. Each line begins with a capital letter as a general rule, though some poets make their own rules. Lines are grouped together to form stanzas, which are like paragraphs for poems.

Words have accented syllables and unaccented syllables. That means that some syllables are stressed more than others are. This gives a certain amount of rhythm to our speech. **Rhythm** is a regular, strong, repeated pattern of sound. Rhythm in poetry is made by writing the words in such a way that the accented and unaccented syllables form a pattern.

Look below at the first stanza from today's poem. The syllables with the ′ mark above them are the accented ones, and the syllables with the ˘ mark above them are the unaccented ones.

> Sun-light, moon-light,
> Twi-light, star-light—
> Gloam-ing at the close of day,
> And an owl call-ing,
> Cool dews fall-ing
> In a wood of oak and may.

The rhythm makes poems easier to read aloud and also much more pleasing to hear. Read today's poem out loud and listen closely to the rhythm.

Dream-Song
By Walter De La Mare

Sunlight, moonlight,
Twilight, starlight—
Gloaming at the close of day,
And an owl calling,
Cool dews falling
In a wood of oak and may.

Lantern-light, taper-light,
Torchlight, no-light:
Darkness at the shut of day,
And lions roaring,
Their wrath pouring
In wild waste places far away.

Elf-light, bat-light,
Touchwood-light and toad-light,
And the sea a shimmering gloom of grey,
And a small face smiling
In a dream's beguiling
In a world of wonders far away.

The Grinding-Stone That Ground Flour by Itself
From *West African Folk-Tales* by William H. Barker

Part II

    When morning came the cousin awoke. Seeing no sign of Spider he very gladly set off alone to the forest, thinking he had got rid of the tiresome fellow. He was no sooner seated by the stone, however, than Anansi appeared, having followed him by the trail of ashes.
    "Aha!" cried he. "Here is plenty of food for all. No more need to starve." "Hush," said his cousin. "You must not shout here. The place is too wonderful. Sit down quietly and eat."
    They had a good meal, and Kofi prepared to return home with enough for his family. "No, no!" cried Anansi. "I am going to take the stone." In vain did his friend try to overcome his greed. Anansi insisted on putting the stone on his head, and setting out for the village.
    "Spider, Spider, put me down, said the stone.
    The pig came and drank and went away,
    The antelope came and fed and went away:
    Spider, Spider, put me down."
    Spider, however, refused to listen. He carried the stone from village to village selling flour, until his bag was full of money. He then set out for home.
    Having reached his hut and feeling very tired he prepared to put the stone down. But the stone refused to be moved from his head. It stuck fast there, and no efforts could displace it. The weight of it very soon grew too much for Anansi, and ground

him down into small pieces, which were completely covered over by the stone. That is why we often find tiny spiders gathered together under large stones.

Exercise

Review memory work. Take your favorite copywork poem and mark the rhythm of the words.

Below are two independent clauses. Show the three ways to join them.

> they could think of nothing but their greedy appetite

> they resembled those vilest of animals far more than they did kings

Copy each sentence below. Double underline the predicate, and underline the subject. Put brackets around any prepositional phrases. Label the part of speech of each word. Noun, N; Proper Noun, PN; Pronoun, PRO; Verb, V; Linking Verb, LV; Adjective, ADJ; Article, ART; Adverb, ADV; Conjunctions, CJ; Prepositions, Prep; Interjections, INJ. Diagram each sentence.

> They saw their own figures in different colored threads.

> "Ha! Do you smell the feast?"

> Serving men brought them dishes of the richest food.

Writing: Commonplace Book

Add the passage below from your model story to your commonplace book.

> The Egyptian began to speculate upon many strange problems that confronted him. Where did the stars come from? Who made the noise of the thunder which frightened him so terribly? Who made the River Nile rise with such regularity that it was possible to base the calendar upon the appearance and the disappearance of the annual floods? Who was he, himself, a strange little creature surrounded on all sides by death and sickness and yet happy and full of laughter?

Dictation

Use part of today's poem for dictation.

102. Historical Narration: The Nile Valley

- This Week: Tanglewood Tales, Circe's Palace

Use your outline to write a narration on this topic. Remember that with a historical topic, you should report the facts without making up new content or adding details.

The **purpose** of your paper is what you wish to accomplish with your writing. Your purpose is to **inform** your reader about this topic.

Red Rooster

By Hilda Conkling

Red rooster in your gray coop,
O stately creature with tail-feathers red and blue,
Yellow and black,
You have a comb gay as a parade
On your head:
You have pearl trinkets
On your feet:
The short feathers smooth along your back
Are the dark color of wet rocks,
Or the rippled green of ships
When I look at their sides through water.
I don't know how you happened to be made
So proud, so foolish,
Wearing your coat of many colors,
Shouting all day long your crooked words,
Loud . . . sharp . . . not beautiful!

Editing

- Did you meet the goal of this writing exercise?

- Look at your word choice. Is there a good mixture of nouns and pronouns? Is the antecedent of each pronoun clear?
- Look at your paragraphs. Are all the sentences related? Does each paragraph focus on a single topic?

103. Rhyme in Poetry

- **This Week:** Tanglewood Tales, The Pomegranate Seeds

Rhythm in poetry is made by writing the words in such a way that the accented and unaccented syllables form a pattern. Oftentimes, poems have both rhythm and rhyme. **Rhymes** are words with similar ending sounds. Rhyme in poetry is made by ending lines in rhyming words. We can assign each rhyme a letter so that we can mark the rhyme in a poem.

At the Seaside

By Robert Louis Stevenson

When I was down beside the sea	A
A wooden spade they gave to me	A
To dig the sandy shore.	B
My holes were empty like a cup.	C
In every hole the sea came up,	C
Till it could come no more.	B

Ferry Me Across the Water

By Christina Rossetti

"Ferry me across the water,	
Do, boatman, do."	A
"If you've a penny in your purse	
I'll ferry you."	A
"I have a penny in my purse,	
And my eyes are blue;	A
So ferry me across the water,	
Do, boatman, do."	A

"Step into my ferry-boat,
Be they black or blue,   A
And for the penny in your purse
I'll ferry you."   A

   In some poems, each stanza has the same number of lines and the same rhyme scheme. Other poems can vary.

   Poems need to be read aloud to best appreciate the rhythm and rhyme. Listen for the rhythm and rhyme of poems when you read them.

Ingratitude

By William Shakespeare

Blow, blow, thou winter wind,
Thou are not so unkind
  As man's ingratitude;
Thy tooth is not so keen
Because thou are not seen,
  Although thy breath be rude.

Freeze, freeze, thou bitter sky,
Thou dost not bite so nigh
  As benefits forgot;
Though thou the waters warp,
Thy sting is not so sharp
  As friend remembered not.

Writing: Oral Narration

   Read your new model story below, and then give your instructor an oral narration of it.

Greek Life

From *The Story of Mankind* by Hendrik Van Loon

   In all matters of government, the Greek democracy recognized only one class of citizens—the freemen. Every Greek city was composed of a small number of free born citizens, a large number of slaves, and a sprinkling of foreigners.

   At rare intervals—usually during a war, when men were needed for the army—the Greeks showed themselves willing to confer the rights of citizenship upon the barbarians, as they called the foreigners. But this was an exception. Citizenship was a matter of birth. You were an Athenian because your father and your grandfather had been Athenians before you. But however great your merits as a trader or a soldier, if you were born of non-Athenian parents, you remained a foreigner until the end of time.

   The Greek city, therefore, whenever it was not ruled by a king or a tyrant, was run by and for the freemen, and this would not have been possible without a large army of slaves who outnumbered the free citizens at the rate of six or five to one and who performed those tasks to which we modern people must devote most of our time and energy if we wish to provide for our families and pay the rent of our apartments. The slaves did all the cooking and baking and candlestick making of the entire city. They were the tailors and the carpenters and the jewelers and the school teachers and the bookkeepers, and they tended the store and looked after the factory while the master went to the public meeting to discuss questions of war and peace or visited the theater to see the latest play of Aeschylus or hear a discussion of the revolutionary ideas of Euripides, who had dared to express certain doubts upon the omnipotence of the great god Zeus.

Indeed, ancient Athens resembled a modern club. All the freeborn citizens were hereditary members, and all the slaves were hereditary servants and waited upon the needs of their masters, and it was very pleasant to be a member of the organization.

But when we talk about slaves, we do not mean the sort of people about whom you have read in the pages of *Uncle Tom's Cabin*. It is true that the position of those slaves who tilled the fields was a very unpleasant one, but the average freeman who had come down in the world and who had been obliged to hire himself out as a farm hand led just as miserable a life. In the cities, furthermore, many of the slaves were more prosperous than the poorer classes of the freemen. For the Greeks, who loved moderation in all things, did not like to treat their slaves after the fashion which afterward was so common in Rome, where a slave had as few rights as an engine in a modern factory and could be thrown to the wild animals upon the smallest pretext.

The Greeks accepted slavery as a necessary institution, without which no city could possibly become the home of a truly civilized people.

The slaves also took care of those tasks which nowadays are performed by the businessmen and the professional men. As for household duties, the Greeks, who understood the value of leisure, had reduced such duties to the smallest possible minimum by living amidst surroundings of extreme simplicity.

To begin with, their homes were very plain. Even the rich nobles spent their lives in a sort of adobe barn, which lacked all the comforts which a modern workman expects as his natural right. A Greek home consisted of four walls and a roof. There was a door which led into the street, but there were no windows. The kitchen, the living rooms, and the sleeping quarters were built around an open courtyard in which there was a small fountain or a statue and a few plants to make it look bright. Within this courtyard the family lived when it did not rain or when it was not too cold. In one corner of the yard the cook, who was a slave, prepared the meal, and in another corner, the teacher, who was also a slave, taught the children the alpha beta gamma and the tables of multiplication, and in still another corner, the lady of the house, who rarely left her domain since it was not considered good form for a married woman to be seen on the street too often, was repairing her husband's coat with her seamstresses, who were slaves, and in the little office, right off the door, the master was inspecting the accounts which the overseer of his farm, who was a slave, had just brought to him.

When dinner was ready, the family came together, but the meal was a very simple one and did not take much time. The Greeks seem to have regarded eating as an unavoidable evil and not a pastime, which kills many dreary hours and eventually kills many dreary people. They lived on bread and on wine, with a little meat and some green vegetables. They drank water only when nothing else was available because they did not think it very healthy. They loved to call on each other for dinner, but our idea of a festive meal, where everybody is supposed to eat much more than is good for him, would have disgusted them. They came together at the table for the purpose of a good talk and a good glass of wine and water, but as they were moderate people, they despised those who drank too much.

The same simplicity which prevailed in the dining room also dominated their choice of clothes. They liked to be clean and well groomed, to have their hair and beards neatly cut, to feel their bodies strong with the exercise and the swimming of the gymnasium, but they never followed the Asiatic fashion which prescribed loud colors and strange patterns. They wore a long white coat, and they managed to look as smart as a modern Italian officer in his long blue cape.

They loved to see their wives wear ornaments, but they thought it very vulgar to display their wealth—or their wives—in public, and whenever the women left their homes, they were as inconspicuous as possible.

In short, the story of Greek life is a story not only of moderation but also of simplicity. Things—chairs and tables and books and houses and carriages—are apt to take up a great deal of their owner's time. In the end they invariably make him their slave, and his hours are spent looking after their wants—keeping them polished and brushed and painted. The Greeks, before everything else, wanted to be free, both in mind and in body. So that they might maintain their liberty and be truly free in spirit, they reduced their daily needs to the lowest possible point.

Exercise

Review memory work. Mark the rhythm and rhyme from the following lines in today's poem.

> Freeze, freeze, thou bitter sky,
> Thou dost not bite so nigh
>   As benefits forgot;
> Though thou the waters warp,
> Thy sting is not so sharp
>   As friend remembered not.

Below are two clauses, one dependent and one independent. Show the two ways to join them.

I will not taste a morsel of food

even if you keep me forever in your palace

Copy each sentence below. Double underline the predicate, and underline the subject. Put brackets around any prepositional phrases. Label the part of speech of each word. Noun, N; Proper Noun, PN; Pronoun, PRO; Verb, V; Linking Verb, LV; Adjective, ADJ; Article, ART; Adverb, ADV; Conjunctions, CJ; Prepositions, Prep; Interjections, INJ. Diagram each sentence.

They prepared her a sumptuous banquet.

"You are a spoiled child, my little Proserpina."

"Will the dog bite me?"

Commonplace Book

With your instructor's approval, add the passage below to your commonplace book, or choose your own passage from a work of fiction. This can be from either school reading or free reading.

> King Pluto had taken a road which now began to grow excessively gloomy. It was bordered on each side with rocks and precipices, between which the rumbling of the chariot wheels was reverberated with a noise like rolling thunder. The trees and bushes that grew in the crevices of the rocks had very dismal foliage; and by and by, although it was hardly noon, the air became obscured with a gray twilight.

Dictation

The black horses had rushed along so swiftly that they were already beyond the limits of the sunshine. But the duskier it grew, the more did Pluto's visage assume an air of satisfaction. After all, he was not an ill-looking person, especially when he left off twisting his features into a smile that did not belong to them. Proserpina peeped at his face through the gathering dusk and hoped that he might not be so very wicked as she at first thought him.

104. Sit and Set

• This Week: Tanglewood Tales, The Pomegranate Seeds

Today we are going to talk about the verbs **to sit** and **to set**. Because these words are so similar, many people get them confused.

To sit means to place oneself in a seated position. You **sit** on your chair or couch. The verb **sit** never has a direct object. It is something that a subject does to himself.

To sit is an irregular verb. Look at the five principal parts of **sit**:

Infinitive	Present	Present Participle	Past	Past Participle
to sit	sit	sitting	sat	sat

Look at the following examples of **sit** from "The Pomegranate Seeds":

"I will **sit** on the footstool."

"What, the young man that always **sits** in the sunshine?

In the chariot **sat** the figure of a man.

Still she continued her search without **sitting** down to rest.

To set means to place, arrange, or leave something. The verb **set** always has a direct object. It is something the subject does to the direct object.

To set is an irregular verb. Look at the five principal parts of **set**:

Infinitive	Present	Present Participle	Past	Past Participle
to set	set	setting	set	set

Look at the following examples of **set** from "The Pomegranate Seeds." Notice how you could replace the form of **set** in these sentences with a form of **place** or another of its synonyms:

"I shall never smile again till you **set** me down at my mother's door."

She **set** forth resolving never to come back until Proserpina was discovered.

He immediately **set** up a grievous cry.

Pluto bade them lose no time in preparing a most sumptuous banquet, and not to fail of **setting** a golden beaker of the water of Lethe by Proserpina's plate.

The Night-Swans

By Walter De La Mare

'Tis silence on the enchanted lake,
And silence in the air serene,
Save for the beating of her heart,
The lovely-eyed Evangeline.

She sings across the waters clear
And dark with trees and stars between,
The notes her fairy godmother
Taught her, the child Evangeline.

As might the unrippled pool reply,
Faltering an answer far and sweet,
Three swans as white as mountain snow
Swim mantling to her feet.

And still upon the lake they stay,
Their eyes black stars in all their snow,
And softly, in the glassy pool,
Their feet beat darkly to and fro.

She rides upon her little boat,
Her swans swim through the starry sheen,
Rowing her into Fairyland—
The lovely-eyed Evangeline.

'Tis silence on the enchanted lake,
And silence in the air serene;
Voices shall call in vain again
On earth the child Evangeline.

'Evangeline! Evangeline!'
Upstairs, downstairs, all in vain.

Her room is dim; her flowers faded;
She answers not again.

How Wisdom Became the Property of the Human Race

From *West African Folk-Tales* by William H. Barker

There once lived, in Fanti-land, a man named Father Anansi. He possessed all the wisdom in the world. People came to him daily for advice and help.

One day the men of the country were unfortunate enough to offend Father Anansi, who immediately resolved to punish them. After much thought, he decided that the severest penalty he could inflict would be to hide all his wisdom from them. He set to work at once to gather again all that he had already given. When he had succeeded, as he thought, in collecting it, he placed all in one great pot. This he carefully sealed and determined to put it in a spot where no human being could reach it.

Now, Father Anansi had a son, whose name was Kweku Tsin. This boy began to suspect his father of some secret design, so he made up his mind to watch carefully. Next day he saw his father quietly slip out of the house, with his precious pot hung round his neck. Kweku Tsin followed. Father Anansi went through the forest till he had left the village far behind. Then, selecting the highest and most inaccessible-looking tree, he began to climb. The heavy pot, hanging in front of him, made his ascent almost impossible. Again and again, he tried to reach the top of the tree, where he intended to hang the pot. There, he thought, Wisdom would indeed be beyond the reach of everyone but himself. He was unable, however, to carry out his desire. At each trial, the pot swung in his way.

For some time Kweku Tsin watched his father's vain attempts. At last, unable to contain himself any longer, he cried out, "Father, why do you not hang the pot on your back? Then you could easily climb the tree."

Father Anansi turned and said, "I thought I had all the world's wisdom in this pot. But I find you possess more than I do. All my wisdom was insufficient to show me what to do, yet you have been able to tell me." In his anger, he threw the pot down. It struck on a great rock and broke. The wisdom contained in it escaped and spread throughout the world.

Writing: Outline

Write or type an outline of the new model story which you read in the last lesson.

Exercise

Review memory work. Mark the rhythm and rhyme from the following lines in today's poem.

> And still upon the lake they stay,
> Their eyes black stars in all their snow,
> And softly, in the glassy pool,
> Their feet beat darkly to and fro.

Copy each sentence below. Double underline the predicate, and underline the subject. Put brackets around any prepositional phrases. Label the part of speech of each word. Noun, N; Proper Noun, PN; Pronoun, PRO; Verb, V; Linking Verb, LV; Adjective, ADJ; Article, ART; Adverb, ADV; Conjunctions, CJ; Prepositions, Prep; Interjections, INJ. Diagram each sentence.

"Where is Proserpina?"

"Tell me, you naughty sea-nymphs."

"I once had a child of my own."

Commonplace Book

With your instructor's approval, add this part of today's poem to your commonplace book, or choose your own poem.

> 'Tis silence on the enchanted lake,
> And silence in the air serene,
> Save for the beating of her heart,
> The lovely-eyed Evangeline.
>
> She sings across the waters clear
> And dark with trees and stars between,
> The notes her fairy godmother
> Taught her, the child Evangeline.

Dictation

Rome wasn't built in a day.

Madame Monet and Child by Claude Monet

Picture Study

1. Read the title and the name of the artist. Study the picture for several minutes, then put the picture away.

2. Describe the picture.

3. Look at the picture again. Do you notice any details that you missed before? What do you like or dislike about this painting? Does it remind you of anything?

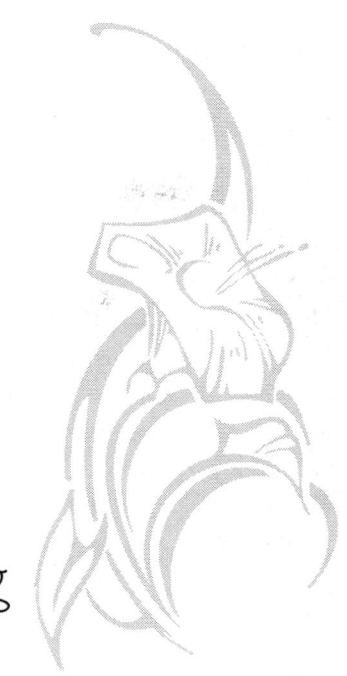

105. Descriptive Writing

• This Week: Tanglewood Tales, The Pomegranate Seeds

Writing: Descriptive Writing

Remember that the purpose of descriptive writing is to describe a person, place, thing, or event so well that an image forms in the mind of the reader.

Your last six picture studies have been on paintings by Claude Monet. Today, choose one of his paintings, either one from this book or one from another source, and write a description of it. Imagine that you are describing the picture to someone who has never seen it before. Get creative if you wish. Write a description for a museum catalog or as part of a police report describing stolen merchandise. Or get really creative. Imagine that the painting is a window to another dimension, and you have just been pulled in. Describe the environment in which you find yourself. Or, write a story about the picture or about your experiences within it. Be as creative as you want. Just do not forget to describe the picture!

Moly

By Edith M. Thomas

Traveler, pluck a stem of moly,
If thou touch at Circe's isle,—
Hermes' moly, growing solely
To undo enchanter's wile!
When she proffers thee her chalice,—
Wine and spices mixed with malice,—
When she smites thee with her staff
To transform thee, do thou laugh!
Safe thou art if thou but bear
The least leaf of moly rare.
Close it grows beside her portal,
Springing from a stock immortal,
Yes! And often has the Witch

Sought to tear it from its niche;
But to thwart her cruel will
The wise God renews it still.
Though it grows in soil perverse,
Heaven hath been its jealous nurse,
And a flower of snowy mark
Springs from root and sheathing dark;
Kingly safeguard, only herb
That can brutish passion curb!
Some do think its name should be
Shield-Heart, White Integrity.
Traveler, pluck a stem of moly,
If thou touch at Circe's isle,—
Hermes' moly, growing solely
To undo enchanter's wile!

When Lion Could Fly

From *South-African Folk-Tales* by James A. Honey

Lion, it is said, used to fly, and at that time nothing could live before him. As he was unwilling that the bones of what he caught should be broken into pieces, he made a pair of White Crows watch the bones, leaving them behind at the kraal while he went a-hunting. But one day Great Frog came there, broke the bones in pieces, and said, "Why can men and animals live no longer?" And he added these words, "When he comes, tell him that I live at yonder pool; if he wishes to see me, he must come there."

Lion, lying in wait for game, wanted to fly up, but found he could not fly. Then he got angry, thinking that at the kraal something was wrong, and he returned home. When he arrived, he asked, "What have you done that I cannot fly?"

Then they answered and said, "Someone came here, broke the bones into pieces, and said, 'If he want me, he may look for me at yonder pool!'"

Lion went and arrived while Frog was sitting at the water's edge, and he tried to creep stealthily upon him. When he was about to get hold of him, Frog said, "Ho!" And diving, he went to the other side of the pool and sat there. Lion pursued him; but as he could not catch him, he returned home.

From that day, it is said, Lion walked on his feet and also began to creep upon his game; and the White Crows became entirely dumb since the day that they said, "Nothing can be said of that matter."

Exercise

Review memory work. Identify each group of words below as either a phrase or a clause. If it is a clause, double underline the predicate and underline the subject.

    which I may judge proper for him

    what the nurse did to her child

    flinging a warm and ruddy light upon the walls

Copy each sentence below. Double underline the predicate, and underline the subject. Put brackets around any prepositional phrases. Label the part of speech of each word. Noun, N; Proper Noun, PN; Pronoun, PRO; Verb, V; Linking Verb, LV; Adjective, ADJ; Article, ART; Adverb, ADV; Conjunctions, CJ; Prepositions, Prep; Interjections, INJ. Diagram each sentence.

Queen Metanira, his mother, shrieked.

The little damsel was not so unhappy.

"Hasten home to your dear mother." [Hint: **home** tells where.]

Commonplace Book

With your instructor's approval, add the passage below to your commonplace book, or choose your own passage from a work of non-fiction. This can be from religious scriptures, a biography, or one of your history or science books.

> So she took up the pomegranate and applied it to her nose; and, somehow or other, being in such close neighborhood to her mouth, the fruit found its way into that little red cave. Dear me! What an everlasting pity! Before Proserpina knew what she was about, her teeth had actually bitten it, of their own accord. Just as this fatal deed was done, the door of the apartment opened, and in came King Pluto, followed by Quicksilver, who had been urging him to let his little prisoner go.

Editing

- Did you meet the goal of this writing exercise?
- Look at your word choice. Is there a good mixture of nouns and pronouns? Is the antecedent of each pronoun clear?
- Look at your paragraphs. Are all the sentences related? Does each paragraph focus on a single topic?

106. Lie and Lay

• **This Week: Tanglewood Tales, The Golden Fleece**

Today we are going to talk about the verbs **to lie** and **to lay**. These are very similar to **sit** and **set**, both in meaning and confusion.

To lie means to place oneself in a prone, lying down position. You **lie** on your bed. The verb **lie** never has a direct object. It's something that a subject does to himself, not something the subject does to something else.

To lie is an irregular verb. Look at the five principal parts of **lie**:

Infinitive	Present	Present Participle	Past	Past Participle
to lie	lie	lying	lay	lain

Lay is the past tense of this irregular verb.
Look at the following examples of **lie** from *Tanglewood Tales*:

"We may as well **lie** down on a bank of soft sponge, under the water."

She could perceive no token of the child's being injured by the hot fire in which he had **lain**.

All the pleasure she had, you know, **lay** in being miserable.

The cow was staring leisurely about her, as other cows do when on the point of **lying** down.

To lay means to place, arrange, set, or leave something. The verb **lay** always has a direct object. It's something the subject does to the direct object.
Look at the five principal parts of **lay**:

Infinitive	Present	Present Participle	Past	Past Participle
to lay	lay	laying	laid	laid

Lay is the present tense of this irregular verb.

Look at the following examples of **lay** from *Tanglewood Tales*. Notice how you could replace the form of lay in these sentences with a form of place or another of its synonyms.

> Medea stayed only long enough to take her son with her, and to steal whatever valuable things she could **lay** hands on.

> They were talking of these schemes, and beguiling the tediousness of the way with **laying** out the plan of the new city.

> Ceres suddenly **laid** him, all naked as he was, in the hollow among the red-hot embers.

The Fairies Dancing

By Walter De La Mare

I heard along the early hills,
Ere yet the lark was risen up,
Ere yet the dawn with firelight fills
The night-dew of the bramble-cup—
I heard the fairies in a ring
Sing as they tripped a lilting round
Soft as the moon on wavering wing.
The starlight shook as if with sound,
As if with echoing, and the stars
Prankt their bright eyes with trembling gleams;
While red with war the gusty Mars
Rained upon earth his ruddy beams.
He shone alone, adown the West,
While I, behind a hawthorn-bush,
Watched on the fairies flaxen-tressed
The fires of the morning flush.
Till, as a mist, their beauty died,
Their singing shrill and fainter grew;
And daylight tremulous and wide
Flooded the moorland through and through;
Till Urdon's copper weathercock
Was reared in golden flame afar,
And dim from moonlit dreams awoke
The towers and groves of Arroar.

Jackal, Dove, and Heron

From *South-African Folk-Tales* by James A. Honey

Jackal, it is said, came once to Dove, who lived on the top of a rock, and said, "Give me one of your little ones."

Dove answered, "I shall not do anything of the kind."

Jackal said, "Give me it at once! Otherwise, I shall fly up to you." Then she threw one down to him.

He came back another day and demanded another little one, and she gave it to him. After Jackal had gone, Heron came and asked, "Dove, why do you cry?"

Dove answered him, "Jackal has taken away my little ones; it is for this that I cry."

He asked her, "In what manner did he take them?"

She answered him, "When he asked me, I refused him; but when he said, 'I shall at once fly up, therefore give me it,' I threw it down to him."

Heron said, "Are you such a fool as to give your young ones to Jackal, who cannot fly?" Then, with the admonition to give no more, he went away.

Jackal came again and said, "Dove, give me a little one."

Dove refused and told him that Heron had told her that he could not fly up. Jackal said, "I shall catch him."

So when Heron came to the banks of the water, Jackal asked him, "Brother Heron, when the wind comes from this side, how will you stand?"

He turned his neck towards him and said, "I stand thus, bending my neck on one side."

Jackal asked him again, "When a storm comes and when it rains, how do you stand?"

He said to him, "I stand thus, indeed, bending my neck down."

Then Jackal beat him on his neck and broke his neck in the middle. Since that day Heron's neck is bent.

Writing: Copia

Take the following sentence and play with it. Remember that the point is not necessarily to make the sentence better. The point is to play with the sentence and make it different. Make a new sentence for each number, using at least one change from that category.

> When dinner was ready, the family came together, but the meal was a very simple one and did not take much time.

1. Change the grammar.
   - Change the nouns from common to proper and vice versa.
   - Change the nouns from singular to plural and vice versa.
   - Change the sentence type.
   - Change the adjectives from articles to descriptive to possessive, etc.
   - Change a quotation from direct to indirect and vice versa.
   - Change the verb tense.

2. Condense the sentence.
   - Remove details.
   - Remove modifiers.
   - Remove phrases or clauses.

3. Amplify the sentence.
   - Add details.
   - Add dialogue.
   - Add modifiers.
   - Add phrases or clauses.

4. Use synonyms and antonyms.
   - Substitute synonyms.
   - Say the opposite thing using antonyms.

5. Point of view.
   - Change the point of view.
   - Slant the sentence.

Exercise

Review memory work. Mark the rhythm and rhyme from the following lines in today's poem.

>I heard along the early hills,
>Ere yet the lark was risen up,
>Ere yet the dawn with firelight fills
>The night-dew of the bramble-cup—

Identify each group of words below as either a phrase or a clause. If it is a clause, double underline the predicate and underline the subject.

when the old dame and her peacock were out of sight

over her shoulder as she departed

after traveling a pretty long distance

Copy each sentence below. Double underline the predicate, and underline the subject. Put brackets around any prepositional phrases. Label the part of speech of each word. Noun, N; Proper Noun, PN; Pronoun, PRO; Verb, V; Linking Verb, LV; Adjective, ADJ; Article, ART; Adverb, ADV; Conjunctions, CJ; Prepositions, Prep; Interjections, INJ. Diagram each sentence.

Argus, the ship builder, built him a galley with fifty oars.

"We are the subjects of King Pelias."

Jason the one-sandaled man had come.

Commonplace Book

With your instructor's approval, add the passage below to your commonplace book, or choose your own passage from a work of fiction. This can be from either school reading or free reading.

> "You will get a handsomer pair of sandals by and by," said the old woman, with a kindly look out of her beautiful brown eyes. "Only let King Pelias get a glimpse of that bare foot, and you shall see him turn as pale as ashes, I promise you. There is your path. Go along, my good Jason, and my blessing go with you. And when you sit on your throne, remember the old woman whom you helped over the river."

Dictation

> With these words, she hobbled away, giving him a smile over her shoulder as she departed. Whether the light of her beautiful brown eyes threw a glory round about her, or whatever the cause might be, Jason fancied that there was something very noble and majestic in her figure, after all, and that, though her gait seemed to be a rheumatic hobble, yet she moved with as much grace and dignity as any queen on earth. Her peacock, which had now fluttered down from her shoulder, strutted behind her in prodigious pomp and spread out its magnificent tail on purpose for Jason to admire it.

107. Well and Good

- This Week: Tanglewood Tales, The Golden Fleece

Good is an adjective. That means it modifies nouns and pronouns.

Well is usually an adverb. That means it can modify verbs, adjectives, and other adverbs. But sometimes, it acts as an adjective. When it's used as an adjective, it means to be in good health.

When you need to decide whether to describe something as **good** or **well**, determine what part of speech the word you're describing is. In the following examples, I've underlined **good** or **well** and the word it modifies in the sentence.

The hot *cocoa* was **good** this morning. You made it **well**.

How are you today? I am **good**. I am doing **well**.

(Note: In the second sentence, **good** modifies the pronoun **I**. In the third sentence, **well** modifies the verb **am doing**.)

Are you feeling ill? No, I am **well**.
(Note: In the second sentence, **well** modifies the pronoun **I**; it is acting as the adjective that means good health.)

Few have gotten a **good** *look* at a Sasquatch. The Sasquatch hides **well**.

Your behavior was **good**. You behaved **well**.

Brookland Road

By Rudyard Kipling

I was very well pleased with what I knowed,
I reckoned myself no fool—

Till I met with a maid on the Brookland Road
That turned me back to school.

Low down—low down!
Where the liddle green lanterns shine—
Oh! maids, I've done with 'ee all but one,
And she can never be mine!
'Twas right in the middest of a hot June night,
With thunder duntin' round,
And I seed her face by the fairy light
That beats from off the ground.

She only smiled and she never spoke,
She smiled and went away;
But when she'd gone my heart was broke,
And my wits was clean astray.

Oh! Stop your ringing and let me be—
Let be, O Brookland bells!
You'll ring Old Goodman * out of the sea,
Before I wed one else!

Old Goodman's farm is rank sea sand,
And was this thousand year;
But it shall turn to rich plough land
Before I change my dear!

Oh! Fairfield Church is water-bound
From Autumn to the Spring;
But it shall turn to high hill ground
Before my bells do ring!

Oh! leave me walk on the Brookland Road,
In the thunder and warm rain—
Oh! leave me look where my love goed
And p'raps I'll see her again!
Low down—low down!
Where the liddle green lanterns shine—
Oh! maids, I've done with 'ee all but one,
And she can never be mine!

The Squirrel and the Spider

From *West African Folk-Tales* by William H. Barker

   A hard-working squirrel had, after much labor, succeeded in cultivating a very fine farm. Being a skilful climber of trees, he had not troubled to make a roadway into his farm. He used to reach it by the trees.
   One day, when his harvests were very nearly ripe, it happened that Spider went out hunting in that neighborhood. During his travels, he arrived at Squirrel's farm. Greatly pleased at the appearance of the fields, he sought for the roadway to it. Finding none,

he returned home and told his family all about the matter. The very next day, they all set out for this fine place and set to work immediately to make a road. When this was completed, Spider—who was very cunning—threw pieces of earthenware pot along the pathway. This he did to make believe that his children had dropped them while working to prepare the farm.

Then he and his family began to cut down and carry away such of the corn as was ripe. Squirrel noticed that his fields were being robbed, but he could not at first find the thief. He determined to watch. Sure enough Spider soon reappeared to steal more of the harvest. Squirrel demanded to know what right he had on these fields. Spider immediately asked him the same question.

"They are my fields," said Squirrel.

"Oh, no! They are mine," retorted Spider.

"I dug them and sowed them and planted them," said poor Squirrel.

"Then where is your roadway to them?" said crafty Spider.

"I need no roadway. I come by the trees," was Squirrel's reply.

Needless to say, Spider laughed such an answer to scorn and continued to use the farm as his own.

Squirrel appealed to the law, but the court decided that no one had ever had a farm without a road leading to it; therefore the fields must be Spider's.

In great glee Spider and his family prepared to cut down all the harvest that remained. When it was cut, they tied it in great bundles and set off to the nearest marketplace to sell it. When they were about halfway there, a terrible storm came on. They were obliged to put down their burdens by the roadside and run for shelter. When the storm had passed, they returned to pick up their loads.

As they approached the spot, they found a great, black crow there, with his broad wings outspread to keep the bundles dry. Spider went to him and very politely thanked him for so kindly taking care of their property.

"Your property!" replied Father Crow. "Who ever heard of anyone leaving bundles of corn by the roadside? Nonsense! These loads are mine." So saying, he picked them up and went off with them, leaving Spider and his children to return home sorrowful and empty-handed. Their thieving ways had brought them little profit.

Exercise

Mark the rhythm and rhyme from the following lines in today's poem.

> I was very well pleased with what I knowed,
> I reckoned myself no fool—
> Till I met with a maid on the Brookland Road
> That turned me back to school.

Writing: Commonplace Book

Add the passage below from your model story to your commonplace book.

> When dinner was ready, the family came together, but the meal was a very simple one and did not take much time. The Greeks seem to have regarded eating as an unavoidable evil and not a pastime, which kills many dreary hours and eventually kills many dreary people. They lived on bread and on wine, with a little meat and some green vegetables. They drank water only when nothing else was available because they did not think it very healthy.

Dictation

Use part of today's poem for dictation.

108. Historical Narration: Greek Life

- **This Week:** Tanglewood Tales, The Golden Fleece

Use your outline to write a narration on this topic. Remember that with a historical topic, you should report the facts without making up new content or adding details.

The **purpose** of your paper is what you wish to accomplish with your writing. Your purpose is to **inform** your reader about this topic.

The Three Beggars

By Walter De La Mare

'Twas autumn daybreak gold and wild,
While past St. Ann's grey tower they shuffled,
Three beggars spied a fairy-child
In crimson mantle muffled.
The daybreak lighted up her face
All pink, and sharp, and emerald-eyed;
She looked on them a little space,
And shrill as hautboy cried:—
"O three tall footsore men of rags
Which walking this gold morn I see,
What will ye give me from your bags
For fairy kisses three?"
The first, that was a reddish man,
Out of his bundle takes a crust:
"La, by the tombstones of St. Ann,
There's fee, if fee ye must!"
The second, that was a chestnut man,
Out of his bundle draws a bone:
"Lo, by the belfry of St. Ann,
And all my breakfast gone!"
The third, that was a yellow man,
Out of his bundle picks a groat,
"La, by the Angel of St. Ann,

And I must go without."
That changeling, lean and icy-lipped,
Touched crust, and bone, and groat, and lo!
Beneath her finger taper-tipped
The magic all ran through.
Instead of crust a peacock pie,
Instead of bone sweet venison,
Instead of groat a white lily
With seven blooms thereon.
And each fair cup was deep with wine:
Such was the changeling's charity,
The sweet feast was enough for nine,
But not too much for three.
O toothsome meat in jelly froze!
O tender haunch of elfin stag!
O rich the odour that arose!
O plump with scraps each bag!
There, in the daybreak gold and wild,
Each merry-hearted beggar man
Drank deep unto the fairy child,
And blessed the good St. Ann.

Editing

- Did you meet the goal of this writing exercise?

- Look at your word choice. Is there a good mixture of nouns and pronouns? Is the antecedent of each pronoun clear?

- Look at your paragraphs. Are all the sentences related? Does each paragraph focus on a single topic?

Exercise Answers

Exercise 2
Common nouns: present, dragon, child, happiness, niece, pleasure, dragon, home, friends

Exercise 3
Common nouns: frock, stuff, curtains, poison, hands, joy
Proper nouns: Harry, Effie, Harry, St. George

Exercise 4
Linking verbs and verbals are not included in my list, though it's fine if the student included them.
Verbs: tumble, cried, fell, fell, crawled, dressed, had

Exercise 5
Linking verbs and verbals are not included in my list, though it's fine if the student included them.
Verbs: boiled, sent, poured, set

Exercise 7
It, the creature; she, Sabrinetta; me, Sabrinetta; I, Sabrinetta

Exercise 8
he, Edmund; it, the new lantern

Exercise 9
me, Black Beauty; they, the six colts; I, Black Beauty; them, the six colts; we, Beauty and the other colts

Exercise 10
I, Black Beauty; me, Black Beauty; he, Squire Gordon; my, Black Beauty's; him, Squire Gordon
In the quote from Squire Gordon, Black Beauty is the antecedent of he.

Exercise 11

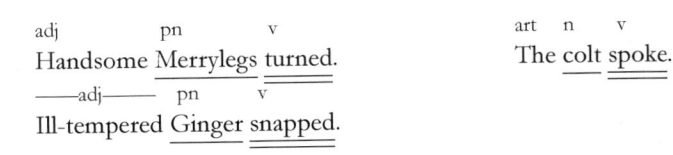

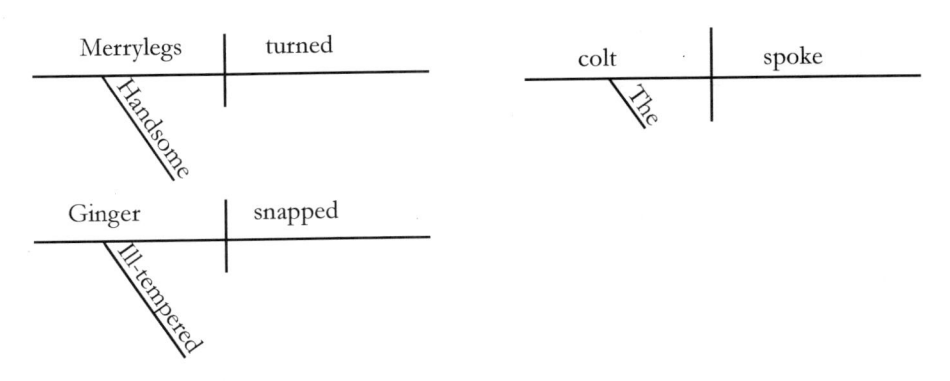

adj   pn   v
Handsome Merrylegs turned.
—adj—   pn   v
Ill-tempered Ginger snapped.

art   n   v
The colt spoke.

Exercise 13

adj   adj   adj   pn   v
Strong, tall, bold Samson boasted.

art   adj   adj   n   v
The kindly old master helped.

```
    adj       adj    pn   v
Steady, thoughtful Job trained.
```

```
   Samson    |    boasted              master   |   helped
    /\ /\ /\                            /\ /\ /\
```

```
   Job       |    trained
    /\ /\
```

Exercise 14

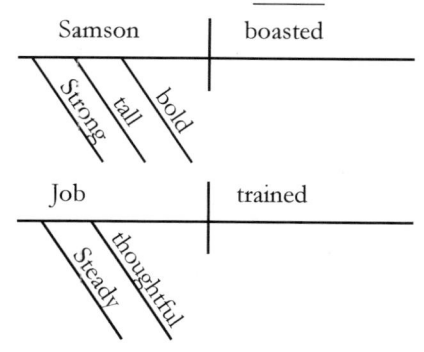

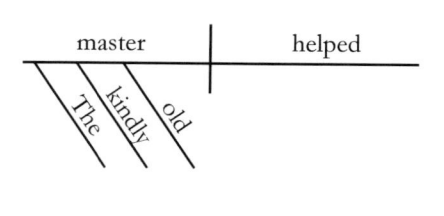

```
pro lv  art adj   ———n———              pro lv   n
"I am the best riding-master."         "We were colts."
pro lv   art adj   n
"He was a good master."
```

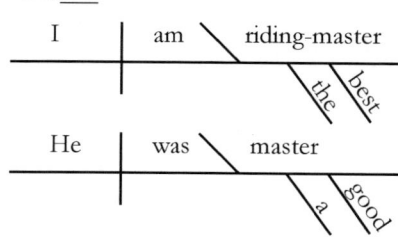

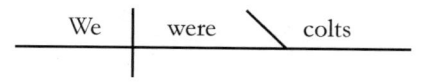

```
    I    |  am  \  riding-master        We  |  were  \  colts
                    \the \best
    
   He   |  was  \  master
                    \a \good
```

Exercise 15

```
pro  lv  art  adj      n                n   lv    n
"They were a valuable kind."           "Men are blockheads."
 n     lv   adj       n
"Blinkers are dangerous things."
```

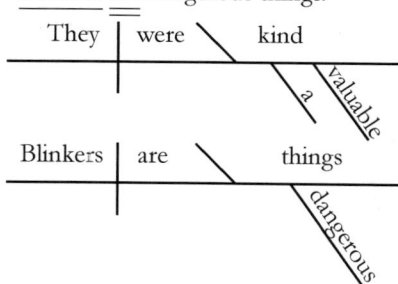

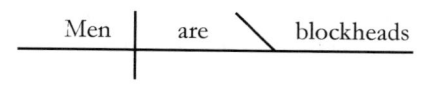

```
   They  |  were  \  kind              Men  |  are  \  blockheads
                     \a \valuable
   
  Blinkers | are  \  things
                     \dangerous
```

Exercise 16

```
pro  lv  art  adj      n
"They are a handsome pair."
pro  lv  art adj    n                  adj  n    v
"You are a military man."              My master rode.
```

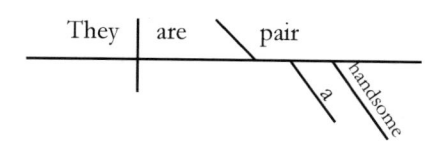

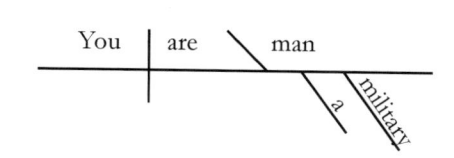

```
   They  |  are  \  pair               You  |  are  \  man
                    \a \handsome                       \a \military
```

```
 master  |  rode
   \My
```

Exercise 17

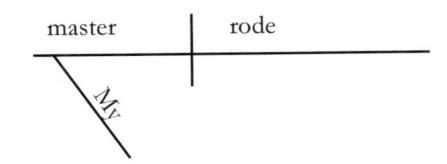

```
 art  n  lv  adj
"The horse is fresh."
 adj   adj   n   lv art n
"That young fellow is a liar."
```

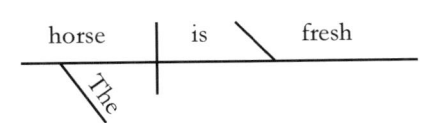

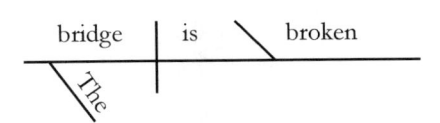

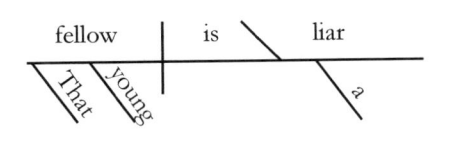

```
 horse  |  is  \  fresh
   \The

 bridge  |  is  \  broken
   \The

 fellow  |  is  \  liar
   \That \young      \a
```

Exercise 19

```
 pro lv art adj  n
"He is a brave lad."
 adj   n     —lv—  adj
Our mistress had been alarmed.

 art adj  n    —v—
A fine horse had died.
```

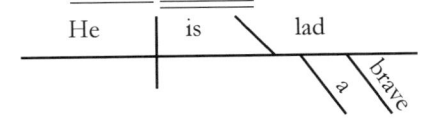

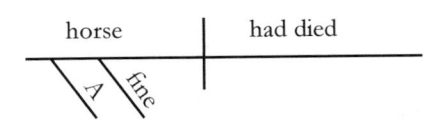

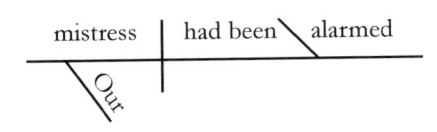

```
 He  |  is  \  lad
            \a \brave

 horse  |  had died
   \A \fine

 mistress  |  had been  \ alarmed
    \Our
```

Exercise 20

kerchiefs, reefs, bluffs; scarves according to the rules, but scarfs is also correct

```
 pro —lv— adj
"I will be ready."
        —pn——   —v—
"Black Beauty will go."
 pro  —v—
We had left.
```

```
  I  |  will be  \  ready

  Black Beauty  |  will go

  We  |  had left
```

Exercise 21

lives, cliffs, roofs; dwarves according the rules, but dwarfs is also correct

```
 art  n  lv  ———adj———
"The boy is broken-hearted."

 pro lv adj  n
"It was only ignorance."
```

489

pro lv adj
He was better.

```
    boy   |  is  \ broken-hearted           It  |  was \ ignorance
  \                                                          \
   \The                                                       \only
```

```
    He    |  was  \ better
```

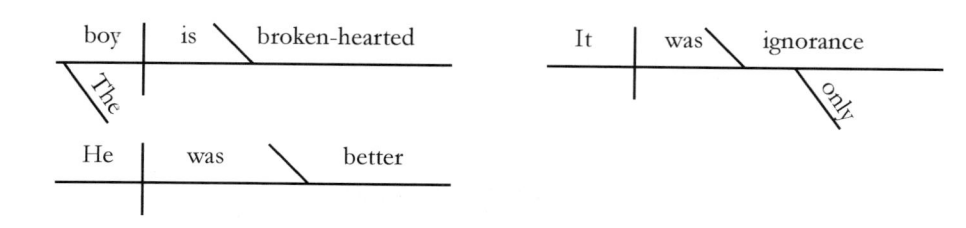

Exercise 22

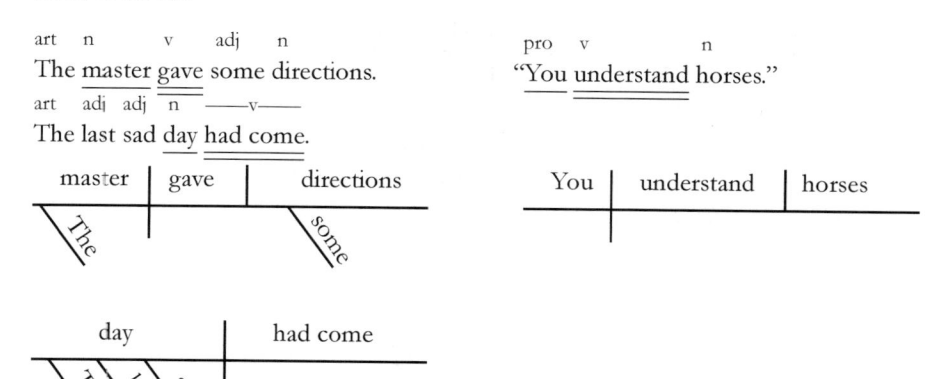

art n v adj n   pro v   n
The master gave some directions.   "You understand horses."
art adj adj n ——v——
The last sad day had come.

```
  master | gave | directions           You | understand | horses
   \            \
    \The         \some
```

```
    day  |  had come
   \ \ \
   The last sad
```

Exercise 23

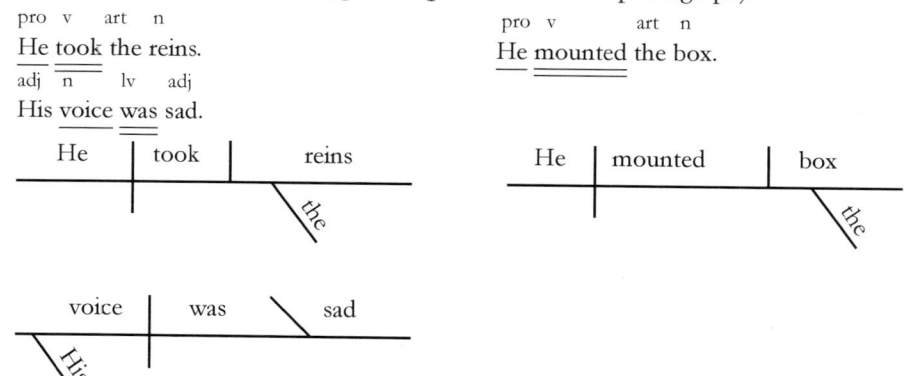

wives, staffs, stereos, tomatoes, photos (photo is short for photograph)

pro v art n   pro v   art n
He took the reins.   He mounted the box.
adj n lv adj
His voice was sad.

```
    He | took | reins                   He | mounted | box
              \                                       \
               \the                                    \the
```

```
   voice | was \ sad
    \
     \His
```

Exercise 25

videos, mangoes or mangos, studios, echoes, heroes

art n lv adj   pro lv art adj   n
The roads were stony.   He was a handsome man.
pro v adj   n
He had pleasant manners.

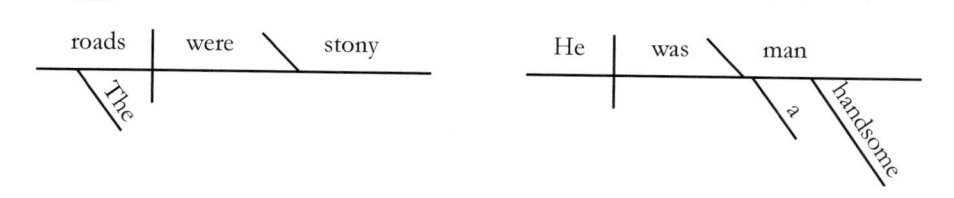

```
   roads | were \ stony                He | was \ man
    \                                           \ \
     \The                                        a handsome
```

490

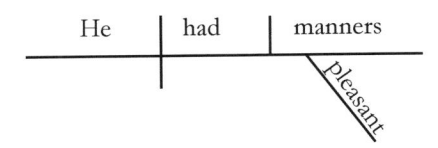

He | had | manners
             \pleasant

Exercise 26

hv pn v   art adj n
Did Beauty enjoy the sweet grass?

lv pn   adj
Was Beauty lonely?

Beauty | Did enjoy | grass
                     \the \sweet

Beauty | Was \ lonely

hv pro v   adj n
Had they become fast friends?

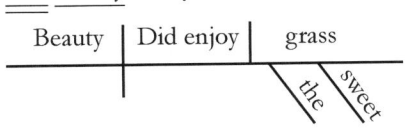

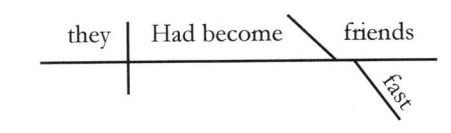

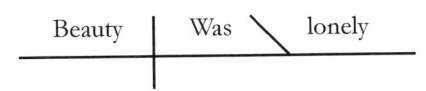

they | Had become \ friends
                     \fast

Exercise 27

adj   n   lv adj
These drivers are careless.

hv pro v art n
Did he have a stone?

drivers | are \ careless
  \These

he | Did have | stone
                 \a

pro v adj n
He lifted his hat.

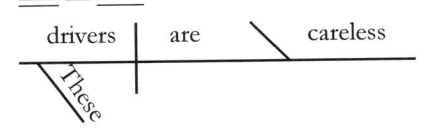

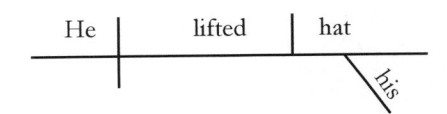

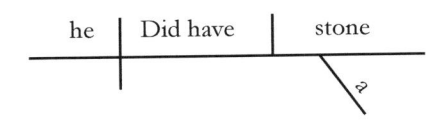

He | lifted | hat
               \his

Exercise 28

hv pro lv adj
"Has he been well?"

pn   art pn   v   art   n
Beauty and Peggy pulled the carriage.

he | Has been \ well

Beauty
   \and | pulled | carriage
Peggy   \the

art n   v   cj v adj n
The farmer dismounted and held his rein.

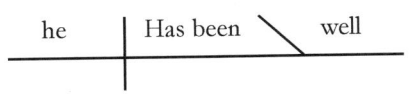

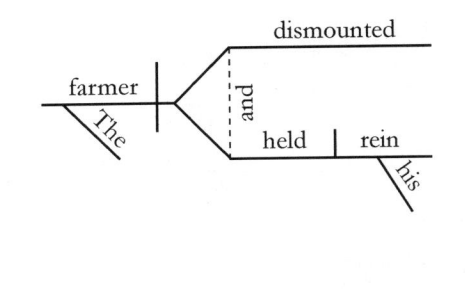

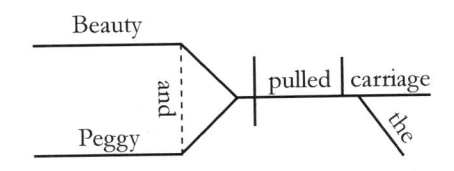

       dismounted
farmer <and
        held | rein
                \his

Exercise 29

pro—v—art n cj v adj n
"I will attend the hoof and direct your man."

pro lv adj   cj   adj
He was ignorant and conceited.

```
art    n      v   cj   v    adj   n
```
The bricklayer came and pulled many bricks.

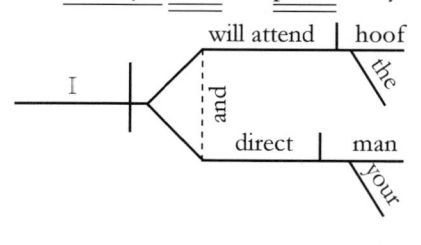

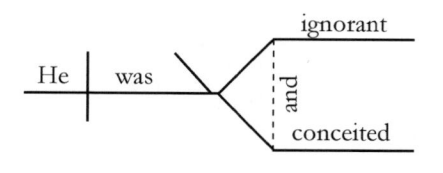

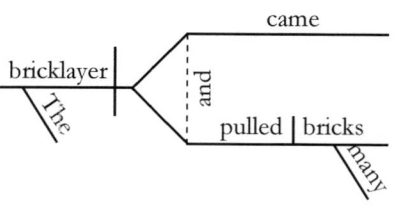

Exercise 31

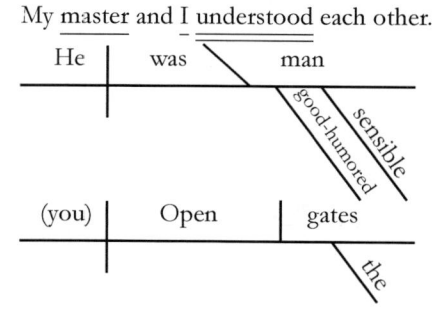

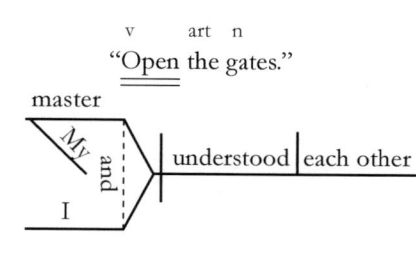

```
pro lv art ———adj——— adj      n
```
He was a good-humored, sensible man.
```
adj  n     cj pro v       ———pro———
```
My master and I understood each other.
```
                  v   art  n
```
"Open the gates."

Exercise 32

```
pro adv  v  art adj   n               pro    lv adv  adj
```
I never knew a better man.   "They are not religious."
```
pro hv  adv  v
```
"I do not believe."

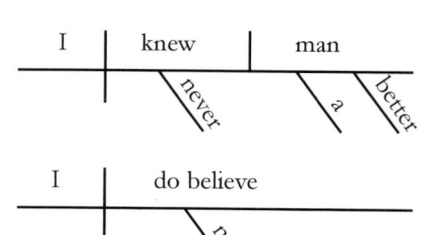

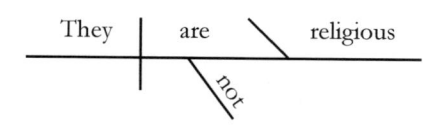

Exercise 33

```
adj    n    lv  adv     adj              pro ——v—— adv
```
"Her mother is dangerously ill."   "She must go directly."
```
pro ——lv—— art adj  n
```
"It would be a rare treat."

492

Exercise 34

n   v   adv
Winter came early.

adj   n   v   adv
Dinah's family lived there.

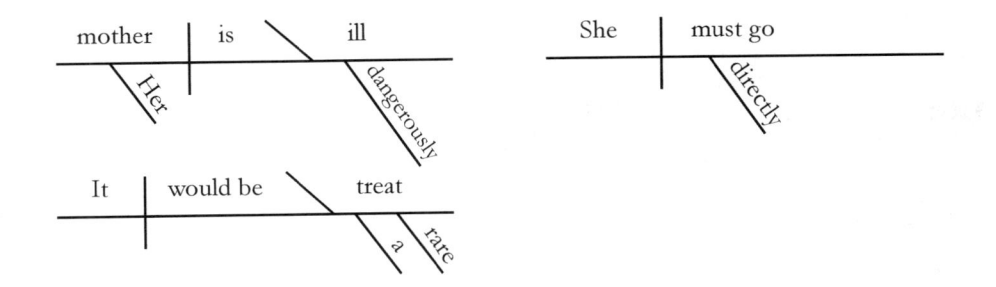

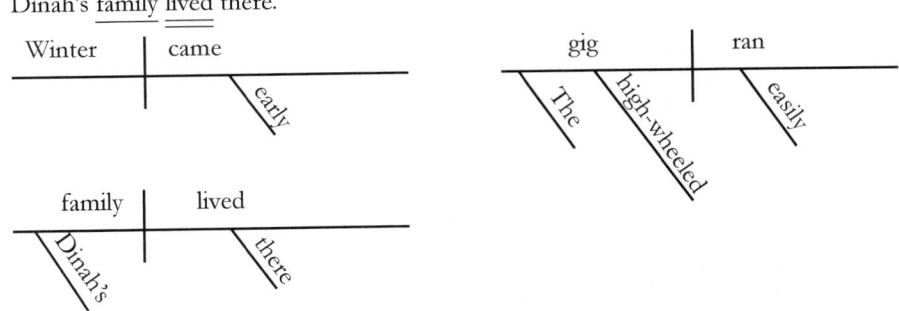

art —adj— n   v   adv
The high-wheeled gig ran easily.

Exercise 35

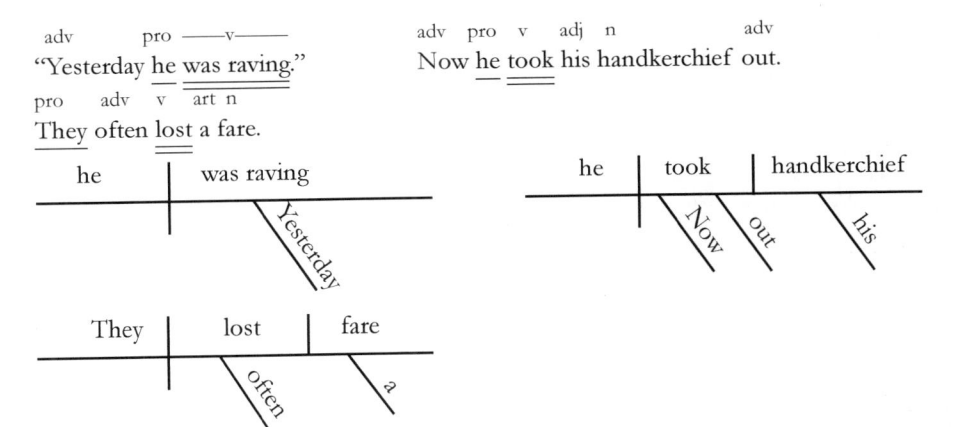

adv   pro —v—
"Yesterday he was raving."

pro   adv   v   art n
They often lost a fare.

adv   pro   v   adj   n   adv
Now he took his handkerchief out.

Exercise 37

pn   cj pro hv adv v   adj   n
Jerry and I had not eaten many mouthfuls.

hv   pro lv   adj   n
Had she been Polly's mistress?

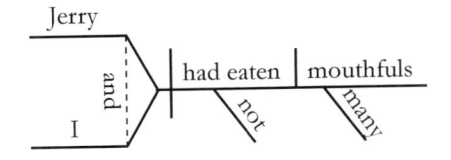

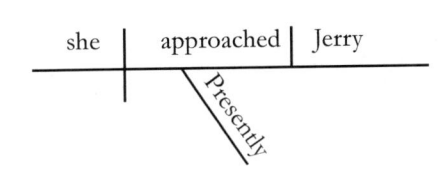

adv   pro   v   pn
Presently she approached Jerry.

493

Exercise 38

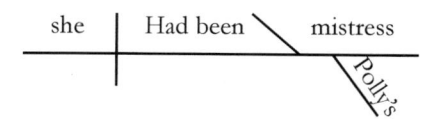

```
art  n   ——lv—— adv  adj
The wind had been very changeable.
hv'adv pro v  pro
"Can't I do something?"
```

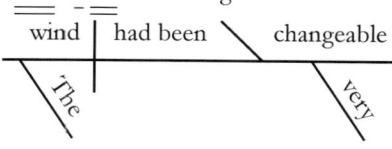

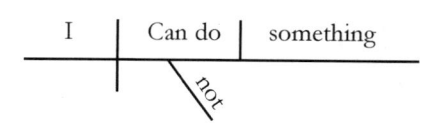

```
adv     n    cj   n   ——v——
Sometimes driver and horse must wait.
```

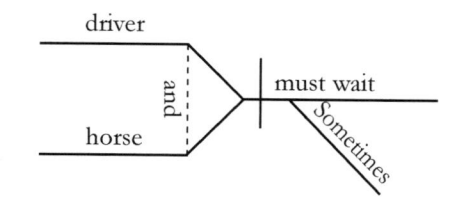

Exercise 39

```
pn    ——v——  cj   v   pro adv
Dolly was crying and kissed me too.
pro ——v—— art  n   adv
He was raising the whip again.
```

```
lv pro art adj  n
"Is it a heavy load?"
```

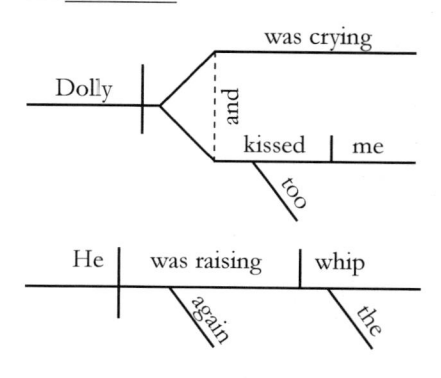

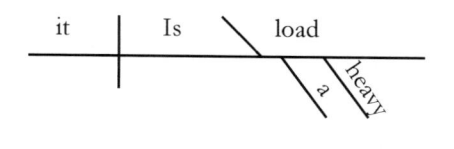

Exercise 40

```
pro v  adj   n  cj art adj    n
He had black eyes and a hooked nose.
——v—— art adj   n
"Do take a second cab."
```

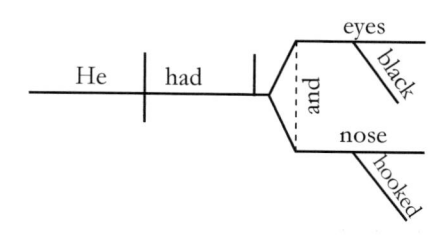

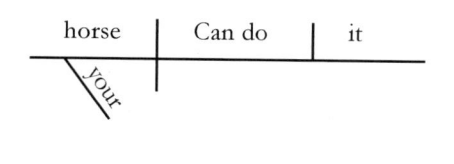

```
hv  adj   n   v  pro
"Can your horse do it?"
```

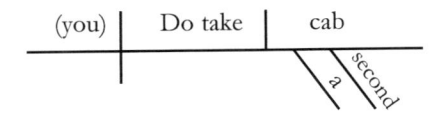

```
         (you) | Do take | cab
                            \
                             \a
                              \second
```

Exercise 41

```
art  n   hv   adv    v   adj  n              art   n     v    cj   v    pro
The boy could hardly control his delight.   The groom cleaned and dressed me.
 v    adj  n
"Check his mouth."
```

```
   boy  | could control | delight
    \The       \hardly      \his

  (you) | Check | mouth
                    \his
```

```
              cleaned
   groom  <          > me
    \The    dressed
         (and)
```

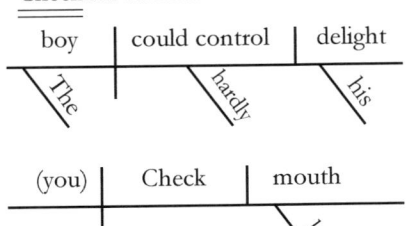

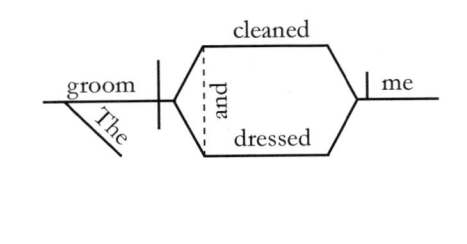

Exercise 43

Phrase: in his little sleeping-berth
Clause: the wind blew hard and joggled the water of the ocean
Clause: she sat down in a corner of the coop

```
 hv  pro  lv  adv  adv           hv pro  v   adv   adv
"Have you been here, too?"      "Do I speak quite properly?"
 pro  ——v——  adj  n
"You may have my egg."
```

```
  you  | Have been              I  | Do speak
           \here \too                    \quite  \properly

  You  | may have | egg
                     \my
```

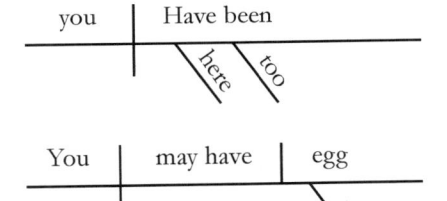

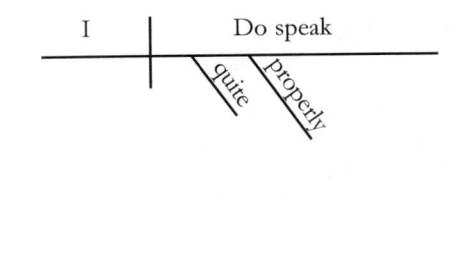

Exercise 44

Clause: while she was speaking
Clause: when Billina suddenly cried
Phrase: upon all fours

```
 hv pro v   n                              v
"Can I tell metal?"                      "Run!"
art   pn      v    art adj   adj  n  cj   v    pro
The Wheeler gave a sharp, wild cry and chased her.
```

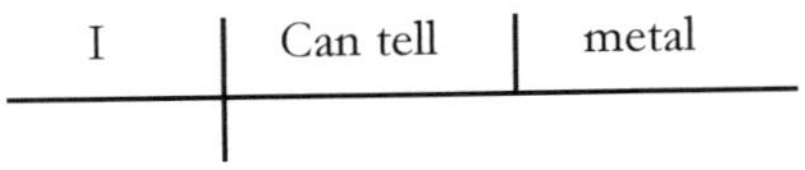

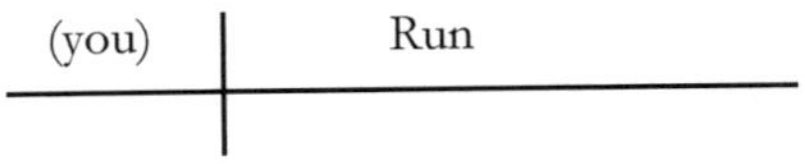

```
   I  | Can tell | metal            (you) | Run
```

495

Exercise 45

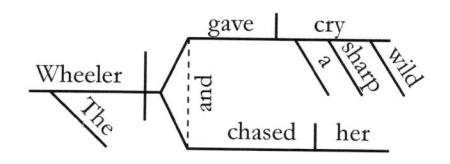

Phrase: that crack in the rock
Clause: so I think
Clause: don't be frightened [understood you is the subject!]

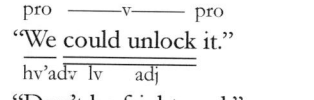

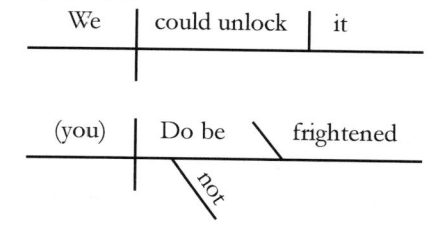

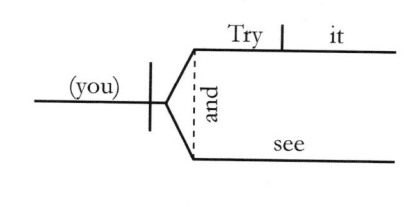

"We could unlock it."
"Don't be frightened."
"Try it and see."

Exercise 46

Clause: until suddenly he became motionless
Phrase: that low bow to you
Clause: she ran around the copper man

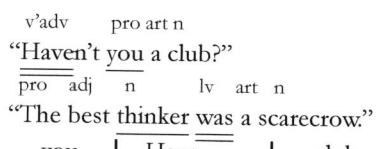

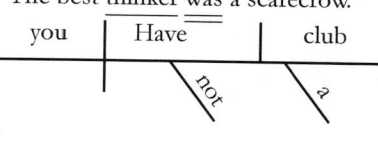

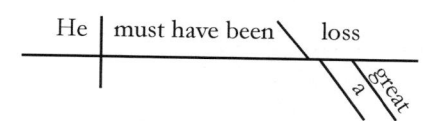

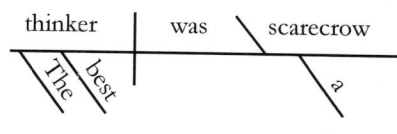

"Haven't you a club?"
"The best thinker was a scarecrow."
"He must have been a great loss."

Exercise 47

Phrase: from those ugly creatures
Clause: and the copper fingers closed firmly over the stout handle
Clause: the yellow hen gave a cackle of delight

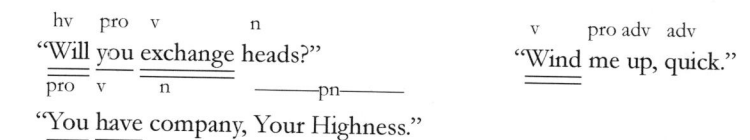

"Will you exchange heads?"
"Wind me up, quick."
"You have company, Your Highness."

Exercise 49

Dorothy was guided to the chicken house by a loud cackling, crowing, and distracting hubbub of sounds.

496

Phrase: as cowardly as ever
Clause: but suddenly the bunch of feathers stopped whirling
Clause: which Dorothy unlatched

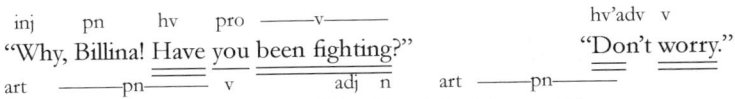

"Why, Billina! Have you been fighting?"   "Don't worry."
The Cowardly Lion introduced his friend the Hungry Tiger.

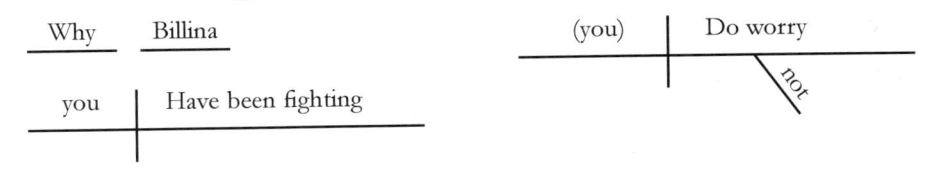

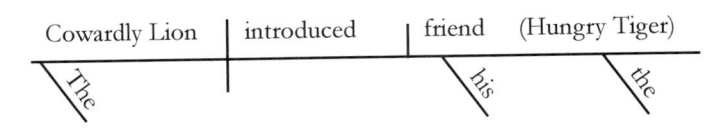

Exercise 50

[In these exercises, the quotation marks around obvious quotations are optional.]
"Please to get me about thirty pounds of tenderloin steak, a peck of boiled potatoes, and five gallons of ice-cream for dessert."

Phrase: a queen mother and her ten children
Phrase: for the sake of the poor prisoners
Clause: I will now retire to my cabinet

"Are you so very hungry?"   He bowed politely and blinked his eyes.
"My uncle, Evoldo, was a very wicked man."

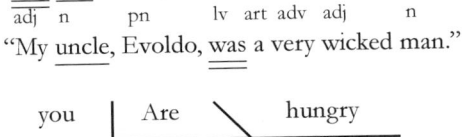

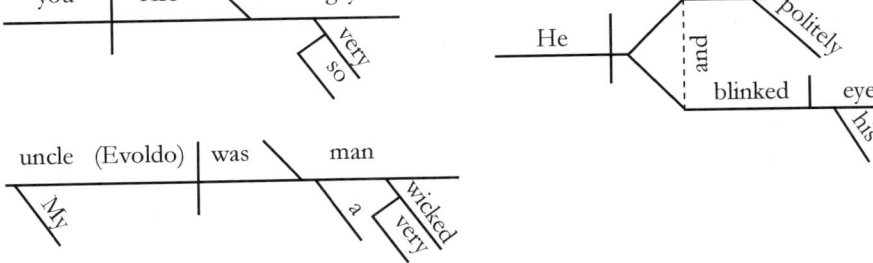

Exercise 51

Clause: she lays one every morning
Phrase: about this time
Clause: although all were restless and anxious

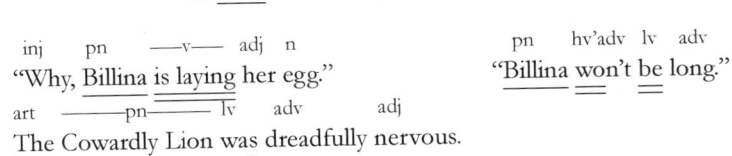

"Why, Billina is laying her egg."   "Billina won't be long."
The Cowardly Lion was dreadfully nervous.

497

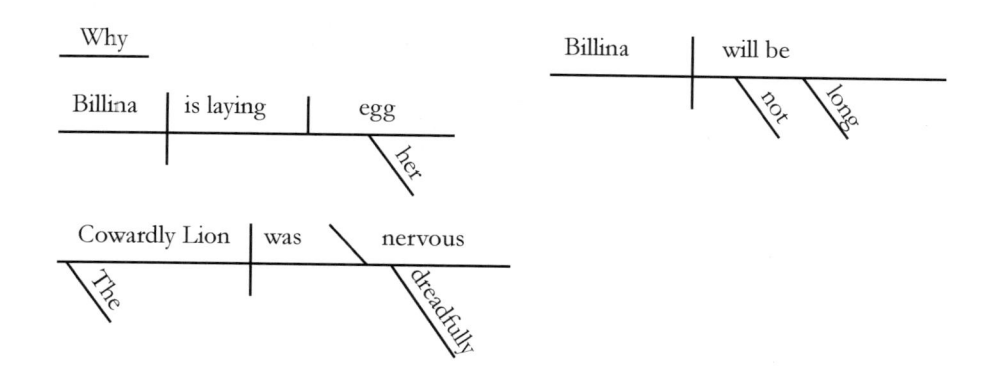

Exercise 52

^{ph} ^{ph}
Ozma and Dorothy were a little awed by the silence.
^{gr} ^{ph}
We will dig him out of his hole, like a fox.

^{inj} ——pn—— ^{v} ^{adv} ^{cj} ^{v} ^{pro} $\quad$ $^{lv'adv\ pro\ art\ n}$
"PLEASE Mr. Nome King, come here and see us." $\quad$ "Isn't it a trick?"
^{art} ——pn—— ^{art} ^{adj} $\quad$ ^{n} $\quad$ ^{v}
The Nome King, the underground monarch, answered.

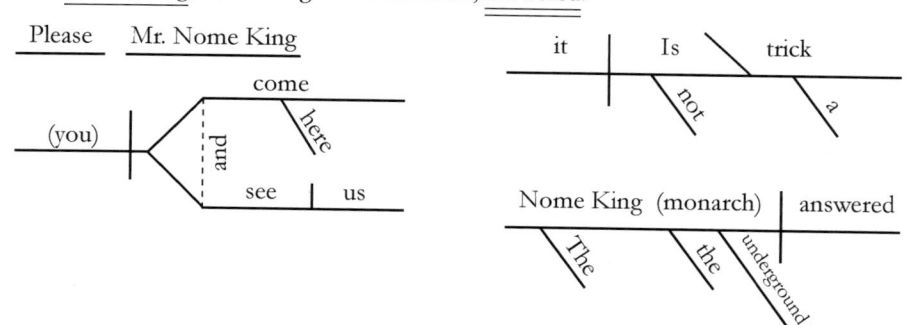

Exercise 53

Dorothy, the Scarecrow, and the Tin Woodman each gave a start of dismay and stared into one another's eyes.

^{ph} ^{ph} ^{ph} ^{ph} ^{ph}
"Surely I ought to guess one object in eleven correctly."
^{ph} $^{ph\ ph}$ $\qquad$ ^{ph} ^{ph}
"It would be weak and cowardly in us to abandon the adventure."

^{pn} $^{art\ adj}$ ^{n} $\quad$ ^{lv} ^{art} ^{n} $\qquad$ ^{hv} ^{pro} ^{v}
Ozma the pretty grasshopper was an emerald. $\quad$ "Has she failed?"
^{art} ——pn—— ^{adv} $\quad$ ^{v} $\quad$ $^{adv\ cj}$ ^{v}
The Nome King suddenly looked up and smiled. [In this sentence, it could be argued that the verb modified both verbs or only the first, so either diagram is acceptable.]

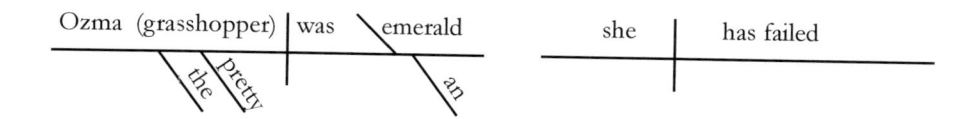

498

Exercise 55

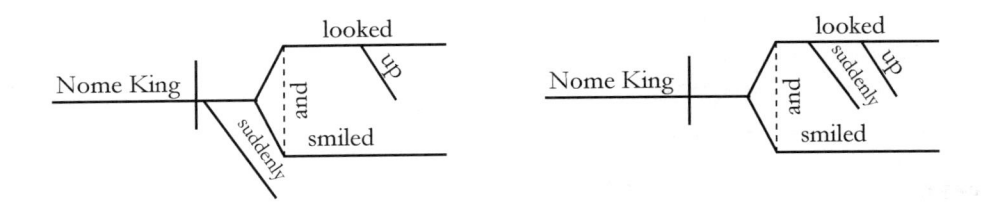

Dorothy, the Lion, and Tiger were given their breakfast in their rooms.

Clause: where he said to the King
Phrase: in so enraged a voice
Phrase: squatting under the throne

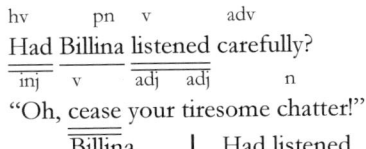

```
hv   pn    v      adv
Had Billina listened carefully?

inj   v    adj   adj     n
"Oh, cease your tiresome chatter!"
```

```
adj    pn    pro lv art n
"Your Majesty, you are a fool."
```

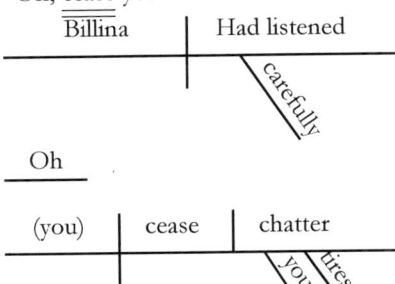

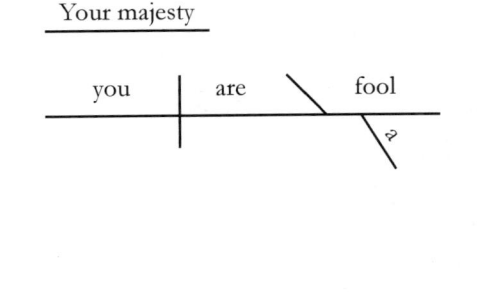

Exercise 56

The Scarecrow, Billina, and the Nome King were in the throne room.
"Why, it's Billina."

```
        ph  ph    ph
"I've got a right to cackle, I guess."

 gr  ph   ph  ph gr    ph
"Well, you'll have to bear this one around."
```

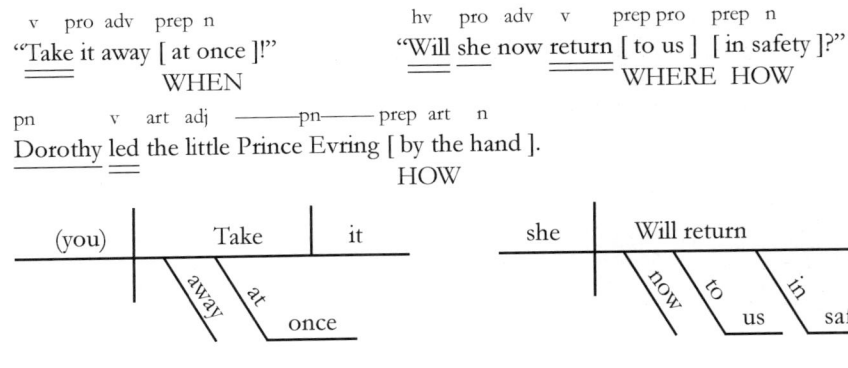

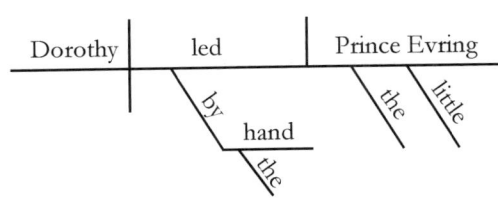

```
 v  pro adv prep n
"Take it away [ at once ]!"
              WHEN
```

```
hv  pro adv  v    prep pro prep  n
"Will she now return [ to us ] [ in safety ]?"
                      WHERE    HOW
```

```
 pn     v  art adj   ——pn—— prep art  n
Dorothy led the little Prince Evring [ by the hand ].
                                          HOW
```

499

Exercise 57

Phrase: with an air of vast importance
Clause: then I thank you for the gracious favor
Clause: don't worry

```
    inj    adj  n   lv  pn  prep   n              lv pro art  adj      n        ———pn———
   "Why, my name is Bill, [ by rights ]."        "Am I a good guesser, Mr. Nome King?"
                                HOW
    pn     art  ——adj——  n     v     prep  pro
   Evanna, a sweet-faced girl, stood [ beside them ].
                                     WHERE
```

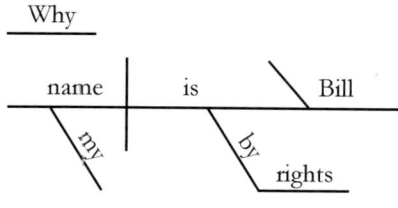

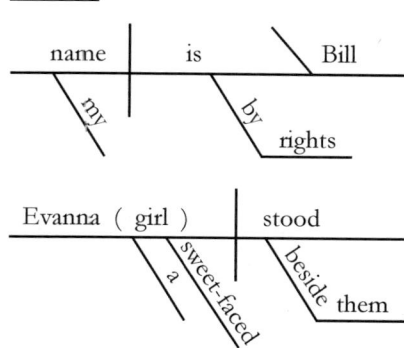

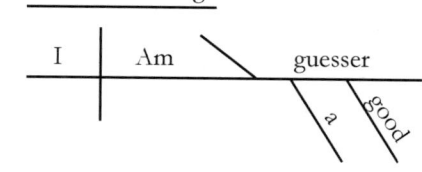

Exercise 58

The generals, the colonels, the majors, and the captains all commanded, "Forward, march!" [Either a period or an exclamation mark is acceptable.]

```
              ph      ph
"The creature is made of wood."

                      ph  ph         ph ph
At once the army filed out in great numbers, led by their captain.

 art    n    ——v—— prep  n                   hv'adv  v    pro
"The creature is made [ of wood ]."        "Don't mind them!"
                      HOW
 hv  pro  v
"Do you surrender?"
```

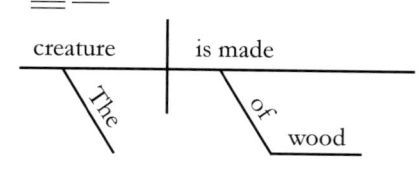

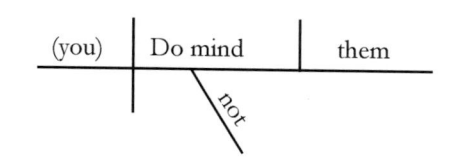

Exercise 59

Clause: although I wonder why
Clause: so the King stopped and looked at them in surprise
Clause: where the king jeered at Dorothy

```
    inj   pro  hv  adv   v      adj  adj    n
  "Why, you are not wearing your magic belt."
```

```
                pn        v       adv     pn    cj   art   pn   prep  pn
              Dorothy welcomed back Ozma and the Queen [ of Ev ].
              art    n    v    prep   pn
              The others went [ with Dorothy ].
                                    WHERE
```

```
          Why
           |
     you  | are wearing | belt
          |      \not    \your  \magic

                                         Ozma
                          Dorothy | welcomed  \and
                                   \back       Queen
                                                \the  \of  Ev

     others | went
      \The   \with
              Dorothy
```

Exercise 61

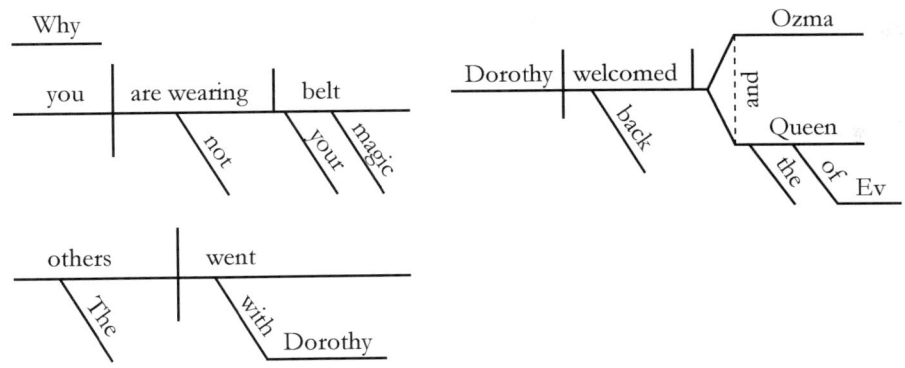

For Ozma of Oz ruled the King of the Munchkins, the King of the Winkies, the King of the Quadlings, and the King of the Gillikins.

```
                  gr   ph                        ph    ph                          ph
              She lives in the Emerald City, which is in the exact center of the four kingdoms
              of the Land of Oz.
                  ph                             ph  gr
              "Now I am happy and contented and willing to lead a quiet life and mind my own business."
```

```
           v    pro  adv  adj    n       prep art   n                  ——pn——  pro  v      pro
          "Have we any other privates [ in the armies ]?"              "Omby Amby, I promote you."
                                           WHERE
           pn   art  pn   prep pn     v      prep art  ——pn——
          Ozma, the Ruler [ of Oz ], returned [ to the Emerald City ].
                          WHAT KIND          WHERE
```

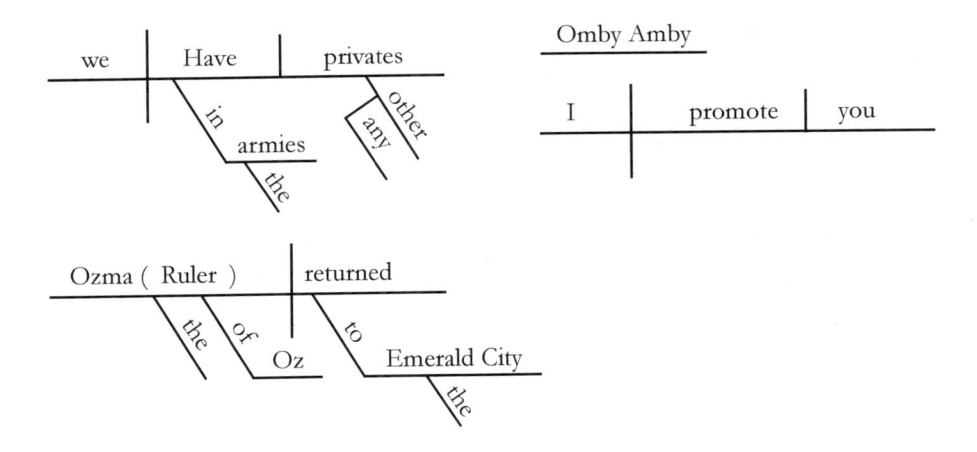

```
     we | Have | privates              Omby Amby
         |      \other
         \in     \any                   I | promote | you
          armies
           \the

     Ozma ( Ruler ) | returned
           \the \of   \to
               Oz     Emerald City
                         \the
```

Exercise 62

"The belt has magical powers only while it is in some fairy country, my little friend."

```
              ——pn——    ——v——  prep art  adj    n
              Uncle Henry was seated [ in an easy chair ].
                                            WHERE
              adv       art    n       v     prep art  n
              Instantly the farmhouse appeared [ in the picture ].
              pn     art  adj    adj     n    ——v——
              Dorothy, the little Kansas girl, might visit.
```

501

Exercise 63

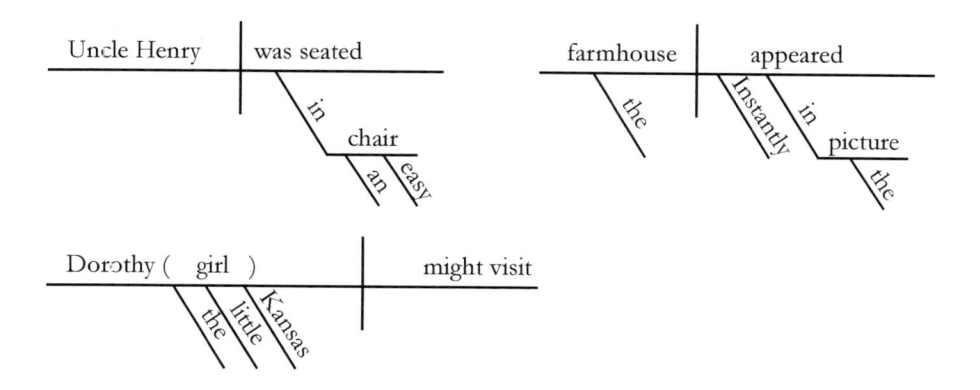

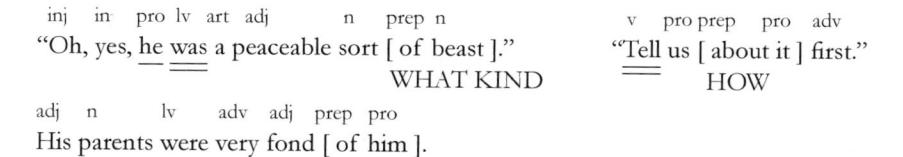

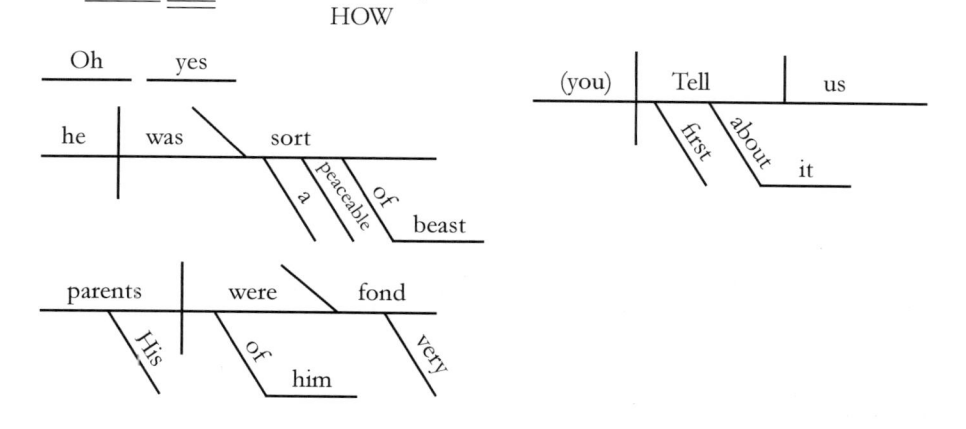

```
inj    in  pro lv  art  adj      n   prep  n
"Oh, yes, he was a peaceable sort [ of beast ]."
         ─── ═══                 WHAT KIND
```

```
       v  pro prep  pro  adv
"Tell us [ about it ] first."
 ═══                   HOW
```

```
adj   n    lv  adv  adj  prep pro
His parents were very fond [ of him ].
    ─────── ════                HOW
```

Exercise 64

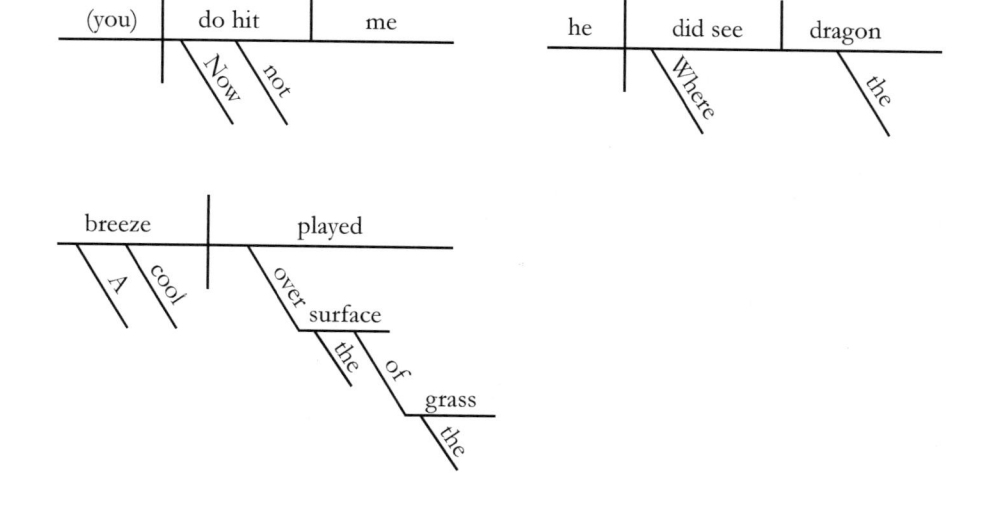

```
adv  hv'adv  v  pro
"Now don't hit me."
         ═══ ═══
```

```
adv     hv pro v  art  n
Where did he see the dragon?
          ── ═══════
```

```
art adj   n    v   prep art   n    prep art  n
A cool breeze played [ over the surface ] [ of the grass ].
       ══════ ══════      HOW/WHERE   WHAT KIND
```

502

Exercise 65

Simple present: hear
Infinitive: to work

```
 adv    lv   ——pn——                    adj  adj  adj   n   adv  v
Where is St. George?               "My dear little man, just understand."
 art   pn   v    adv  prep adj  n
The Boy jumped round [ in sheer delight ].
                     HOW
```

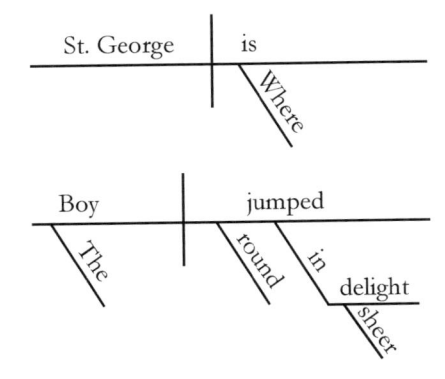

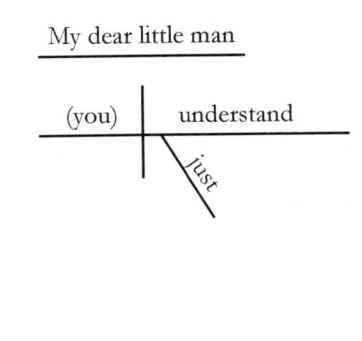

Exercise 67

Infinitive: to make
Present participle: am going

```
art  pn   ——v—— art  adj   adj   n      pn   hv'adv pro  v    art  pn
The Boy had secured a good front place.  "Boy, can't you arrange a Princess?"
adv   hv  ——pn—— art  adj    n     v
When did St. George the dragon slayer arrive?
```

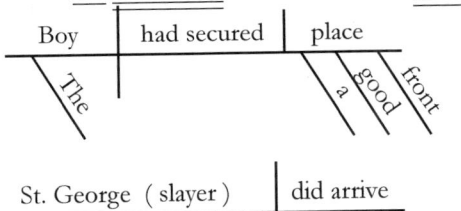

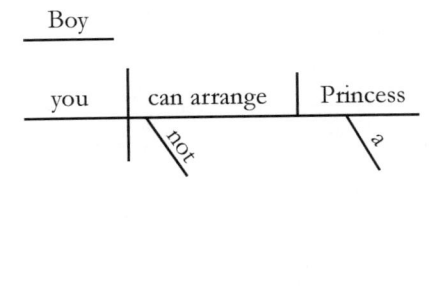

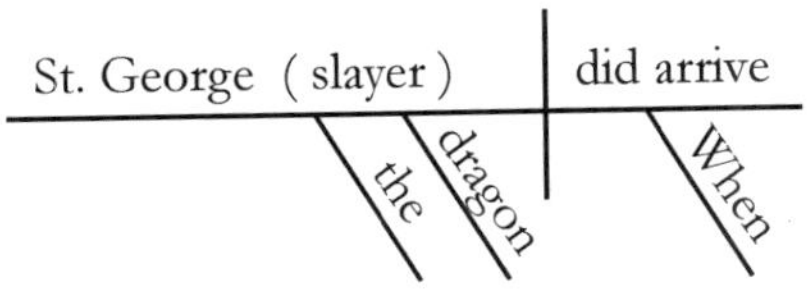

Exercise 68

Simple past: looked
Past participle: have noticed

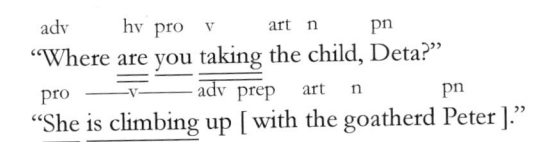

```
 adv    hv  pro  v   art  n   pn        adv  lv adj  n  adv adj
"Where are you taking the child, Deta?" "Why are his eyes so fierce?"
 pro  ——v—— adv prep art    n    pn
"She is climbing up [ with the goatherd Peter ]."
```

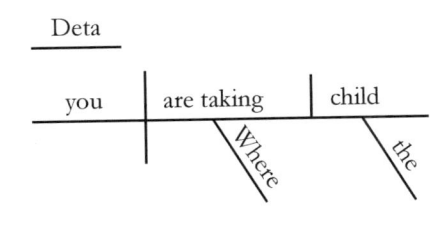

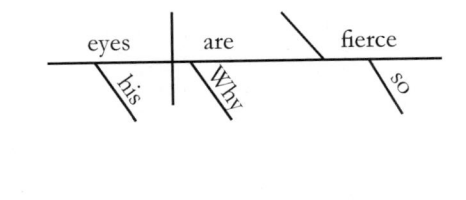

503

[Diagram: she | is climbing \ up \ with goatherd (Peter) \ the]

Exercise 69

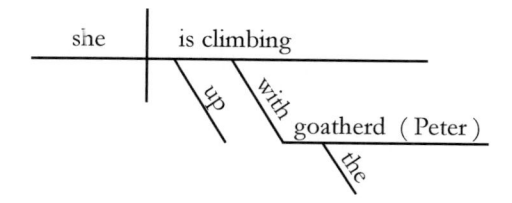

Phrase: after looking around attentively in the room
Clause: Heidi followed him into a fairly spacious room
Clause: when he opened it

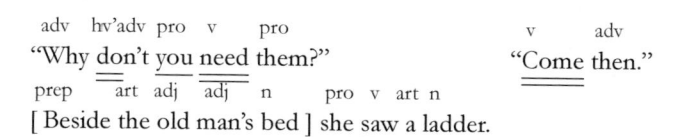

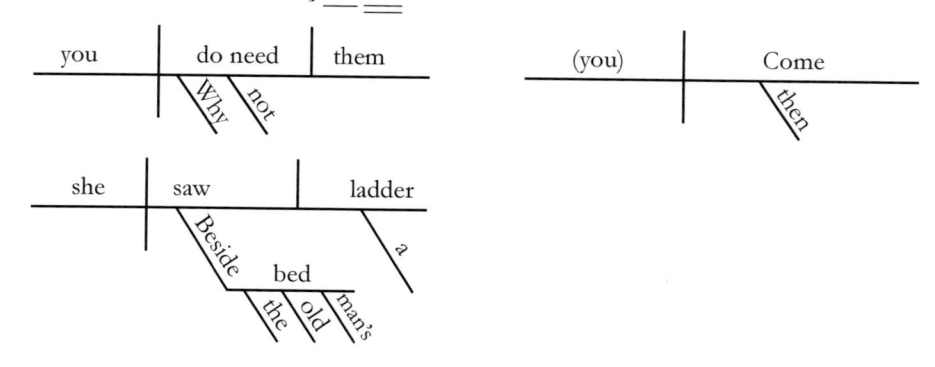

adv hv'adv pro v pro
"Why don't you need them?"

v adv
"Come then."

prep art adj adj n pro v art n
[Beside the old man's bed] she saw a ladder.

[Diagram: you | do need | them \ Why \ not]

[Diagram: (you) | Come \ then]

[Diagram: she | saw | ladder \ Beside bed the old man's / a]

Exercise 70

Infinitive: to call
Past participle: had happened

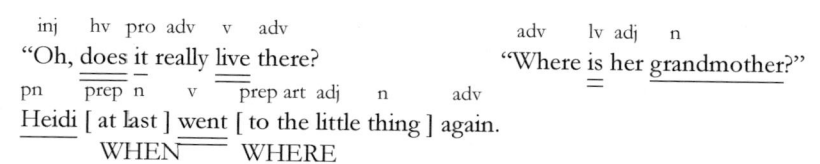

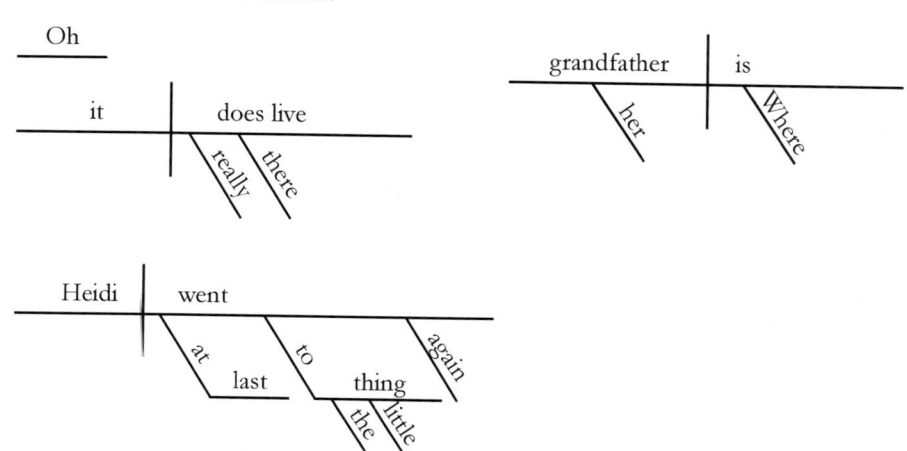

inj hv pro adv v adv
"Oh, does it really live there?"

adv lv adj n
"Where is her grandmother?"

pn prep n v prep art adj n adv
Heidi [at last] went [to the little thing] again.
         WHEN   WHERE

[Diagram: Oh]

[Diagram: it | does live \ really \ there]

[Diagram: grandfather | is \ her \ Where]

[Diagram: Heidi | went \ at last \ to thing \ the \ little \ again]

Exercise 71

adv lv pro adj
"How is it possible?"

inj n hv'adv pro v art n
"Why, grandmother, can't you see the shutter?"

```
      pn ───v─── prep  adj  n
Heidi would talk [ about her life ].
                            HOW
```

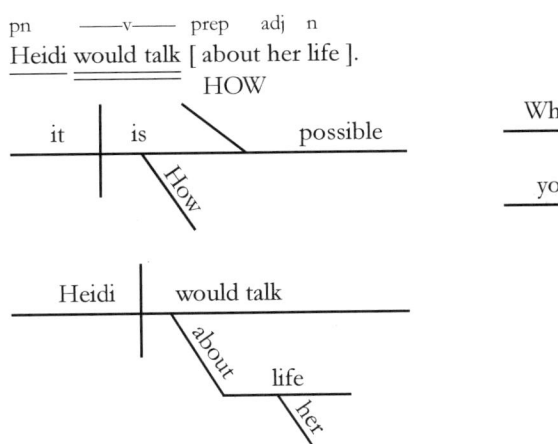

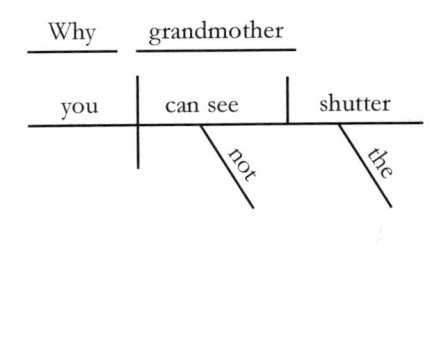

[Diagram: "it | is \ possible" with "How" below is]

[Diagram: "Heidi | would talk" with "about \ life / her"]

[Diagram: "Why grandmother / you | can see | shutter" with "not" under can see and "the" under shutter]

Exercise 73

Present participle: is sitting
Simple past: grumbled

```
pn         art  n   adv   v   prep  pro
Sebastian, the butler, soon stood [ before her ].
  ──pn──  adv hv  pro  v    adj   n
"Miss Deta, how could you bring this child?"
pro hv  adv    v    art  n   adv
"I have never heard the name before."
 -  ══          ═══
```

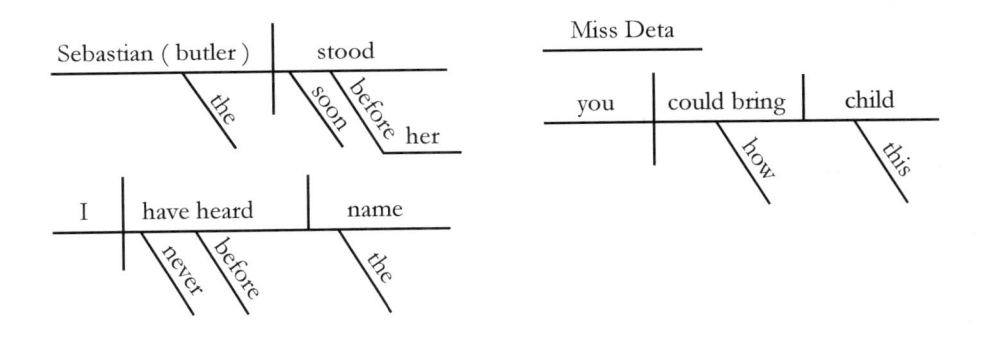

[Diagram: "Sebastian (butler) | stood" with "the" under Sebastian, "soon" and "before \ her" under stood]

[Diagram: "I | have heard | name" with "never", "before" under have heard, and "the" under name]

[Diagram: "Miss Deta / you | could bring | child" with "how" under could bring and "this" under child]

Exercise 74

Simple present: brings
Simple present: hear

```
adv    hv  pro v
Where has she gone?
 ══    ═══     ═══

adv  lv art  n   prep art adj    n
"Where is the tower [ with the golden dome ]?"
  =                         WHAT KIND

hv   pro  v    art  n    prep pro
"Can you open a window [ for me ]?"
 ══       ═══                HOW
```

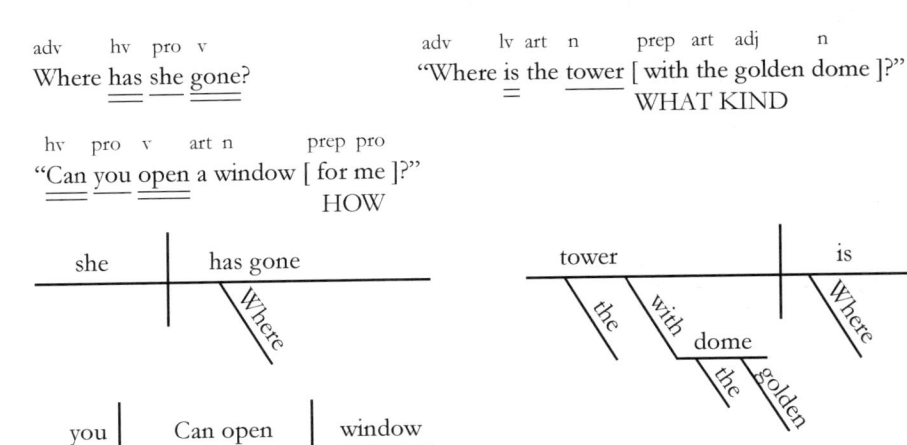

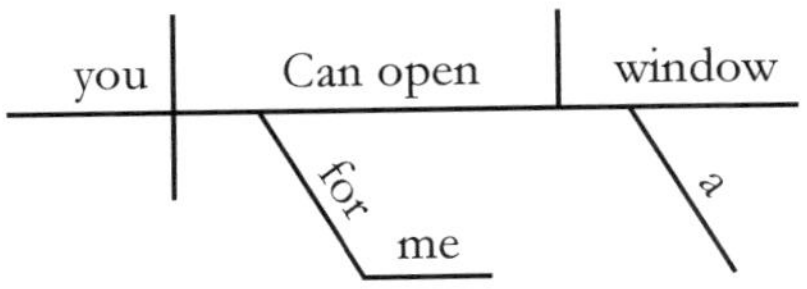

[Diagram: "she | has gone" with "Where" below]

[Diagram: "you | Can open | window" with "for \ me" and "a"]

[Diagram: "tower | is" with "the", "with \ dome / the / golden", and "Where"]

505

Exercise 75

"Oh, please, Mr. Candidate, can't we just peep in?"

Clause: the furious lady proceeded
Clause: whispered the frightened child
Phrase: for mercy's sake

```
pn        adv     v    art  n  prep  pro
Sebastian obediently pulled the boy [ after him ].
                                       WHERE
```

```
pn    prep art  n       v     adj  adj    n
Clara, [ on the contrary ], enjoyed her companion's society.
              HOW
```

```
 v   art  adj    n   adv
"Bring the unlucky child up!"
```

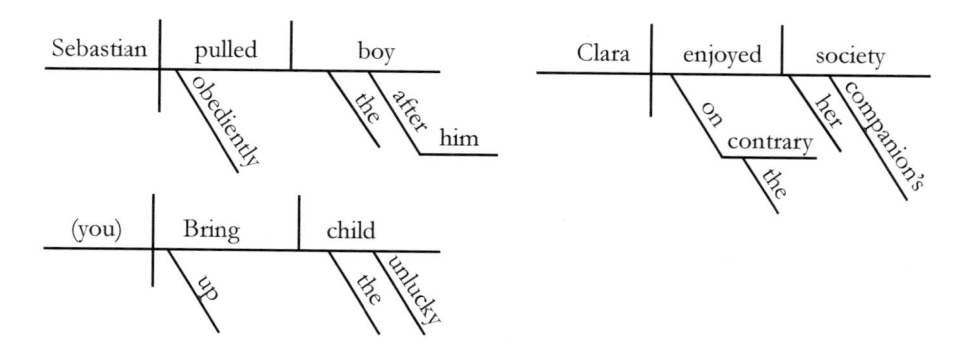

Exercise 76

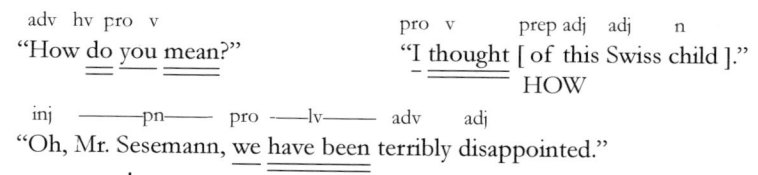

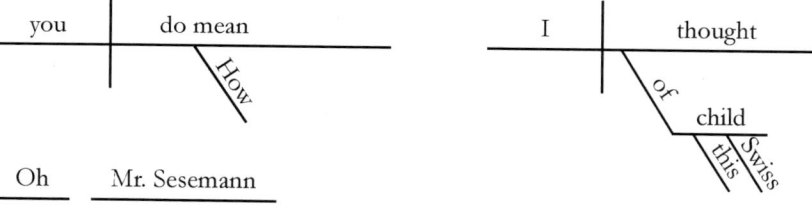

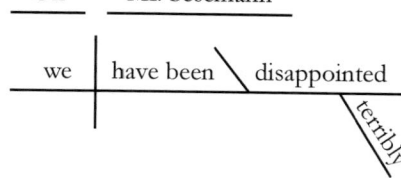

```
adv hv pro  v
"How do you mean?"
```

```
pro  v    prep adj   adj   n
"I thought [ of this Swiss child ]."
                   HOW
```

```
inj    ——pn——     pro ——lv—— adv      adj
"Oh, Mr. Sesemann, we have been terribly disappointed."
```

Exercise 77

Past participle: have learned
Present participle: am going

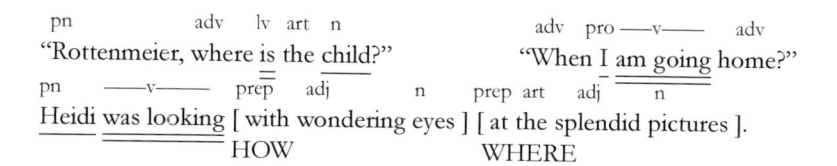

```
pn         adv  lv art  n
"Rottenmeier, where is the child?"
```

```
adv pro ——v—— adv
"When I am going home?"
```

```
pn    ——v—— prep  adj      n   prep art  adj       n
Heidi was looking [ with wondering eyes ] [ at the splendid pictures ].
                        HOW                       WHERE
```

506

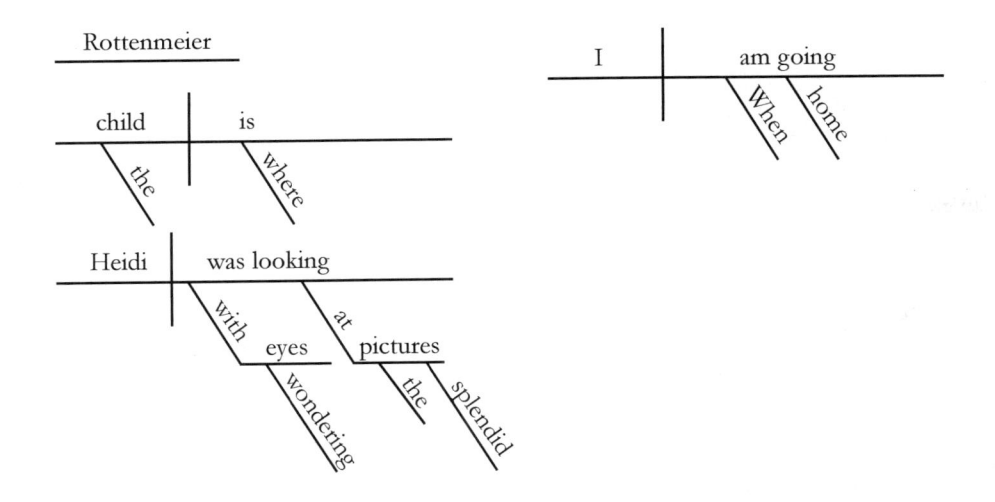

Exercise 79

Infinitive: to speak
Past participle: have played

adj n lv adj cj adj
His eyes were lively and kind.

v n adj adj n
"Have patience, my old friend."

art adj n prep n v prep art n
A few bottles [of wine] stood [on the table].
⎯⎯⎯⎯⎯ WHAT KIND WHERE

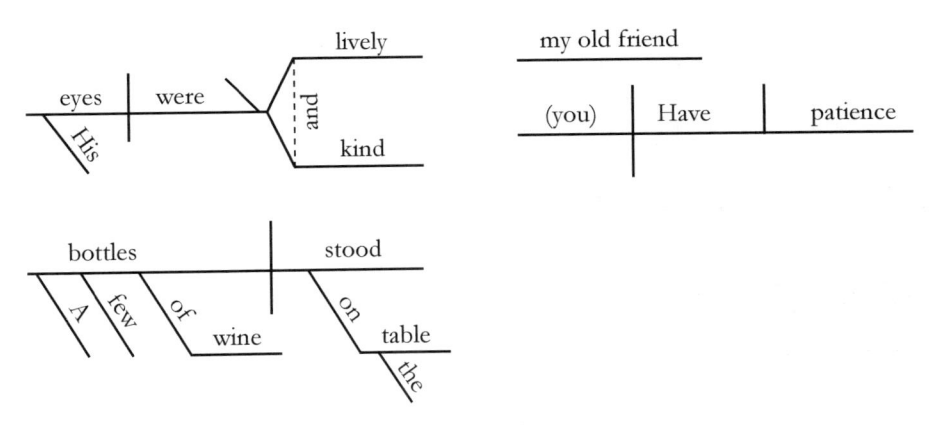

Exercise 80

Simple past: called
Present participle: is feeling

pn v –prep– pro prep n
Heidi looked [up to him] [in amazement].

pro v prep adj adj n
Heidi was dressed [in her Sunday frock].
⎯⎯⎯⎯⎯ HOW

adv hv'adv pro v pro prep pro
"Why don't you give it [to me]?"
⎯⎯ ⎯⎯ ⎯⎯ HOW/WHERE

507

[Diagram: Heidi | looked, with "up to him" and "in amazement" as prepositional phrases]

[Diagram: Heidi | was dressed, with "in frock" modified by "her" and "Sunday"]

[Diagram: you | do give | it, with "Why", "not", and "to me" as modifiers]

Exercise 81

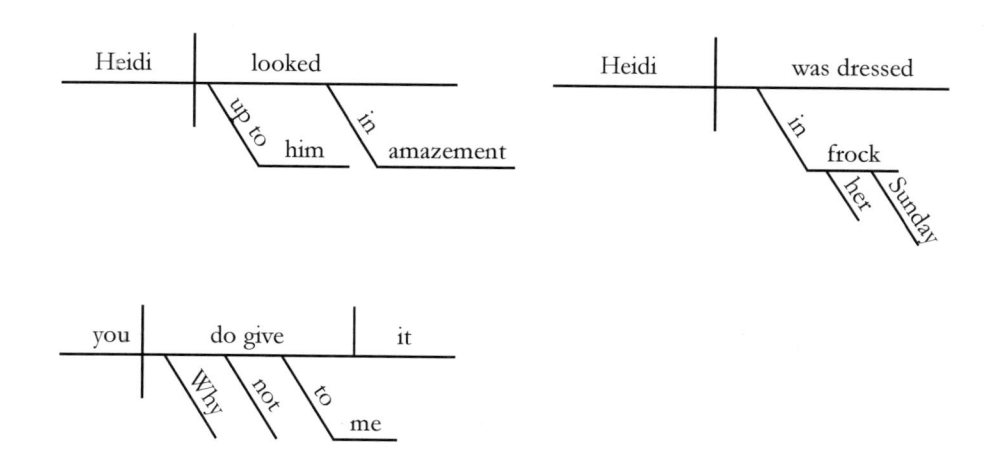

Phrase: to mar the happiness of the child
Clause: after she had carefully wiped it off
Clause: shall I read you a song from your book now

    hv   pro   v   adv   n
"Have you come again, child?"
adj   n   v   prep art adj   n
Grandmother's face changed [to a joyous expression].
                                HOW

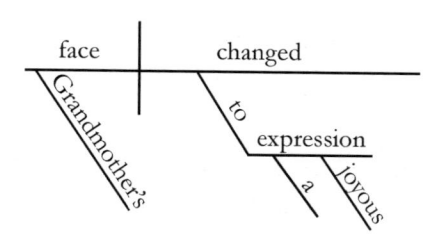

[Diagram: child (vocative); you | have come, with "again" modifier]

[Diagram: face | changed, with "Grandmother's" and prepositional phrase "to expression" modified by "a" and "joyous"]

Exercise 82

   ——inj——   n   ——v—— prep pn
"Oh please, doctor, do go [to Heidi]."
prep   adj   n   art n   v
[With shrugging shoulders] the doctor replied.
adj   n ——v—— prep   n
Clara's eyes had filled [with tears].

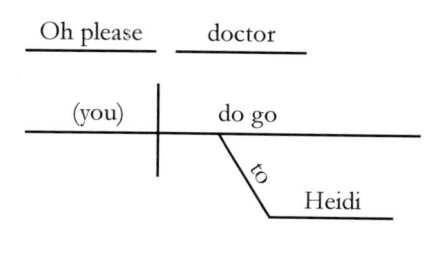

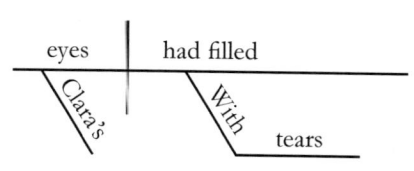

[Diagram: Oh please | doctor; (you) | do go, with "to Heidi" as prepositional phrase]

[Diagram: doctor | replied, with "the" modifier and "With shoulders" prepositional phrase modified by "shrugging"]

[Diagram: eyes | had filled, with "Clara's" modifier and "With tears" prepositional phrase]

Exercise 83

Simple past: reached

508

Simple past: caressed

```
                    lv   adj   n    adj   adv
```
"Are your eyes bright already?"

```
       prep  art adj  n   pro ——v—— art  n    cj   n
```
[With an old rag] she would rub the chairs and table.
        HOW

```
art    n        ——v—— adj prep adj adj  n
```
The grandfather had been busy [in his little shop].
                                    WHERE

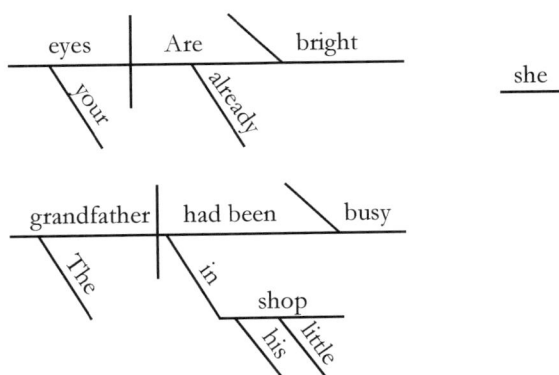

Exercise 85

"Oh, grandfather, I have found my bedroom."
[An exclamation point would also be acceptable.]

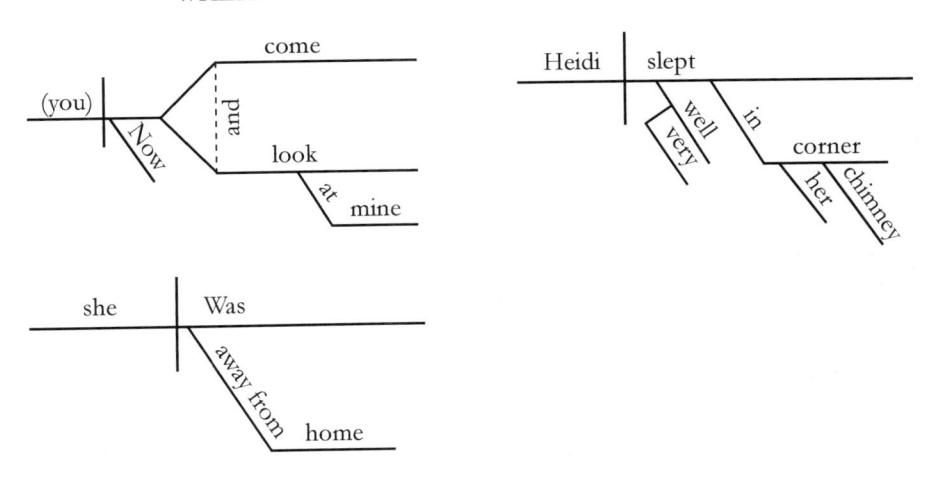

```
    adv   v   cj  v    prep pro        pn    v   adv adj prep adj  adj    n
```
"Now come and look [at mine]."   Heidi slept very well [in her chimney corner].
            HOW/WHERE   WHERE

```
lv   pro adv  prep  n
```
Was she away [from home]?
              WHERE

Exercise 86

Simple past: began
Infinitive: to read

```
     v   cj   v    art  adj   n         pro  v   adv prep pro prep adj  n
```
"Hurry and learn the three letters."   He came daily [to her] [for his lesson].
                                                     WHERE   HOW

```
   inj     lv  pro adj
```
"What, is it possible?"

509

Exercise 87

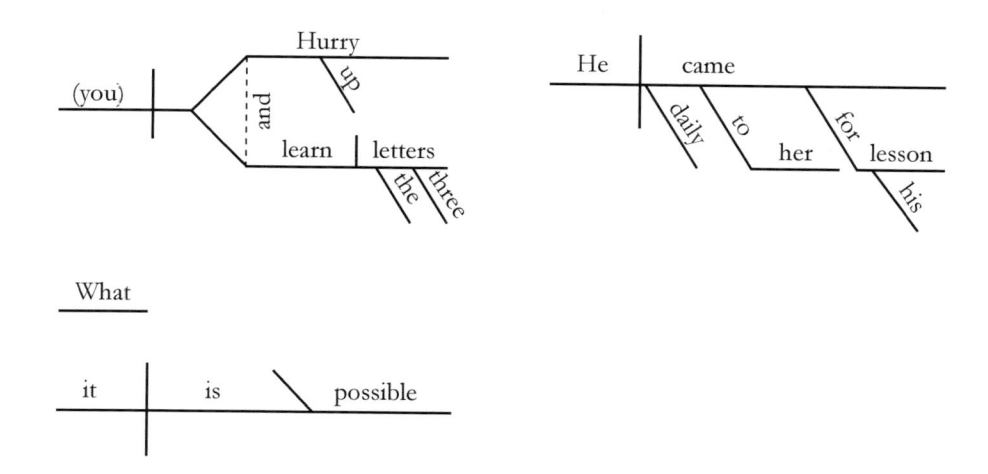

Phrase: thoughtfully looking at the backless chairs
Clause: what the grandfather had meant
Phrase: but not with us

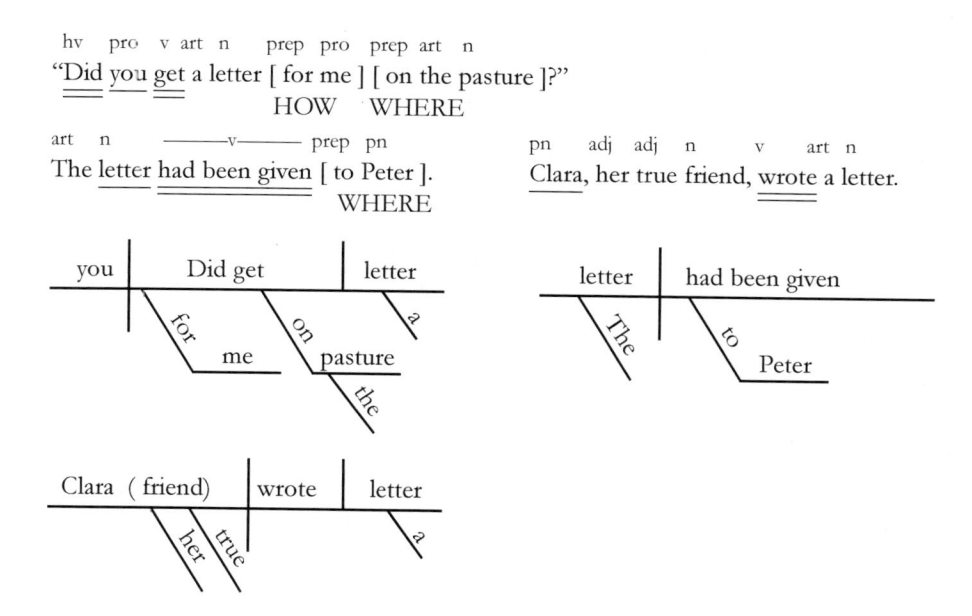

```
   hv   pro   v  art  n    prep pro   prep art  n
"Did you get a letter [ for me ] [ on the pasture ]?"
                             HOW      WHERE

 art   n    ———v———  prep  pn          pn  adj  adj  n    v  art  n
The letter had been given [ to Peter ].   Clara, her true friend, wrote a letter.
                          WHERE
```

Exercise 88

The grandfather, Heidi, and Clara were all in the mountain home.

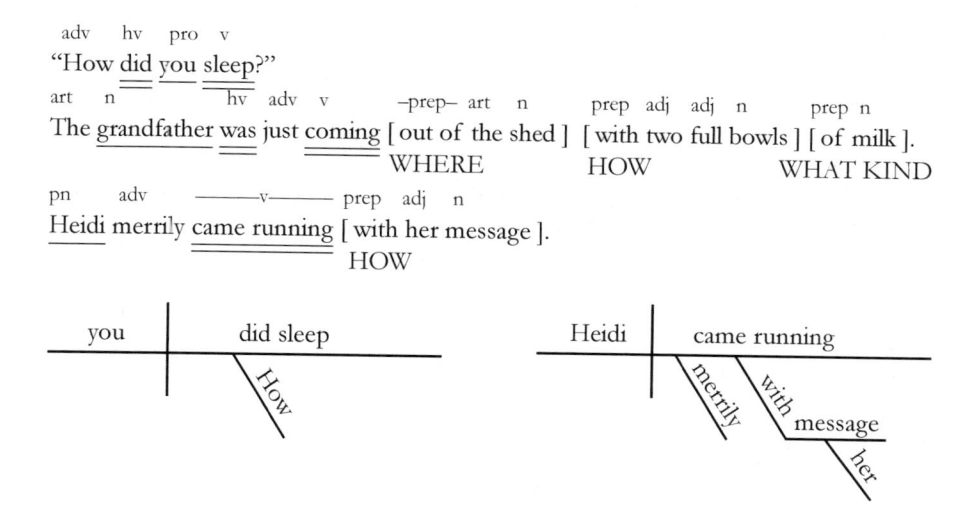

```
 adv  hv  pro   v
"How did you sleep?"
 art    n      hv  adv   v    —prep— art   n     prep adj  adj   n    prep n
The grandfather was just coming [ out of the shed ] [ with two full bowls ] [ of milk ].
                                      WHERE              HOW                WHAT KIND
 pn   adv   ———v———  prep  adj    n
Heidi merrily came running [ with her message ].
                                 HOW
```

510

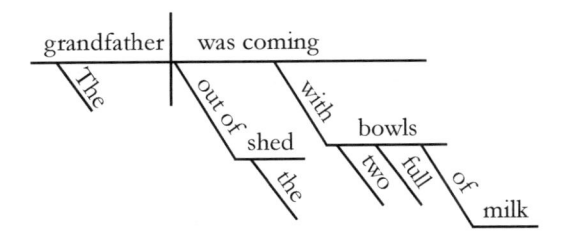

[Diagram: "The grandfather was coming out of the shed with bowls two full of milk"]

Exercise 89

"Grandfather, the wind has done it!" exclaimed Heidi eagerly.
[A comma would also be acceptable instead of the exclamation mark.]

```
pn    —v—   pn  prep art  n     prep art  n
```
Heidi had told Clara [of the flowers] [on the pasture].
                      HOW   WHAT KIND

[This sentence might be a little tricky. In some sentences, "on the pasture" could tell where. However, we know it's modifying the flowers because if we take out the phrase "of the flowers," "on the pasture" no longer makes sense: Heidi had told Clara on the pasture. What kind of flowers? The ones on the pasture.]

```
hv  pro  v  art  n              inj  pn   hv  pro  lv  adj
```
"Have you seen the chair?"   "Oh, Clara, would you be angry?"

[Diagram: "you | Have seen | chair \ the"]

[Diagram: "Oh Clara / you | would be \ angry"]

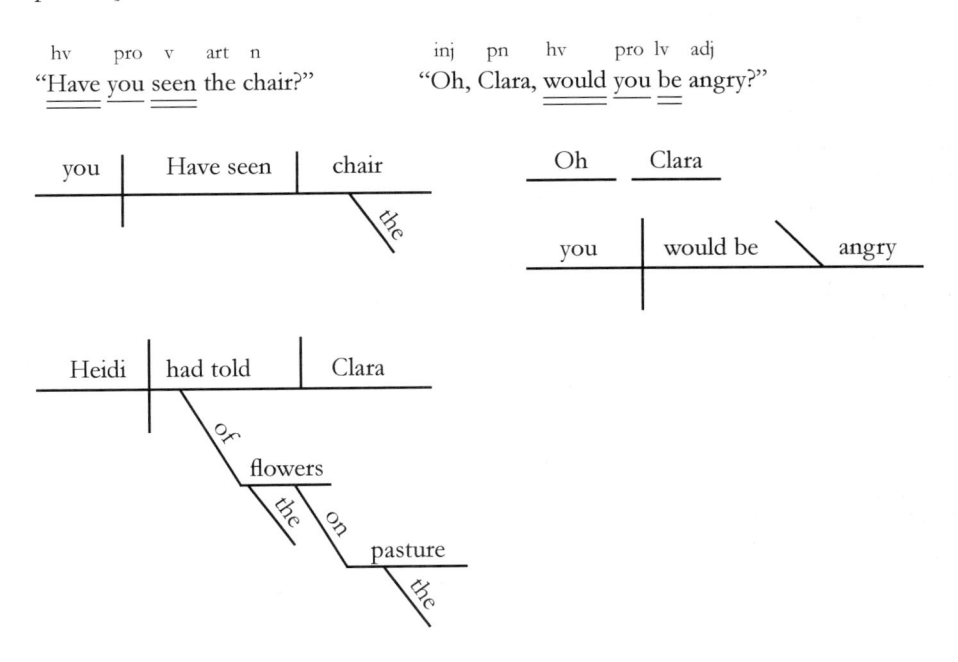

[Diagram: "Heidi | had told | Clara \ of \ flowers \ the \ on \ pasture \ the"]

Exercise 91

In this first sentence, any coordinating conjunction is technically correct, though some would produce an odd sentence. In my household, making the sentence odd would be a bonus.

She began to be conscious that her son was no longer a child**, so** she must soon send him forth among the perils and troubles of the world.

She began to be conscious that her son was no longer a child**.** She must soon send him forth among the perils and troubles of the world.

She began to be conscious that her son was no longer a child**;** she must soon send him forth among the perils and troubles of the world.

```
 lv   adj   cj   v
```
"Be patient and see."

```
adv  hv   adv pro v  prep adj  adj   n    prep  pn
```
"Why can not I go [to this famous city] [of Athens]?"
                      WHERE   WHICH ONE

```
art  n   prep pn     v    prep   n
```
The eyes [of Theseus] glowed [with enthusiasm].
           WHICH ONE   HOW

511

Exercise 92

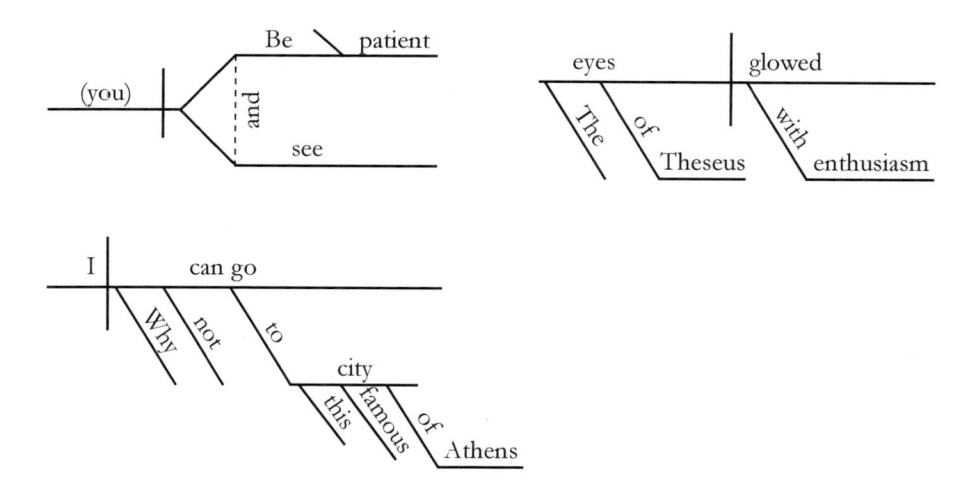

It was not more than a year afterwards. They were again sitting on the moss-covered stone.
It was not more than a year afterwards, **and** they were again sitting on the moss-covered stone.
It was not more than a year afterwards; they were again sitting on the moss-covered stone.

```
pn         —v—    adj   adj   n   prep  adj   adj          n
Theseus had done many valiant deeds [ with his father's golden-hilted sword ].
     v      pn    adj  adj           adj    n     prep adj    n
"Admit Theseus, this evil-minded young man, [ to your presence ]."
 inj   pro —lv— art adv  adj    adj    n     adv
"Why, he must be a very wicked young fellow indeed!"
```

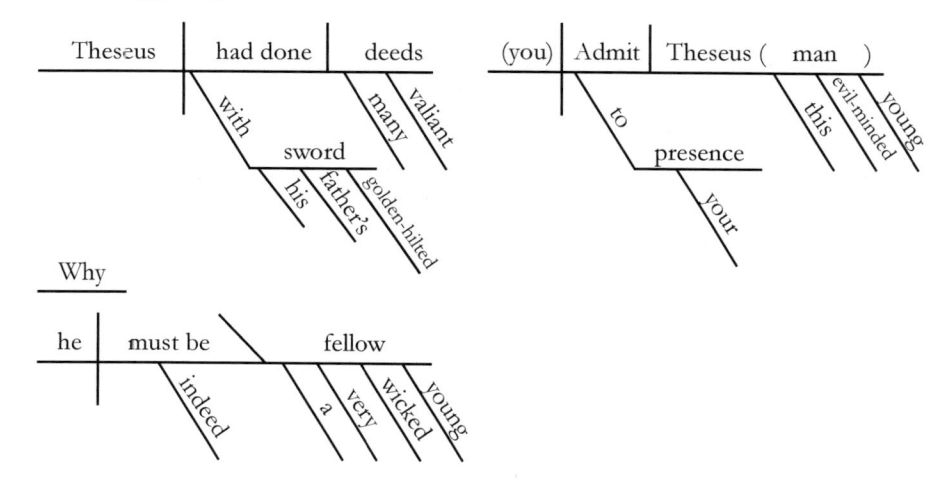

Exercise 93

Do but let me put a single drop into the goblet. Let the young man taste it.
Do but let me put a single drop into the goblet; let the young man taste it.
Do but let me put a single drop into the goblet, **and** let the young man taste it.

```
 adv   v    pro prep pro        pro  v   adv art  n
"How came you [ by it ]?"       He drew back the goblet.
 adj  n   —v—  prep art   adj        n
His eyes had fallen [ on the gold-hilted sword ].
                WHERE
```

Exercise 94

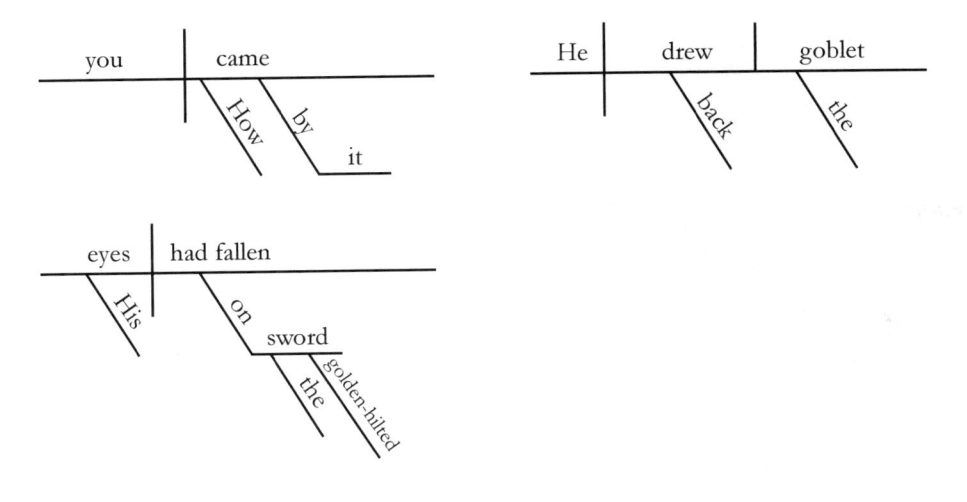

I shall probably have to teach you a little civility before we part.
Before we part, I shall probably have to teach you a little civility.

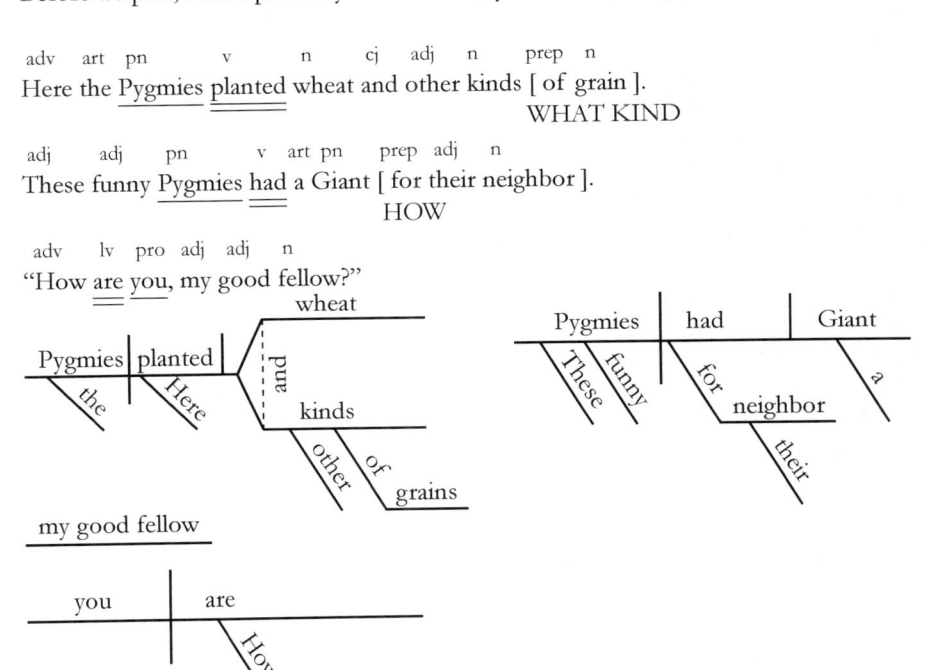

adv art pn v n cj adj n prep n
Here the Pygmies planted wheat and other kinds [of grain].
                                                    WHAT KIND

adj adj pn v art pn prep adj n
These funny Pygmies had a Giant [for their neighbor].
                                    HOW

adv lv pro adj adj n
"How are you, my good fellow?"

Exercise 95

The figure looked all the more terrible because it carried an enormous brass club on its shoulder.
Because it carried an enormous brass club on its shoulder, the figure looked all the more terrible.

art pn v pro adj adj n
The Giant gave them his brotherly kindness.

pro v art pn art n prep adj n
He gave the Pygmies a breeze [with his breath].
                                HOW

art pn v pro n prep n
The Pymies built themselves structures [of clay].
                                        WHAT KIND

513

Exercise 97

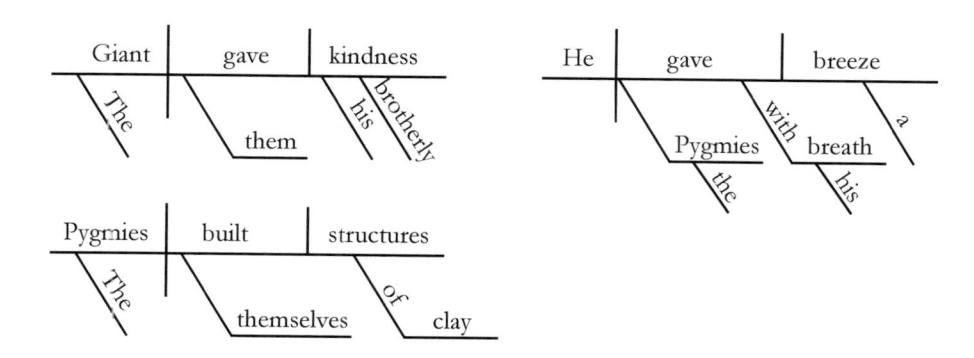

Because he wanted to be friends with the child, he ate them out of her hand.
He ate them out of her hand because he wanted to be friends with the child.

```
 adv   lv   pro
"Where are you?"
  v    adv  adj   n
"Come back, pretty creature!"
  v    pro adv adj adj  pn
"Bring me back my little Europa."
```

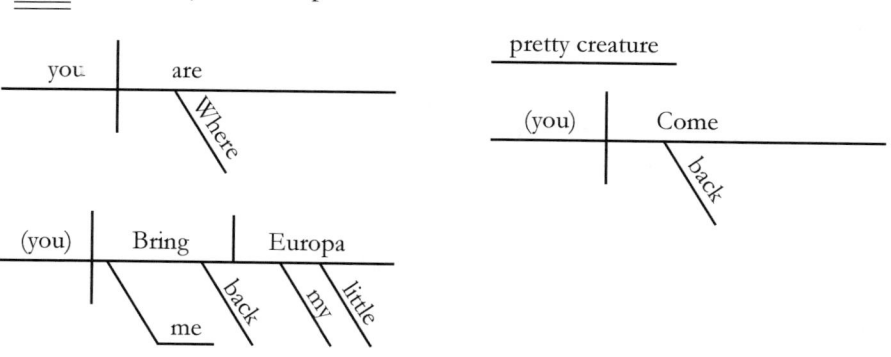

Exercise 98

It was delightful to witness the gratitude of this amiable bull; he capered higher than ever.
It was delightful to witness the gratitude of this amiable bull. He capered higher than ever.
It was delightful to witness the gratitude of this amiable bull, **for** he capered higher than ever.

```
  v    cj    v    adv  adj  n
"Come and drive away this bull!"
 adv   hv  art  n    v   pn
Where did the bull take Europa?
——pn——   adj    n    v   pro
King Agenor, Europa's father, said this.
```

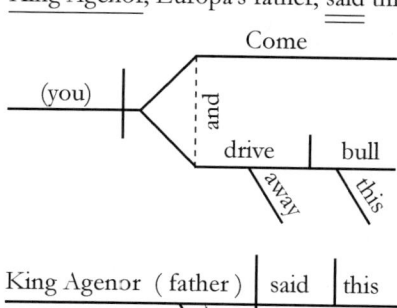

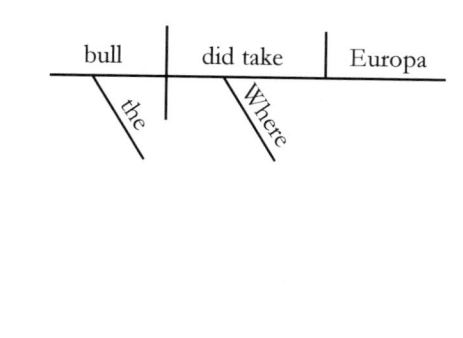

514

Exercise 99

Telephassa threw away her crown because it chafed her forehead.
Because it chafed her forehead, Telephassa threw away her crown.

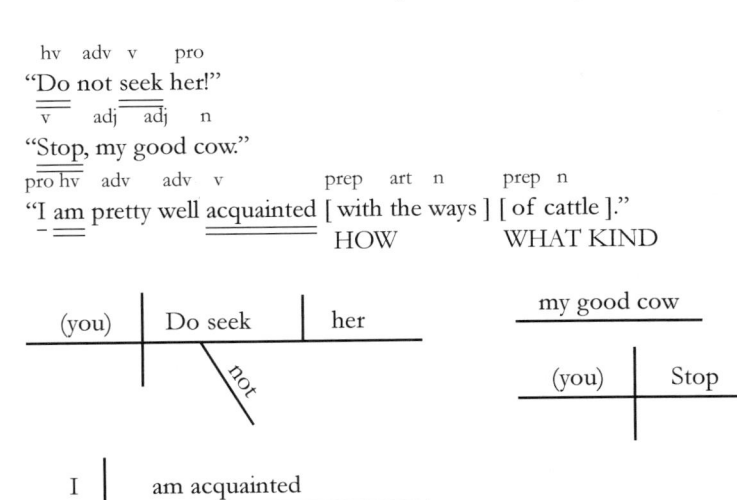

```
 hv  adv  v   pro
"Do not seek her!"
  v   adj  adj  n
"Stop, my good cow."
pro hv  adv    adv       v        prep  art  n   prep  n
"I am pretty well acquainted [ with the ways ] [ of cattle ]."
                                    HOW          WHAT KIND
```

Exercise 100

When they bade him farewell, Poenix shed tears.
Poenix shed tears when they bade him farewell.

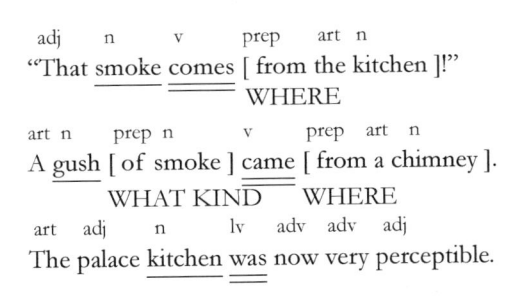

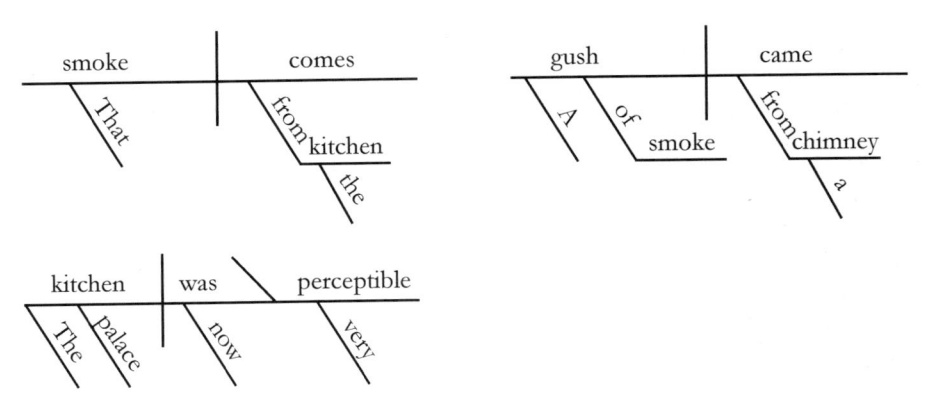

```
adj   n    v    prep art  n
"That smoke comes [ from the kitchen ]!"
                        WHERE
art  n   prep  n    v   prep art   n
A gush [ of smoke ] came [ from a chimney ].
    WHAT KIND           WHERE
art  adj    n    lv  adv  adv   adj
The palace kitchen was now very perceptible.
```

Exercise 101

They could think of nothing but their greedy appetite; they resembled those vilest of animals far more than they did kings.
They could think of nothing but their greedy appetite. They resembled those vilest of animals far more than they did kings.

515

They could think of nothing but their greedy appetite**, and** they resembled those vilest of animals far more than they did kings.

```
       pro   v   adj  adj  n      prep  adj      adj     n
       They saw their own figures [ in different colored threads ].
                                        WHERE
```

```
       inj  hv  pro  v   art  n
       "Ha! Do you smell the feast?"
       adj      n      v    pro   n   prep art   adj      n
       Serving men brought them dishes [ of the richest food ].
                                             WHAT KIND
```

```
   They │ saw    │ figures              Ha
         ╲their╲own                  ──────────────────────
          in                          you │ Do smell │ feast
           ╲threads                                    ╲the
            ╲colored
             ╲different
```

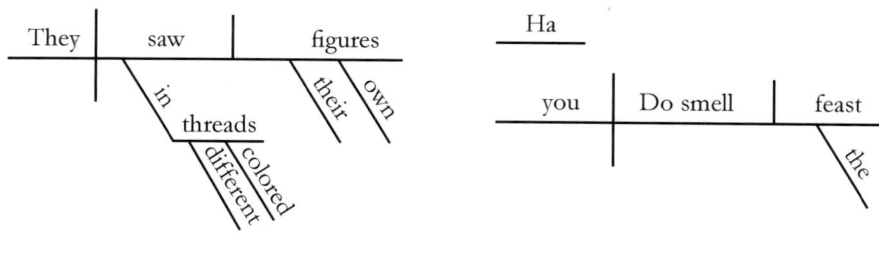

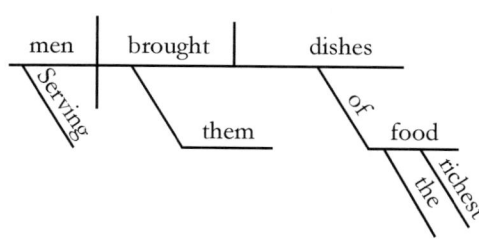

```
   men │ brought │ dishes
    ╲Serving  ╲them   ╲of
                       ╲food
                         ╲the
                          ╲richest
```

Exercise 103

Freeze, freeze, thou bit-ter sky,   A
Thou dost not bite so nigh   A
 As ben-e-fits for-got;   B
Though thou the wat-ers warp,   C
Thy sting is not so sharp   C
 As friend re-mem-bered not.   B

I will not taste a morsel of food even if you keep me forever in your palace.
Even if you keep me forever in your palace, I will not taste a morsel of food.

```
       pro   v        pro art  adj       n
       They prepared her a sumptuous banquet.
       adj  lv  art adj    n   adj  adj  pn
       "You are a spoiled child, my little Proserpina."
       hv   art  n   v   pro
       "Will the dog bite me?"
```

516

```
     They  | prepared | banquet                    my little Proserpina
              \        \                            ─────────────────
               \her     \a \sump.                  You | are \ child
                                                              \a \spoiled
  dog | Will bite | me
   \the
```

Exercise 104

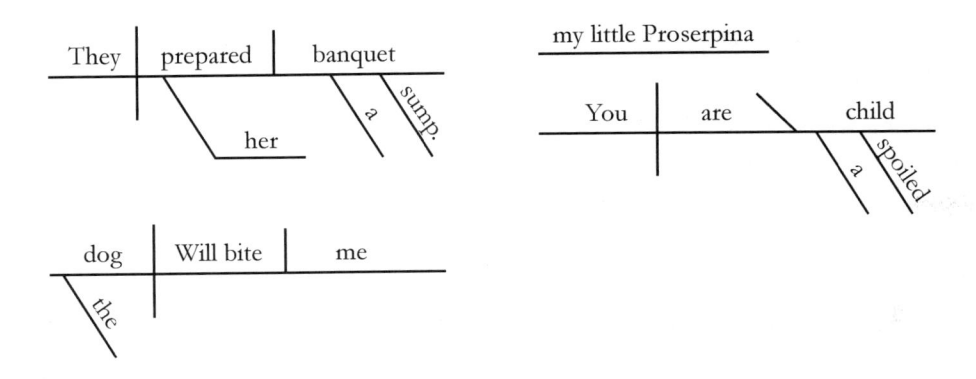

And still up-on the lake they stay,   A
Their eyes black stars in all their snow,   B
And soft-ly, in the glas-sy pool,   C
Their feet beat dark-ly to and fro.   B

```
 adv  lv  pn
"Where is Proserpina?"
 v   pro pro adj    ──n──
"Tell me, you naughty sea-nymphs."
pro adv  v  art  n   prep adj  n
"I once had a child [ of my own ]."
                        WHAT KIND
```

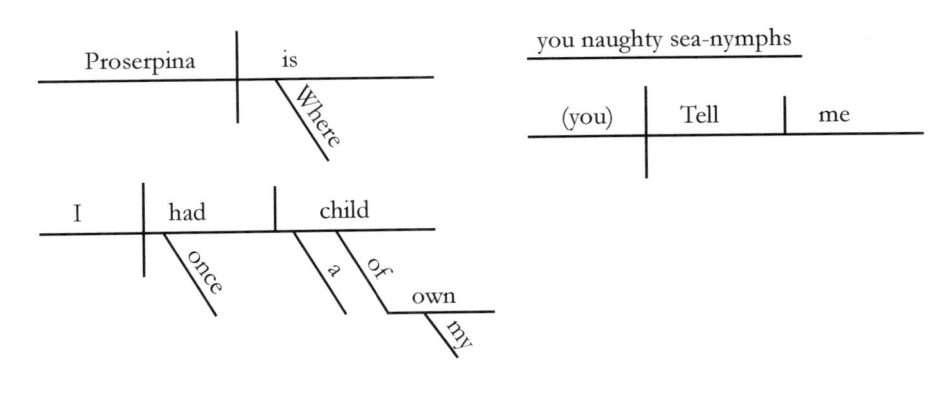

```
   Proserpina | is                     you naughty sea-nymphs
                 \Where                ─────────────────────
                                       (you) | Tell | me
     I | had | child
          \once \a \of
                     \own
                     \my
```

Exercise 105

Clause: which I may judge proper for him
Clause: what the nurse did to her child
Phrase: flinging a warm and ruddy light upon the walls

```
   ────pn────    adj  n       v
Queen Metanira, his mother, shrieked.
 art  adj    n    lv  adv adv  adj
The little damsel was not so unhappy.
  v     adv prep adj   adj    n
"Hasten home [ to your dear mother ]."
```

517

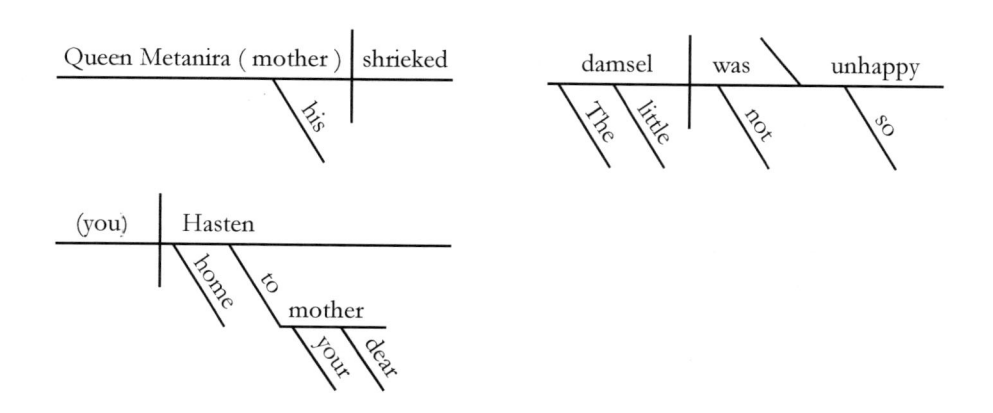

Exercise 106

I heard a-long the ear-ly hills,   A
Ere yet the lark was ris-en up,   B
Ere yet the dawn with fire-light fills   A
The night-dew of the bram-ble-cup—   B

Clause: when the old dame and her peacock were out of sight
Phrase: over her shoulder as she departed
Phrase: after traveling a pretty long distance

```
pn     art  adj  n      v    pro art  n    prep  adj   n
Argus, the ship builder, built him a galley [ with fifty oars ].
                                      WHAT KIND

pro lv  art  n        prep ——pn——
"We are the subjects [ of King Pelias ]."
                         WHAT KIND

pn    art  ———adj——   n   ——v——
Jason the one-sandaled man had come.
```

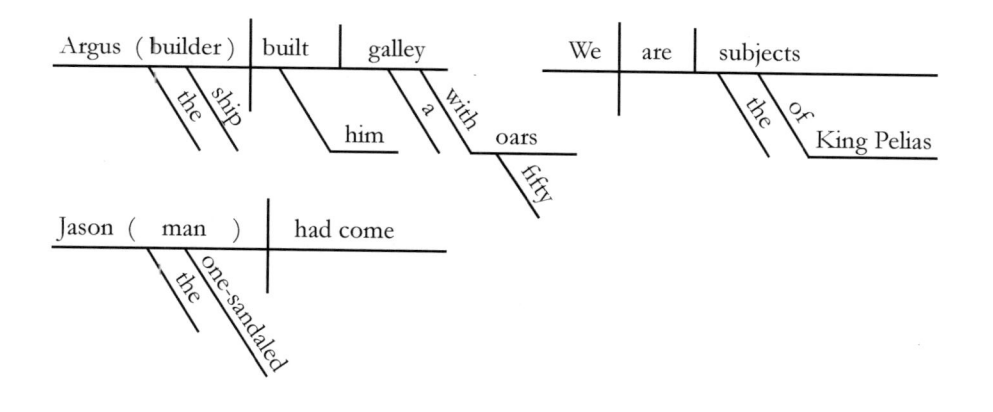

Exercise 107

′ ˘ ′ ˘ ′ ′ ˘ ′ ˘ ′	
I was ver-y well pleased with what I knowed,	A
′ ˘ ′ ˘ ′ ˘ ′	
I reck-oned my-self no fool—	B
′ ˘ ′ ˘ ˘ ′ ˘ ˘ ′ ˘ ′	
Till I met with a maid on the Brook-land Road	A
˘ ′ ˘ ′ ˘ ′	
That turned me back to school.	B

Appendix A: Memory Work

Appendix A contains memory work which will make the study of grammar easier, and Appendix B contains sentences to read in order to imprint the correct use of certain problem words in your mind. Below, each definition or list appears with the ELTL level title in which it was first introduced, though in some cases, it may be a more advanced version of what actually appeared in that level. Ideally, you should know all of the definitions and lists in Appendix A, so study the memory work through the level you are currently in. You can approach this material in a couple of ways.

My preferred way is to simply read the material each week. ELTL is a three-day per week program, so on Day 1, read half of Appendix A; on Day 2, read the second half of Appendix A; and on Day 3, read Appendix B. In this way, you would memorize or at least become very familiar with the material over the course of the school year.

If you would prefer, you can actively work on memorizing the material in Appendix A instead. If you are new to ELTL and have never learned the definitions and lists from the lower levels, first focus on the ones from the level you are currently in. However, you should also spend some time working on the definitions and lists from lower levels. You can work on memorizing several at a time. Say each of them three times each day until it is memorized, and then move on to the next item. Regularly review items which you have already memorized by reciting them once a month.

You do not need to wait until you have completed the lesson in which the definition or list occurs. In fact, if you have already memorized the definition or list, you may find the lesson easier.

Level B

A noun is the name of a person, place, thing, or idea.

A pronoun is a word used in the place of a noun.

An antecedent is the noun that a pronoun replaces.

A verb is a word that shows action or a state of being.

The state of being verbs are am, are, is, was, were, be, being, been.

The linking verbs are am, are, is, was, were, be, being, been, become, seem.

The helping verbs are
am, are, is, was, were, be, being, been,
do, does, did, have, has, had, may, might, must,
can, could, shall, should, will, would.

A conjunction is a word that joins words or groups of words together. The three types of conjunctions are coordinating, subordinating, and correlative.

An adjective is a word that modifies a noun or a pronoun. Adjectives tell what kind, how many, which one, and whose.

The articles are: a, an, the. Articles are adjectives.

A preposition is a word that shows the relationship between a noun or a pronoun and another word in the sentence.

Some of the most common prepositions are
>aboard, about, above, across, after, against, along, among, around, at,
before, behind, below, beneath, beside, between, beyond, by,
down, during, except, for, from, in, inside, into, like, near, of, off,
on, onto, outside, over, past, round, since, through, throughout, till, to, toward,
under, underneath, until, up, upon, with, within, without.

An interjection is a word or group of words that shows sudden or strong feeling.

An adverb is a word that modifies a verb, an adjective, or another adverb. Adverbs tell how, when, where, why, how often, and to what extent.

A sentence is a group of words that expresses a complete thought.

Synonyms are words that have the same meaning.

Antonyms are words that have opposite meanings.

Homophones are words that sound the same but are spelled differently.

Level C

The Four Types of Sentences:

>A declarative sentence makes a statement. It ends with a period.

>An interrogative sentence asks a question. It ends with a question mark.

>An exclamatory sentence shows sudden or strong feeling. It ends with an exclamation mark.

>An imperative sentence gives a command or makes a request. It ends with a period.

Personal Pronouns:

>The first person pronouns are I, me, my, mine, we, us, our, ours.

>The second person pronouns are you, your, yours.

>The third person pronouns are he, him, his, she, her, hers, it, its, they, them, their, theirs.

A predicate nominative is a noun or pronoun which follows a linking verb and renames the subject.

A predicate adjective is an adjective which follows a linking verb and modifies the subject.

A direct object is the noun or pronoun that receives the action of the verb.

A paragraph is a group of sentences on a single topic.

The object of the preposition is a noun or pronoun which teams up with the preposition and completes its meaning.

The four properties of nouns and pronouns are number, gender, person, and case.

> Number tells whether nouns and pronouns are singular or plural.
>
> Gender tells whether nouns and pronouns are masculine, feminine, or neuter.
>
> Person tells the identity of the subject—first person, second person, or third person.
>
> Case is the change in form based on a noun or pronoun's job in a sentence.

The nominative case pronouns are I, we, you, he, she, it, they.

The objective case pronouns are me, us, you, him, her, it, them.

The possessive case pronouns are my, mine, our, ours, your, yours, his, her, hers, its, their, theirs.

Comparative adjectives and adverbs compare two things.

Superlative adjectives and adverbs compare three or more things.

An appositive is a noun, a noun phrase, or a noun clause that sits next to another noun and renames it.

Homographs are words that are spelled the same but have different origins and meanings.

The interrogative adverbs are when, where, why, how.

Level D

Point of view is the perspective from which a writer tells a story or presents information.

A phrase is a group of related words which does not include a subject-predicate pair.

A clause is a group of words which contains a subject-predicate pair. The four types of clauses are independent, subordinate, relative, and noun.

The seven coordinating conjunctions are: for, and, nor, but, or, yet, so (FANBOYS).

A noun of direct address is the name or other reference directly to the person being addressed.

The five principal parts of the verb are the infinitive, the present tense, the present participle, the past tense, and the past participle.

The five properties of verbs are: person, number, tense, voice, mood.

A collective noun is a noun which refers to a group of individuals. Collective nouns are usually treated as singular nouns in American English.

Some common subordinating conjunctions are after, although, as, as if, as long as, as though, because, before, even if, even though, if, if only, in order that, now that, once, provided that, rather than, since, so that, than, that, though, till, unless, until, when, whenever, where, whereas, wherever, whether, while.

An indirect object is a noun or pronoun that tells TO or FOR whom/what the action of the verb is performed.

The four sentence structures are simple, complex, compound, and compound-complex.

A complex sentence is a sentence with one independent clause and at least one dependent clause.

The relative pronouns are that, which, who. (Memorize these three and you can spot the others easily. The full list includes: that, which, whichever, who, whoever, whom, whomever, whose, whosever.)

Level E

A dependent clause begins with a subordinating conjunction, a relative pronoun, or a relative adverb. It contains a subject-predicate pair, but it does not form a complete sentence.

Inversion is the reversal of normal word order in a sentence.

An expletive is word that performs a syntactic role but contributes nothing to meaning of the sentence.

An indefinite pronoun is a pronoun which does not refer to any definite person, place, thing, or idea in particular.

Parallel structure uses equal grammatical units to show that two or more ideas have the same level of importance.

The relative adverbs are when, where, why.

The interrogative pronouns are what, which, who. (Memorize these three and you can spot the others easily. The full list includes: what, whatever, which, whichever, who, whoever, whom, whomever, whose, whosever.)

Level F

The perfect tense shows actions which have been completed. Perfect tenses always use the helping verb "to have" with the past participle of the verb.

   The present perfect tense is **have** or **has** plus the past participle.

   The past perfect tense is **had** plus the past participle.

   The future perfect tense is **will have** plus the past participle.

The singular indefinite pronouns are everybody, everyone, everything, anybody, anyone, anything, nobody, no one, nothing, somebody, someone, something, each, either, neither, one, another. They will always take a singular verb.

The plural indefinite pronouns are both, few, several, and many. They will always take a plural verb.

The indefinite pronouns which may be either singular or plural, depending on the context, are all, any, most, none, and some.

A verbal is a word which is formed from a verb but acts as a different part of speech. The three types of verbals are gerunds, participles, and infinitives.

> A gerund is a verbal which ends in *-ing* and acts as a noun in a sentence. A gerund has the same form as the present participle.
>
> A participle is a verbal which acts as an adjective in a sentence. Both present participles and past participles can act as adjectives.
>
> An infinitive is a verbal which can act as a noun, adjective, or adverb in a sentence.

A simile is a figure of speech which compares two different things using the words **like** or **as**.

A metaphor is a figure of speech which makes a comparison between two things by saying that one thing is the other.

An onomatopoeia is a word which imitates the sound which it names.

Personification is a figure of speech which gives human characteristics to nonhuman things.

Hyperbole is an exaggerated statement which is used for emphasis and is not meant to be taken literally.

Alliteration is the repetition of beginning consonant sounds within a group of words.

Assonance is the repetition of vowel sounds, anywhere in a word, within a group of words.

Consonance is the repetition of consonant sounds, anywhere in a word, within a group of words.

Appendix B: Correct Use of Words

This is like copywork in that it is intended to imprint certain grammatical concepts into the child's mind just through repetition. Have you ever said, or heard another say, that something just "sounds" right? Saying these sentences aloud regularly will help the correct forms "sound" right to our children and to ourselves.

My advice is to read these sentences approximately once a week for the school year. That could mean all of them once a week, or it could mean a page a day. By the time you get to the actual lessons on these topics, your child will already know these forms and the lessons will be reviews.

Predicate nominatives are in the nominative/subjective case.

It is I.
This is he.
This is she.
It is we.
It was I.
It was not I; it was she.
I think it was he.
I am sure it is she.
It was we.
It might have been they.
It was he and I.
It was they.
No, it is not she.
Yes, it is he.

Objects are in the objective case.

Did you call her?
Did you call me?
Did you call him and me?
Mother bought a ball for you.
Mother bought a ball for me.
Mother bought a ball for you and me.
Between you and me, I really wanted a dinosaur.

Some irregular past participles are never used without a helping verb.

I came.
I saw.
I conquered.
I have come.
I have seen.
I have conquered.
I did my chores.
I am done with chores.
She did her quiz.
He is done with his quiz.
We did the work.
We have done the work.
They did fine.

They have done fine.
I go to the store.
She goes to the store.
He went to the store.
It has gone to the store.
We have gone on vacation.
They went on vacation.
You go on vacation.
I see the bird.
We did see the bird.
They saw the bird.
The bird has seen us.

Double Negatives: Use only one negative word per sentence.

I have never heard that. I had not ever heard that.
I know nothing about that. I do not know anything about that.
Nobody is home. No one is at home.
None of our relatives live near. Not any of our relatives live near.
The train went nowhere. The train did not go anywhere.

Well vs. Good

The hot cocoa was good this morning. You made it well.
How are you today? I am good. I am doing well.
Are you feeling ill? No, I am well.
Few have gotten a good look at a Sasquatch. The Sasquatch hides well.
Your behavior was good. You behaved well.

Sit vs. Set

I sit in my favorite chair.
He is sitting in my favorite chair.
She sat in my favorite chair yesterday.
You have sat in my favorite chair.
I will sit in my favorite chair today.
They are sitting on the couch.
I set my book on the table.
You set your book on the table yesterday.
He will set his book on the table tomorrow.
They are setting books on the table.
We have set our books on the table.

Lie vs. Lay

I lie on the couch.
He lay on the ground.
She will lie in the flowers.
They are lying in the field.
I have lain here on the couch.
I lay the book on the table.
He laid the book on the table earlier.
She will lay the book on the table later.
We are laying the books on the table.
They have laid books on the table before.

Rise and Raise

I rise from bed each morning.
The sun is rising.
He rose from bed yesterday.
The sun has risen.
In the morning, we raise the windows.
She is raising her hand.
He raised his hand.
They have raised money for charity.

Accept and Except
I accept this package.
She is accepting an award.
He accepted the apology.
Her son has been accepted to college.
The study excepts children; they are not included.
He likes hot drinks except tea.
She likes cool weather except when it is raining.

Affect vs. Effect

The ear infection affects her balance.
She affected a British accent.
The events he witnessed affected him.
He had affected surprise at the news.
The medicine has some side effects.
An example of the Doppler effect is the change in pitch of a siren.
The special effects were outstanding.
Before leaving the hotel, they gathered their personal effects.

Advise vs. Advise

I advise you to read Appendix B each week during your lessons.
The doctor was advising his patients to eat a healthy diet.
He also advised them to exercise regularly.
He had advised them of this in the past.
Her advisor gives good advice.

Principle vs. Principal

World religions often have varied beliefs, but similar principles.
People often struggle to live according to their principles.
The head of the school was the principal, our pal.
He had visited the principal cities in Europe.
She spent the interest, but she would not touch the principal.

Appendix C: Diagramming Reference

Procedure for analyzing sentences (skip parts you haven't learned yet):

Put brackets around prepositional phrases.

What is the predicate? The main verb is often easier to find than its subject, so find it first. Double underline it. Is it an action verb or a linking verb? Label it.

What is the subject? Underline it once.

For action verbs, is there a direct object which receives the action of the verb by answering the question **whom** or **what**? IF THERE IS A DIRECT OBJECT (DO), is there an indirect object between the DO and the verb which identifies the recipient of the direct object by answering the question **to whom or what**, or **for whom or what**, the action of the verb is performed?

For linking verbs, is there a subject complement—a predicate nominative or a predicate adjective—which renames or modifies the subject?

Basic sentence.

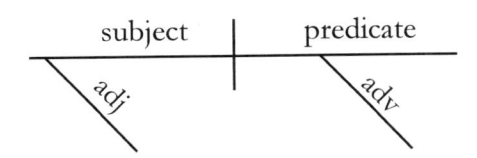

Sentences with subject complements. Note that the predicate nominative can be modified by an adjective, and the predicate adjective can be modified by an adverb.

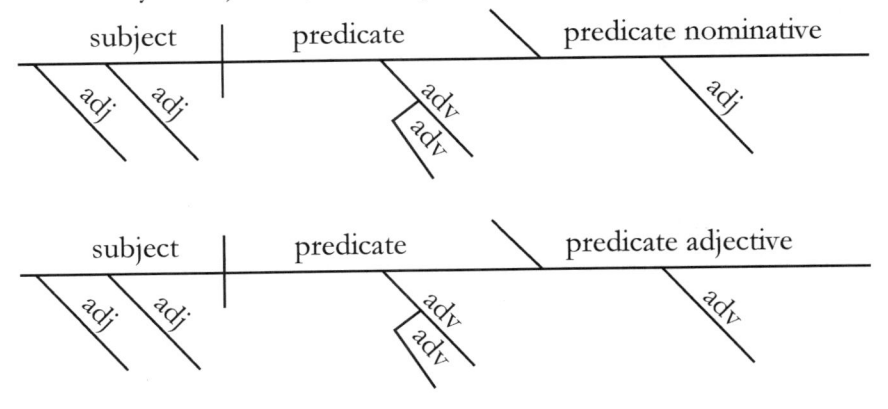

Sentence with a direct object.

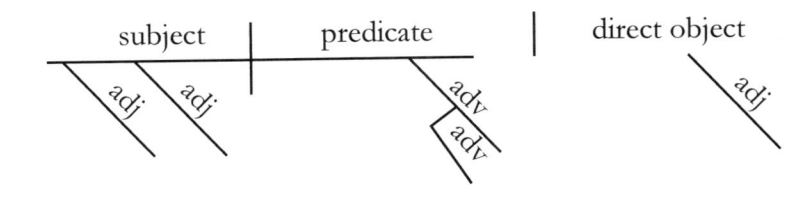

531

Sentences with compound structures.

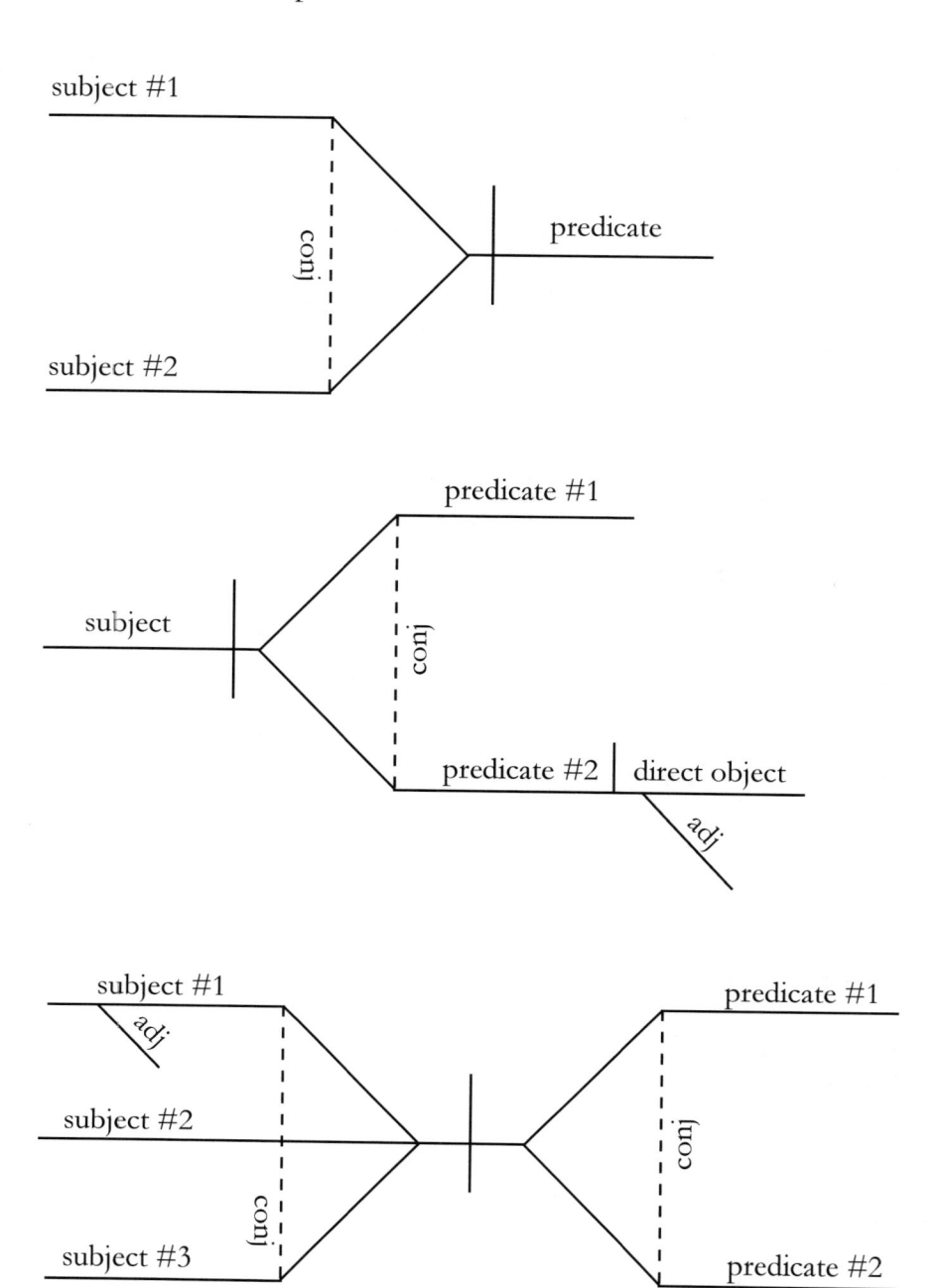

Compound direct object.

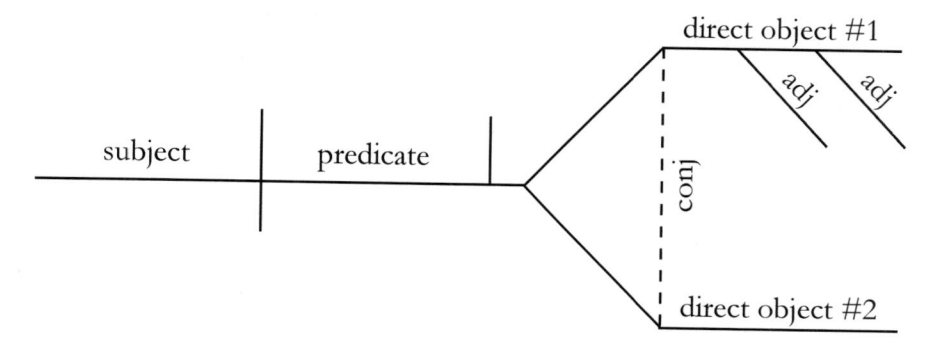

Compound predicate with shared direct object.

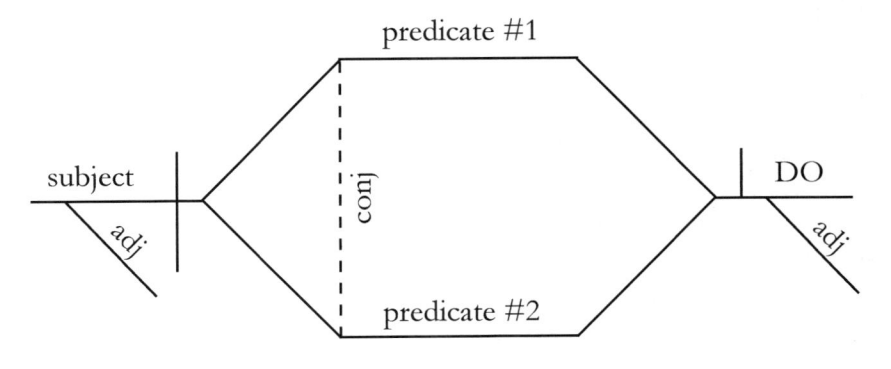

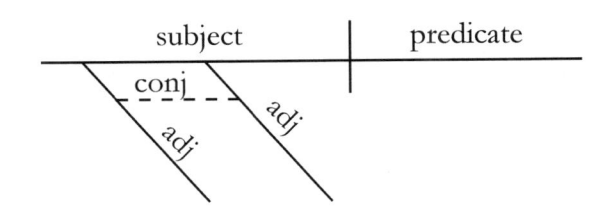

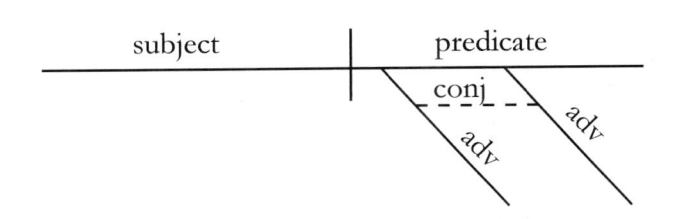

Command with understood you.

Prepositional phrases.

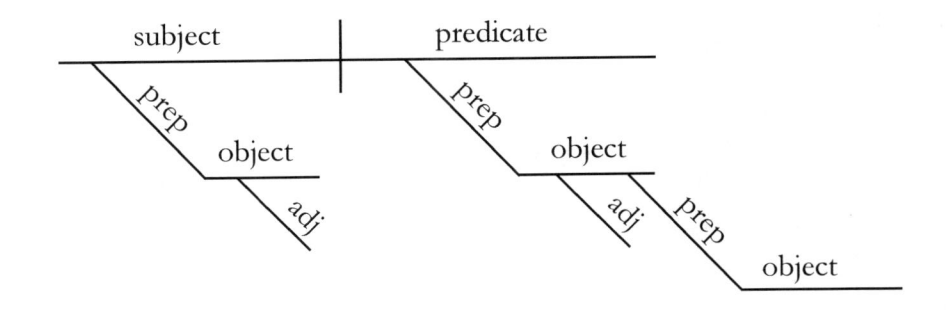

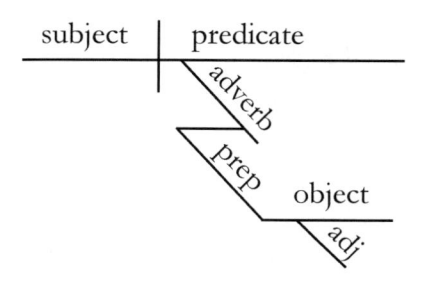

```
   subject  |  predicate
            |\
            | \adverb
            |  \
            |   \prep
            |    _____object
            |           \
            |            \adj
```

Interjections and nouns of direct address.

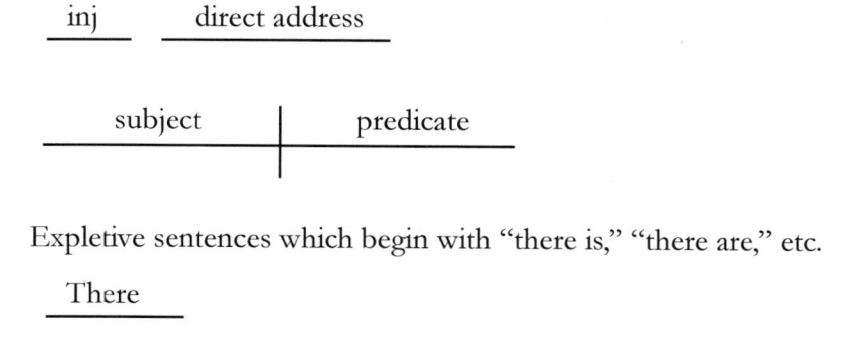

```
  inj   |   direct address
```

```
   subject  |  predicate
            |
```

Expletive sentences which begin with "there is," "there are," etc.

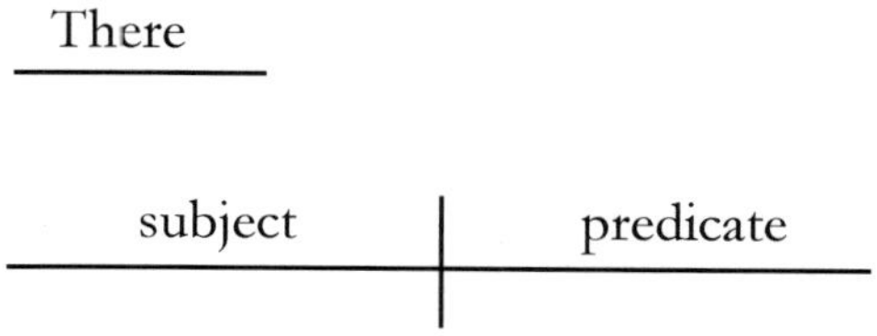

```
   There
```

```
   subject  |  predicate
            |
```

Complex sentence with a subordinate clause, which begins with a subordinating conjunction. Subordinating conjunction connects the verbs.

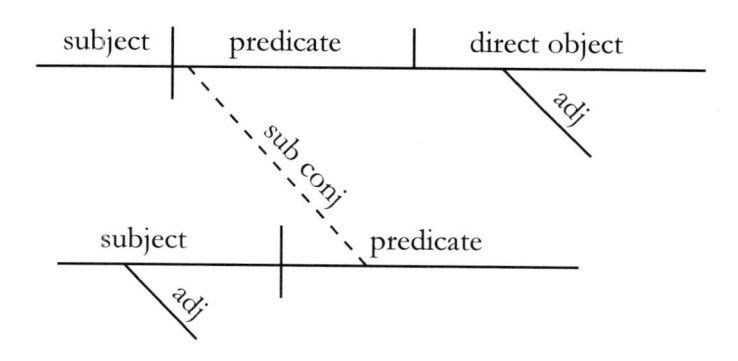

```
   subject  |  predicate  |  direct object
            \                       \
             \                       \adj
              \sub conj
               \
   subject  |  predicate
            \
             \adj
```

Complex sentence with a relative clause, which begins with a relative pronoun or relative adverb. Dotted line connects the relative clause to the word it modifies. The relative pronoun can act as the subject or object of the relative clause, or it can modify the subject of the relative clause.

```
       subject  |  predicate
          ¦
          ¦
          ¦
   relative pronoun  |  predicate
                     |
```

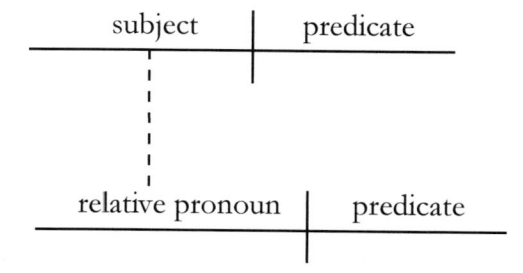

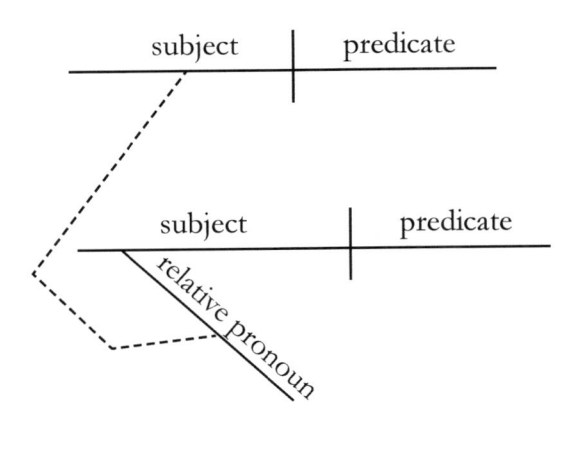

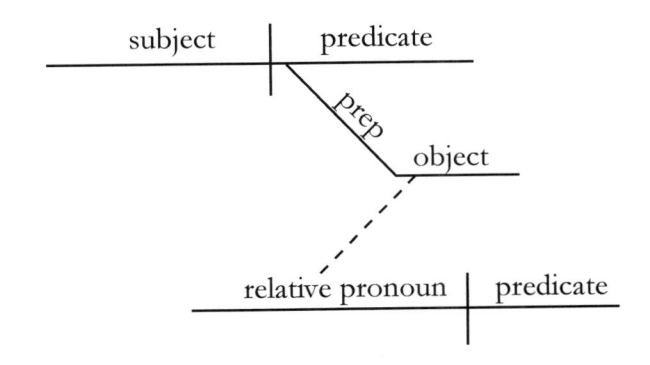

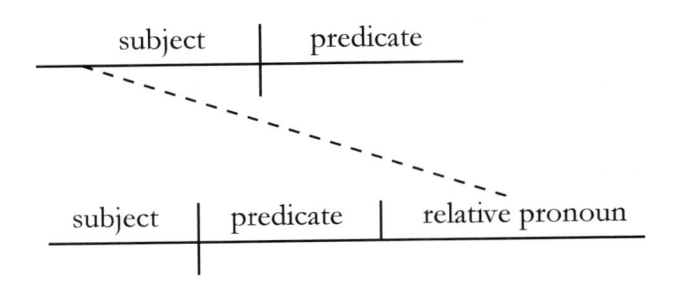

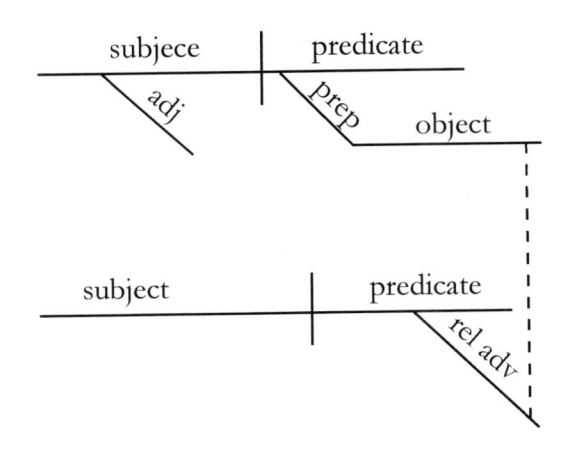

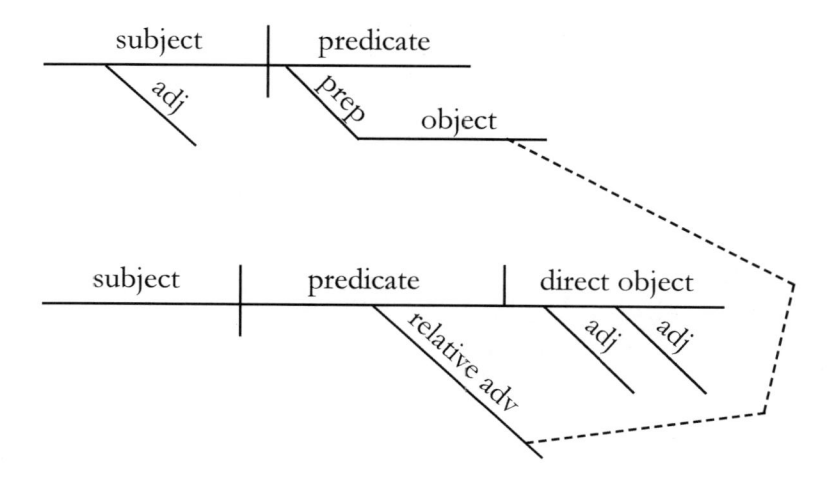

Indirect object.

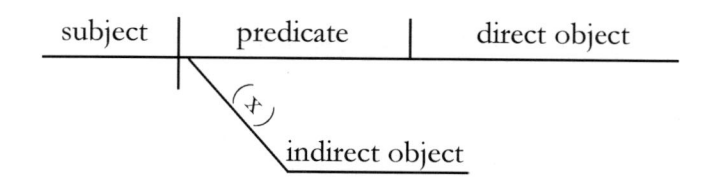

Compound indirect object.

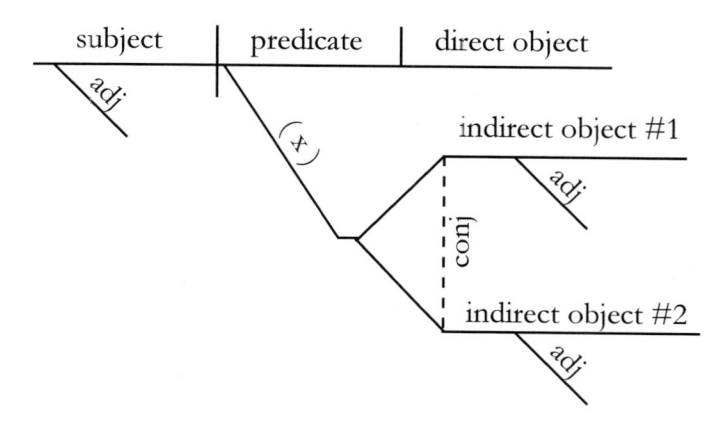

Compound sentence.

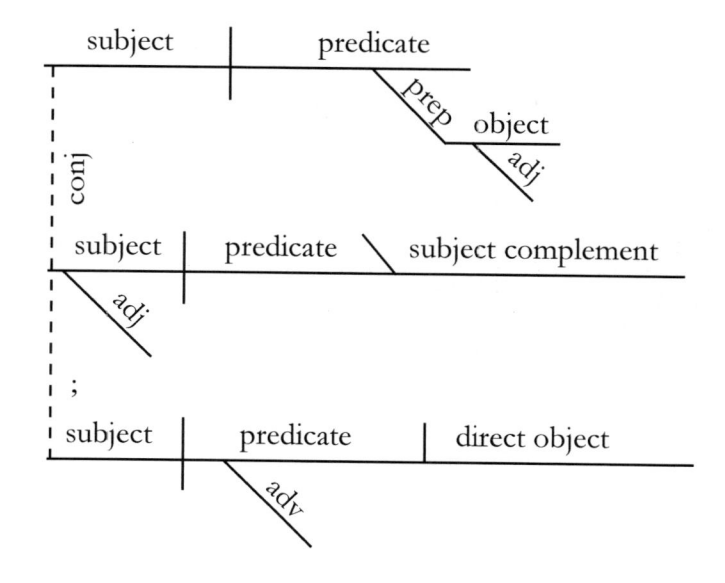

Compound-complex sentence. Dependent clauses are connected to independent clauses in the normal ways, which depend on whether the clause begins with a subordinating conjunction or a relative pronoun.

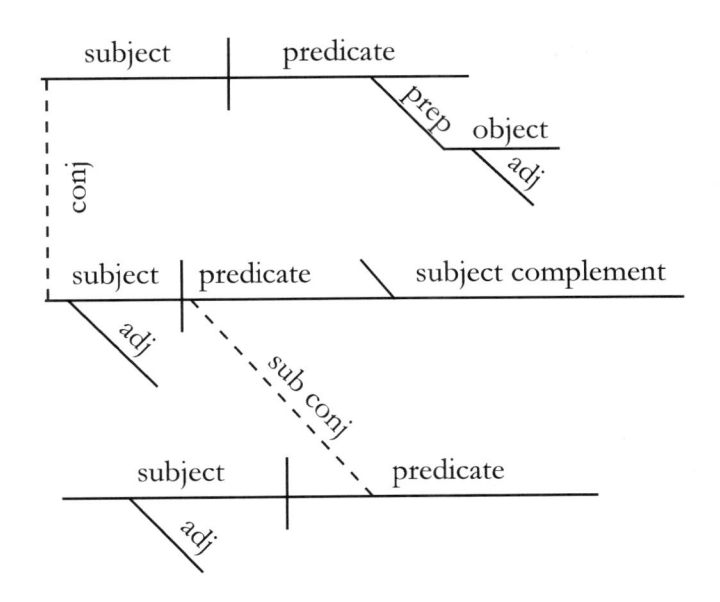

Appositive. Modifiers for the appositive go under it.

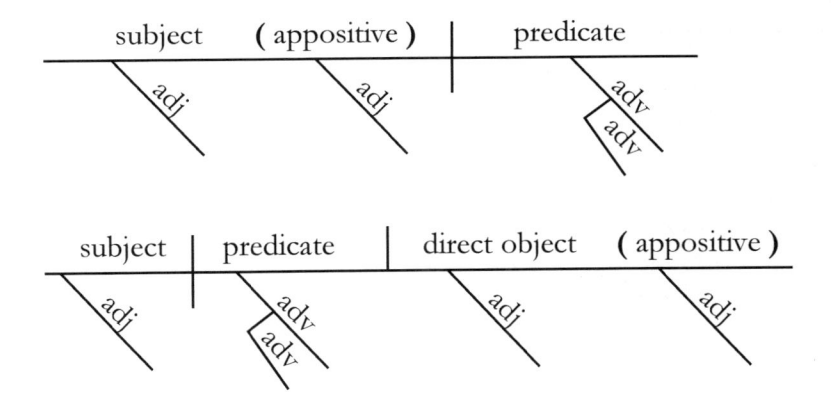

Correlative conjunctions.

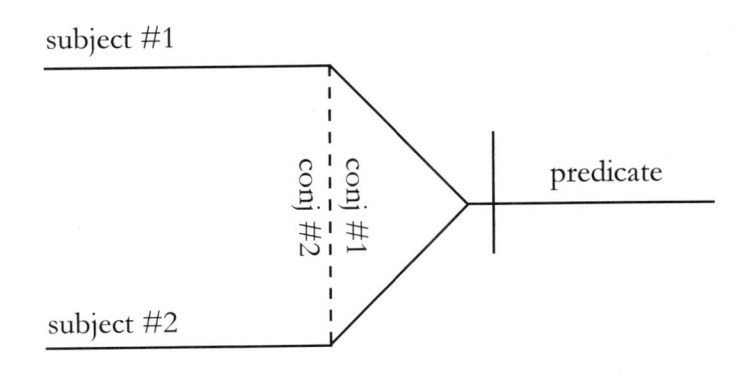

537

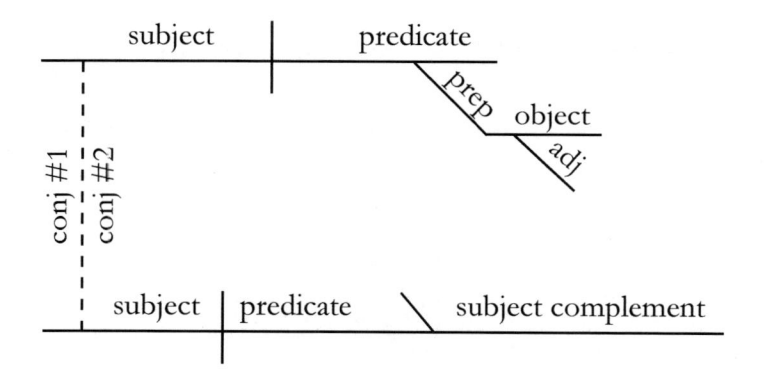

Appendix D: Irregular Verbs

Use the chart on the following pages to become familiar with common irregular verbs. But when in doubt, use the dictionary. It will list the various forms of the verb.

Infinitive	Simple Present	Present Participle	Simple Past	Past Participle
to arise	arise(s)	arising	arose	arisen
to awake	awake(s)	awaking	awoke or awaked	awaked or awoken
to be	am, is, are	being	was, were	been
to bear	bear(s)	bearing	bore	borne or born
to beat	beat(s)	beating	beat	beaten
to become	become(s)	becoming	became	become
to begin	begin(s)	beginning	began	begun
to bend	bend(s)	bending	bent	bent
to bet	bet(s)	betting	bet	bet
to bid	bid(s)	bidding	bid	bid
to bid	bid(s)	bidding	bade	bidden
to bind	bind(s)	binding	bound	bound
to bite	bite(s)	biting	bit	bitten or bit
to blow	blow(s)	blowing	blew	blown
to break	break(s)	breaking	broke	broken
to bring	bring(s)	bringing	brought	brought
to build	build(s)	building	built	built
to burst	burst(s)	bursting	burst	burst
to buy	buy(s)	buying	bought	bought
to cast	cast(s)	casting	cast	cast
to catch	catch(es)	catching	caught	caught
to choose	choose(s)	choosing	chose	chosen
to cling	cling(s)	clinging	clung	clung
to come	come(s)	coming	came	come
to cost	cost(s)	costing	cost	cost
to creep	creep(s)	creeping	crept	crept
to cut	cut(s)	cutting	cut	cut
to deal	deal(s)	dealing	dealt	dealt
to dig	dig(s)	digging	dug	dug
to dive	dive(s)	diving	dived or dove	dived
to do	do(es)	doing	did	done

539

to draw	draw(s)	drawing	drew	drawn
to dream	dream(s)	dreaming	dreamed or dreamt	dreamed or dreamt
to drink	drink(s)	drinking	drank	drunk
to drive	drive(s)	driving	drove	driven
to eat	eat(s)	eating	ate	eaten
to fall	fall(s)	falling	fell	fallen
to feed	feed(s)	feeding	fed	fed
to feel	feel(s)	feeling	felt	felt
to fight	fight(s)	fighting	fought	fought
to find	find(s)	finding	found	found
to flee	flee(s)	fleeing	fled	fled
to fling	fling(s)	flinging	flung	flung
to fly	flies, fly	flying	flew	flown
to forbid	forbid(s)	forbidding	forbade	forbidden
to forget	forget(s)	forgetting	forgot	forgotten or forgot
to forgive	forgive(s)	forgiving	forgave	forgiven
to forsake	forsake(s)	forsaking	forsook	forsaken
to freeze	freeze(s)	freezing	froze	frozen
to get	get(s)	getting	got	got or gotten
to give	give(s)	giving	gave	given
to go	go(es)	going	went	gone
to grow	grow(s)	growing	grew	grown
to hang	hang(s)	hanging	hung	hung
to have	has, have	having	had	had
to hear	hear(s)	hearing	heard	heard
to hide	hide(s)	hiding	hid	hidden
to hit	hit(s)	hitting	hit	hit
to hurt	hurt(s)	hurting	hurt	hurt
to keep	keep(s)	keeping	kept	kept
to know	know(s)	knowing	knew	known
to lay	lay(s)	laying	laid	laid
to lead	lead(s)	leading	led	led
to leap	leap(s)	leaping	leaped or leapt	leaped or leapt
to leave	leave(s)	leaving	left	left
to lend	lend(s)	lending	lent	lent
to let	let(s)	letting	let	let
to lie	lie(s)	lying	lay	lain

to light	light(s)	lighting	lighted or lit	lighted or lit
to lose	lose(s)	losing	lost	lost
to make	make(s)	making	made	made
to mean	mean(s)	meaning	meant	meant
to pay	pay(s)	paying	paid	paid
to prove	prove(s)	proving	proved	proved or proven
to quit	quit(s)	quitting	quit	quit
to read	read(s)	reading	read	read
to rid	rid(s)	ridding	rid	rid
to ride	ride(s)	riding	rode	ridden
to ring	ring(s)	ringing	rang	rung
to rise	rise(s)	rising	rose	risen
to run	run(s)	running	ran	run
to say	say(s)	saying	said	said
to see	see(s)	seeing	saw	seen
to seek	seek(s)	seeking	sought	sought
to send	send(s)	sending	sent	sent
to set	set(s)	setting	set	set
to shake	shake(s)	shaking	shook	shaken
to shine	shine(s)	shining	shone	shone
to shoot	shoot(s)	shooting	shot	shot
to show	show(s)	showing	showed	shown or showed
to shrink	shrink(s)	shrinking	shrank	shrunk
to sing	sing(s)	singing	sang	sung
to sink	sink(s)	sinking	sank or sunk	sunk
to sit	sit(s)	sitting	sat	sat
to slay	slay(s)	slaying	slew	slain
to sleep	sleep(s)	sleeping	slept	slept
to sling	sling(s)	slinging	slung	slung
to sneak	sneak(s)	sneaking	sneaked or snuck	sneaked or snuck
to speak	speak(s)	speaking	spoke	spoken
to spend	spend(s)	spending	spent	spent
to spin	spin(s)	spinning	spun	spun
to spring	spring(s)	springing	sprang or sprung	sprung
to stand	stand(s)	standing	stood	stood
to steal	steal(s)	stealing	stole	stolen

to sting	sting(s)	stinging	stung	stung
to stink	stink(s)	stinking	stank or stunk	stunk
to stride	stride(s)	striding	strode	stridden
to strike	strike(s)	striking	struck	struck
to strive	strive(s)	striving	strove	striven
to swear	swear(s)	swearing	swore	sworn
to sweep	sweep(s)	sweeping	swept	swept
to swim	swim(s)	swimming	swam	swum
to swing	swing(s)	swinging	swung	swung
to take	take(s)	taking	took	taken
to teach	teach(es)	teaching	taught	taught
to tear	tear(s)	tearing	tore	torn
to tell	tell(s)	telling	told	told
to think	think(s)	thinking	thought	thought
to throw	throw(s)	throwing	threw	thrown
to understand	understand(s)	understanding	understood	understood
to wake	wake(s)	waking	woke or waked	waked or woken
to wear	wear(s)	wearing	wore	worn
to weave	weave(s)	weaving	wove or weaved	woven or wove
to weep	weep(s)	weeping	wept	wept
to wring	wring(s)	wringing	wrung	wrung
to write	write(s)	writing	wrote	written

Appendix E: Tenses

Simple Tense

Infinitive	Simple Past	Simple Present	Simple Future
to be	I was	I am	I will be
to move	I moved	I move	I will move

Pefect Tense

Infinitive	Past Perfect	Present Perfect	Future Perfect
to be	I had been	I have been	I will have been
to move	I had moved	I have moved	I will have moved

Appendix F: Editing

- Did you meet the goal of this writing exercise?

- Check for sentence fragments, reading the paper backwards if necessary.

- Check for expletive construction and remove any instances of it.
  Reference lessons: E Lesson 49; F Lesson 19

- If you gave an opinion, did you support it with evidence? Did you use quotations properly? Reference Lessons: E Lesson 38; F Lesson 26

- Did you include all the important details from the story? Did you keep the narrative in the proper order?

- If applicable, did you write an introduction and a conclusion (Appendix D)?

- Look at your word choice. Is there a good mixture of nouns and pronouns? Is the antecedent of each pronoun clear? Did you use different ways to say **said**? Reference Lessons: E Lesson 23; F Lesson 25

- Are your verb tenses consistent?

- Did you check your punctuation? Did you maintain parallel structure?

- Do your paragraphs have unity? Does each paragraph have a clear topic? Do the sentences in the paragraph all support the main topic?

- Do your paragraphs have coherence? Are the thoughts organized? Does each sentence follow logically from the one before? Did you use transitions?
  Reference lessons: F Lessons 11 and 14

Made in the USA
Middletown, DE
04 May 2020